I0881890

Patent Law and Intellectual Property in the Medical Field

Rashmi Aggarwal
Institute of Management Technology Ghaziabad, India

Rajinder Kaur
Panjab University, India

A volume in the Advances in Healthcare Information Systems and Administration (AHISA) Book Series

IGI GLOBAL
DISSEMINATOR OF KNOWLEDGE
www.igi-global.com

Published in the United States of America by
IGI Global
Medical Information Science Reference (an imprint of IGI Global)
701 E. Chocolate Avenue
Hershey PA, USA 17033
Tel: 717-533-8845
Fax: 717-533-8661
E-mail: cust@igi-global.com
Web site: http://www.igi-global.com

Copyright © 2017 by IGI Global. All rights reserved. No part of this publication may be reproduced, stored or distributed in any form or by any means, electronic or mechanical, including photocopying, without written permission from the publisher.
Product or company names used in this set are for identification purposes only. Inclusion of the names of the products or companies does not indicate a claim of ownership by IGI Global of the trademark or registered trademark.

Library of Congress Cataloging-in-Publication Data

Names: Aggarwal, Rashmi, 1974- editor. | Kaur, Rajinder, 1976- editor.
Title: Patent law and intellectual property in the medical field / Rashmi Aggarwal and Rajinder Kaur, editors.
Description: Hershey PA : Medical Information Science Reference, [2017] | Includes bibliographical references.
Identifiers: LCCN 2017001258| ISBN 9781522524144 (hardcover) | ISBN 9781522524151 (ebook)
Subjects: | MESH: Patents as Topic--legislation & jurisprudence | Health Care Sector--legislation & jurisprudence | Drug Industry--legislation & jurisprudence | Drugs, Generic | India
Classification: LCC T211 | NLM QV 33 JI4 | DDC 352.7/49--dc23 LC record available at https://lccn.loc.gov/2017001258

This book is published in the IGI Global book series Advances in Healthcare Information Systems and Administration (AHISA) (ISSN: 2328-1243; eISSN: 2328-126X)

British Cataloguing in Publication Data
A Cataloguing in Publication record for this book is available from the British Library.

All work contributed to this book is new, previously-unpublished material.
The views expressed in this book are those of the authors, but not necessarily of the publisher.

For electronic access to this publication, please contact: eresources@igi-global.com.

Advances in Healthcare Information Systems and Administration (AHISA) Book Series

ISSN:2328-1243
EISSN:2328-126X

Editor-in-Chief: Anastasius Moumtzoglou, Hellenic Society for Quality & Safety in Healthcare and P. & A. Kyriakou Children's Hospital, Greece

MISSION

The **Advances in Healthcare Information Systems and Administration (AHISA) Book Series** aims to provide a channel for international researchers to progress the field of study on technology and its implications on healthcare and health information systems. With the growing focus on healthcare and the importance of enhancing this industry to tend to the expanding population, the book series seeks to accelerate the awareness of technological advancements of health information systems and expand awareness and implementation.

Driven by advancing technologies and their clinical applications, the emerging field of health information systems and informatics is still searching for coherent directing frameworks to advance health care and clinical practices and research. Conducting research in these areas is both promising and challenging due to a host of factors, including rapidly evolving technologies and their application complexity. At the same time, organizational issues, including technology adoption, diffusion and acceptance as well as cost benefits and cost effectiveness of advancing health information systems and informatics applications as innovative forms of investment in healthcare are gaining attention as well. **AHISA** addresses these concepts and critical issues.

COVERAGE

- Medical informatics
- E-Health and M-Health
- Rehabilitative Technologies
- IT Applications in Physical Therapeutic Treatments
- IT security and privacy issues
- Nursing Expert Systems
- Role of informatics specialists
- Measurements and Impact of HISA on Public and Social Policy
- Management of Emerging Health Care Technologies
- IT Applications in Health Organizations and Practices

IGI Global is currently accepting manuscripts for publication within this series. To submit a proposal for a volume in this series, please contact our Acquisition Editors at Acquisitions@igi-global.com or visit: http://www.igi-global.com/publish/.

The Advances in Healthcare Information Systems and Administration (AHISA) Book Series (ISSN 2328-1243) is published by IGI Global, 701 E. Chocolate Avenue, Hershey, PA 17033-1240, USA, www.igi-global.com. This series is composed of titles available for purchase individually; each title is edited to be contextually exclusive from any other title within the series. For pricing and ordering information please visit http://www.igi-global.com/book-series/advances-healthcare-information-systems-administration/37156. Postmaster: Send all address changes to above address. ©© 2017 IGI Global. All rights, including translation in other languages reserved by the publisher. No part of this series may be reproduced or used in any form or by any means – graphics, electronic, or mechanical, including photocopying, recording, taping, or information and retrieval systems – without written permission from the publisher, except for non commercial, educational use, including classroom teaching purposes. The views expressed in this series are those of the authors, but not necessarily of IGI Global.

Titles in this Series

For a list of additional titles in this series, please visit:
https://www.igi-global.com/book-series/advances-healthcare-information-systems-administration/37156

Design, Development, and Integration of Reliable Electronic Healthcare Platforms
Anastasius Moumtzoglou (P&A Kyriakou Children's Hospital, Greece)
Medical Information Science Reference • ©2017 • 357pp • H/C (ISBN: 9781522517245) • US $205.00

Cloud Computing Systems and Applications in Healthcare
Chintan M. Bhatt (Charotar University of Science & Technology, India) and S. K. Peddoju (Indian Institute of Technology Roorkee, India)
Medical Information Science Reference • ©2017 • 282pp • H/C (ISBN: 9781522510024) • US $205.00

Handbook of Research on Healthcare Administration and Management
Nilmini Wickramasinghe (Epworth HealthCare, Australia & Deakin University, Australia)
Medical Information Science Reference • ©2017 • 825pp • H/C (ISBN: 9781522509202) • US $345.00

Reshaping Medical Practice and Care with Health Information Systems
Ashish Dwivedi (University of Hull, UK)
Medical Information Science Reference • ©2016 • 399pp • H/C (ISBN: 9781466698703) • US $150.00

M-Health Innovations for Patient-Centered Care
Anastasius Moumtzoglou (P&A Kyriakou Children's Hospital, Greece)
Medical Information Science Reference • ©2016 • 438pp • H/C (ISBN: 9781466698611) • US $235.00

For an enitre list of titles in this series, please visit:
https://www.igi-global.com/book-series/advances-healthcare-information-systems-administration/37156

IGI GLOBAL
DISSEMINATOR OF KNOWLEDGE
www.igi-global.com

701 East Chocolate Avenue, Hershey, PA 17033, USA
Tel: 717-533-8845 x100 • Fax: 717-533-8661
E-Mail: cust@igi-global.com • www.igi-global.com

Table of Contents

Detailed Table of Contents

In this chapter, we review the legal effects of patent rights and specifically address the legal aspects of the patent system. The production and dissemination of new knowledge is fraught with market failures because knowledge is a public good. Patents provide a second-best solution to the resulting appropriability problem. We review the main benefits, types and costs of the patent system, focusing on the role that patents play in providing incentives for innovation, in promoting the dissemination of knowledge, and in helping technology transfer and commercialization of new technology. From a more normative perspective, we address the questions of what the features of an optimal patent system are and whether the patent system is socially desirable. We examine the problem of the optimal length and scope of patent protection, both for the case of a single innovation and for the richer case of cumulative innovations. Finally, we review the recent changes in patent regime and it is based on the view that stronger patents would boost innovation and the issues related to how the patent system influences the market structure and research and development investments.

There is a great deal of disparity between the availability and affordability of medicines in least developed, developing and developed nations. Patents are one of the major

People often say that the world is not only "Black and White" but there are many other shades which pose difficult question. Parallel import, which is also known as "Grey area" is one of them. Parallel imports are goods produced genuinely under protection of a trademark, patent, or copyright, placed in one market, and then imported into another market without the approval of the Intellectual Property Right holder. Through this chapter, the Author(s) have tried to give an insight on parallel imports by discussing all possible national and international issues related to it. Some principal concepts like exhaustion, regional and global have acquired considerable space in the chapter. A brief contemporary view on parallel import has also been taken by the author(s). The contradictory views; one which favours the Parallel imports by endorsing that it enhances the local competition; and another which condemns parallel imports are covered in the later part of the chapter.

Exclusion of patentability finds its justification in philanthropy and public welfare. Time and again this approach has been endorsed and upheld by the eminent jurists. However, the "US Supreme Court in the case of Diamond v. Chakrabarty" endorsed a controversial view holding that "anything under the sun made by man" is patentable, but the situation was however rectified subsequently in "Diamond v. Dier." The Boards have gone a step forward in being very selective while granting patents excluding "Plant and Animal varieties" and also other immoral procedures, for example the process of cloning human beings etc. from the scope of patentability. The chapter will take up the study relating to the provisions of exclusions in patentability in international and national regime. The chapter will further highlight the emerging grey areas on the exclusions of patentability.

The issue of patenting is a contentious issue. Different stakeholders hold opposite views. The pharmaceutical giants demand for stricter and longer Intellectual Property Protection for the promotion of research and development. They contend IP protection to be the "bedrock of their business". While the health activists and governments of developing nations want greater flexibility in intellectual property protection and shorter patent period protection. Article 31 of the TRIPs agreement provides certain flexibilities to cater to certain situations. The countries are free to determine the grounds to issue provisions like compulsory licensing. But despite the provisions very few countries have used them. Pharmaceuticals giants with the backing of developed countries always try to denounce the practice of compulsory licensing with economic and political pressure. This chapter explains the concept and significance of Intellectual Property with reference to Pharmaceuticals. It also traces the little history of TRIPs agreement and explains the concept of Compulsory Licensing with trends in its use. It also discusses the few instances where compulsory License has been issued in different countries and tries to find the reasons of non issuance of Compulsory License.

Compulsory licensing is defined generally as the granting of a license by a government to use a patent without the patent-holder's permission. As applied to international intellectual property rights, it allows governments to grant licenses for patent use in situations where the patent-holder is either not using the patent within the country or is not using it adequately. Most of the drugs for which compulsory licenses have been granted in India are used for treatment of life-threatening diseases. The pharmaceutical companies however object on the ground of violation of their patent rights. This chapter discusses the provisions for compulsory licensing in TRIPs and the India patent system.

Traditional knowledge and Intellectual Property Rights (IPR), both are supplementary and complementary to each other. The aim of traditional knowledge is to promote community interest and protect indigenous rights against bio-piracy and bio-prospecting. On the other hand, IPR guarantees monopoly of a product or service to an organization and empowers it to profit from it. This article studies the present Indian IPR system to understand whether it is capable to handle traditional knowledge or should it be amended to incorporate a separate law to protect traditional knowledge. Besides, a large-scale commercialization and unauthorized use of traditional knowledge has been observed, which gives rise to the need to screen and protect it. This article also takes into consideration the Bonn guidelines and Indian Biodiversity Act 2002 and the issues related to traditional knowledge, and finds that the current issues cannot be resolved by the existing IPR regime.

By creating a robust intellectual property structure, a high-quality job future can be secured and sustained. Therefore, promotion to innovation/invention requires adequate protection. The multinational giant Colgate- Palmolive can be seen caught up into legal dispute where accusation is over the company for having purloined an archaic formula to have its roots to ancient times, and also being used by Indians for generations. India foiled an attempt by consumer goods giant Colgate-Palmolive to patent a mouthwash formula containing herb extract by citing ancient texts that show it was traditionally used in ancient medicinal practices. Traditional Knowledge Digital Library of Council of Scientific & Industrial Research (CSIR-TKDL) had submitted proof in the form of references from ancient books, which said the herb and its extracts in Indian systems of medicine. The proactivness of Indian community to safeguard its traditional knowledge obstructed the profit-making strategy of the company.

Preface

The TRIPs agreement of the WTO envisaged a global IPR regime with major consensus on best practices and policy framework on all IPRs for the WTO members. India signed the TRIPS agreement in 1995 and committed to being TRIPs compliant by 2005. This led to notification of The Patents (Amendment) Act, 2005 which came into effect on April 3, 2005 fulfilling the TRIPs agreement. There was a direct implication on the medical patents regime in India. The rationale behind this amendment as emphasized by the then Government of India was that it will increase R&D in the country- the only way to survive in this competitive globalized economy to which India had opened up in mid 1990s. Indian pharma industry had been manufacturing high quality generic medicines at an affordable cost under the previous process patent regime. With effect from January 1, 2005, India began recognizing product patents, an important step towards complying with its TRIPS obligation. This had put an end to 'reverse engineering' practiced by the Indian companies paving the way for innovation and research in the pharma industry. It might not have severally changed the fate and face of the Indian pharma industry immediately but it was inevitable that in the times to come the number of new product launches had to be under the product patent provisions as against the process patents. Thereby, the domestic companies had to gain significant breakthroughs in their R&D efforts. At the same time the interest of the consumer, who in case of the pharma industry is a patient, needed medical care and access to medicines at most reasonable prices could not be diluted.

The patent protection is the statutory right granted under the national patent acts, to the patentee to exercise his absolute right on his invention and thereby it casts a duty on the part of the legislature to ensure that there are requisite laws to guarantee these protections. Though it's a monopoly right granted for a limited period of time, the right of exclusion of other stakeholders has to be carefully construed. Hence, any patent regime has to deal with following contentions:

1. Any patent protection leads to a limited monopoly in favor of the patentee which is justified on the ground that when the patentee is given exclusive right to ascertain this protection to ensure commercial viability of his invention. The commercial gains are primary benefits for the patentee and provides motivation to incentivize and encourage further R&D for technological and other advancements.
2. Patents guarantee a statutory right only for inventions and not prior art. Though the grant is national, investigation whether it is an invention or not is global. These are proprietary rights of an investor for a limited period but the knowledge is a public property, a common heritage of the people and hence can these inventions be declared as private properties of the inventors and exclusive right of use can be bestowed on them under the patent regime?

In India, this differentiation was adopted in The Patents Act, 1970. The architect of The Indian Patent Law of 1970, S Vedaraman, the then Director of the Indian Patent Office had summarized the spirit of the patent legislation as "We are not against patents. And we are prepared to pay decent license fees. But we in India cannot afford monopolies." From 1970 till 2005, India had a process for the pharma, agrochemicals and food industry and laid down that the patents shall not be granted for the claims or the products but for the manufacturing of these products. This provision was very well received by the Indian pharma industry and it rigorously indulged in 'reverse engineering'. Over a period of time the local pharma industry flourished so much that 85% of the pharma products were produced and distributed by these local manufacturers.

With the opening of Indian economy in early 1990's, the pharma multinationals felt threatened by this practice of their Indian counterparts. They did not find much merit in the grant of process patents for pharma inventions though the protection of inventions through products patents in their own countries was developed only in the last 30 years. For example, in Switzerland, the Swiss pharma industry fought for the enactment of a patent law at the end of the 19th century to imitate the foreign drugs, such as Aspirin. It was in 1978 after many deliberations that the product patent was introduced in Switzerland for pharma products. Such patents protect the interest of technology exporters, which shield them from low-cost competition. The erstwhile Indian Patents Act 1970, was perceived as a balanced legislation that helped the growth of the domestic pharma industry and also adequately covered the public interests. The Indian pharma industry produced high quality products of almost all therapeutic groups and that helped exports of generic pharma products to the developing and developed countries at competitive prices. The strong base of the Indian pharma industry did not find any favor with the multinational companies. A group of these companies banded together, and worked relentlessly behind the scenes, first to work out what they called was an "ideal", "Global" patent regime, and then to "sell" it to the US administration and then to have it put on the WTO agenda and through the courtesy of this body have on the international trade to incorporate it in the TRIPS agreement in accordance with which all national Patents Acts of the member states of the WTO had to be amended. The thrust of their whole effort was to overturn the 1970 Act in India and similar legislation elsewhere in the world.

In India, the erstwhile Patents Act, 1970 provided the process patents under Section 5 which served to legalize "copying" of the drugs that were patented in developed countries as newly invented products but were unprotected in India. These Indian pharma companies were paying for licenses and royalties, hence that could access the newest molecules from all over the world and reformulate them for sale in the domestic market. Further, it provided for the general principles of working of the patentable inventions. The provision on these principles emphatically laid down the intention of the legislature to grant the patents to encourage inventions and to secure that the inventions are worked in India on a commercial scale. Thus, the inventions to be patentable had a commercial utility to it and further, the patentee ensured that the product is not kept to himself and that he should explore the marketing aspect of the patented process without any unreasonable delays. The law made it mandatory for the patentee to manufacture the process as only dealing in the imports of the process was not permitted under this provision. These trends lead to the share of the multinationals decline to 40% of the Indian market. The Patents Act, 1970 was amended three times in 1999, 2002 and finally in 2005 to bring it in line with the TRIPS agreement. In the amending process, some safeguard provisions had been incorporated. However, some provisions were beyond the TRIPS requirements and were called as TRIPs plus, the contentious of was Section 3(d). A critical evaluation of these amendments needs to be done in order to understand its impact on the Indian pharma industry.

Another provision which finds special mention here is on Compulsory License (CL) which permitted a third party to approach the Controller of patents, the official-in-charge of the grant of patents in the Patent office to grant a CL at any time after the expiration of three years from the date of the sealing of a patent. The pre-requisites for the grant of the CL were:

1. Reasonable requirements of public with respect to the patented invention have not been satisfied and there is a shortage of goods
2. Patented invention is not available to the public at a reasonable price

These two conditions though broadly covered the grounds on which the CL could be granted but a lot of other grounds could have been covered through this provision. A special ground in relation to the pharma industry where if there is a shortage of certain essential medicines and the patentee is manufacturing the patented medicine to the best of his ability but could not cater to the demands of the market. Or when the production cost is more than the profits which can be generated from the manufacturing of the drug than the Government can intervene and grant a CL to the generic company which can provide the same drug at a reasonable cost. The Controller could grant the CL to achieve certain purposes such as that the patented inventions worked on a commercial scale in India without undue delay and to the fullest extent that is reasonably practicable and that the CL should not be given against the interests of any persons for the time being working or developing an invention in India.

These provisions envisaged that the right given to any person through a patent protection should not be diluted by the grant of the patent protection if it is likely to prejudice the patentee rights. How did these rights get prejudiced was not clear from the reading of the provision. A more elaborate description of these interests was required so that the balancing between the better interests of the public by the grant of the CL to a third-party vis a vis infringement of the third party could be maintained.

The TRIPS agreement was an endeavor, using the WTO forum, to re-impose on the third world a regime of monopoly domination by the multinational companies from which the third world countries had been trying to escape, through the enactment of suitable legislation from their respective States. The TRIPS agreement did not represent some sort of an "ideal" or "optimum" regime. It represented nothing intrinsically sacrosanct but only an imposition reflecting, the unequal bargaining strengths of the participants in the Uruguay Round Negotiations at that time. TRIPS provided a three-stage frame for countries such as India which did not grant product patent rights in pharmaceuticals, when TRIPS came into force on 1 January, 1995:

1. Introduction of a facility ("mail box") from January 1, 1995 to receive and hold product patent applications in the fields of pharmaceuticals (and agricultural chemicals). Such applications will not be processed for the grant of a patent until the end of 2004. Exclusive Marketing Rights (EMRs) could be obtained for the application if a patent has been granted in some other WTO member country and the application has not been rejected in the country as not being an invention.
2. Compliance, from January 1, 2000 with other obligations of TRIPS, namely, those related to rights of patentee, term of patent protection, compulsory licensing, reversal of burden of proof etc.

3. Introduction of full product patent protection in all fields including pharmaceuticals from January 1, 2005. All the product patent applications held in the mail box are also required to be taken up for examination from January 1, 2005.

The important changes incorporated in The Patents (Amendment) Act, 2005 are:

1. Grant of patents for pharmaceutical, chemicals and food substances *per se* which were non-patentable vide Sections 3 and 5 of The Patents Act, 1970.
2. The grant of patents for the products and hence a shift from the process patent regime to the product patent regime.
3. Recognition of micro- organisms as a patentable subject matter.
4. Reversal of burden of proof in cases where infringement of a process for producing a novel compound where it prima facie appears that no other process could have been used.

The provisions on inventions which were patentable under the earlier act have not been amended except clause (d) of Section 3 of the principal Act. It first ruled out patenting of any discovery of a new form of a known substance which does not result in the enhancement of the known efficacy of that substance. This provision could also be interpreted in the light of the inventions *per se* where there has to be a technological improvement in the known property of an object for it to be entitled for the grant of patents. In the pharma sector if a medicine is invented and it is only an improvement of the earlier drug it shall not be subjected to the grant of the patents under this provision.

Further, this provision also covers the mere discovery of any new property or new use for a known substance or of the mere use of a known process or a machine or apparatus unless such known process results in a new product or employs at least one new reactant. The discoveries *per se* are not patentable and hence this provision is rather not required in such details. Did the exhaustive list of the different types of discoveries complicated the grant of pharma patents?

The explanation attached to the clause is just to clarify the different components of the pharma inventions which may involve salts, esters, ethers, polymorphs, metabolites, pure form, particle size, isomers, mixtures of isomers, complexes, combinations and other derivatives of known substance shall be considered to be the same substance, unless they differ significantly in properties with regard to efficacy. Based on case to case basis the various constituents of any medicine had to differ significantly in regard to efficacy for it to be granted a patent and mere improvements cannot be granted patents. Only non-obvious and significant changes in the composition of the pharmaceutical substances can be considered for the grant of patents. The final decision on whether the substance is an invention and thereby should be granted a patent was subject to the discretionary understanding of the patent office. Should this provision be made objective and will it have a direct bearing on the patent files by the MNCs in India?

This provision further incorporates the term "new use" of already known property of the medicine. For example, if there is a medicine which can be injected and if one manipulates the composition, it can also be used as an oral medicine then this new use is not patentable. However, if the second medical indication of a known drug molecule passes the test than it is patentable. Consequently, if a discovery of a new form of a new drug molecule, results in an enhancement of its known efficacy, it is patentable. Similarly, the mere discovery of a new use of a known substance is not patentable. The pharma companies incur a major expenditure on the discovery of a new use of a known substance which is now made non-patentable.

The language of the provision 'differs significantly in properties with regard to efficacy' is the final test of patentability as regards all inventions around a drug molecule. It seems that this explanation will keep a huge amount of R&D outside the scope of patentability, because the properties concerning efficacy will have an overriding effect over the standard tests of patentability when it comes to pharma inventions. The pharma companies will restrain themselves from indulging in R&D relating to better efficacy which may not be significant efficacious. As the patent protection is granted only for the latter there might not be improved versions of available medicines in the market any more. Either there will be new inventions or medicines which are significantly different from the available drugs.

The objective behind such an elaborate explanation in Section 3(d) is probably to check what the Indian generic drug makers alleges as ''ever greening''. "Ever greening" is a phrase in currency in relation to updating of a patented product and protecting it as new. It is when the patent owner attempts to extend the patents monopoly by seeking a new patent that updates the first one before its expiration. This is usually done by claiming things such as "inventive" method for administering the pharma company covered by the base patent. For the pharma products, this means an extended monopoly that excluded generic drugs from the market. The act thereby makes it clear to the domestic companies that the new use of previously patented entities will not qualify for patents. How far reaching have been the consequences of this provisions needs to be assessed as it has been more than a decade since India made patents to be TRIPs compliant and more.

The objective of present edited volume is to understand the Indian patent laws, impact of all three amendments on the Indian medicine industry and subsequently on the consumers, the real stakeholders. Further, can we question whether IP policy was means to an end or an end in itself? Should there be unilateral approach within the context of more innovation more IP or more IP and thereby more innovations or should there by plurality of approaches? Can there be a thematic permeation to the IP regulations? There are many arms to these contentions. The book has been divided into 11 chapters.

Chapter 1, "Patents: An Overview and Legal Aspects," provides comprehensive understanding of Indian patents law and reviews the legal effects of patent rights. It reviews the main benefits, types and costs of the patent system, focusing on the role that patents play in providing incentives for innovation, in promoting the dissemination of knowledge, and in helping technology transfer and commercialization of new technology, problem of the optimal length and scope of patent protection, both for the case of a single innovation and for the richer case of cumulative innovations.

Chapters 2 and 3 provide a comparative between specific pricing policies of medicines as main contention against grant of patents for life saving medicines have been on the availability and affordability of medicines in least developed, developing and developed nations. The chapters cover various techniques pharmaceutical industry adopt to control price of patented products such as proliferation of me-too drugs, product reformulation, prolonging patent rights, biasing research and large promotional expenditures.

Chapter 4, "Impact of National and International Regulations on Indian Generic Drugs Industry," is an analysis. The chapter is a study on evolution of the IP laws in India with regard to pharma products and their impact on the pharma industry in India. It analyses the amendments to Indian Patents Act 1970 as a result of India's obligations towards the TRIPS agreement while balancing the need to safeguard the interests of its population, domestic industry, international laws and treaties.

Chapter 5, "Parallel Import in India: A Study," covers the concept of parallel importing when there the patented drugs are not either affordable or there is a shortage of goods in the market. As a fall out the national regulators allows for parallel importing of drugs without seeking permission of the patentee.

Chapter 6, "Exclusions on Patentability," provides detailed understanding on exclusion of patentability with reference to Diamond v. Chakrabarty where the U.S. Supreme court endorsed a controversial view holding that "anything under the sun made by man" is patentable, but the situation was rectified subsequently in Diamond v. Dier. The chapter will take up the study relating to the provisions of exclusions in patentability in international and national regimes while highlighting the emerging grey areas on the exclusions of patentability.

Chapters 7 and 8 are a study on the issue of patenting vis-a-vis stakeholder perspectives holding diverse views. On one hand the pharma companies demand for rigid patent protection on the context of R&D spending's and on the other hand the health activists and governments of developing nations want greater flexibility in the IP protection and shorter patent period protection. It explains the concept of CL, its use and provides illustrations on issuance and denial of CL in different countries.

In Chapter 9, traditional knowledge and IPR, both are supplementary and complementary to each other but the aim of traditional knowledge is to promote community interest, protect indigenous rights against bio piracy and bio prospecting, on the other hand IPR provides monopoly and profit. These chapters also cover the effects of Bonn guidelines and Biodiversity Act, 2002 and the issues related to traditional knowledge and how those issues cannot be handled by the existing IPR laws.

Chapter 10, "Colgate-Palmolive's Attempt of Patenting Toothpaste Formula," is a case study of Colgate-Palmolive, legal dispute on allegations of purloining of an archaic formula to be used for a mouthwash product by the company which was a prior art and traditional know-how in India.

Chapter 11, "Various Tools Available to Access Patent Information in India," is a comprehensive study on search engines to establish the credentials on whether the patent application can be granted a patent or not by the national patent offices. For the patent grant, technical information about the invention must be disclosed to the public in the patent application. This information is available from both free and fee-based sources across globe. This chapter is a study on different databases and tools available in India for the patent search.

Chapter 1
Patents:
An Overview and Legal Aspects

Rita Ghial
Panjab University, India

ABSTRACT

In this chapter, we review the legal effects of patent rights and specifically address the legal aspects of the patent system. The production and dissemination of new knowledge is fraught with market failures because knowledge is a public good. Patents provide a second-best solution to the resulting appropriability problem. We review the main benefits, types and costs of the patent system, focusing on the role that patents play in providing incentives for innovation, in promoting the dissemination of knowledge, and in helping technology transfer and commercialization of new technology. From a more normative perspective, we address the questions of what the features of an optimal patent system are and whether the patent system is socially desirable. We examine the problem of the optimal length and scope of patent protection, both for the case of a single innovation and for the richer case of cumulative innovations. Finally, we review the recent changes in patent regime and it is based on the view that stronger patents would boost innovation and the issues related to how the patent system influences the market structure and research and development investments.

INTRODUCTION

Intellectual property is the intangible product of the mind's work. The United States and other developed nations generally recognize four different routes for protecting intellectual property: copyright, trademark, trade secret and patent (Auerbach, 2006). A patent is a document, issued, upon application, by a government office (or a

DOI: 10.4018/978-1-5225-2414-4.ch001

Copyright © 2017, IGI Global. Copying or distributing in print or electronic forms without written permission of IGI Global is prohibited.

regional office acting for several countries), which describes an invention and creates a legal situation in which the patented invention can normally only be exploited (manufactured, used, sold, imported) with the authorization of the owner of the patent. Patents play an increasingly important role in innovation and economic performance (Peters, 2006). Between 1992 and 2002, the number of patent applications filed in Europe, Japan and the United States increased by more than 40% (Brown, 2009). The increasing use of patents to protect inventions by businesses and public research organisations is closely connected to recent evolutions in innovation processes, the economy and patent regimes (Durham, 1999). Scientific and technological advances have created new waves of innovation, notably in information and communications technology (ICT)[1] and biotechnology, and innovation processes themselves have become centred less on individual firms and more dependent on interactions among global networks of actors in the public and private sectors (Moursund, 2005). Shifts in the legal and regulatory frame work of patent regimes have resulted in more expansive domains of patentable subject matter (patent regimes in many countries now include biotechnology and software), and more robust and more valuable patents (Arnold, 2007). Like a deed to real property, most governments require a patent to specify the metes and bounds of the property claimed to constitute the invention. This legal description of the invention is found in the patent's claims. Unlike real property whose borders can be measured with precision, the precise boundaries of an invention cannot be precisely determined. Thus, a patent often presents a set of claims of varied scope which extend inward from a broad description of the invention to a narrow description of the patent's core invention (Pilani. Entrepreneurship Development and IPR unit, n. d.). A patent endows its owner with a limited term of years in which the patent owner may exclude others from making, selling, using or importing the invention claimed in the patent. It is important to recognize that a patent provides only a right to exclude others from practicing an invention (i.e., manufacture, use, sale or importation). It does not confer an affirmative right on the patent holder to actually make, use, sell, or import the invention claimed in the patent. The patentee's ability to practice the patented invention may be restricted by the patents of others (Pilani. Entrepreneurship Development and IPR unit, n. d.).

The right conferred by the patent grant is, in the language of the statute and of the grant itself, "the right to exclude others from making, using, offering for sale, or selling" the invention in the United States or "importing" the invention into the United States.[2] What is granted is not the right to make, use, offer for sale, sell or import, but the right to exclude others from making, using, offering for sale, selling or importing the invention. Once a patent is issued, the patentee must enforce the patent without aid of the USPTO. There are three types of patents:

1. Utility patents may be granted to anyone who invents or discovers any new and useful process, machine, article of manufacture, or composition of matter, or any new and useful improvement thereof;
2. Design patents may be granted to anyone who invents a new, original, and ornamental design for an article of manufacture; and
3. Plant patents may be granted to anyone who invents or discovers and asexually reproduces any distinct and new variety of plant (Khaliq & Winarski, 2014).

A patent has two important functions:

- **Protection:** A patent allows the patent holder to exclude others from commercially exploiting the invention covered by the patent and as specified in the claims in a certain country or region in which the patent was granted and for a specific period of time, generally not exceeding 20 years from the filing date (Hall, 2007).
- **Disclosure:** The publication of a patent and in many countries patent applications give the public access to information regarding new technologies in order to stimulate innovation and contribute to economic growth (Hall, 2007).

Protection

A patent application may be filed via one of the following routes:

- **National:** An application for a patent is generally filed at a national patent office and a patent for an invention may be granted and enforced only in that country in which patent protection is requested, in accordance with the law of that country. Corresponding applications covering the same invention can be filed in accordance with the respective national patent laws in different countries on an individual country-by-country basis (Chakroun, 2016).
- **Regional:** In some regions, regional patent applications may be filed at a regional patent office, for example the African Regional Intellectual Property Organization (ARIPO)[3] or the European Patent Office (EPO)[4]. Regional patent applications have the same effect as applications filed in the member states of the respective regional patent agreement. In certain regions, patents are granted centrally as a bundle of national patents. In some other regions, a single regional patent granted by the regional patent office has effect in the entire territory of that region. In order to validate regional patents in the Member States, submission of a translation of the granted patent into the national language may be required (Regional Patents, n. d.).

- **International**: International applications may be filed with the national or certain regional patent offices of Contracting States of the Patent Cooperation Treaty (PCT)[5] or the International Bureau of the World Intellectual Property Organization (WIPO) by any resident or national of a PCT Contracting State. A single international patent application has the same effect as national or certain regional applications filed in each Contracting State of the PCT (Merrill, Levin, & Myers, 2003). Although, the major part of the patent application procedure is carried out within the international phase, a patent can only be granted by each designated State within the subsequent national phase (Poltorak & Lerner, 2001).

Although procedures vary amongst patent offices, the following illustrates a much-generalized procedure for granting a patent:

- **Filing:** An applicant chooses a filing route, i.e. national, regional or international, and files an application. The initial filing is considered the "priority filing" from which further successive national, regional or international filings can be made within the "priority period" of one year under the Paris Convention for the Protection of Industrial Property (WIPO, n. d.).
- **Formal Examination:** The patent office ensures that all administrative formalities have been complied with, e.g., that all relevant documentation is included in the application, and that a filing fee has been paid.
- **Prior Art Search:** In many countries, but not all, the patent office carries out a search of the prior art, i.e., of all relevant technological information publicly known at the time of filing of the patent application or when applicable, at the time of the priority filing (USPTO, 2014). Using extensive databases, expert examiners draft a "search report", which lists relevant prior art.
- **Publication:** In most countries, the patent application is published 18 months after the priority date, i.e., after the filing date or the priority filing. In general, a patent is also published once granted.
- **Substantive Examination:** Not all offices conduct substantive examination and some only do so if requested within a specified time. The examiner checks that the application satisfies the requirements of novelty and inventive step (non-obviousness) against the prior art listed in the search report. Further, he/she checks whether the invention is susceptible of industrial application and within the scope of patentable subject matter. In many countries, prior art search and substantive examination are conducted consecutively.

- **Grant/Refusal:** In general, if the patentability requirement is not met, the applicant is given an opportunity to amend the application. If the examination process reaches a positive outcome, the patent is granted and the office issues a certificate of grant. Otherwise, the patent application is refused.
- **Opposition:** Within a specified period, many patent offices allow third parties to oppose the granted patent on the grounds that it does not in fact satisfy patentability requirements. In some countries, third party observations and opposition may also be allowed in a certain time frame before the grant of a patent.
- **Appeal:** In general, decisions of grant or refusal of a patent and decisions of opposition boards can be challenged before an administrative body or a court (USPTO, 2014).

Disclosure

The second important function of the patent system is disclosure, i.e., a patent gives the public access to information regarding new technologies in order to stimulate innovation and contribute to economic growth.

Though the protection offered by a patent is territorial, covering only the jurisdiction in which the patent has been granted, the information contained in a patent document is global, available as a disclosure to any individual or organization worldwide, thus allowing anyone to learn from and build on this knowledge.

UNDERSTANDING PATENT PLEDGES: AN OVERVIEW OF LEGAL CONSIDERATIONS

The Legal Theories Underlying Patent Pledges and Covenants

Patent pledges and covenants made by Contributors to the Patent Commons are not licensed to the Open Source Community as a whole, nor are they licensed to any particular individual or company. Instead, ownership of the patents remains with the pledgor or promisor, but subject to an enforceable pledge or promise governing how the owner or holder will or will not enforce the patents in the future.

Individuals and others who take advantage of these promises or covenants ("users") to facilitate innovation do so in reliance on the legal doctrines of implied license,[6] equitable estoppel,[7] or laches[8] to protect themselves against a claim of patent infringement by the pledgers and promisors (collectively, "Contributors").[9]

These doctrines allow users to rely on the representations for the uses described in the pledges and covenants (collectively, "Commitments"). Understanding the basics of these theories is the first step in using the Patent Commons safely.

Patent Infringement Liability

Affirmative Acts of the Infringer

In general, two conditions must be met before liability will attach for patent infringement: (1) an affirmative act of the infringer, typically unlawful use of claimed, patented technology, and (2) an affirmative act of the patentee[10] putting the alleged infringer on notice of the allegedly infringing act.

Secondary References

An affirmative act on the part of the alleged infringer may include using technology disclosed in a patent cited as a Secondary Reference in order to make, use, or sell a particular device such as a piece of software.[11] To avoid liability, the alleged infringer must demonstrate how and why her technology is different from the patented technology disclosed as a Secondary Reference.

Generally, patents as Secondary References are disclosed in three different ways. First, almost all patents have one or more patents cited on the cover page under the heading "References cited." The patents disclosed under this heading are typically patents identified by the patent applicant on an information disclosure statement provided to the patent examiner examining the patent when it is first filed as an application. In some instances, these references are supplied by third parties in protest[12] to the filing of the initial patent application. The references usually contain information about the Secondary Reference such as patent number, date of issuance, and the inventor's name. In addition to the patents disclosed under the References Cited section, patents may also be disclosed via a mechanism known as incorporation by reference (Massey, 1994). Using this disclosure mechanism, a patentee can cite various United States patents, and have the technological disclosures in those patents included with the filed application to assist in complying with the enablement, best-mode, and/or written-description requirements for the patentee's own patent application (USPTO, 2014).

The third type of Secondary Reference is a prior art citation made in the patent application itself. This occurs when the drafter of a patent application wants to premptively distinguish certain types of prior art patents[13] to reduce the likelihood that a patent examiner will use that prior art against the applicant. In distinguishing a prior art patent, the patent drafter may provide details regarding the technology, such as how it is produced, how it works, and other related information in order to distinguish adequately the patented prior art technology from the technology claimed in the patent application.

In all of these cases, an alleged infringer must be able to explain how and why their technology is distinct from the patented technology in the Secondary Reference. If the technology cannot be distinguished, then once the patentee puts the alleged infringer on notice it becomes easier for her to claim that the alleged infringer deliberately copied the ideas or designs of a patent. That, in turn, may result in a higher damage award if infringement is found.[14]

In sum, the more an alleged infringer knows about a patent that is claiming the technology of a product that she is making, using or selling, the greater the likelihood that she will be liable for damages for patent infringement.[15] If an alleged infringer merely knows the patent number, date of issuance, and the inventor's name from a patent cited in a References Cited section, this would more than likely not constitute an affirmative act that, in turn, could support a finding of liability for damages. If, however, the alleged infringer knows how to implement a particular technology by reading, for example, a prior art citation within a patent, it becomes more likely to be deemed an affirmative act that would support a finding of liability for damages[16] (assuming she is making, using or selling the technology). A formal, competent legal opinion[17] such as an infringement opinion from a patent attorney may assist an alleged infringer in distinguishing her technology from technology disclosed in a Secondary Reference.

Blocking Patents

Another affirmative act that may serve as a basis for patent infringement liability is improving on patented technology the alleged infringer is legally entitled to use, yet the improvements are already patented. Again, an alleged infringer must be able to explain how and why her improvements to the existing patented technology are distinct from the patented technology of another. This problem is exemplified in the Blocking Patent[18] scenario, described below.

A patent grants the right to exclude others from a particular area of claimed technology, but does not confer the right to practice an invention.[19] In the Blocking Patent scenario, patent infringement liability may attach when the scope of the claims in the patent are exceeded and infringe on the patented technology of another patentee. If, for example, Patent A claims a method of using a particular algorithm with a particular type of processor, and someone legally entitled to use[20] Patent A tries to improve the scalability of the algorithm so that it can be used with a second processor, it is possible that a second patent, Patent B, already claims this improvement. The result is that someone legally entitled to use the Patent A must obtain a license to use the technology claimed in Patent B, and an individual entitled to use the technology claimed in Patent B must obtain a license to use the technology claimed in Patent A. Without those licenses, both individuals are prevented, or "blocked," from practicing the other party's claimed invention, and both are potentially liable for patent infringement if they do so.[21]

RECENT CHANGES IN PATENT REGIMES

Patent regimes have gone through important changes in the past two decades, most in the direction of strengthening patent rights, in the sense of reinforcing the exclusive rights conferred to patent holders, expanding their coverage and easing their enforcement. This upward shift in most countries coincided with upward international harmonisation of patent regimes. It was based on the view that stronger patents would boost innovation (Rossi & Pammouli, n. d.).

The design and enforcement of patent policies is increasingly the responsibility of new and more powerful governing bodies. Reforms were initiated in the United States in the late 1970s, and the centralised court system set up in 1982 (Court of Appeal of the Federal Circuit, CAFC) has been instrumental in strengthening the rights of patent holders in the United States. The EPO, with Europe wide coverage and a centralised examination system, was also set up in the late 1970s (Harrison & Sullivan, 2011). In 2002, the Japanese government created the Strategic Council on Intellectual Property under the Prime Minister's Cabinet with the aims to establish a national strategy for intellectual property (IP) and to implement the corresponding policies (an IP strategic programme was issued in July 2003) (Encaoua, 2005). At the global level, IPRs were included in international trade negotiations, and WTO was given enforcement power at the Uruguay Round in 1986-1994, resulting in the signature of TRIPS in 1994, which is considered as an important milestone in international harmonisation efforts. Negotiations are currently taking place at WIPO to increase international harmonisation of substantive patent law across countries, and some efforts have been initiated at the trilateral level to increase co-ordination among the three major patent offices in the world: the USPTO[22], JPO[23] and EPO[24].

Major changes experienced by patent regimes in the United States, Japan and Europe in the past two decades can be summarised as follows (Martinez & Gullec, 2004):

- **Extended Coverage of Intellectual Property Protection:** Areas that used to fall outside the patent subject matter are now partially or totally included, notably software, business methods and some inventions close to basic science, although differences remain across jurisdictions (which are significant in the case of business.

- **Patents Confer Broader Protection, Especially in New Areas:** Patent claims in new areas often cover far more than what the inventor actually discovered or invented. Some of the current patenting practices in new areas may extend protection to a broad range of applications unknown at the time of patenting (e.g. uses of genes) (Martinez & Gullec, 2004).
- **Filing Procedures Are Increasingly Flexible and Less Costly, Notably at the International Level:** Several mechanisms to defer filing and examination procedures at patent offices, such as the system introduced by the Patent Cooperation Treaty (PCT)[25], have transformed the initial application into a sort of option to patent that allows inventors to retain the right to patent in foreign countries for longer periods of time.
- **The Rights of Patent Holders Are More Frequently and Strongly Enforced in Court:** Since the creation of the CAFC in 1982, the rate of invalidation of patents by courts has substantially decreased in the United States. Efforts to create specialised courts are ongoing in other jurisdictions: legislation is expected to be passed next year in Japan in order to create a high court specialised in IPRs, and the implementation of a centralised patent litigation system is currently under discussion in Europe. Moreover, damage awards in patent litigation trials have substantially increased in recent years.
- **Restrictions on the Exemption for Research Use:** Recent developments indicate that the conditions to apply research exemptions may become increasingly restrictive in the future. In 2002, the CAFC held that research exemptions would be granted in the United States when research is solely for amusement, to satisfy idle curiosity, or for strict philosophical inquiry.

The main factors underlying changes to patent regimes in the past few years have been as follows:

- Great recognition that Intellectual property has major influence on innovation and growth. The conventional wisdom that has driven policy changes in recent years considers patents as an essential instrument to foster R&D investment and economic growth.
- Emergence of new governing bodies. The design and enforcement of patent policy has lain increasingly in the hands of international organizations such as the World Trade Organization (WTO)[26] and the World Intellectual Property Organization (WIPO)[27], major patent offices and courts specialized in Intellectual Property Rights (IPR)[28] issues such as the Court of Appeals for the Federal Circuit (CAFC)[29] in the United States.

- International harmonisation of patent regimes. Patent laws have followed an upward harmonisation process across countries via bilateral and multilateral treaties and especially since the inclusion of IPRs as an essential issue in international trade negotiations with the agreement on Trade Related Aspects of Intellectual Property Rights (TRIPS)[30].

CONCLUSION

The Contributors who have made Commitments to the Patent Commons Project understand the importance of providing the open source community with a safe place to innovate and create. The users who take advantage of the Commitments have at their disposal various legal doctrines that allow them to use these contributed patents without fear of facing liability for patent infringement by the Contributors, provided the users comply with the terms of the applicable Commitment (Rao, 2013). Those legal doctrines, like all legal doctrines, have limits that need to be understood and respected by users if they are to innovate safely (Bar-Shalom & Cook-Deegan, 2002). Patent law is so crucial to the economic system and because patent doctrines play such an important role in shaping how patent law promotes innovation while minimizing problems associated with the power to exclude, the economic role of patent law deserves greater attention from the courts (Bar-Shalom & Cook-Deegan, 2002). Although the Federal Circuit is by design a specialized court, we can anticipate that that court will become more explicit about the economic underpinnings of patent doctrines (Golden, 2008). At a time when public focus on technology and the role of government in promoting it has never been higher, it would serve neither the patent system nor public policy toward technology to obscure the role of the patent system in a thicket of technical patent law rules unapproachable by those unskilled in that arcane art.

Another factor seen missing from the obviousness analysis is the consideration of the inventor's subjective mental state and creative process. Understanding the process of creation/invention would assist in understanding the motivation of the inventor. This would require a better understanding of creativity and the manner in which scientists and engineers come up with innovations (Narayan, 2013). The Obviousness standard came into the foray when the lawmakers and the courts sought to define with precision, inventions which should be patentable. The patent theories proposed lay down the foundation for the several theories behind innovation. In this context the evolution of Obviousness standard is appreciated as an outcome of judicial activism and common sense. Courts and lawmakers have used several indices and introduced the hypothesis of person having ordinary skill in the art, to arrive at this elusive definition. At the apex of these indices and hypotheses underlies a determination of "sufficiently creative" versus "ordinarily creative".[31] This distinction of "sufficiently creative" versus "ordinarily creative", has through the years lost touch with how inventions are truly created. The abstract and subjective definition of Obviousness standard has been shown to cause indeterminacy in awarding patents, and thereby appreciating innovation (Maxwell, 2010).

REFERENCES

A Patent System for the 21st Century. (n. d.). Washington. The National academics Press.

Arnold, C. M. (2007). Protecting Intellectual Property in the Developing World: Next Stop—Thailand. Retrieved 11 July 2016 from http://scholarship.law.duke.edu/cgi/viewcontent.cgi?article=1156&context=dltr

Auerbach, J. I. (2006). Patent Law Principles & Strategies. *Edell, Shapiro & Finnan, LLC.* Retrieved 14 August 2016 from http://euro.ecom.cmu.edu/program/law/08-732/Patents/PatentLawPrinciples.pdf

Bar-Shalom, A., & Cook-Deegan, R. (2002). Patents and Innovation in Cancer Therapeutics: Lessons from CellPro. *The Milbank Quarterly*, *80*(40). PMID:12532643

Brown, D. A. (2009). Protecting Intellectual Property Right from the Start. *Eurostat.* Retrieved 22 July 2016 from http://ec.europa.eu/eurostat/statistics-explained/index.php/Patent_statistics

Chakroun, N. (2016). *Patents for Development Improved Patent Information Disclosure and Access for Incremental Innovation*. United Kingdom: Edward Elgar Publishing.

Durham, A. A. (1999). *Patents Law Essentials: A Concise Guide*. London: Greenwood Publishing Group.

Encaoua, D. (2005). The economics of patents: from natural rights to policy instruments.

Golden, J. M. (2008) The Federal Circuit and the D.C. Circuit: Comparative Trials of Two Semi Specialized Courts. Retrieved 24 November 2016 from http://www.gwlr.org/wp-content/uploads/2012/08/78-3-Golden1.pdf

Gov.uk. (n. d.). Intellectual property and your work. Retrieved 24 September 2016 from https://www.gov.uk/intellectual-property-an-overview/what-ip-is

Hall, B. H. (2007). Contribution to the New Palgrave: A Dictionary of Economics. Retrieved 22 June 2016 from http://web.mit.edu/e-club/hadzia/the-importance-of-patents.html

Harrison, S. S., & Sullivan, H. P. (2011). *Other Boardroom Revised How Leading Companies Realise Value From Their Intellectual Property*. Hoboken: Wiely & Sons. Inc.

Khaliq, I., & Winarski, T. (2014) USF School of Law. *Patent Licensing and Monetization Law*. Retrieved 21 July 2016 from http://www.uspto.gov/sites/default/files/inventors/edu-inf/BasicPatentGuide.pdf

Martinez, C., & Gullec, D. (2004). Overview of recent changes and comparison of patent regimes in the United Retrieved 23 October 2016 from https://www.researchgate.net/publication/250615452_Overview_of_recent_changes_and_comparison_of_patent_regimes_in_the_United_States_Japan_and_Europe

Massey., ... (1994). Distributed intelligence engineering casualty and damage control management system using an AC power line carrier-current lan. Retrieved 11 November 2016 from http://www.patents.com/us-5349644.html

Maxwell (2010). *Maxwell on the Interpretation of Statutes*. Lexis Nexis

Merrill, S. A., Levin, R. C., & Myers, M. B. (Eds.). (2003) Committee on Intellectual Property Rights in the Knowledge-Based Economy; Board on Science, Technology, and Economic Policy; Policy and Global Affairs; National Research Council.

Moursund, D. (2005). Introduction to Information and Communication Technology in Education. *Introduction to Information and Communication Technology in Education*. Retrieved 16 August 2016 from http://pages.uoregon.edu/moursund/Books/ICT/ICTBook.pdf

Narayan, P. (2013). *Intellectual Property Law*. Mumbai, India: Eastern Book Company.

Patents, R. (n.d.) Protecting Industrial Property Right. Retrieved 13 July 2016 from http://kipi.go.ke/index.php/regional-patents-aripo

Peters, D. M. (2006) Understanding Patent Pledges: An overview of legal considerations. Open Source Development Labs. Inc. Retrieved 12 August 2016 from http://www.patent-commons.org/publications/OSDL_Whitepaper_Final_final_4-12-06.pdf

Poltorak, A. I., & Lerner, P. J. (Eds.). (2001). *Essentials of Intellectual Property, Law, Economics and Strategy*. Hoboken: Wiley John Wiley & Sons, Inc.

Rao, V. G. (2013). *Intellectual Property Rights in India*. India: SSDN Pub.

Rossi, M. A., & Pammolli, F. (n. d.). Intellectual Property. Technological Regimes and Market Dynamics. Retrieved 23 November 2016 from http://www.who.int/intellectualproperty/submissions/IP-tech-reg-final.pdf

USPTO. (2014). General information concerning patents. United States Patent and Trademark Office. Department of commerce. Retrieved 23 July 2016 from http://www.uspto.gov/sites/default/files/inventors/edu-inf/BasicPatentGuide.pdf

USPTO. (2014). General Information Concerning Patents. Retrieved 15 November 2016 from http://Www.Uspto.Gov/Patents-Getting-Started/General-Information-concerning-patents

WIPO. (n. d.). WIPO Guide To Using patent information. Retrieved 26 August 2016 from http://www.wipo.int/edocs/pubdocs/en/patents/434/wipo_pub_l434_03.pdf

ENDNOTES

1 Information and communications technology (ICT) is an extended term for information technology (IT) which stresses the role of unified communication and the integration of telecommunications (telephone lines and wireless signals), computers as well as necessary enterprise software, middleware, storage, and audio-visual systems, which enable users to access, store, transmit, and manipulate information.

2 US Patent Office definition of Patent: The right conferred by the patent grant is, in the language of the statute and of the grant itself, "the right to exclude others from making, using, offering for sale, or selling" the invention in the United States or "importing" the invention into the United States. What is granted is not the right to make, use, offer for sale, sell or import, but the right to exclude others from making, using, offering for sale, selling or importing the invention." Retrieved from http://www.the-business-of-patents.com/definition-of-patent.htmt.

3 The African Regional Intellectual Property Organization (ARIPO), formerly African Regional Industrial Property Organization, is an intergovernmental organization for cooperation among African states in patent and other intellectual property matters. ARIPO was established by the Lusaka Agreement of 1976.

It has the capacity to hear applications for patents and registered trademarks in its member states who are parties to the Harare (patents), Banjul (marks) and Arusha (plant varieties) protocols ARIPO also features a protocol on the protection of traditional knowledge, the Swakopmund Protocol, signed in 2010 by 9 member states of the organization. However, that has not come into force yet, as of July 2013.

4 The European Patent Office (EPO) is one of the two organs of the European Patent Organisation (EPOrg), the other being the Administrative Council. The EPO acts as executive body for the Organization while the Administrative Council acts as its supervisory body as well as, to a limited extent, its legislative body. The actual legislative power to revise the European Patent Convention lies with the Contracting States themselves when meeting at a Conference of the Contracting States.

5 The Patent Cooperation Treaty (PCT) is an international patent law treaty, concluded in 1970. It provides a unified procedure for filing patent applications to protect inventions in each of its contracting states. A patent application filed under the PCT is called an international application, or PCT application.

6 See Wang Labs v. Mitsubishi, 103 F.3d 1571, 1582 (Fed. Cir. 1997) (finding an implied license where the accused infringer relied on patentee's public statements and conduct, showing acquiescence, in creating the infringing goods for the purpose of promoting an industry standard). See also AT&T Corp. v. Microsoft, 2004 U.S. Dist. LEXIS 1214, 15 (granting AT&T's motion for partial summary judgment dismissing Microsoft's affirmative defense of implied license where Microsoft failed to proffer evidence showing a nexus between AT&T's course of conduct or alleged waiver of patent rights and Microsoft's actions.

7 See B. Braun Medical Inc. v. Abbott Laboratories et al., 124 F.3d 1419, 1425-1426 (Fed. Cir. 1997) (reversing a finding of equitable estoppel where the evidence did not support a finding that the patentee stated that they would not sue the defendant for patent infringement). See generally Ecolab, Inc. v. Envirochem, Inc., 264 F.3d 1358, 1371 (Fed. Cir. 2001) (citing Scholle Corp. v. Blackhawk Molding Co. Inc., 133 F.3d 1469, 1473 (Fed. Cir. 1998)) ("Three elements must be established to bar a patentee's suit by means of equitable estoppel: 1) the patentee, through misleading conduct, leads the alleged infringer to reasonably infer that the patentee does not intend to enforce its patent against the alleged infringer, 2) the alleged infringer relies on that conduct, and 3) due to its reliance, the alleged infringer will be materially prejudiced if the patentee is allowed to proceed with its claim").

8 See Odetics, Inc. v. Storage Technology Corp et al., 185 F.3d 1259, 1272-1273 (Fed. Cir. 1999) (affirming the trial court's grant of summary judgment based upon laches and denying plaintiff's appeal seeking injunctive relief despite the finding of laches). See generally Mainland Industries, Inc. v. Standdal's Patents Ltd., 799 F.2d 746, 748 (Fed. Cir. 1986) ("In order to assert the defense of laches successfully [the accused infringer] must prove (1) unreasonable and inexcusable delay in the assertion of the claim and 2) material prejudice resulting from the delay."); 6 Donald S. Chisum, Chisum on Patents § 19.05[3][a] (2000) (noting that the doctrines of equitable estoppel and laches differ in that equitable estoppel precludes the recovery of damages by a patentee that occur after a lawsuit is filed, while laches bars the recovery of damages that arise prior to a lawsuit being filed.

9 Patent infringement liability is not limited to those who produce an infringing product, but extends to anyone who makes, uses, offers to sell, sells, or imports a patented article, or actively induces one of these proscribed activities. See 35 U.S.C. § 271 et seq.

10 The term "patentee" as defined herein includes an assignee and, in some cases, an exclusive licensee. See generally 35 U.S.C. § 100(d). The word 'patentee' includes not only the patentee to whom the patent was issued but also the successors in title to the patentee.

11 These Secondary References can arguably serve as the basis for putting someone on inquiry notice, whereupon a duty of care arises to investigate whether she is infringing the patented technology of another. See generally John E. Wright, Comment: Willful Patent Infringement and Enhanced Damages- Evolution and Analysis, 10 Geo. Mason L. Rev. 97, 108 (2001) (describing a spectrum of inquiry notice where at one end of the spectrum one has no knowledge of the infringed patent, and there is no duty to investigate, while at the other end of the spectrum, one is told of a patent and is offered a license, thus creating an affirmative duty to investigate). These Secondary References fall somewhere on the spectrum described above by Wright.

12 *Supra* note 2.

13 See 35 U.S.C. §§ 102 et seq. and 103. outlining what constitutes prior art for the purpose of rejecting the claims in a patent application.

14 The amount of liability for damages may be proportional, in some instances, to the amount of technological knowledge gleaned from a particular Secondary Reference as disclosed in a contributed patent. See Read Corp. et al. v. Portec Inc., 970 F.2d 816, 826 (Fed. Cir. 1992) (describing enhanced liability for damages as based upon the egregiousness of the defendants conduct in, for example, copying the patented invention). See generally Honeywell International, Inc.

et al. v. Hamilton Sundstand Corporation, 166 F. Supp. 2d 1008, 1040 (D. Del 2001) (outlining the factors for a totality of the circumstances test for determining whether enhanced damages are appropriate, with the first factor being evidence that the infringer deliberately copied the ideas or designs of the patentee.

15 This fact has led some commentators to note that the patent system promotes an atmosphere of "willful ignorance" or "willful blindness" when it comes to reviewing and reading patents. See Note, The Disclosure Function of the Patent System (or Lack Thereof), 118 Harv. L. Rev. 2007, 2023 (2005) (discussing the problems associated with the present willful infringement regime and the use of "willful ignorance" as a solution, whereby employees are instructed not to read patents); Mark A. Lemley and Ragesh K. Tangri, Ending Patent Law's Willfulness Game, 18 Berkeley Tech. L.J. 1085, 1102 (2003) (discussing "willful blindness" as a protection against enhanced damages based upon a finding of willful infringement).

16 Compare Studiengesellschaft Kohle Gmbh v. Dart Industries, 829 F.2d 1075, 1084 (Fed. Cir. 1987) ("an appreciation of the technological and commercial significance of Suessen's patent rights . . . put Schubert on notice to exercise due care prior to initiating any activity which had the possibility of infringing."); with Great Northern Corp. v. Davis Core & Pad Co., 782 F.2d 159, 167 (Fed. Cir. 1986) ("At the May 1980 meeting between Joel T. Davis of Davis Core and Thomas Roellchen of Ace Polymers, Roellchen inquired whether Davis Core wanted to manufacture Rollrider and advised that there was a similar patented product on the market but that the patent was invalid. . .Davis Core had an affirmative duty, on the facts of this case, to obtain a validity and infringement opinion.").

17 But see Stryker Corp. et al. v. Intermedics Orthopedics, Inc. et al., 96 F.3d 1409, 1415 (Fed. Cir. 1996) (affirming the trial court's finding of actual notice, even where patent counsel for the defendant did not believe that actual infringement was taking place due to the failure of patent counsel to adequately investigate the alleged infringement).

18 See Prima Tek II LLC et al. v. A-Roo Company, 222 F.3d 1372, 1379 (Fed. Cir. 2000) ("A 'blocking patent' is an earlier patent that must be licensed in order to practice a later patent. This often occurs, for instance, between a pioneer patent and an improvement patent."). See generally Amgen, Inc., v. Hoechst Marion Roussel, Inc. et al., 339 F. Supp. 2d 202, 288 (D. Mass. 2004) ("A blocking patent situation occurs when an improvement is patented but the improvement patent infringes on the original patent. Lemley, Economics, at 1009-1010. The original patent owner is entitled to damages from past

infringement and an injunction against future use of the infringing invention. Id. At the same time, however, the original patent owner cannot use the patented improvement without risking liability for damages and a potential injunction. Id. Thus, the original patent owner can prevent the improver from using his patented technology but the improver can prevent the original patent owner from using the improvement. Unless the parties bargain, no one gets the benefit of the improvement.").

19 See Phillips v. AWH Corp., 415 F.3d 1303, 1312 (Fed. Cir. 2005) (en banc) ("It is a 'bedrock principle' of patent law that 'the claims of a patent define the invention to which the patentee is entitled the right to exclude.'") (quoting Innova/Pure Water, Inc. v. Safari Water Filtration Systems, Inc., 381 F.3d 1111, 1115 (Fed. Cir. 2004).

20 The right to use a patent may be granted in a patent license or, for example, relying on a Commitment to use a patent contributed to the Patent Commons. As of the date of this writing, the enforceability of Commitments made by Contributors to the Patent Commons Project has not been tested in court.

21 See Catalina Mktg. Int'l v. Coolsavings, 289 F.3d 801, 809-810 (Fed. Cir. 2002) (providing a hypothetical example illustrating the use of a blocking patent).

22 The United States Patent and Trademark Office (USPTO) is an agency in the U.S. Department of Commerce that issues patents to inventors and businesses for their inventions, and trademark registration for product and intellectual property identification. The USPTO is "unique among federal agencies because it operates solely on fees collected by its users and not on taxpayer dollars". Its "operating structure is like a business in that it receives requests for services—applications for patents and trademark registrations—and charges fees projected to cover the cost of performing the services.

23 The Japan Patent Office is a Japanese governmental agency in charge of industrial property right affairs, under the Ministry of Economy, Trade and Industry. The Japan Patent Office is located in Kasumigaseki, Chiyoda, and Tokyo and is one of the world's largest patent offices. The Japan Patent Office's mission is to promote the growth of the Japanese economy and industry by administering the laws relating to patents, utility models, designs, and trademarks.

24 The European Patent Convention (EPC), also known as the Convention on the Grant of European Patents of 5 October 1973, is a multilateral treaty instituting the European Patent Organization and providing an autonomous legal system according to which European patents are granted. The term *European patent* is used to refer to patents granted under the European Patent Convention. However, a European patent is not a unitary right, but a group of essentially.

25 The Patent Cooperation Treaty (PCT) is an international patent law treaty, concluded in 1970. It provides a unified procedure for filing patent applications to protect inventions in each of its contracting states. A patent application filed under the PCT is called an international application, or PCT application.

26 The World Trade Organization (WTO) is an intergovernmental organization which regulates international trade. The WTO officially commenced on 1 January 1995 under the Marrakesh Agreement, signed by 123 nations on 15 April 1994, replacing the General Agreement on Tariffs and Trade (GATT), which commenced in 1948. The WTO deals with regulation of trade between participating countries by providing a framework for negotiating trade agreements and a dispute resolution process aimed at enforcing participants' adherence to WTO agreements, which are signed by representatives of member government and ratified by their parliaments. Most of the issues that the WTO focuses on derive from previous trade negotiations, especially from the Uruguay Round (1986–1994).

27 The World Intellectual Property Organization (WIPO) is one of the 17 specialized agencies of the United Nations. WIPO was created in 1967 "to encourage creative activity, to promote the protection of intellectual property throughout the world. WIPO currently has 188 member states, administers 26 international treaties, and is headquartered in Geneva, Switzerland. The current Director-General of WIPO is Francis Gurry, who took office on October 1, 2008,186 of the UN Members as well as the Holy See and Niue are Members of WIPO. Non-members are the states of Marshall Islands, Federated States of Micronesia, Nauru, Palau, Solomon Islands, South Sudan and Timor-Leste. Palestine has observer status.

28 Intellectual property (IP) refers to creations of the intellect for which a monopoly is assigned to designated owners by law. Intellectual property rights (IPRs) are the protections granted to the creators of IP, and include trademarks, copyright, patents, industrial design rights, and in some jurisdictions trade secrets. Artistic works including music and literature, as well as discoveries, inventions, words, phrases, symbols, and designs can all be protected as intellectual property.

29 The United States Court of Appeals for the Federal Circuit (Federal Circuit; in case citations, Fed. Cir. or C.A.F.C.) is a United States court of appeals headquartered in Washington, D.C. The court was created by Congress with passage of the Federal Courts Improvement Act of 1982, which merged the United States Court of Customs and Patent Appeals and the appellate division of the United States Court of Claims, making the judges of the former courts into circuit judges. The Federal Circuit is particularly known for its decisions on patent law, as it is the only appellate-level court with the jurisdiction to hear patent case appeals.

30 The Agreement on Trade-Related Aspects of Intellectual Property Rights (TRIPS) is an international agreement administered by the World Trade Organization (WTO) that sets down minimum standards for many forms of intellectual property (IP) regulation as applied to nationals of other WTO Members. It was negotiated at the end of the Uruguay Round of the General Agreement on Tariffs and Trade (GATT) in 1994.

31 *Supra* note 59.

Chapter 2
Influence of Patent Law on Price of Medicines:
A Comparative Analysis of Various Countries

Naina Singh
Panjab University, India

Rajinder Kaur
Panjab University, India

Rashmi Aggarwal
Institute of Management Technology Ghaziabad, India

ABSTRACT

There is a great deal of disparity between the availability and affordability of medicines in least developed, developing and developed nations. Patents are one of the major reasons of this difference. The pharmaceutical industry spends over US$10 billion to fund some 90% of 40,000-80,000 randomised controlled trails being conducted across the world at any given time. A United Nations AIDS study reported that the number of people in poor countries who have access to anti-retroviral medicines remains extremely low; only 30,000 received medication in 2002, out of an estimated 5 million in need. The proposed chapter aims to study effect of patent law on pricing of medicines. The legal and regulatory policies such as TRIPs jointly introduced by various nations to regulate the pricing of patented products will be elaborated in this chapter. Apart from national and international policies, the behaviour of pharmaceutical companies also affect price of patented products. The chapter will also cover various techniques pharmaceutical industry adopt to control price of patented products such as proliferation of me-too drugs, product reformulation, prolonging patent rights, biasing research and large promotional expenditures.

DOI: 10.4018/978-1-5225-2414-4.ch002

Copyright © 2017, IGI Global. Copying or distributing in print or electronic forms without written permission of IGI Global is prohibited.

INTRODUCTION

Patent monopoly creates a lot of problems. It allows the patentee to charge the maximum to consumers. This may not be a problem if the patented product is a luxury item, like parts that go into a smartphone, but can violate basic human rights if it involves things such as life-saving drugs. -By Ha-Joon Chang (2016)

Each year millions of human lives end in death from poverty-related causes, such as respiratory infections, HIV/AIDS, tuberculosis, malaria, measles, and tropical diseases.[1]Many of these are treatable, if not curable, conditions. Lybecker (2011) further suggests that the numbers of such deaths are overwhelming and mandate an examination of the barriers to accessing medicines in developing countries, where the majority of these deaths occur. Admittedly this is an immense and complicated issue, and the economics behind pharmaceutical innovation and access is but one facet of a complete understanding of the problem.

While dwelling on the economics aspect of the pharmaceutical industry, DiMasi, Caglarcan, and Wood-Armany (2001) found out that the investment of societies around the world on biomedical research leads to important developments including the continuous discovery of new pharmaceutical compounds. It is not clear, however, whether newly developed and approved drugs cover all therapeutic areas in a relatively uniform manner. Different reasons might be postulated with respect to the driving forces of drug development.

Of all the goods and services traded in the market economy, pharmaceuticals are perhaps the most contentious. Though produced by private companies, they constitute a public good, both because they can prevent epidemics and because healthy people function better as members of society than sick ones do. They carry a moral weight that most privately traded goods do not, for there is a widespread belief that people have a right to health care that they do not have to smartphones or trainers. Innovation accounts for most of the cost of production, so the price of drugs is much higher than their cost of manufacture, making them unaffordable to many poor people. Firms protect the intellectual property (IP) that drugs represent and sue those who try to manufacture and sell patented drugs cheaply. For all these reasons, pharmaceutical companies are widely regarded as vampires who exploit the sick and ignore the sufferings of the poor (The Economist, 2014).

In Least developed and developing nations it is a cruel sight to watch our patients die because they cannot afford the drugs that could improve, extend, or save their lives. Price is not the only reason why people do not get the medicines they need, but it is a major barrier. The high cost of many life-saving drugs not only keeps patients from getting treatment, but also discourages health ministries from improving the quality of patient care through the use of newer and better medicines. While the $406 billion-strong drug industry researches, develops, markets, and prices medicines for the industrialised world, there is no mechanism to make newer medicines affordable to developing countries. Newer drugs, which are usually under patent and more expensive than those off-patent and this vicious circle has no end and keeps on playing with the lives of all those people who have poor paying capacity.[2]

The Dilemma of Pharmaceutical Patents: Policy Framework Aspect

In 1994, the World Trade Organization (WTO)[3] completed the Trade-Related Aspects of International Property Rights agreement (TRIPS)[4], which called for the standardization of IP law among all WTO members. Most of the countries prior to the WTO regime did not have a very strong Intellectual Property rights protection. However, the WTO introduced a mandatory product patent regime. As a result, most of the developing countries amended their patent laws to comply with the WTO.

Figure 1. Comparison of the top 10 causes of deaths across income groups

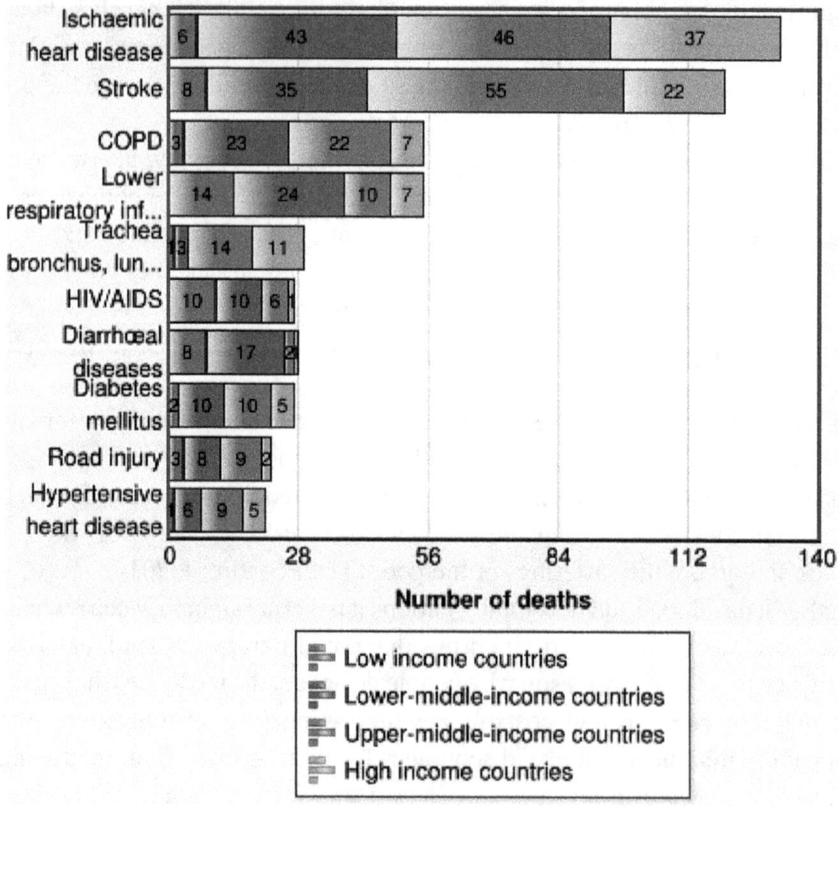

Nevertheless, concerns regarding access to medicines were voiced at many of these WTO forums by developing country members. In 2001, the Doha Declaration[5] was instrumental in concretizing these concerns into a policy debate. As a result of these deliberations, the developing country members lead by Brazil and India were able to negotiate for flexibilities within the TRIPS regime. There are instruments within TRIPS that national governments can use to "break" patent monopolies and ensure a supply of affordable generic drugs. One such instrument is compulsory licensing[6], which allows generic manufacturers to produce pharmaceutical products (in cases of national emergency or public non-commercial use) that are currently subject to patent protection.

Kobori (2002) comments that while all countries signed the agreement during the Uruguay Round, the country with the most to gain from TRIPS was clearly the United States, which earns large amounts of money from American patents in foreign markets.

Pharmaceutical patents are often held out as an example of the patent system at its best.[7] It is widely accepted that patents play an essential role in motivating private investment in pharmaceutical R&D[8], and those investments have yielded tremendous social gains through the resulting introduction of new drugs. For this reason, pharmaceutical innovation is thought to be the patent system's greatest success story.

Over the years, the role that intellectual property play in the development of and access to medicine has be examined extensively. The importance of patents to pharmaceutical innovation has been demonstrated by numerous economists and policymakers. The usual explanation of why patents are more important to pharmaceutical firms in appropriating benefit from innovation directly flows from the characteristics of the pharmaceutical R&D process (Benoliel & Chirwa, n.d.).

As *Roy Levy* and *Abraham Wickelgren* of the Federal Trade Commission observed in an article:

It is hard to think of many industries that have contributed as much to human welfare as the pharmaceutical industry. The importance of the industry makes the job of competition authorities that much more difficult and important (Kettler, 2011).

THE NECESSITY FOR PATENTING DRUGS: WHY PATENTS?

The explanation for why patents are more important to pharmaceutical firms in appropriating the benefits from innovation flows directly from the characteristics of the pharmaceutical R&D process. In essence it takes lot of time, money and sweat

Figure 2.

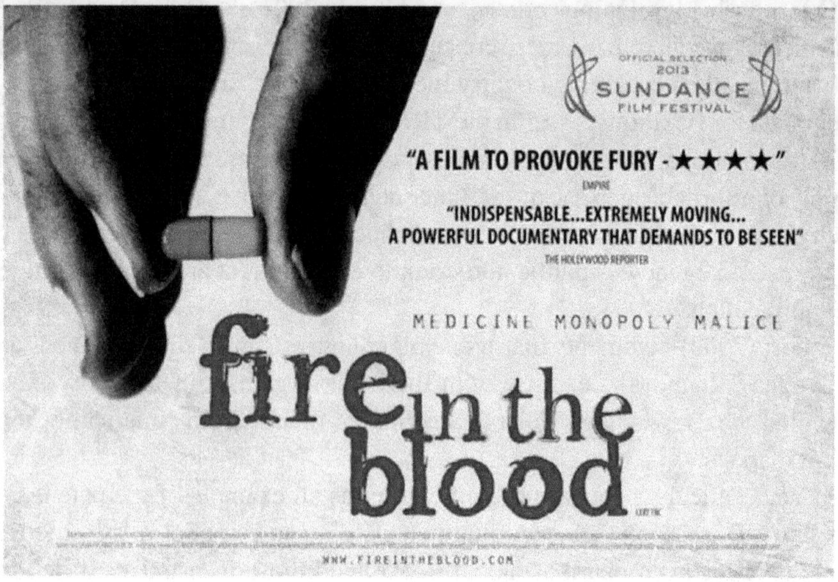

to discover, develop and gain regulatory approval for a new medicine. Absent patent protection, or some equivalent barrier, imitators could free ride on the innovator's FDA approval and duplicate the compound for a small fraction of the originators costs. In essence, imitation costs in the pharmaceutical industry are extremely low relative to the innovator's costs for discovering and developing a new compound which runs into millions of dollars due to the brains involved and the field trials which occur for the testing of the newly developed medicines.

DiMasi (1995) while discussing the success rates of new drugs entering the clinical testing phase comments that one of the reasons R&D is so costly in pharmaceuticals is that most new drug candidates fail to reach the market. Failure can result from toxicity, carcinogenicity, manufacturing difficulties, inconvenient dosing characteristics, inadequate efficacy, economic and competitive factors and various other problems. Typically, fewer than 1% of the compounds examined in the pre-clinical period make it into human testing. Only 22% of the compounds entering clinical trials survive the development process and gain FDA approval. Furthermore, a study conducted by Kaitin and DiMasi (2000) shows, that the full R&D process from synthesis to FDA approval involves undertaking successive trials of increasing size and complexity. The pre-clinical and clinical testing phases generally take more than a decade to complete.

In stark contrast to this the development costs of generic compounds are relatively modest. The probability of success is also very high as reflected by the fact that many generic firms typically receive FDA approval and enter the market within a short time of the patent expiration of the pioneer brand.

Kuosmanen (2016) states that while the necessity of IPR in general has been the subject of debate, but the major focus will be on the pharmaceutical industry and pharmaceutical products for two reasons. Firstly, the R&D process in pharmaceuticals differs radically from other industries. Secondly, pharmaceutical products, and especially essential medicine, differ radically from other goods, e.g. computers or smart phones, due to their paramount importance in public health. The countries of focus of this chapter could be rather loosely considered to be developing countries dealing with public health crises and a need for access to essential medicines. While the most prominent proportion of such countries, and the largest burden of disease, is located in Sub-Saharan Africa, Brazil is also included in this group of target countries for the purposes of this thesis due to their public health crises, healthcare reform, and prominent role in the access debate.

As intellectual property has become an important part of trade, which itself had become increasingly international, TRIPS was negotiated to establish common standards of IPR in order to provide order and predictability to international trade. Following the entry into force of TRIPS, trade disputes and public debate ensued on the topic of access to medicine. Developing countries have been hit hardest by disease, the region of Sub-Saharan Africa carrying arguably the heaviest burden of disease. Despite efforts being made to ensure access to medicine, it continues to be a major obstacle to treating epidemics of AIDS, Malaria and Tuberculosis.

Medicines Shouldn't Be a Luxury: The Downside of Patenting Drugs

Parker (2007) remarks that the Intellectual Property (IP) rights were created in order to reward innovation and allow inventors to recoup the research and development (R&D) costs incurred during product development. Companies assert that without this kind of protection, they would not be guaranteed to make profits of a successful invention.

Patents can have a dramatic impact on access to medicines when they are used to prevent competition. A drug company that holds patents on a medicine has the right to prevent others from manufacturing it and therefore can charge an artificially high price. When a company is selling CD-ROMs or toy dolls for example, this might be of no great significance. But when life-saving treatments for diseases such as HIV/AIDS or cancer become unaffordable to those that need them, the consequences can be - and are - devastating. In developing countries, where people pay for drugs out of their own pockets and very seldom have health insurance, the high price of medicines becomes a question of life and death (Access Campaign, n. d.).

The HIV/AIDS pandemic and an increasing awareness of global diseases have brought heightened scrutiny to the international pharmaceutical industry and the structure of international trade. Both industry representatives and public health advocates are fiercely focused on the role of pharmaceutical patents in the development of new therapies and the availability of medical technologies to the world's most vulnerable populations. The industry perspective is a supply-side story in which patents are seen as essential to protecting and preserving innovation on a global scale.[9] In contrast, public health advocates argue that patents amount to a principal barrier to affordable medicines for consumers in developing countries, a demand-side story.[10]

Some Statistical Overview

A bare perusal of the global statistics will make the situation clear and help us in analysing the drug patenting issue in a more pristine manner.

Figure 3. Adult HIV prevalence rate, 2014
Goldsmith, 2015.

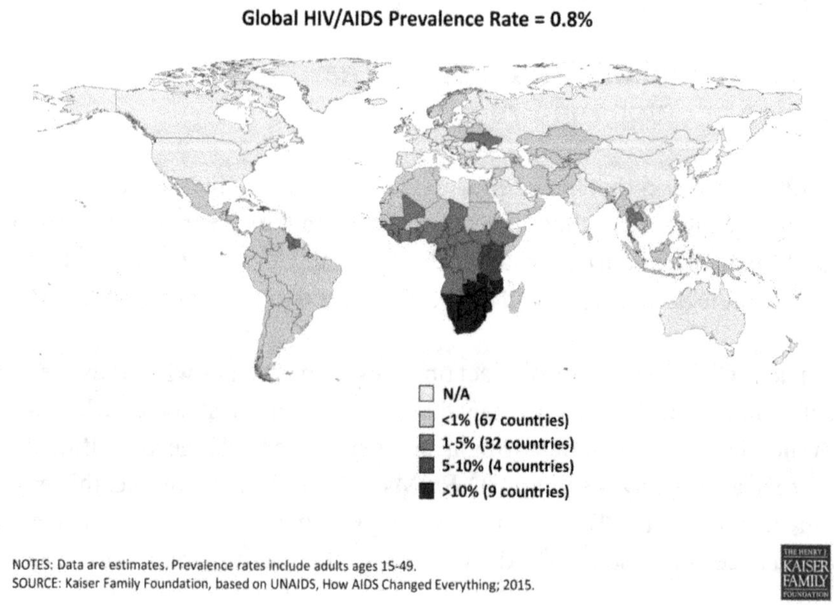

- In 2015, there were 36.7 million [34.0 million–39.8 million] people living with HIV.
- In comparison to this there were 19 million [17.7 million–20.5 million] people living with HIV in eastern and southern Africa alone (Women account for more than half the total number of people living with HIV in eastern and southern Africa) and 470 000 [390 000–560 000] people died of AIDS-related causes in 2015.
- Further in 2015, there were 6.5 million [5.3 million–7.8 million] people living with HIV in western and central Africa. (Women account for nearly 60% of the total number of people living with HIV in western and central Africa) and 330 000 [250 000–430 000] people died of AIDS-related causes in 2015.
- Lastly in 2015, there were 5.1 million [4.4 million–5.9 million] people living with HIV in Asia and the Pacific and Treatment coverage was 41% [35–47%] of all people living with HIV in Asia and the Pacific (UNAIDS, 2016).

On examination of the above statistics the stark reality of the global North-South divide in matters as pristine as medicine is well apparent.

Pharmaceutical Companies Profiteering Ways: Food for Thought

This claim of pharmaceutical company's connivance with patents is further fortified after we make an estimate of its fiscal multiplier effect. Hence worth pondering over is also the profit-making aspect of the pharmaceutical industry. The industry which is responsible for the development of medicines to save lives and alleviate suffering and has such benign intentions is not supposed to function for mere generation of profits.

Pharmaceutical companies have developed the vast majority of medicines known to humankind, but they have profited handsomely from doing so, and not always by legitimate means. Last year, US giant Pfizer, the world's largest drug company by pharmaceutical revenue, made an eye-watering 42% profit margin. Richard Anderson (2014), an industry veteran understandably says: "I wouldn't be able to justify [those kinds of margins]." This is very rightly asserted by the statistics listed below.

Patents leads to monopolisation of the end product and when such results are applied to the health care sector the end result would only be devastating. The statistics below would only invigorate the claims stated above.

Figure 4. The most profitable sectors in 2016
Zdravko, 2015.

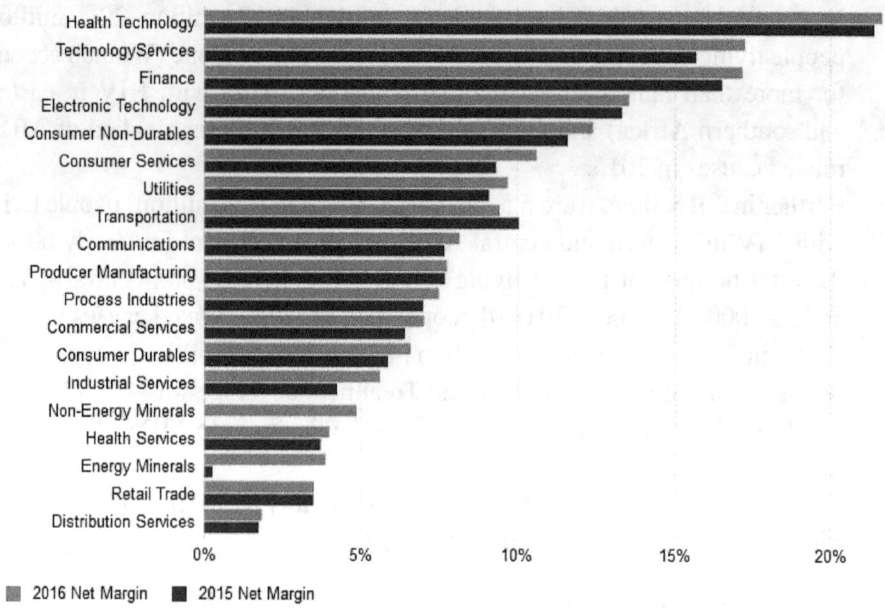

Figure 5. Pharmaceutical manufacturers in the 2015 Fortune 500 list
Fein, 2015.

Company (stock symbol)	2014 Revenues ($B)	Revenues, % vs. 2013	2015 Fortune 500 Rank	Profit as % of Revenues	Profit as % of Assets	Annualized Return to Investors (2004-2014)	Total Return to Investors (2014)
Johnson & Johnson (JNJ)	$74.3	4.0%	37	22%	12%	8%	17%
Pfizer (PFE)	$49.6	-7.0%	56	18%	5%	5%	5%
Merck & Co. (MRK)	$42.2	-4.0%	71	28%	12%	10%	17%
Gilead Sciences (GILD)	$24.9	122.0%	118	48%	34%	26%	25%
Amgen (AMGN)	$20.1	7.0%	145	25%	7%	10%	42%
AbbVie (ABBV)	$20.0	6.0%	146	8%	6%	n.a.	27%
Eli Lilly and Company (LLY)	$19.6	-15.0%	151	12%	6%	6%	39%
Bristol-Myers Squibb Company (BMY)	$15.9	-3.0%	195	12%	5%	13%	14%
Biogen (BIIB)	$9.7	40.0%	298	30%	20%	17%	21%
Celgene (CELG)	$7.7	18.0%	369	26%	11%	32%	32%
Allergan (AGN)	$7.2	12.0%	380	21%	12%	18%	91%
Average	**$26.5**	**16.4%**	**179**	**22.7%**	**11.8%**	**14.5%**	**30.0%**
Median	**$20.0**	**6.0%**	**146**	**22.0%**	**11.0%**	**11.5%**	**25.0%**

Source: Pembroke Consulting analysis of 2015 *Fortune* 500 list
Published on Drug Channels (http://www.DrugChannels.net) on June 24, 2015.

DRUG CHANNELS INSTITUTE

Figure 6. Monopoly profits can be very high: profit margin of top 10 global pharmaceutical companies in 2013
Basics of the economics monopoly, n.d.

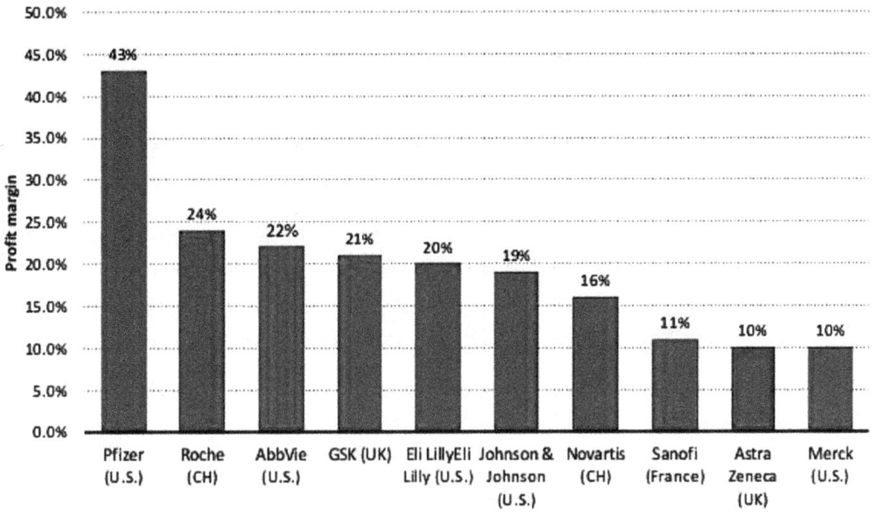

INNOVATIVE ARM-TWISTING TECHNIQUES USED BY PHARMACEUTICAL INDUSTRIES

In the present super competitive era pharmaceutical companies are now-a-days involved in a new rat race altogether which is just to edge out the other competitors. Charles Darwin would have never fathomed that his "Survival of the fittest"[11] ideology when applied in the pharmaceutical industry would have such devastating effect.

Concept of Me-Too Drugs

The first brand-name drug using a particular therapeutic mechanism of action is called a "breakthrough drug"; brand-name drugs that use the same mechanism of action but enter after the breakthrough drug are called "me-too drugs." Hence they are not new at all but merely variations of older drugs already on the market.

The idea is to grab a share of an established, lucrative market by producing something very similar to a top-selling drug. For instance, we now have six statins (Mevacor, Lipitor, Zocor, Pravachol, Lescol, and the newest, Crestor) on the market to lower cholesterol, all variants of the first. As Dr. Sharon Levine (n. d.), associate executive director of the Kaiser Permanente Medical Group, put it,

If I'm a manufacturer and I can change one molecule and get another twenty years of patent rights, and convince physicians to prescribe and consumers to demand the next form of Prilosec, or weekly Prozac instead of daily Prozac, just as my patent expires, then why would I be spending money on a lot less certain endeavor, which is looking for brand-new drugs?

Since we live in laissez faire era the pharmaceutical giants are free to decide which drugs to develop (me-too drugs instead of innovative ones, for instance), and it is free to price them as high as the traffic will bear, but it is utterly dependent on government-granted monopolies—in the form of patents and Food and Drug Administration (FDA)–approved exclusive marketing rights. If it is not particularly innovative in discovering new drugs, it is highly innovative—and aggressive—in dreaming up ways to extend its monopoly rights.[12]

Product Reformulations

Over the past fifteen years, a number of reformulations of psychotropic medications, such as Remeron Soltab and Paxil Controlled Release (CR), have been introduced. The reformulations often involve less frequent or easier-to-administer dosing. From 1999 through 2004, the FDA approved 510 new drug applications (NDAs), including both new molecular entities (NMEs) and reformulations. Development of reformulations can also expand a firm's market share by creating an improved version of an existing drug or effectively extending patent exclusivity beyond the initial patent period. For example, within a year of patent expiration for Eli Lilly's blockbuster antidepressant Prozac, the firm released Prozac Weekly, a once-weekly formulation of Prozac, and Sarafem, a form of Prozac with an indication for premenstrual dysphoric disorder. The market shares of Prozac Weekly and Sarafem are each less than 1 percent of antidepressant retail sales in June 2003, so this strategy has not allowed Lilly to maintain a large market share for Prozac (Huskamp, 2006).

The Secret Pacts: TPP Repercussions

Trans-Pacific Partnership or TPP in a nutshell involves 12 countries: the US, Japan, Malaysia, Vietnam, Singapore, Brunei, Australia, New Zealand, Canada, Mexico, Chile and Peru. The pact aims to deepen economic ties between these nations, slashing tariffs and fostering trade to boost growth. Member countries are also hoping to foster a closer relationship on economic policies and regulation. The agreement could create a new single market something like that of the EU (BBC News, 2017).

THE NOT SO NOBEL IDEA BEHIND TPP

The TPP member states have surrendered their sovereign right to define 'patentability' criteria. Not only have they have surrendered their right, they have agreed to grant patents for:

1. New uses of a known product
2. New methods of using a known product
3. New processes of using a known product

This would lead to the "evergreening" of patents[13] and result in an average extension of monopoly by at least five years. Some can stretch it beyond five years, as was done by Novartis AG for *Gleevec* (imatinib). This would encourage innovators to go for low-hanging fruits at the cost of more difficult-to-succeed efforts. Generics[14] will slow down and patients will have to wait longer for affordable treatments. If this was not enough to wreak havoc in the developing and least developed countries the TPP member states have agreed to adjust the term of the patent for "unreasonable"[15] delays in the issuance of patents[16]and last but not the least it even approves of patent linkages which would further benefit the innovators and delay launch of generics, depriving patients of affordable alternative.[17]

THE WAY FORWARD: EQUITY PRICING OF DRUGS

Essential medicines should be priced in developing countries based on the principle of "equity." MSF[18] uses the term "equity pricing" to describe policies that ensure that, from the point of view of the community and the individual, the price of a drug is fair, equitable and affordable, even for a poor population and/or the health system that serves them. Equity pricing is based on the principle that the poor should pay less for, and have access to, essential medicines.[19]

Various terms are often used synonymously with, or are related to, pricing of medicines which are "tiered pricing"[20], including "differential pricing, " "market segmentation, " "price discrimination, " and less frequently "Ramsey pricing" (Danzon & Towse, 2003).

Moon, Jambert et al (2011) suggests that equity pricing emphasizes the perspective of the consumer, i.e, whether a price is affordable and acceptable to him or her. In contrast, tiered pricing emphasizes the perspective of the producer, i.e., whether a fair profit can be sustained while charging lower prices to lower-income populations.

While tiered pricing may lead to equitable prices, the concepts are not equivalent and there is no guarantee that tiered prices are affordable.

To verify that equity pricing is a better alternative HIV/AIDS: Antiretrovirals case study would be appropriate. Among different therapeutic areas, the availability of data and analysis on tiered pricing is greatest for HIV/AIDS. In a review of over 7,000 developing-country purchase transactions from 2002-2007, Waning, Kaplan et al. (2009) found that the tiered prices for 15 of 18 antiretroviral (ARV) drugs were 23-498% higher than the generic price.

CONCLUSION

There were times not long ago that drug companies were merely the size of nations. Now, after a frenzied two-year period of pharmaceutical mega-mergers, they are behemoths, which outweigh entire continents. The combined worth of the world's top five drug companies is twice the combined GNP of all sub-Saharan Africa and their influence on the rules of world trade is many times stronger because they can bring their wealth to bear directly on the levers of western power. -The Guardian (2001)

Nothing can more aptly sum up this eye-opening aspect of the pharmaceutical industries than the anecdote above. The present era of globalization and appreciation of human rights has forced a deeper cognizance of the relationship between intellectual property (IP) law and global health.

The stark reality is that in their vulnerability to treatable diseases, the rich and the poor live in different worlds. Every year, millions of people in developing countries die of illnesses that they would likely have survived had they lived in Europe or the United States. A key factor in the enormous global disparities in death rates is poor people's lack of access to needed drugs. The case of HIV AIDS and its wide prevalence only in the developing and lead developed world and which has now reached critical alarming proportions. At present, only a tiny minority of HIV-positive people in poor countries have access to anti-retroviral drugs. For most people in the least developing world, as well as marginalized populations in developing countries, the cost of treatment remains prohibitively high.

In the United States and other rich countries, since the advent of effective anti-retroviral drug treatment, AIDS has become a manageable disease, not a death sentence. But for the millions living with HIV in the developing world, prospects for effective treatment remain dim. This only consolidates the stand that patent protection and racketeering has some deep connivance and the far-reaching effects of which no developed country likes to discuss or even refer about. Something needs to be done real soon before we reach a situation from where there is no looking back as this atrocity meted out by the large pharmaceutical MNC's in the name of R&D is nothing less than crime against humanity at large. As goes the apt saying that "Prevention is better than cure" hence the need of the hour is action or else the result would be the opening of the Pandora's Box.

REFERENCES

Access Campaign. (n. d.). The impact of patents on access to medicines. *Access Campaign*. Retrieved July 31, 2016 from http://www.msfaccess.org/content/impact-patents-access-medicines

Basics of the economics of monopoly". Retrieved August 8, 2016, from http://image.slidesharecdn.com/monopolywebinar-150529100216-lva1-app6892/95/basics-of-the-economics-of-monopoly-23-638.jpg?cb=1432893806

Benoliel, D., & Chirwa, T. J. (n. d.). The Impact of Pharmaceutical Patents on Health Expenditures in Least-Developed Countries. Retrieved July 31, 2016 from http://weblaw.haifa.ac.il/he/Faculty/BenOliel/Publications/BenolielChirwa.pdf

Chang, H. J. (2013, April 13). Company profits depend on the 'welfare payments' they get from society. The Guardian. Retrieved July 31, 2016, from <https://www.theguardian.com/commentisfree/2013/apr/05/company-profits-welfare-payments-society>

Danzon, P. M., & Towse, A. (2003). Differential pricing for pharmaceuticals: Reconciling access, R&D and patents. *International Journal of Health Care Finance and Economics*, *3*(3), 183–205. doi:10.1023/A:1025384819575 PMID:14625999

DiMasi, J. A. (1995). Success Rates for New Drugs entering Clinical Testing in the United States. *Clinical Pharmacology and Therapeutics*, *58*(1), 1–14. doi:10.1016/0009-9236(95)90066-7 PMID:7628176

DiMasi, J. A., Caglarcan, E., & Wood-Armany, M. (2001). Emerging role of pharmacoeconomics in the research and development decision-making process. *PharmacoEconomics*, *19*(7), 753–766. doi:10.2165/00019053-200119070-00004 PMID:11548911

Fein, A. J. (2015). Profits in the 2015 Fortune 500: Manufacturers vs. Wholesalers, PBMs, and Pharmacies. Retrieved August 8, 2016 from http://www.drugchannels.net/2015/06/profits-in-2015-fortune-500.html

Goldsmith, B. (2015). Is the end of AIDS in sight? *World Economic Forum.* Retrieved August 5, 2016 from https://www.weforum.org/agenda/2015/12/is-the-end-of-aids-in-sight/

Huskamp, H. A. (2006). Prices, Profits, and Innovation: Examining Criticisms Of New Psychotropic Drugs' Value. *Healthaffairs.org.* Retrieved August 8, 2016 from http://content.healthaffairs.org/content/25/3/635.full#xref-ref-15-1

Kaitin, K. I., & DiMasi, J. A. (2000). Measuring the Place of New Drug Development in the User Free Era. *Drug Information Journal*, 34(3), 673–680.

Kobori, S. (2002). TRIPS and the Primacy of Public Health. *Asia-Pacific Review, 9*(1), 10–19. doi:10.1080/13439000220141550

Kuosmanen, L. (2016). *TRIPS and Pharmaceutical Patents: Effects on Access to Essential Medicine and Innovation* [Thesis]. Helsinki Metropolia University of Applied Sciences. Retrieved July 31, 2016, from http://www.theseus.fi/bitstream/handle/10024/112464/Kuosmanen_Lauri.pdf?sequence=1

Levine, D. (n. d.). On ABC Special with Peter Jennings (2002). Bitter Medicine: Pills, Profit, and the Public Health. Retrieved August 8, 2016 from http://www.dklevine.com/archive/bitter-medicine.htm

Levy, R. & Wickelgren, A. (2001). Competition Policy Issues for Regulators: A U.S. Perspective on Pharmaceutical Industry Cases before the Federal Trade Commission. In H. Kettler (Ed.), *Consolidation and Competition in the Pharmaceutical Industry* (pp. 106-117). London: Office of Health Economics.

Lybecker, K. M. (2011). The Economics of Access to Medicines: Meeting the Challenges of Pharmaceutical Patents, Innovation, and Access for Global Health. An Article from the Symposium: Developments and Challenges in International Intellectual Property Law. *Harvard International Law Journal Online, 53*, 25-26.

Moon, S., Jambert, E., Childs, M., & Schoen-Angerer, T. V. (2011). A win-win solution?: A critical analysis of tiered pricing to improve access to medicines in developing countries. *Globalization and Health, 7*(1), 39. doi:10.1186/1744-8603-7-39 PMID:21992405

BBCNews, (2017). TPP: What is it and why does it matter? Retrieved from http://www.bbc.com/news/business-32498715

The Economist. (2014). The New Drugs War. Retrieved July 31, 2016 from http://www.economist.com/news/leaders/21592619-patents-drugs-are-interests-sick-well-industry-protection-should-not

The Guardian. (2001). Pharmaceutical Industry: Sector Overview. Retrieved August 8, 2016 from https://corporatewatch.org/company-profiles/pharmaceutical-industry

UNAIDS. (2016) Fact Sheet 2016 UNAIDS. *Global Statistics*. Retrieved August 5, 2016, from http://www.unaids.org/sites/default/files/media_asset/UNAIDS_FactSheet_en.pdf

Waning, B., Kaplan, W., King, A. C., Lawrence, D. A., Leufkens, H. G., & Fox, M. P. (2009). Global strategies to reduce the price of antiretroviral medicines: Evidence from transactional databases. *Bulletin of the World Health Organization*, *87*(7), 520–528. doi:10.2471/BLT.08.058925 PMID:19649366

Zdravko. (2015). Industries you should look at in 2016! *P&BC Consulting*. Retrieved February 8, 2017 from http://pbconsulting.co/industries-you-should-look-at-in-2016/

ENDNOTES

1 Data from WHO which shows causes of death across various income groups. Figure 1. It can easily be analysed that diseases like HIV/AIDS, diarrheal diseases, etc., are causes of death mostly in the low income (Least Developed Countries) and middle income countries (developing countries) unlike the high income countries (developed countries). WHO Data (2012) has been retrieved from http://www.who.int/mediacentre/factsheets/fs310/en/index3.html

2 A grueling account for the same can be witnessed after watching an intricate tale of 'medicine, monopoly and malice', *Fire In The Blood* tells the story of how Western pharmaceutical companies and governments aggressively blocked access to low-cost AIDS drugs for the countries of Africa and the global south in the years after 1996 - causing ten million or more unnecessary deaths - and the improbable group of people who decided to fight back. Shot on four continents and including contributions from global figures such as Bill Clinton, Desmond Tutu and Joseph Stiglitz, FIRE IN THE BLOOD is the never-before-told true story of the remarkable coalition which came together to stop 'the Crime of the Century' and save millions of lives in the process. As the film makes clear,

however, this story is by no means over. With dramatic past victories having given way to serious setbacks engineered far from public view, the real fight for access to life-saving medicine is almost certainly just beginning. Retrieved from http://fireintheblood.com/ accessed on July 31, 2016, 11am. Figure 2. The poster of the film has been retrieved July 31, 2016, from http://www.carnegiecouncil.org/publications/ethics_onfilm/0011.html The trailer of the film shows how Multi National Companies are making a mockery of the most benign industry in the world. The embed code for watching the trailer of the documentary is given below: <iframe src= “http://fireintheblood.com/player/” frameborder= “0” width= “640” height= “470”></iframe>.

3 The World Trade Organization (WTO) is an international organization designed to supervise and liberalize international trade. The WTO came into being on January 1, 1995, and is the successor to the General Agreement on Tariffs and Trade (GATT), which was created in 1947, and continued to operate for almost five decades as a de facto international organization.

4 The Agreement on Trade Related Aspects of Intellectual Property Rights (TRIPS) is an international agreement administered by the World Trade Organization (WTO) that sets down minimum standards for many forms of intellectual property (IP) regulation. It was negotiated at the end of the Uruguay Round of the General Agreement on Tariffs and Trade (GATT) in 1994.

5 The November 2001 Doha Declaration on the TRIPS Agreement and Public Health was adopted by the WTO Ministerial Conference of 2001 in Doha on November 14, 2001. It reaffirmed flexibility of TRIPS member states in circumventing patent rights for better access to essential medicines. In Paragraphs 4 to 6 of the Doha Declaration, governments agreed that: The TRIPS Agreement does not and should not prevent Members from taking measures to protect public health. Accordingly, while reiterating our commitment to the TRIPS Agreement, we affirm that the Agreement can and should be interpreted and implemented in a manner supportive of WTO Members’ right to protect public health and, in particular, to promote access to medicines for all. In this connection, we reaffirm the right of WTO Members to use, to the full, the provisions in the TRIPS Agreement, which provide flexibility for this purpose. Accordingly and in the light of paragraph 4 above, while maintaining our commitments in the TRIPS Agreement, we recognize that these flexibilities include: (a) In applying the customary rules of interpretation of public international law, each provision of the TRIPS Agreement shall be read in the light of the object and purpose of the Agreement as expressed, in particular, in its objectives and principles. (b) Each Member has the right to grant compulsory licences and the freedom to determine the grounds upon which such licences are granted.

(c) Each Member has the right to determine what constitutes a national emergency or other circumstances of extreme urgency, it being understood that public health crises, including those relating to HIV/AIDS, tuberculosis, malaria and other epidemics, can represent a national emergency or other circumstances of extreme urgency. (d) The effect of the provisions in the TRIPS Agreement that are relevant to the exhaustion of intellectual property rights is to leave each Member free to establish its own regime for such exhaustion without challenge, subject to the MFN and national treatment provisions of Articles 3 and 4, 6. "We recognize that WTO Members with insufficient or no manufacturing capacities in the pharmaceutical sector could face difficulties in making effective use of compulsory licensing under the TRIPS Agreement. We instruct the Council for TRIPS to find an expeditious solution to this problem and to report to the General Council before the end of 2002." These provisions in the Declaration ensure that governments may issue compulsory licenses on patents for medicines, or take other steps to protect public health.

6 Compulsory licensing is a technique in which a government can grant someone other than the patent owner the right to produce the patented product or process. This allows a government to prevent patent owners from abusing their patents by blocking trade or the international transfer of technology. The drugs produced under compulsory licensing are generic drugs, or drugs that are identical to a brand-name drug in safety, strength, quality, and dosage form. Article 31 of TRIPS states that a generic firm can obtain a compulsory license as long as: • it first tries to negotiate a commercial license from the patent owner • it produces predominantly for the domestic market • the remunerations paid to the patent owner are subject to judicial review. For Additional Reading refer to Westerhaus, M. and Castro, A. (2006). How Do Intellectual Property Law and International Trade Agreements Affect Access to Antiretroviral Therapy?. *PLoS Medicine, 3*(8). Compulsory licenses are considered by many as an effective tool to control monopolies by patent holders. The provision has been used by a number of countries in the last few years. Indonesia, Malaysia and recently Thailand are the notable ones. They are particularly significant for countries like India that export drugs to other developing countries.

7 See, e.g., Bessen, J. and Meurer, M.J. (2008). Patent failure: How Judges, Bureaucrats, and Lawyers put innovators at risk. (noting the great importance of patents in the pharmaceutical industry in comparison to most other industries); Jaffe, A.B. & Josh Lerner, J. (2004). Innovation and its discontents: How our broken patent system is endangering innovation and progress, and what to do about it. (noting that patents provide incentives for costly drug development that would not otherwise occur).

8 The importance of patents to pharmaceutical innovation has been demonstrated in several studies by economists. To quote here such a study conducted by Richard C. Levin, Alvin K. Klevorick et. al would be worthwhile. In their study conducted by analysing responses of 650 respondents the benefits of patent system for R&D was observed. To quote a paragraph from this study would help in evaluating the convenience of the patent system: "To have the incentive to undertake research and development, a firm must be able to appropriate returns sufficient to make the investment worthwhile. The benefits consumers derive from an innovation, how-ever, are increased if competitors can imitate and improve on the innovation to ensure its availability in favorable terms. Patent aw seeks to resolve this tension between incentives or innovation and widespread diffusion of benefits. A patent confers, in theory, perfect appropriability (monopoly of the invention) for a limited time in return for a public disclosure that ensures, again in theory, widespread diffusion of benefits when the patent expires." Levin, R.C. Klevorick, A.K. et al. (1987). Appropriating the returns from Industrial Research and developments. *Brookings Papers on Economic Activity*, *3*, 783-784.

9 This perspective is well represented in Bale, H.E., Jr. (1994). IP and Pharmaceuticals: A Decade of Progress. *Managing Intellectual Property, 4* (Pharmaceuticals Supplement).

10 Consider, for example, the words of Goemare, E. (2011): "I am revolted when I hear claims that patent rights do not constitute a barrier to treatment here in South Africa. I have seen young men and women die from an AIDS-related brain tumour provoking unbearable headaches. I have seen children covered with scars due to AIDS-related dermatitis, unable to sleep for the pain. I knew that all of them could have been helped with antiretroviral therapy, but the cost of the patented drugs was the only barrier." MSF and Patents, Medecins Sans Frontieres. Retrieved July 31, 2016, from <http://www.msfaccess.org/content/msf-patents>

11 It has been claimed that "the survival of the fittest" theory in biology was interpreted by late 19th century capitalists as "an ethical precept that sanctioned cut-throat economic competition" and led to the advent of the theory of "social Darwinism" which was used to justify laissez-faire economics, war and racism.

12 For further reference see also Angell, M. (2004). The Truth About the Drug Companies. Retrieved August 8, 2016, from <http://www.nybooks.com/articles/2004/07/15/the-truth-about-the-drug-companies/#fnr-4>

13 Ever greening is a method by which technology producers keep their products updated, with the intent of maintaining patent protection for longer periods of time then would normally be permissible under the law. It refers to increasing

the life of the patent or the patent term beyond 20 years to reap the benefits for a much longer period of time. Drug patent ever greening is the single most important strategy that multinational pharmaceutical companies have been using. One form of ever greening occurs when the original manufacturer "stockpiles" patent protection by obtaining separate 20 year patents on multiple attributes of a single product. These patents can cover everything from aspects of the manufacturing process to tablet color, or even a chemical produced by the body when the drug is ingested and metabolized by the patient. The ultimate consequence could be that the generic equivalents of the drug would be prohibited from entering the market so the price of the drug of the innovator company will be higher even after the patent expiry in absence from competition from generic drug makers.

14 New drugs, like other new products, are developed under patent protection. The patent protects the investment in the drug's development by giving the company the sole right to sell the drug while the patent is in effect. When patents or other periods of exclusivity expire, manufacturers can apply to the FDA to sell generic versions. A generic drug is hence identical--or bioequivalent--to a brand name drug in dosage form, safety, strength, route of administration, quality, performance characteristics and intended use. Although generic drugs are chemically identical to their branded counterparts, they are typically sold at substantial discounts from the branded price. According to the Congressional Budget Office, generic drugs save consumers an estimated $8 to $10 billion a year at retail pharmacies. To gain FDA approval, a generic drug must: • contain the same active ingredients as the innovator drug(inactive ingredients may vary) • be identical in strength, dosage form, and route of administration • have the same use indications • be bioequivalent • meet the same batch requirements for identity, strength, purity, and quality • be manufactured under the same strict standards of FDA's good manufacturing practice regulations required for innovator products Retrieved August 9, 2016, from http://www.fda.gov/Drugs/ResourcesForYou/Consumers/BuyingUsingMedicineSafely/UnderstandingGenericDrugs/ucm144456.htm

15 The "unreasonable" period is defined as "more than five years from the date of filing of the patent application." Likewise, any delay in granting marketing approval for a drug will entitle the rights holder to extension of the patent term.

16 The repercussions of the patent term adjustment provision are mentioned below. Firstly, it would enable the rights holder to delay launch of the product in relatively low-priced markets, particularly developing countries. Secondly, to delay the launch, the innovators may furnish even incomplete data to the drug regulator to show the approval process look tardy and inefficient. Thirdly, it

would thus deny access to a new medicine in the lower priced markets. Fourthly, even after the expiry of a patent in the developed countries, the product would retain monopoly status in the developing countries. This could on an average give at least two years of extended monopoly, further impacting generic growth and patient access.

17 For a detailed study on the same refer to Shah, D.G. (2015) Inside Views: Impact Of The TPP On The Pharma Industry. Retrieved August 9, 2016, from http://www.ip-watch.org/2015/12/02/impact-of-the-tpp-on-the-pharma-industry/

18 Médecins Sans Frontières (MSF): Doctors without Borders.

19 "PILLS AND POCKETBOOKS: Equity Pricing of Essential Medicines in Developing Countries. "(Adapted from a presentation made by Ellen 't Hoen, Médecins Sans Frontières, at the WHO/WTO Workshop on Differential Pricing and Financing of Essential Drugs, Høsbjør, Norway, April 2001) Retrieved August 9, 2016, from <https://www.wto.org/english/tratop_e/trips_e/hosbjor_presentations_e/15thoen_e.pdf>.

20 We use the term "tiered pricing" to refer to the practice of systematically setting higher prices in higher-income markets and lower prices in lower-income markets, such that there is some positive correlation between price and income. Notably, tiered pricing does not necessarily imply that a price is equitable or affordable; rather, it simply means that different prices are charged to different segments of the market for the same product.

Chapter 3
Medical Patents and Impact on Availability and Affordability of Essential Medicines in India

Kishore Dulam
IMT Ghaziabad, India

ABSTRACT

This paper discusses the Pharmaceutical patents in India and its effects. The definition of patents and its aspects, registration patent bodies, and the time period aspects are studied. The need of patents in the pharmaceutical industry is discussed in detail with cases. Regulatory bodies and their relevance as the majority of revenue for Indian pharmaceutical companies are studied. The intent of the government is to control the prices of a few drugs and to make basic drugs affordable to the common public.

INTRODUCTION

When expanding businesses, industries are forced to evolve their business models according to recent changes in the operating market. In January 2005, India implemented a patent law that reinstated product patents. The legislation started on the timeline set by the Trade-Related Aspects of Intellectual Property Rights (TRIPS) agreement. It mandated the patent protection on both products and processes for a period of 20 years. Under this new law, India is forced to recognize not only new patents, but also all patents filed after 1 January 1995. Companies in India achieved their status in the market by infringement of these patents. They are expected to lose $650 million of the local generics market to the original patent-holders. This change has a significant impact on Indian pharmacy companies.

DOI: 10.4018/978-1-5225-2414-4.ch003

Copyright © 2017, IGI Global. Copying or distributing in print or electronic forms without written permission of IGI Global is prohibited.

Requirement for Getting a Patent

To become patentable, an invention should meet the subsequent criteria

- It should be novel.
- It should have an ingenious step or it should be non-obvious
- It should be capable of commercial application.

The basic obligation of a patent is that the invention altogether branches technology. Not whether the product or processes are patentable meets the 3 tests: being a novelty, an inventive step, and being capable of commercial application. Additionally, to the overall security exemption that applies to the whole TRIPS (Trade-Related Aspects of Intellectual Property Rights) Agreement, specific exclusions are permissible from the scope of the patentability of inventions; the hindrance of whose business exploitation is critical to guard public order or morality, human, animal, plants or health; or to avoid serious prejudice to the setting. Further, members can also exclude the patentability of diagnostic, therapeutic, and surgical ways of the treatment of humans, plants, and animals aside from micro-organisms and basic biological processes for the assembly of plants and animals.

The visits agreement provides a minimum term of protection of twenty years beginning from the date of filing. However, in the case of applications filed under PCT the term of 20 years begins from the International filing date. The government of India had already enforced the requirements in Articles 70.8 and 70.9 of the TRIP Agreement.

Ministry administering the IPR:

- Department Industrial Policy and Promotion
- Ministry of Commerce & industry

The main workplace is in Kolkata and 4 branches of the Patent Offices are in Kolkata, Mumbai, Delhi, and Chennai. Mumbai supervises jurisdiction of Maharashtra, Gujrat, Madhya Pradesh and Goa, Daman and Diu, Dadra, and Nagar Haveli. In Chennai's jurisdiction, the States of Andhra Pradesh, Kerala, Tamil Nadu, Mysore and Pondicherry, Laccadive, Minicoy and the Aminidivi Islands are included. The New Delhi branch looks over the jurisdiction of Haryana, Himachal Pradesh, Jammu, Kashmir, Punjab, Rajasthan, Chandigarh, and Delhi City. The remainder of the Republic of India comes under the jurisdiction of Delhi.

Patent protection is a territorial right and thus it's effective solely inside the territory of the Republic of India. However, filing an application in the Republic of India allows anybody to file a corresponding application for the same invention in convention countries, during or before the end of the twelve month filing period in the Republic of India. Therefore, separate patents ought to be obtained in every country wherever the applicant needs the protection of his or her invention in those countries. No patent is valid worldwide.

An application can be filed by either the true and initial discoverer or his or her recipient, alone, or conjointly with the other person. Also, the personal representative of an associate decedent can create a patent application.

Counterfeiting

India's Pharmacy industry stands 4th in the world in terms of production volumes and more than 55% of exports are too highly regulated in the market. India's drug exports were $14.6 billion (around Rs.82, 730 Crore) in the financial year up to March 31, 2012. India is a classic example of developing a country through a strong pharmaceutical industry, which also has effective drug regulatory and control systems. However, at the same time, the Pharmacy Industry in India is tormented by the problem of counterfeiting. The business of drug counterfeiting in India is getting bigger and bigger day by day because of various reasons such as the growing pharmaceutical industry, poor pharmaceutical regulation, high drug prices, value added tax, prescription of drugs without registration, lack of public awareness, weak enforcement of legislations, and flexibility in the current legal framework. Drug counterfeiting in India is a very lucrative business. India's image as a low-cost manufacturing base has opened up the gates for counterfeiters. Counterfeiting is the making of fraudulent copies of something valuable. This does nothing but cheat the consumers as well as the manufacturers running parallel operations.

The World Health Organization (WHO) defines counterfeiting of medicine as, "A counterfeit medicine is one which is deliberately and fraudulently mislabeled with respect to identity and/or source. Counterfeiting can apply to both branded and generic products and counterfeit products may include products with the correct ingredients or with the wrong ingredients, without active ingredients, with insufficient active ingredients or with fake packaging."

The counterfeit drug industry receives money to the tune of $200 billion globally every year. The counterfeit drug industry has been defined as "The crime of the 21st century" (ACG Report, 2003). At present, it occurs in almost every industry, especially in Asia which appears to be the single largest producing region for counterfeit drugs. Almost three-fourths of all counterfeit drugs supplied in the world have direct or indirect origins in India. According to BASCAP, the "Pharmaceutical industry is the most counterfeited industry in India". A report by Rama Lakshmi suggests that an estimated 12 to 25 percent of all drugs sold within the boundaries of India are counterfeited.

The World Health Organization (WHO) estimates that up to 30 percent of branded drugs sold in developing nations are counterfeit. This can have dangerous and fatal implications for patients. For example, tuberculosis and Malaria counterfeits, which mostly originate in India and China, are estimated to kill around 700,000 people a year. Counterfeiters, similar to legitimate drug manufacturers, are keen to benefit from cheaper manufacturing costs in India that are around 40 percent lower in price than other markets. According to reports, it is estimated that about 1 out of 5 medicines sold in India is counterfeited, accounting for about 14 percent share in the domestic market. Also, fake products with a "Made in India" label manufactured in China have been floating in the global market at an alarming rate, which brings disrepute to the Indian domestic Industry and causes loss to the tune of $5 billion.

Remedies Against Counterfeiting of the Patents Are as Follows

A suit for infringement of a patent may be instituted in the district court or High court having original jurisdiction to try the suit (section 104). The procedure followed in conducting a suit for infringement is governed by the provision of the code of Civil procedure. The reliefs which may be awarded in such a suit may include an interlocutory/interim injunction, damages or account of profits, or permanent injunction.

Impact on Research and Development Expenditures

The development of a new drug typically takes around 10 to 12 years and can cost as much as $1.5 billion. Each year only around 26 new chemical entities enter the drug market. These figures prove beyond a doubt that pharmacy companies have a difficult road ahead for drug development. This makes the new patented drug costlier and out of reach for general lower middle-income group and BPL group. However, counterfeiting takes the essence out of it and makes it available at the cheap rates for general strata of the population. This makes the Indian Pharmaceutical companies reluctant to spend large ransom amounts on the R&D part.

It is estimated that the top 25 Indian Pharmaceutical companies spend around 6,103 Crore INR on Research and Development. Pharmacy companies enjoy a significant tax benefit on R&D expenditure. The government allows a weighted deduction of up to 200 percent of such spending in India. Even after the increased investment, market leaders such as Ranbaxy and Dr. Reddy's Laboratories spend only 5–10% of their revenues on R&D. This disparity is too great to be explained by cost differentials and it comes when advances in genomics have made research equipment more expensive than ever.

Problem of Pricing the Patented Drugs

The cost incurred by Pharmacy companies is huge and spans for anywhere between 10-20 years. Hence, their investments in resources, time, and efforts should be aptly rewarded by allowing them a monopoly in the form of patent protection for a stipulated time period. However, the reality is something very much different.

Pharmaceutical companies in India have been constrained to live with a continuing focus from the government and also from the civil society on 'reasonably affordable medicines' irrespective of the fact whether they are generic or patented. Pharmaceuticals being covered under the 'Essential Commodities Act' 1955, empower the government to announce the 'administered price' for essential medicines. Drugs fall under the sub-section 2[IV (a)] of "Essential Commodities Act". In India, 70 percent of expenditures on healthcare are out-of-pocket, which has led the government and its judiciary to take steps to promote the use of generic products to prevent prices of lifesaving drugs being set by market forces. This has caused a number of issues for multinational companies, leading some to question the commercial viability of India. In April 2013, Novartis lost a six-year legal battle. The Supreme Court ruled that because of small changes to its leukemia drug Glivec, the drug would not get a new patent. Recently, India upheld a compulsory license of Bayer's cancer drug Nexavar, effectively allowing generics firms to copy the patented drug. The patent for Pfizer's cancer drug Sutent was revoked and Roche's patent on Pegasys, a hepatitis C drug, was denied.

Off-Patented Drugs

An off-patented is a drug defined as "a drug product that is comparable to a brand/ reference listed drug product in dosage form, strength, quality and performance characteristics, and intended use, which patent is expired and became generic. Generic drugs are subject to the regulations of the governments of India. Generic drugs are labeled with the name of the manufacturer and the adopted name of the drug.

When the drugs become off-patented, the market competition often leads to substantially lower prices for both the original brand name product and the generic forms. In India, patents give 20 years of protection. Many countries/regions such as the European Union and the USA may grant up to 5 years of additional protection for drugs ("patent term restoration") if manufacturers meet specific goals such as conducting clinical studies for pediatric patients. But India does not give this extension.

Once the patent of a drug expires, the manufacturer can't take advantage of being the inventor of that particular medicine. Many companies will come up with the same composition and as supply in the drug industry increases, the price goes down.

Generic manufacturers do not incur the cost of drug discovery. Sometimes, reverse-engineering is used to develop bioequivalent versions to existing drugs. Generic manufacturers also do not bear the burden of proving the safety and efficacy of the drugs through clinical trials, since these trials have already been conducted by the brand name company. For as long as a drug patent lasts, a brand name company enjoys a period of monopoly in which the company is able to set the price of the drug at a level which maximizes profitability.

The World Generic Medicines Congress Europe 2015 indicates that drugs valued at $170 billion in annual sales will lose patents in 2015, leaving concerned companies trying to calculate the imminent damage. Aripiprazole by Otsuka Pharmaceuticals, glatirame by TevaPharma, albuterol-ipratropium inhalation by Boehringer Ingelheim, imatinib mesylate by Novartis, memantine HCI by Forrest Labs, etc. are some of the off-patent drugs. These drugs treat conditions like neuro-psychiatry, Multiple Sclerosis, cancer, Alzheimer's, sleep disorders, COPD, anti-viral, and HIV (Bengaluru, 2014). The Indian pharmacy collects much of its revenues from exports. Now companies, including Sun pharmacy, Dr. Reddy's Labs, Glenmark, Cipla, Lupin, Torrent, etc will be able to grab business opportunities from global markets. In the US alone, the post-patent cliff demand for generics is expected to be at 86-87% (Bengaluru, 2014). There are around five Indian companies in the list of top 20 global generic companies. The patent expiry drugs are a massive opportunity for Indian pharmacy. All big players in the country have been extremely proactive and well prepared by lining up their pipeline to propel growth (Bengaluru, 2014).

"The promising market opportunity needs ample long-term planning and research efforts. Indian pharmacy companies would have made efforts to timely file the ANDAs", said Kaushik Desai, pharmacy consultant, Hon General Secretary, Indian Pharmaceutical Association and Chairperson, Industrial Pharmacy Section, Federation of Asian Pharmaceutical Associations (FAPA) (Bengaluru, 2014).

The off-patent drug also provides room for alternative growth paths as indicated by World Generic Medicines Congress Europe 2015. Indian pharmacies will need to fast track orphan drugs, work on new drug delivery devices and develop drugs with different forms of the new molecule, pointed out Desai (Bengaluru, 2014).

Price Decay After Patent Expiration

Every branded drug will lose their exclusivity when the patented duration gets over and generics will begin to compete for market share. Even though it impacts brands, they try to stay in the market by promoting commercial departments whose main function is to maintain value in the brand years after the loss of exclusivity. Both generic and innovator companies have tried to understand the ways in which prices change once a patent has expired and a generic product is launched. Generic companies have to plan their production scheduling, need to estimate how quickly the price might decline, and will make a stab at predicting the length of their product's profitability window. Branded companies, on the other hand, need to understand how well any price equalization against the generic product might work.

Scalloped Decay

It has long been recognized that prices paid by chemists and dispensing doctors for a generic product would decline in the weeks and months after generic launch, but how quickly this would happen could only be guessed at. Typically, the product price follows a 'scalloped' curve as the price initially declines rapidly as generics firms compete for market share, but then flattens out as the price approaches their cost of goods. In some cases, the decline is extremely rapid, whilst for others, the decline can take many years. Some generic companies still use 'rules of thumb', which states that 'if there are more than three generic license holders the price will decline rapidly and the profits will be low. However, if the brand is worth many millions of dollars, they focus on this and seem to forget that the value of the market is likely to decline massively. Thus, the value of the brand in the year prior to generic launch has an effect on the speed of price decay. In other words, the larger the value of the brand, the more generic companies there are likely to be competing for this new market.

Figure 1. Cetirizine price decline after off-patenting

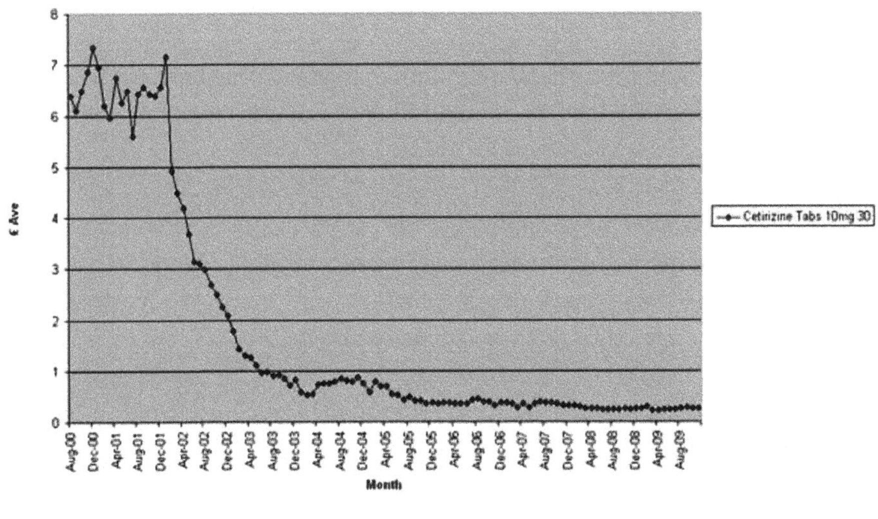

Bouncing in the Prices

The number of off-patented manufacturers is also important as if the generic price approaches a generic company's cost of goods, some are able to get a price decrease from their supplier whilst others are not. The difference is that if the price is not flexible as there is only one supplier, the market price may then decline to a level at which some license holders decide not to schedule further batches and withdraw from the market. As the number of license holders' declines, the price rises or bounces, resulting in some changing of minds and market re-entry. These bounces happen in about 20% of products, and the remaining 80% continue to follow the 'scalloped' curve.

Regulations That Govern the Operations of Pharmaceutical Companies

USFDA

USFDA (United States Food & Drug Administration), headquartered in Maryland is the regulatory agency which regulates the food and drugs that are imported into the USA.

USFDA regulates more than US $1 trillion worth of consumer goods, about 25% of the expenditure on consumer goods in the United States. This includes $466 billion in food sales, $275 billion in drugs, $60 billion in cosmetics, and $18 billion in vitamin supplements. Much of these expenditures are for goods imported into the United States; the FDA is responsible for monitoring imports. USFDA proposal for the federal budget in 2014 is $4.7 billion, out of which major part is paid by the pharmaceutical companies that export drugs into the United States (The Indian Express, n. d.).

Any new drug or improvement/ alteration to existing drug needs to be approved by the FDA to be imported into the United States. There are two types of approvals by the FDA:

- **FDA Approved:** This is applicable for new drugs or new substitutions that are made and these drugs need to be proven "safe and efficacy" to be certified.
- **FDA Cleared:** FDA clearance pertains to drugs which are modifications to drugs that are already, otherwise approved by the FDA.

Any company that proposes to export drugs to the USA needs to file a "new drug application" to test the drug and submit the report to prove its safety and efficacy for consumption (The Indian Express, n.d.).

Impact on Indian Pharmaceutical Market

As the US market contributes to 25-55% of the revenue to Indian pharmaceutical companies, the necessity to comply with FDA standards and get clearances from regular scrutiny is essential. Given the level of importance of compliance and hygiene is less in India, there is an increasing trend in the number of pharmaceutical units that are coming under the scrutiny of the FDA is increasing and the same trend is evident in the number of warning Indian pharmaceutical companies are receiving (from 2 warnings in 2008 to 8 in 2014).

An extract from recent JP Morgan report:

Regulatory headwinds remain one of the key risks to the Indian pharmaceutical sector, especially in light of the increasing scrutiny by the FDA to ensure quality and compliance. While the volume of warning letters issued by FDA has increased 10x over the last four years, there has been a higher impact on Indian companies recently from the increasing activities of the US regulator (import alerts, warning letters, Form 483s)

A recent example of the impact of FDA on Indian major Ranbaxy:

Ranbaxy Laboratories has been sued in US district court on the allegations of manipulating US Food and Drug Administration (USFDA) rules for years to keep rival generic drugs out of the market. Ranbaxy being the largest supplier of generic drugs into the US market, is currently prohibited to supply drugs due to the noncompliance to the standards. This is not the first time that this major paid price for noncompliance (Reuters, 2015).

In 2013, Ranbaxy was proven guilty for lawbreaking on the charges related to drug safety and agreed to civil and criminal compensation of $500 million in a settlement with the US to resolve claims that it sold substandard drugs and made false statements to the FDA about manufacturing practices at its plants. In the recent tests by FDA, the tablets from Ranbaxy were found to have 'black fiber' and black marks black spots which were subsequently observed to be hair strands and oil marks (Reuters, 2015; Business Standard, 2013).

Observation from USFDA 2012 report "black fiber embedded in a tablet was likely either tape remnants on the nozzle head of the machine or a hair from an employee's arm that could be exposed on loading the machine" (Business Standard, 2013). It was also observed that the plant lacked basic facilities like hand wash for employees and managers and also proper toilets for workers. This followed a series of actions by the US authorities and the FDA, which in 2008 banned the import of

30 generic drugs produced by Ranbaxy at its Dewas and Paonta Sahib plants for violation of manufacturing norms (Business Standard, 2013).

EMEA

EMEA is a European Union agency for the evaluation of medicinal products. The EMEA was set up in 1995 on the lines similar to USFDA to check and control the drugs that are entering the European market from various importers. The European Medicines Agency operates as a decentralized scientific agency (as opposed to a regulatory authority) of the European Union and its main responsibility is the protection and promotion of public and animal health through the evaluation and supervision of medicines for human and veterinary use. More specifically, it coordinates the evaluation and monitoring of centrally authorized products and national referrals, developing technical guidance and providing scientific advice to sponsors. Its scope of operations is medicinal products for human and veterinary use, including biologics and advanced therapies, and herbal medicinal products.

The centralized procedure allows companies to submit a single application to the Agency to obtain from the European Commission a centralized (or 'Community') marketing authorization (MA) valid in all EU and European Economic Area (EEA)-European Free Trade Association (EFTA) states (Iceland, Liechtenstein, and Norway). The centralized procedure is compulsory for all medicines derived from biotechnology and other high-tech processes, as well as for human medicines for the treatment of HIV/AIDS, cancer, diabetes, neurodegenerative diseases, autoimmune and other immune dysfunctions, and viral diseases, and for veterinary medicines for use for growth or yield enhancers. The centralized procedure is also open to products that bring a significant therapeutic, scientific, or technical innovation, or is in any other respect in the interest of patient or animal health. As a result, the majority of genuinely novel medicines are authorized through the EMA.

Compliance Issues With EMA

European regulatory officials have expressed concern that dozens of medicines may have been approved in the EU based on fraudulent data conducted by a contract testing facility in Hyderabad, India (Gaffney, 2014). In September 2014, French regulator ANSM raised concerns about GVK Biosciences, saying a good clinical practice (GCP) inspection had "raised serious concerns regarding the GCP compliance of the conduct of the clinical part of bioequivalence trials" at the company's Hyderabad facility (Gaffney, 2014). Then, on 5 December 2014, German regulator BfArM said it had suspended the marketing authorisations (MAs) for all products whose approval was based on bioequivalence data conducted by GVK, giving ANSM's allegations further weight (Gaffney, 2014). To counter this, GVK has agreed to re-do its tests in another facility or to refund the money of the customers.

Regulatory Bodies

- Central Drug Standard Control Organization (CDSCO)
- Government of India Directory of Health and Family Welfare
- Indian Council of Medical Research (ICMR)
- Ministry of Health and Family Welfare

The essential administrative body for the pharmaceutical division is the Central Drugs Standard Control Organization (CDSCO) started in 1940. The Bureau of Chemicals and Petrochemicals (DCP) was initiated in 1991 to handle the strategy and arranging part of chemical, petrochemical, and pharmaceutical commercial enterprises. So as to alter and modify the costs of controlled bulk drugs, the National Pharmaceutical Pricing Authority (NPPA) was initiated in 1994 (D&B, n.d.).

An outline of regulatory and policy environment in Indian Pharmaceutical industry is given underneath:

Price

- DPCO allows government to control prices of 74 bulk drugs and their formulation
- NPPA does price fixation/revision and updating the list of drugs under price control
- Direct price control discourages the industry from producing these medicines (D&B, n. d.)

Product and Quality

- CDSCO lays down standards for the drugs, cosmetics, diagnostics, and devices that manufacturers should follow
- Good Manufacturing Practices (GMP) for plants and materials
- National Pharmaceutical Policy seeks to strengthen the GMP norms patents
- Patent Act, 1970 Patent (Amendment) Act 2005 (D&B, n. d.)

TRIPS and Compulsory Licensing

Article 31(f) of the TRIPS Agreement explains that products made under compulsory licensing must be "predominantly for the supply of the domestic market ". This puts an upper limit on the exports of medicines made under compulsory licensing. Consequently, it has an effect on nations that do not manufacture medicines and need to import generics. It becomes increasingly difficult for them to find suppliers of drugs manufactured under compulsory licensing. Due to the Patents (Amendment) Act 2005, there has been a movement in the method followed by leading Indian organizations; they are proceeding onward to growing new medications, exporting to regulated markets, and getting into helpful concurrences with MNCs. This attempt further bolsters India's good fortune because of the issues confronted by MNCs. For example, drowsy offers of patented drugs in home markets, diminishing R&D incomes, and increasing costs. To manage these issues and to concentrate on their core competency, i.e. drug discoveries and advertising of the medication, MNCs have progressively taken an interest in CRAMS, co-showcasing collusions, and outsourcing of research and trials.

The Supreme Court judgment that rejected the Novartis patent plea (for the cancer drug Glivec) was momentous for its vision, when it said: "We certainly do not wish the law of patent in this country to develop on the lines where there may be a vast gap between the coverage and the disclosure under the patent; where the scope of the patent is determined not on the intrinsic worth of the invention but by the artful drafting of its claims by skillful lawyers, and where patents are traded as a commodity, not for production and marketing of the patented products but to search for someone who may be sued for infringement of the patent."

Following this order by the Supreme Court, there has been a serious weight on India from the US pharmacy organizations. The US business and trade bodies have attempted to portray India as an IP-maverick though the truth was that India constantly consented to multilateral agreements.

The idea of a better-ordered world is one in which medical discoveries will be free of patents and there will be no profiteering from life and death." -Indira Gandhi at the World Health Assembly in 1982

India arrangements to broaden the extent of value controls on pharmaceuticals, a senior government authority said, "making another potential obstacle for multinational medication organizations working together in the nation. The new proposition would broaden value limitations past bland solutions to apply interestingly to licensed medications. That would be a noteworthy test for medication organizations that as of now are concerned that India isn't doing what's necessary to secure their licensed innovation."

"Most nations take after some type of value control. We have to guarantee that extravagant medications are accessible at reasonable rates to poor people," said D.S. Kalha, the secretary of India's Pharmaceuticals Department. The arrangements come as Bayer AG is battling a request from India's patent power that obliged the Germany organization to issue a permit permitting an Indian nonspecific medication organization to offer a less costly duplicate of Bayer's licensed malignancy drug Nexavar. India's patent office referred to the high cost of the malignancy drug as the explanation for the request. India's Intellectual Property Appellate Board heard contentions for the situation this week and is relied upon to issue a decision soon.

India sets costs for 74 nonspecific drugs and is considering expanding the quantity of solutions secured by value tops to 348a level not seen following 1979. The administration contends that the cost of lifesaving medications shouldn't be dictated by business sector constraints, however, rather ought to be managed. Indians pay just about 70 percent of their human services costs out of pocket in light of the fact that not very many individuals have protection and the greater part of the spending is on medications.

Any endeavor to limit costs of licensed medications likely will irritate remote pharmaceutical organizations. Securing protected items is urgent to encourage advancement, so "any value control around there will smother [research and development] activities genuinely, unfavorably influencing patients' hobbies over the long haul," said Tapan Ray, chief general of the Organization of Pharmaceutical Producers of India, an exchange gather that speaks to multinational medication organizations.

Ranjit Shahani, India overseeing executive of Novartis AG, said remunerating imaginative protected medications, in the end, helps the generics business. "Today's protected medications are truth be told the bland business' pipeline," he said. The Swiss drug producer has been battling for a patent on its malignancy drug Glivec in India since the nation's patent power rejected Novartis' patent application in 2006. The organization's allure against the decision is pending in India's Supreme Court. India in 2005 started perceiving licenses on pharmaceutical items and past patent law had secured assembling procedures. The move brought reasons for alarm up in India because without value controls protected medications may become excessively expensive for a lion's share of the nation's 1.2 billion individuals.

An interagency government council was set up in 2007 to consider how to set costs of licensed medications. That gathering has finished broad thoughts and the Pharmaceuticals Department is relied upon to discharge a report to the general population in coming weeks to gather criticism. That info will be considered when formal regulations are drafted and brought before Parliament.

The counseling firm Ernst & Young and the Federation of Indian Chambers of Commerce and Industry said in a late report that costs of protected medications ought to consider a nation's buying force and the per capita salary of its kind. "For licensed items, development should be regarded. In any case, similarly as valuing of these items are concerned, we have to take an exceptionally comprehensive general visibility instead of an extremely limit item view," said Murali Nair, an Ernst & Young accomplice. India's patent office additionally has rejected a patent application from US-based Gilead Sciences Inc. for its HIV solution Viread. Furthermore, Roche Holding AG has not been able to get Indian courts to stop the offer of duplicates of the Swiss organization's tumor drug Tarceva, which has patent assurance in numerous other Western countries. Both nations have appealed.

The Drugs Prices Control Order, 1995, is a request issued by the Government of India under Section 3 of the Essential Commodities Act, 1955 to manage the costs of medications. Its essential structure stays the same as that under the earlier two requests of '79 and '87, however, it did change the compass of control impressively. With the end goal of executing procurements of DPCO, forces of the administration have been vested in National Pharmaceutical Pricing Authority (NPPA) according to warning S.O. 637(E) dated 04.09.1997.

A center advisory group of industry specialists had been set up by the Department of Pharmaceuticals, and following two years of discussions, the council settled on a rundown of medications considered vital taking into account 'local the study of disease transmission' and mulling over expense adequacy, well-being, and viability. It went into specifics to cover 27 remedial fragments and dose shapes with the qualities determined. This was the genesis of the 652 details under the NLEM.

While the overarching objective of providing 'affordable medicines for all' is laudable, particularly in India, industries argue that there must be sufficient profit margins for the industry and price control is justifiable only 'under extraordinary circumstances' like an emergency, epidemic, or where a monopoly situation exists. "Price control does not make drugs accessible to the poor or needy but having an NLEM as per standard guidelines is critical,'' Mr. Shah said. The government's role in procuring drugs and providing it at low cost to the masses has been underplayed. The government role in developed markets like the U.K. through the Universal Healthcare program of the National Healthcare Service (NHS) or even in the U.S. has established models. Closer to home, governments in Tamil Nadu and Kerala have successful models in place to supply free drugs to government hospitals. Tamil Nadu Medical Supply Corporation's program covers 40 percent of the State's population and has been implemented in a cost-effective manner. The recent protracted stand-off with trade saw wholesalers and retailers drive a hard bargain with manufacturers for higher margins. The highly competitive scenario too does not allow companies to reduce drug prices below certain levels and continue to maintain scale and profits.

"The recent developments are not in the right direction. There has tended to be a one-sided view and there has not been an adequate dialogue between the pricing authority and industry," Mr. Piramal said. "India has a strong manufacturing base for pharmaceuticals and growth of the industry must be encouraged but if pricing makes it unviable, then companies will not be attracted to manufacture here." The top companies lose the freedom to upcharge on a few drugs and thereby subsequently will hit revenues and thereby hit the R &D expenses.

RECOMMENDATIONS

On one hand, the worldwide weight on healthcare is expanding, and on the other, the public-sector expenditure on well-being is diminishing. Compulsory Licensing (CL) is one such adaptability that can be utilized by the Indian government to get access to affordable medicines. One major limitation of Compulsory Licensing is that the MNCs may pull back new products from the market. Furthermore, the procurement of issuing "utility model" patents or basically "petty patents" would control or lessen the act of getting insignificant patents or expanding the patent duration of the original chemical composition. Issuance of "petty patents" was constrained to small inventions, simple to get and were only required to be registered and not examined. Further, "petty patents" were granted for a brief time of only three years contrasted with the regular twenty years of patent life. The move towards granting of "petty patents" would attempt to strike a balance between the opposing forces-innovation and access to reasonably priced medicines. To avoid overpricing of medicines the government and makers can mutually decide on the price of patented medicines. Individuals should be made aware of the benefits of medical insurance and be encouraged to invest in the same. A differential pricing system that envisages companies with patented drugs to recover most of the costs in the developed world and at the same time license or sells at lower prices in the poor countries is one. Perhaps licensing out to a company in developing country for manufacture could be a better option as local manufacturing would ensure sustainability, the lowest price and strengths the local technical competence. A differential pricing framework that visualizes organizations with patented medications to recoup a large portion of the expenses in the developed countries and in the meantime permit or sell at lower costs in under-developed/developing nations can be put in place. Maybe licensing out to an organization for production could be a superior alternative as local production would guarantee sustainability and most reduced value other than reinforcing local specialized competence.

REFERENCES

Bengaluru, N. V. (2014) Patent expiries valued at $170 bn set Indian pharma to accelerate its complex generic programmes. *Pharmabix.com.* Retrieved from http://www.pharmabiz.com/NewsDetails.aspx?aid=85348&sid=1

D&B. (n. d.) Pharmaceuticals – Indian regulatory & policy environment. *D&B.* Retrieved from http://www.dsir.gov.in/reports/isr1/Pharmaceuticals/7_5.pdf

Gaffney, A. (2014). EU regulators concerned about drug data fraud by Indian company. *Regulatory Affairs Professional Society.* Retrieved from http://www.raps.org/Regulatory-Focus/News/2014/12/08/20924/EU-Regulators-Concerned-About-Drug-Data-Fraud-by-Indian-Company/

Ghai, D. (2010). Patent protection and Indian pharmaceutical industry. *International Journal of Pharmaceutical Sciences Review and Researches, 3*(2). Retrieved from http://www.globalresearchonline.net/journalcontents/Volume3issue2/Article%20008.pdf

Ibis. (n. d.). Astra pharma receives USFDA approval for Vadodara plant. *IBIS.* Retrieved from http://pharma.industry-focus.net/usfda-approvals.html

Intellectual Property India. (n. d.). *Office of the Controller General of Patents, Designs & Trade Marks. Government of India.* Retrieved from: http://ipindia.nic.in/

PharmaPhorum. (n. d.) Articles. Retrieved from http://www.pharmaphorum.com/articles

Press Trust of India. (2013). Ranbaxy import ban: USFDA found suspected hair, oil in tablets. Retrieved from http://www.business-standard.com/article/companies/ranbaxy-import-ban-usfda-found-suspected-hair-oil-in-tablets-113091800573_1.html

Reuters. (2015). Ranbaxy sued for manipulating USFDA rules. *The Times of India.* Retrieved 11 October 2016 from http://timesofindia.indiatimes.com/india/Ranbaxy-sued-for-manipulating-USFDA-rules/articleshow/47289866.cms

Satyanarayana, K. (2005). TRIPS, patens & HIV/AIDS drugs. *The Indian Journal of Medical Research, 121*, 211–214. Retrieved from http://icmr.nic.in/ijmr/2005/April/editorial2.pdf PMID:15817937

The Indian Express. (n. d.). USFDA alerts to have no impact on pharmacy exports. Retrieved from http://indianexpress.com/article/business/business-others/usfda-alerts-to-have-no-impact-on-pharmacy-exports/

U.S Food & Drug Administration. (n. d.). How Drugs are Developed and Approved. Retrieved 11 November 2016 from http://www.fda.gov/Drugs/DevelopmentApprovalProcess/HowDrugsareDevelopedandApproved/

Chapter 4
Impact of National and International Regulations on Indian Generic Drugs Industry

Surabhi Singh
Trident ET Group of Institutions, India

ABSTRACT

This article looks at evolution of the intellectual property right laws in India with regard to pharmaceutical drugs, and their impact on the pharmaceutical industry in India. The amendments to Indian Patents Act 1970 as a result of India's obligations towards the TRIPS agreement while balancing the need to safeguard the interests of its population and domestic industry have also been looked at. International laws and treaties that impact the Indian industry have been analysed.

DEFINITION OF GENERIC DRUGS

A generic pharmaceutical drug is equivalent to a brand-name product in dosage, strength, route of administration, quality, performance, and intended use. E.g. Paracetamol, a painkiller, is the generic name for branded drugs like Crocin. In most countries, the original inventor of a new medicine or drug can file a patent and assert monopoly rights on the commercial exploitation of his invention or discovery for a certain number of years – such a drug is generally called a brand-name drug. Other companies can produce and sell generic drugs after the patent protections afforded to the drug's original inventor expire.

DOI: 10.4018/978-1-5225-2414-4.ch004

Copyright © 2017, IGI Global. Copying or distributing in print or electronic forms without written permission of IGI Global is prohibited.

Generic drugs go through a similarly rigorous (as a brand name drug) national and international regulatory approval before they can be released in the market. They are required to have the same active ingredient, strength, dosage form, and route of administration as the brand name product. The generic drug manufacturer must prove its drug is the same as (bioequivalent) and performs the same the brand name drug. All generic manufacturing, packaging, and testing sites must pass the same quality standards as those of brand name drugs, and the generic products must meet the same exacting specifications as any brand name product. In fact, many generic drugs are made in the same manufacturing plants as brand name drug products.

Cost Difference Between Generics and Brand-Name

The average cost of discovering, testing, and obtaining regulatory approval for a new drug, with a new chemical entity, was estimated to be as much as $800 million (all figures in US Dollars) in 2003 by DeMasi (2003) and $2.6 billion in 2014 by Tufts University (2014). Patent protection is provided to incentivise innovation and new drug development. With patent protection, pharmaceutical companies developing new (brand-name) drugs can exclude competition from the market, recoup their costs to develop the drug and make a profit.

Generic drugs are usually sold for significantly lower prices than their branded equivalents and at lower profit margins. One reason for this is that competition increases among producers when a drug is no longer protected by patents. Also, generic companies have to incur only the cost of manufacturing, and not the costs of drug discovery and development. They are thus able to maintain profitability at a lower selling price. According to FDA (Food and Drug Administration, U.S.A.) in 2010 alone, the use of FDA-approved generics saved $158 billion, an average of $3 billion every week. In a sample study of five commonly used medicines in India, Singhal, Nanda and Kotwani (2011) found that price-to-patient for the branded version of cetirizine, fluoxetine, ciprofloxacin, lansoprazole, and alprozolam was higher by 41%, 33%, 0%, 14%, and 31% than branded-generics. Numerous other studies have corroborated such results – generic drugs reduce the cost of medicines for patients significantly.

Acceptance of Generics

Today in the US, generic drugs account for 88% of all prescriptions filled and according to latest IMS report, generics may account for 91%-92% of prescription volumes by 2020 (as cited on nasdaq.com). In a study by Bronnenberg, Dubé, Gentzkow, & Shapiro (2015), researchers looked at over 66 million over-the-counter drug purchases in the U.S. and found that pharmacists and doctors buy generics 91% of the time, while "regular" people bought generics 74% of the time.

In India, generic substitution is legally not allowed so patients' awareness about generics is limited and doctors and patients do not want pharmacist to change the trade name written by doctor. For this reason, the consumer awareness of generics and the wide variety of trade names, and price variation available in the market is very limited. Government has taken initiatives to increase the prevalence of generic drugs, and reduce the overall cost of healthcare for the citizens and made it mandatory for doctors to prescribe drugs by their chemical or technical (generic) name rather than brand name. However, the uptake of this policy is mixed as per different news sources. More needs to be done in order to increase the prevalence of generics (from the current 70%) in India.

Equivalence With Brand-Name Drugs

It has been clearly shown in innumerable studies that, at least at a physiological level, generic medicines behave very similarly to their originator counterparts. Davit et al (2009) published an assessment of 12 years of bioequivalence data submitted to the FDA, comparing 2070 single-dose clinical bioequivalence studies of orally administered generic medicine products approved by the FDA from 1996 to 2007, demonstrated that the products did not differ significantly. Kesselheim et al (2008) published an extensive systematic review and meta-analysis related to clinical efficacy that were favourable towards use of generic drugs in treating cardiovascular disease (as cited on fda.gov). Further, many studies have demonstrated that initiation of treatment with generic medicines or switching to generic medicines are not associated with poorer patient outcomes. Specifically, Amit et al. in 2004 showed that a generic formulation of propafenone, used to treat atrial fibrillation, was found to be at least as safe as the originator drug (as cited by Dunne et al (2013)).

Economics of Generic Drugs

According to a report by IMS Health, from 2013-2018 generic drugs are expected to account for 52% of global pharmaceutical spending growth, compared to 35% for branded drugs. Overall, sales of generic drugs are forecast to increase from $267 billion in 2013 to $442 billion in 2017, an annualized growth rate of 10.6%. Major factors driving this growth include popular branded drugs losing their patent protection – blockbuster drugs with $150 billion of annual sales are set to lose patents between 2010 and 2017 (known as a "patent cliff"), support for generics from governments, new complex generics coming into the market, and industry consolidation (as cited on nasdaq.com).

The US is the largest pharmaceutical market in the world. It is also the world's largest generics market, accounting for a share of around 45% in the global Generics market. According to rncos.com's US Generic Drug Market Outlook 2018 report, the US Generics market, which was $ 43.5 Billion in 2013, is anticipated to grow at a CAGR of around 11% during 2013-2018. Japan, India and China are the other large markets, as well as producers of generic drugs. The top ten global generic companies account for 56% market share. The top eight global markets comprise 80% of the total generic sales.

According to IBEF (India Brand Equity Foundation) data, India is the largest provider of generic drugs globally with the Indian generics accounting for 20 per cent of global exports in terms of volume. Generic drugs form the largest segment of the Indian pharmaceutical sector with 70% market share (in terms of revenues). Over the years, India has established itself as one of the major producers of affordable generic drugs. The Indian pharmaceutical industry today is considered the world's third-largest by volume and, as of 2010, produces approximately 20% of the world's generic drugs. Experts anticipate India's pharmaceutical industry to grow to a value of $74 billion by 2020, solidifying India as a global leader in the pharmaceutical industry. Bennett (2014) states that India is not only a chief exporter of drugs, but also the primary producer of drugs for its own population. India is one of only two countries in the world (other being Japan) where generic drug manufacturers control a larger share of the domestic pharmaceutical market than big MNCs (Multi-National Companies). A few indigenous firms are capable of both generic drug production and research and development, while many smaller companies specialize exclusively in reverse-engineering drugs from overseas.

INDIAN PATENT LAWS ON PHARMACEUTICAL PRODUCTS

First Phase

Zacharias and Farias (2002), and Bennett (2014) have very well recorded the evolution of Patents laws in India, specifically provisions related to pharmaceuticals. India's patent regime can be broadly categorised into three phases – before independence to 1970, 1970 to 1995, and after 1995. India passed its first patent law in 1856 during British colonial rule. This law was based on the British Patent Law of 1852, which provided privileges to inventors for a period of 14 years. Following a number of amendments, this law later gave way to the Inventions and Designs Act of 1888. In 1911, the British replaced this act with the Indian Patents and Design Act, 1911. The 1911 Act established India's first modern system of patent administration. As with the 1856 Act and all subsequent acts, the 1911 Act provided for the patentability of pharmaceutical products.

During this phase, the Indian market was dominated by foreign companies, with little domestic participation. Patent applications by foreign nationals exceeded those of Indians by 340% with foreigners holding 80-90% of the pharma patents in India, acquired not for manufacturing but for protecting their imports. There was relative inaccessibility and unaffordability or even non-availability of essential lifesaving medicines.

Second Phase

After Indian independence in 1947, the country faced the challenge of providing affordable healthcare to all of its citizens. Because affordable healthcare naturally entails affordable pharmaceuticals, Indian officials began an extensive review of the 1911 Indian Patents and Design Act shortly after independence. The Government of India appointed two committees to spearhead this effort: the Tek Chand Patents Enquire Committee (1948–50) and the Ayyangar Patents Revision Committee (1957–59). The goal was to review the patent laws in India with a view to ensure that the patent system was more conducive to national interests. The reports of the two expert committees paved the way for the eventual enactment of the Patents Act of 1970, repealing all previous legislations. This Act provided that any invention that satisfies the criteria of newness, non-obviousness and usefulness can be the subject matter of a patent. The key change from the previous legislation were the provisions disallowing patent protection for certain categories of goods. Some of the non-patentable inventions under the Patents Act included processes for the medicinal, surgical, curative, prophylactic, therapeutic or other treatment of human beings, animals or plants or substances obtained by a mere admixture, resulting only in the aggregation of the properties of the components, etc. With regard to pharmaceuticals, substances intended for use or capable of being used as food, drugs or medicines or substances produced by chemical processes, patents were granted only for the processes of manufacture of such substances and not for the substances themselves. This exclusion of pharmaceutical products was introduced to reduce India's dependence on imports and support development of an indigenous pharmaceutical industry.

In addition, the Patents Act provided a number of safeguards to prevent abuse of patent rights and provide better access to drugs. The term of patents related to pharmaceuticals is reduced to a period of seven years from the date of filing or five years from the date of sealing the patent, whichever is less. Patents relating to all other inventions are granted for a period of 14 years from the date of filing. The Act also had provisions relating to compulsory licensing - on completion of three years from the date of sealing the patent, any person interested in the patented invention may apply for a compulsory license related to the invention. The controller of patents may direct the patent holder to grant such a license upon terms as may be deemed fit, only if he or she is satisfied that the reasonable requirements of the public with respect to the patented invention have not been met or that the patented invention is not available to the public at a reasonable price. In addition to compulsory licensing, the Patents Act included a provision for "licenses of right" where, in certain cases, the central government could, after the expiration of three years from the date of the sealing of the patent, apply for an order that the patent may be endorsed with the words "licenses of right", on the grounds that the reasonable requirements of the public with respect to the patented invention have not been satisfied or that the patented invention is not available to the public at a reasonable price. Patents for certain substances that are not food items or drugs as such but that are capable of being used as food items or drugs were deemed to be endorsed with the words "license of right" immediately on completion of three years from the date of the sealing of the patent. The effect of endorsing a patent with the words "licenses of right" is that any person who is interested in working the patented invention in India may request the patentee to grant a license. The granting of a license would be on terms that have been mutually agreed upon, even if he/she is already the holder of a license under the patent. In case the parties are unable to agree on the terms of the license, they can apply to the controller of patents to arrive at a settlement of terms.

Under these new patents laws, Indian drug manufacturers could copy pharmaceutical products that were patented in foreign countries and this is because of the lack of protection for product patents in pharmaceutical industry which resulted in the development of considerable expertise in reverse engineering of drugs that are patented in the other countries but unprotected in India. This resulted to a boom in the production of generic drugs in India. From a base of $604 million in 1974-75, production more than doubled to $1.21 billion by 1977-78 and increased to $2.2 billion in 1993-94. By 1993, Indian companies dominated over 70% of the domestic market in contrast to the world-wide trend of MNCs from the developed nations engulfing local markets. The number of pharmaceutical producing units in India increased from 2,257 in 1970 to more than 23,790 in 1996 according to the data from Organisation of Pharmaceutical Producers of India. The country went from being a net importer to exporting about $ 1 billion worth of finished formulations and bulk drugs annually in 1995-96.

The phase spanning the second half of 1970s to the early 1990s was a period during which the industry experienced structural transformation through the growth of the Indian generic industry. This development was a direct result of the adoption of the Patents Act of 1970. Firms belonging to Indian promoters began to take roots in the industry during the 1970s, and by the 1990s, these firms had consolidated their position in the industry. Without product patents with which to contend, Indian pharmaceutical companies were able to churn out countless generic drugs, establishing India as one of the leading generic drug manufacturers in the world. The relative affordability of these generic drugs compared to their patented counterparts has not only enabled India to provide cheap medicines for its citizens, but has also made India the de facto pharmacy for many developing countries.

Third Phase

India signed the General Agreement on Tariffs and Trade (GATT) on 15 April 1994, thereby making it mandatory to comply with the requirements of GATT, including the agreement on Trade-Related Aspects of Intellectual Property Rights (TRIPS). In 1995, India became a member of the World Trade Organisation (WTO). As a member, India was required to modify its domestic intellectual property laws in order to comply with the TRIPS agreement. Although India had to implement certain provisions of TRIPS immediately, article 65.2 of the agreement granted developing countries like India a transition period for the implementation of other provisions. One such provision gave nations without patent protection for pharmaceutical products a ten year period to bring their laws into compliance with TRIPS. Thus, India had until January 1, 2005, to make its patent laws relating to pharmaceuticals and agricultural chemicals TRIPS-compliant. Indian law went through three stages between 1995 and 2005 in order to conform with TRIPS. First, in 1999, India instituted the "mailbox" requirement of article 70.9, which enabled entities to submit product patent applications for pharmaceuticals and agricultural chemicals to the patent office that would be held until examination in 2005. Second, India introduced the Patents (Amendment) Act of 2002, which further integrated Indian law by extending patent terms to twenty years as stipulated by TRIPS. Third, and lastly, the Patents (Amendment) Act of 2005 brought India into compliance with TRIPS by giving full patent protection to pharmaceutical products.

While India made the necessary adjustments to its laws to satisfy the requirements of TRIPS, criticism and concern about the effect of pharmaceutical patents on domestic drug prices compelled the Indian government to retain legitimate means for balancing innovation incentives against the social costs of pharmaceutical product patents. A significant means by which the Indian government can "limit the reach of product patent protection" is section 3(d) of the Patents (Amendment)

Act of 2005. Section 3(d) essentially provides for a tougher standard for securing patents. Companies that introduce new versions of their pharmaceutical products must demonstrate that the new versions are "therapeutically more beneficial than earlier versions on which patents had expired." Through section 3(d), India is able to prevent "ever-greening," which critics characterize as a "common abusive patenting practice" where pharmaceutical companies attempt to extend patent protection by making minor changes to existing drugs.

India is also a signatory to the Paris Convention for the protection of industrial property, 1883, and the Patent Cooperation Treaty, 1970. Rahalkar (2012) provides an excellent historical as well as contemporary overview of the gamut of Indian laws and regulatory frameworks related to pharmaceutical and drug affairs.

IMPACT OF CURRENT PATENTS LAW AMENDMENTS ON INDIAN PHARMACEUTICAL INDUSTRY

The 1970 Act, denying product patent to pharmaceutical products, medicines, food products and chemical processes gave impetus to the practice of reverse engineering and large pharmaceutical companies emerged in India by successfully marketing generic versions of brand-name drugs and exporting them the world over. Reversing these trends among the developing countries and protecting the economic interests of their large multi-national pharmaceutical companies was top priority for the developed nations like US. Developing countries rebelled against strict imposition of this stand from developed countries as they sought compromise. Many provisions were made to protect the interests of the Indian consumers, public health and Indian pharmaceutical industry.

Preventing "Ever-Greening" of Patents

Section 3(d) of the Indian Patent Act 1970 (as amended in 2005) does not allow patent to be granted to inventions involving new forms of a known substance unless it differs significantly in properties with regard to efficacy. This provides a strong defense against the ever-greening of patents. The provisions have been amended to remove the ambiguity of what can be patented and what cannot be patented i.e. the ambiguity related to the scope of patentability. These amendments are very critical in Indian context for creating awareness of what cannot be patented as there are many healing techniques of different ethnic systems and societies of medicines like Ayurveda, Unani etc. which could not be patented.

Compulsory License

Compulsory licences are critical to curb the abuse of the patents rights. Further clarifications have been made in obtaining compulsory licence to facilitate export of patented pharmaceutical products by Indian companies to countries that do not have adequate production capacities. TRIPS gave this instrument of compulsory licensing to governments so that they can allow domestic manufacturers to manufacture patented products within 3 years of their introduction. This would open an opportunity for manufacturers to export the medicines to other countries which are not in manufacturing of drugs. India has the opportunity to emerge as world leader in the field of export of drugs as India is rich in cost effective and intellectually competitive manpower and other resources.

Immunity for Generic Production

This act enables the manufacturers of Generic drugs to continue production of generic version of new drugs. For doing so, the generic companies are required to pay the patent holder a reasonable royalty. With respect to the reasonable royalty it creates the problem of excessive demands from the patent holder and litigation. Because of the provision, India is likely to become the production hub of generics because of cheap and skilled labour. Over a period, Indian drug companies may become dependent on multinational companies for technology to produce new drugs because they will lose the opportunity to develop processes for patent protected drug in the country. Large MNCs have returned to the Indian market, e.g. Merck opened its fully owned subsidiary after a gap of 20 years. The domination of MNCs in the Indian drug market may increase with a loss of Indian companies which may give the liberty to MNCs to increase prices for drugs in Indian market.

Regulation of Prices

Indian pharmaceutical market is drug controlled. The fight between the regulators and the industry started way back in 1970s when he first DOPC (Drugs Price Control Order) was issued. Since 1997, National Pharmaceutical Pricing Authority (NPPA), a government regulatory agency, controls the prices of pharmaceutical drugs in India. It can fund studies regarding pricing of drugs. It also monitors drug shortages and take appropriate actions to rectify it. It usually regulates the prices of essential drugs through National List of Essential Medicines (NELM). Recently there was an uproar over NPPA regulating prices of over 100 drugs outside the NELM which was upheld by the Supreme Court of Indian. Drug price control, though controversial, falls within the legal limits of the government in the interests of public health.

As a means to cope with the change in regulatory landscape, Indian pharmaceutical industry increased its R&D activities with increase in public-private partnerships with academic institutions. They ventured into contract research with large MNCs, and increased filings with the US FDA. The industry has continued to prosper with exports increasing from $3.9 billion in 2004-05 to more than $12.5 billion in 2014-15.

The Indian pharmaceutical industry that has developed has a three-tier structure. It consists of a large private sector, which can be further divided into two categories of firms, viz. firms that are affiliates of foreign firms in India and those that have Indian promoters and produce generic drugs; and the small scale units. Yet another way of looking at the Indian pharmaceutical industry is in terms of scale of operations – it can be characterized as "long tailed", i.e. there are a relatively small number of large firms and a large number of small firms. In 2006, nearly 80% of the net worth of the pharmaceutical industry was accounted for by the largest 18 firms.

During 1990s, the Indian pharmaceutical industry performed strongly on all fronts. Total production of the industry (large firms and the small-scale units taken together) expanded more than four times in value (in Rupees). The dollar value of exports too had a similar increase. There was strong evidence that the Indian industry was getting increasingly outward oriented – the share of exports in total production almost doubled during the decade. But it was in the post-1995 phase that the large firms in the industry have performed strongly on all fronts. During this phase, generic producers were relatively more active as compared to the affiliates of foreign firms. While in 1995, five of the top ten pharmaceutical firms (in terms of sales) were foreign affiliates, in 2004 GlaxoSmithKline was the only foreign affiliate in the top ten list.

The privatisation and globalisation policy has made India a place for R&D in the pharmaceutical industry. So far. Indian companies have only been manufacturing the drugs. Now, government policies are aimed at making India the place to set up research and development, including soft loans for pharma R&D, joint research projects between industry and government academic institutions, and regulatory support.

Impact of International Policies

Generic drugs play a vital role in healthcare by improving accessibility as well as affordability of drugs. Generic drugs occupy a significantly higher share of the drug market globally as compared to reference drugs. The same is true even in developed economies of the world. It is important to take a holistic view of the prevailing policy framework covering generic drugs globally, making it possible to analyse the effects of these policies on the generic pharmaceutical industry.

The vicinity of a substantial number and mixture of generic drugs puts weight on regulatory powers. The regulatory powers are in charge of surveying, institutionalizing, valuing and approbation of the generic drugs. Alongside the current obligations, they are confronting with difficulties because of the increment in the mixed bag, detail and use of the generic drugs, the mind boggling supply chains and circulation systems over the globe. These difficulties were in charge of the requirement for regulatory joining. Regulatory joining alludes to a procedure of adjusting the regulatory prerequisites and systems of diverse nations to shape a standard and investigative regulatory structure for the audit and endorsement of the generic drug applications. This prompted the dispatch of the universal Generic Drug Regulators Pilot (IGDRP) in a meeting of regulatory powers from Australia, Brazil, Canada, the European Union, Korea, Singapore, US and the World Health Organization in October 2011. The fundamental target of the IGDRP is to create methodology and systems for approval and accessibility of value and safe generic drugs, and set up data and work sharing environment universally. This reduces the regulatory weight on pharmaceutical companies across countries; duplication of drugs can be controlled; increase the accessibility of generic drugs increments, in the event that they are not enlisted in specific markets. It also makes the audit and support methodology reliable and more productive. However, some challenges still remain: the legal meaning of terms like generic, varieties, and so forth are diverse under distinctive legal systems. The treatment techniques differ because of diverse conventions in societies. The technique and time of evaluation may change across nations.

The first pertinent area of global pharmaceutical policy is funding of research in life sciences. This pertains primarily to reference drugs rather than generic drugs. Globally, there is no overarching framework in this area. This has happened only in the event of a global challenge in the form of HIV/AIDS in the 1980s, Avian influenza and Ebola in recent times. At the national level, biomedical research bodies like the NIH (National Institute of Health) in the US, the MRC (Medical Research Council) in the UK, and the DST (Department of Science and Technology) in India control and incentivise medical research. The effect is seen in terms of quality control issues in the manufacture of generic drugs from time to time. There have been several instances of sales and distribution bans on pharmaceutical companies from the developing world by US FDA and the European Medicines Agency (EMA) for CGMP (Current Good Manufacturing Practice) violations.

Patent law is another area with regard to a divergence of interests between the developed and developing world, thereby rendering it difficult for policy makers to converge on a common agenda. The legal instrument driving international patent protection is the Agreement on Trade-Related Aspects of Intellectual Property Rights (TRIPS) under the auspices of the World Trade Organization. The TRIPS framework sets out minimal standards for intellectual property protection modelled after those in developed nations with which all WTO members must comply. Patent law is already well established in western countries, so most of the efforts to comply with the TRIPS are concentrated in the developing world.

Multinational pharmaceutical giants have challenged the validity of a key provisions the Patent laws of developing countries on multiple occasions. Many of these countries have legislative provisions to ensure that frivolous 20-year patent monopolies are not granted at the cost of public health. Also, the status of many developing countries, such as India, as suppliers of low-cost essential medicines to the developing world will be jeopardised. More fundamentally, a complete alignment with global patent standards will mark the first time in history that a multinational corporation succeeds in legally abrogating a country's sovereign right to implement its obligations under the Agreement on Trade-Related Aspects of Intellectual Property (TRIPS) in a manner consistent with the protection of public health. With regard to licensing, drugs that are imported into a country without the authorization of the intellectual property right holder for that country, but after having been legally placed on sale in another country is illegal, at best falling into a legally contestable grey area. Allowing the reintroduction of price competition, parallel importation and compulsory licensing provide safeguards against a patent holder charging excessively high prices in a particular market. They are recognized as TRIPS public health safeguards because they enhance the affordability and availability of medicines. At the national level, governments may issue a licence to allow the use of a patented drug without the consent of the patent holder in situations of public interest like national emergency, anti-competitive practices or for public, non-commercial use.

With regard to pricing, most multinational pharmaceutical companies follow 'Tiered pricing', the practice of selling drugs to different countries at different prices depending on their socioeconomic status, allowing pharmaceutical companies to maximise profit in all countries, as prices are determined according to the highest a country is prepared to pay. With their emerging middle classes now firmly on the pharmaceutical industry's radar, middle-income countries are often left paying excessively high prices. Even poorer countries can lose out, as tiered pricing does not reflect the true lowest price potential of drugs, and acts against generic competition, which tends to deliver a lower sustainable price over the long term. In terms of making drugs accessible as well as affordable to the majority of the global population, generic medicines are absolutely critical. For example, generic competition brought the price of first-line HIV drugs down by close to 99 percent from over $10,000 per person per year a decade ago to $120 today, tiered pricing leaves middle-income countries paying as much as $740 per person per year for second-line drug lopinavir/ritonavir – over 60% more than what pharmaceutical companies like Abbott are charging low-income countries. The higher price is unsustainable for countries with large numbers of poor people living with HIV, such as Brazil. There have been recent proposals by the Global Fund to establish a new pricing regime for medicines to fight AIDS, Tuberculosis and Malaria. International medical humanitarian organisation Médecins Sans Frontières (MSF) have staunchly opposed the move.

The effect on the pricing of reference drugs plays into the hands of an elite group of pharmaceutical companies globally, while any competition from generic drugs is sought to be cut off at the very outset.

The next area of significance of policy making is formulary management. A formulary is a list of prescription drugs covered under a plan. It is created, reviewed and updated by a team of doctors and pharmacists. It applies to a wide range of generic as well as brand-name drugs that have been approved by the World Health Organization (WHO), and bodies like US FDA at the national level. Drugs are chosen because first, they're safe and effective, and second, they save money. The effect on generic drugs is twofold - in terms of price, generic drugs tend to be cheaper compared to reference drugs. The second issue of ensuring that these drugs are safe and effective is a far bigger challenge, as it covers the entire process of value addition, manufacture and sale of drugs.

Pharmacy services is possibly the final area of concern to global policy makers. In this regard, the umbrella organization covering all significant areas of pharmacy is the International Pharmaceutical Federation (FIP). The FIP, founded in 1912, is the global body representing over three million pharmacy and pharmaceutical sciences. The goal of any policy covering pharmacy services is to improve global health by advancing pharmacy practice and science to enable better discovery, development, access to and safe use of appropriate, cost-effective, quality medicines worldwide. Recognising the need to support and strengthen pharmacy education worldwide, in November 2007, FIP, in collaborated with the WHO and UNESCO (United Nations Educational, Scientific and Cultural Organization), forming the Pharmacy Education Taskforce. Though the goal of the global pharmacy services framework is to bring uniformity in the access and use of medicines worldwide, the reality is far from the norm. With differences in national policy and legislative frameworks, occurrence of a variety of diseases and disparate levels of education, training and evaluation of pharmacy professionals, there is a need to device a policy and institutional arrangement which can substantially homogenise the global regime of pharmacy services.

CONCLUSION

Generic drugs play an essential role in health care by increasing the accessibility and affordability of the modern day pharmaceuticals domestically and globally. Drug prices in India are one of the cheapest in the world today and are affordable to the population. On an average, drugs manufactured in India are more than 100% cheaper than the same drug in U.S. While the production of drugs is not a problem in India, general access to drugs is. The affordability of pharmaceuticals and lack of a comprehensive health insurance system have heavily influenced the evolution and development of India's patent laws. The patent policy pursued by India has enabled it to become a big international player in the generic drug market. The patent policy of 1970 dramatically impacted the industry. In the subsequent 30 years, it is valued at $ 70 billion compared to a mere $ 2.1 million before 1970.

The concern for securing access to affordable drugs is a real one, and there are strong moral arguments for why increasing patent protection for the products of powerful MNCs works only to hurt the common man. The reality, however, is that the protection of intellectual property rights provides these corporations with the needed incentive to invent and manufacture the drugs on which patients around the world rely, whether branded or generic. The current regulatory environment in India, heavily influenced by its TRIPS obligations, attempts to strike a balance between the long term social objective of providing incentives for future inventions and creation, and the short term objective of allowing people to use existing inventions and creations. In theory, India could continue down its current path where its generics industry simply reverse-engineers the pharmaceuticals that are researched and developed elsewhere. But if India desires to grow into its role as a major scientific and technological powerhouse, then it must work to protect intellectual property rights, while balancing public health concerns of its large and poor populace. It should also simultaneously work towards developing in-house capabilities for genuine new drug development.

REFERENCES

Bennett, W. J. (2014). Indian Pharmaceutical Patent Law and the Effects of Novartis Ag v. Union of India. *Washington University Global Studies Law Review*, *13*(3).

Bronnenberg, B. J., Dubé, J. P., Gentzkow, M., & Shapiro, J. M. (2015). Do Pharmacists Buy Bayer? Informed Shoppers and the Brand Premium. Retrieved Dec. 21, 2016 from https://www.brown.edu/Research/Shapiro/pdfs/generics.pdf

Davit, B. M., Nwakama, P. E., Buehler, G. J., Conner, D. P., Haidar, S. H., Patel, D. T., ... & Woodcock, J. (2009). Comparing generic and innovator drugs: a review of 12 years of bioequivalence data from the United States Food and Drug Administration. *Annals of Pharmacotherapy*, *43*(10), 1583-1597.

DiMasi, J. A., Hansen, R. W., & Grabowski, H. G. (2003). Hansen, & Grabowski (2003). The price of innovation: New estimates of drug development costs. *Journal of Health Economics*, *22*(2), 151–185. doi:10.1016/S0167-6296(02)00126-1 PMID:12606142

Dunne, S., Shannon, B., Dunne, C., & Cullen, W. (2013). A review of the differences and similarities between generic drugs and their originator counterparts, including economic benefits associated with usage of generic medicines, using Ireland as a case study. *BMC Pharmacol Toxicol*, *14*(1), 1. doi:10.1186/2050-6511-14-1 PMID:23289757

USA Food and Drug Administration. (n. d.). Facts about Generic Drugs. Retrieved from http://www.fda.gov/Drugs/ResourcesForYou/Consumers/BuyingUsingMedicineSafely/UnderstandingGenericDrugs/ucm167991.htm

India Brand Equity Foundation. (2015). Indian Pharmaceutical Industry. Retrieved Jan. 19, 2017 from http://www.ibef.org/industry/pharmaceutical-india.aspx and http://www.ibef.org/download/Pharmaceuticals-March-2015.pdf

Indxx. (2016). Generic Drugs: Revolutionary Change in the Global Pharmaceutical Industry. Retrieved Dec. 8, 2016 from http://www.nasdaq.com/article/generic-drugs-revolutionary-change-in-the-global-pharmaceutical-industry-cm576603#ixzz4YqQmvtoK

Kesselheim, A. S., Misono, A. S., Lee, J. L., Stedman, M. R., Brookhart, M. A., Choudhry, N. K., & Shrank, W. H. (2008). Clinical equivalence of generic and brand name drugs used in cardiovascular disease: A systematic review and meta-analysis. *Journal of the American Medical Association*, *300*(21), 2514–2526. doi:10.1001/jama.2008.758 PMID:19050195

Médecins Sans Frontières (MSF). (2013). Global Fund: Proposed shake-up to drug pricing framework risks middle-income countries paying more. Retrieved Jan. 19, 2017 from http://www.msf.org/en/article/global-fund-proposed-shake-drug-pricing-framework-risks-middle-income-countries-paying-more

Rahalkar H (2012). Historical Overview of Pharmaceutical Industry and Drug Regulatory Affairs. *Pharmaceutical Regulatory Affairs*, *11*. doi:10.4172/2167-7689.S11-002

RNCOS. (2018). US Generic Drug Market Outlook 2018. Retrieved Jan. 19, 2017 from http://www.rncos.com/Market-Analysis-Reports/US-Generic-Drug-Market-Outlook-2018-IM731.htm

Singal, G. L., Nanda, A., & Kotwani, A. (2011). A comparative evaluation of price and quality of some branded versus branded-generic medicines of the same manufacturer in India. *Indian Journal of Pharmacology*, *43*(2), 131-136.

Tufts Center for the Study of Drug Development. (2014). Cost to Develop and Win Marketing Approval for a New Drug Is $2.6 Billion. Retrieved Nov. 18, 2016 from http://csdd.tufts.edu/news/complete_story/pr_tufts_csdd_2014_cost_study

Zacharias, N., & Farias, S. (2002). Patents and the Indian Pharmaceutical Industry. Retrieved Jan. 19, 2017 from http://www.nishithdesai.com/fileadmin/user_upload/pdfs/Patents_and_the_Indian_Pharmaceutical_Industry.pdf

ADDITIONAL READING

Akhtar, G. (2013). Indian Pharmaceutical Industry: An Overview. *IOSR Journal Of Humanities And Social Science*, *13*(3), 51-66.

Choudhary, K. & Ritiraj (2013). India: the trickle-down effect of product patent in India and on the developing world. Retrieved Jan. 19, 2017 from http://www.mondaq.com/india/x/262416/Patent/The+TrickleDown+Effect+Of+Product+Patent+In+India+And+On+The+Developing+World

Dhar, B., & Gopakumar, K. M. (n.d.). Effect of Product Patents on the Indian Pharmaceutical Industry. Retrieved Jan. 19, 2017 from http://wtocentre.iift.ac.in/Papers/3.pdf

Generic Pharmaceutical Association (GPhA) (2011). Savings: An Economic Analysis of Generic Drug Usage in the U.S.

Ghai, D. (2010). Patent protection and Indian pharmaceutical industry. *International Journal of Pharmaceutical Sciences Review and Research*, *3*(2), 008.

GPhA (2015). Generic Drug Savings in the U.S.

Janodia, M. D., Rao, J. V., Pandey, S., Sreedhar, D., Ligade, V. S., & Udupa, N. (2009). Impact of Patents on Indian Pharma Industry's Growth and Competency: A Viewpoint of Pharmaceutical Companies in India. *Journal of Intellectual Property Rights*, *14*, 432–436.

Lakshminarasimha, A., & Shrishti, N. (2008). The Phenomenal Growth of Pharma Industry in India. *Marketing Mastermind, 2008*(September), 49–53.

Meléndez-Ortiz, R. (2009). *Intellectual Property and Sustainable Development Development Agendas in a Changing World.* doi:10.4337/9781849803458

Nair, G. G. (2008). Impact of TRIPS on Indian Pharmaceutical Industry. *Journal of Intellectual Property Rights, 13*, 432–441.

Puranik, S. B., Sangamesh, M., & Golshan, M. S. (2010). Patent Laws In India And Its Impact On Pharmaceutical Industry. *International Journal of Pharma and Bio Sciences, V1*(2), 2010.

Ramanna, A. Dr. (n. d.). India's Patent Policy and Negotiations in TRIPs: Future Options for India and other Developing Countries. Retrieved Jan. 19, 2017 from https://www.iprsonline.org/ictsd/docs/ResourcesTRIPSanita_ramanna.doc

Sarkar, S. (n. d.). Product Patent for the Indian Pharmaceutical Sector under the TRIPS regime. Retrieved Jan. 19, 2017 from http://www.legalserviceindia.com/articles/ppch.htm

Chapter 5 Parallel Import in India: A Study

Dinesh Kumar
Panjab University, India

Gurjinder Singh
Panjab University, India

ABSTRACT

People often say that the world is not only "Black and White" but there are many other shades which pose difficult question. Parallel import, which is also known as "Grey area" is one of them. Parallel imports are goods produced genuinely under protection of a trademark, patent, or copyright, placed in one market, and then imported into another market without the approval of the Intellectual Property Right holder. Through this chapter, the Author(s) have tried to give an insight on parallel imports by discussing all possible national and international issues related to it. Some principal concepts like exhaustion, regional and global have acquired considerable space in the chapter. A brief contemporary view on parallel import has also been taken by the author(s). The contradictory views; one which favours the Parallel imports by endorsing that it enhances the local competition; and another which condemns parallel imports are covered in the later part of the chapter.

DOI: 10.4018/978-1-5225-2414-4.ch005

Copyright © 2017, IGI Global. Copying or distributing in print or electronic forms without written permission of IGI Global is prohibited.

INTRODUCTION

Inventions are not mechanical process; a lot of hands and minds are involved every time. Success and failure are the ultimate results, but the hidden labour cannot be ignored rather appreciated and stimulated for next time. Inventions[1] and innovations[2] are key points while explaining economic growth and must be protected to facilitate the human life. Invention protection systems, which confer monopoly rights to the originators of new ideas for a limited period of time, can be traced back to the Greek colonial city of Sybaris in 500 B.C. With the advent of time the same system has converted into intellectual property rights.[3] To bring more clarity, Intellectual property (IP) refers to creations of the mind, such as inventions; literary and artistic works; designs; and symbols, names and images used in commerce. IP is protected in law by, for example, patents[4], copyright[5] and trademarks[6], which enable people to earn recognition or financial benefit from what they invent or create. By striking the right balance between the interests of innovators and the wider public interest, the IP system aims to foster an environment in which creativity and innovation can flourish.[7] Intellectual property rights (IPRs), for example patents, play an important role in this innovative market, affecting the diffusion of knowledge, innovation process and economic efficiency. These IPRs have usually been granted by Governments as a way to protect inventions and then promote further innovation through a limited monopoly (Lewell, 2009).

The relationship between innovations and IPRs laws has paved the way for economic development. It is assumed that the IPRs laws have positively contributed in the socio-economic regime. IPRs laws are not abstract and futile concepts which are confined to law textbooks, but these laws play an important role in everyday life. For example, patent is a reward for every new idea and technology, which encourage the development in innovation and inventions. As we know patent, copyright and trademark has various dimensions and reach, and gives valuable protection to works done various fields like Biotech, computer software, medical science or nanotechnology etc. Like other fields of law, IPRs laws are also struggling with some problems and issues in all these fields. But some of the concerns are very crucial and complex too.

The pharmaceutical sector has unusual prominence in debates about IP policy, and has served as the front line for national and international controversies about the relationship between IPRs, R&D (Research and Development) incentives, pricing and access to medicines (Cockburn, 2009a). Two basic areas which impact the pharmaceuticals are, first, the pricing and access, and availability of medicine. Second is the issue of R&D. These two areas pose some very difficult economic and legal questions. Despite the Governments at global level are doing their best but, the balance between these two areas is very important not only for economic growth but also for invaluable human life.

The first issue of pricing and access to medicine has further opened doors to some complex issue like Parallel Importing. The same has also impacted on the second one i.e. R&D. In this chapter, author(s) have discussed the core issue i.e. parallel importing along with its roots and results.

MEDICINE AND PATENT LAWS

Access to medicine cannot be taken lightly, it directly impacts the life of a human being. The issue of patents in the medical field that how much it is impacting human life has significantly increased. There is no doubt that medical field needs much more attention for R&D as compare to others, but the balance between accessibility and R&D should be the prior question for nations. The puzzle between access and research in medicine created a very complex situation for world leaders. History is witnessed that for developing countries access to life saving drugs has remained a big goal to achieve. Today, most of the developing countries do not have the luxury to decide whether to provide patents on drugs. TRIPS[8] mandates the patent protection, including on drugs for WTO member countries. Such mandatory patent protection is likely to significantly impact access to medicine in countries where resources are already limited (Ho, 2011a). A nation's ability to promote access to drugs is especially of importance to low income countries in which the cost of drugs may be a significant barrier to obtaining access to medicine (Ho, 2011b). Expenditure on medicines accounts for a major proportion of health costs in developing countries. This means that access to treatment is heavily dependent on the availability of affordable medicines. Although trade in medicines is increasing rapidly, most of it takes place between wealthy countries, with developing countries accounting for just 17% of imports and 6% of exports. It is estimated that one-third of the developing world's people are unable to receive or purchase essential medicines on a regular basis.[9] The unavailability or denial to drugs resulted in many alternative ways like Parallel Importing, compulsory licensing, etc., which further created havoc among the countries.

PARALLEL IMPORTS

Between "black and white" people often say, there are many other shades which pose difficult questions. Parallel import, which is also known as "Grey area" is one of them. Parallel imports are goods produced genuinely under protection of a trademark, patent, or copyright, placed in one market, and then imported into another market without the approval of the Intellectual Property Right holder. In a free-trade environment parallel trade prevents monopoly suppliers from engaging in international price discrimination. However, when the goods are protected by an intellectual property right, such as a patent or trademark, this right may permit the owner to prohibit international arbitrage. Parallel imports are imports of a patented or trademarked product from a country where it is already marketed. For example, in South Africa 100 units of Bayer's ciprofloxacin (500mg) costs US$740, but in India Bayer sells the same drug for US$15 (owing to local generic competition). South Africa can import the product from India without Bayer's consent (Example available at WHO glossary). Sometimes referred to as "grey market" imports, parallel imports often take place when there is differential pricing of the same product - either brand-name or generic drugs - in different markets (usually owing to local manufacturing costs or market conditions). Important here is that, goods produced and marketed are genuine good not counterfeit goods. If we look at the whole concept from different angle, goods produced and sold legally are not "Gray" the distribution channel may be called gray.

In a simple note, Parallel Import refers to the resale of goods between countries without the authorization of the owner of the intellectual property (IP) rights associated with those goods. It is a response to international price discrimination, whereby an identical product is sold at different prices in different countries (K. Kyle, 2009a). Parallel Import is the entering of goods in the market in ways which are not intended by the manufacturer or licensee. So, the debate over Parallel Import and price discrimination has divided the public discourse into two blocks. Those who favour the Parallel Importing, cite the socio-economic welfare agenda as defense, and argue that it is important for every country to be able to purchase drugs from the cheapest possible sources, requiring an open regime of PI. Whether or not such imports actually occur, the threat that they might come in could force distributors to charge lower prices (Maskus, 2001a). On the other side, opponents argue that Parallel Importing impeaches the Research and Development in the medical field, which ultimately reduce the ability of pharmaceutical industries and slow down the innovation process.

Apparently, Parallel Importing builds up tensions between achieving price reduction and incentivising innovation in new products. Even in a single-country context, the use of IPRs to reach an appropriate balance between "static" gains to consumers from low prices and competitive supply of drugs with "dynamic" gains from innovative new products presents serious challenges. On the one hand, industry feels acute financial pressure from rising R&D costs and decreasing effective patent life. On the other, notwithstanding very substantial economic and health benefits associated with innovation in pharmaceuticals, even in relatively wealthy countries high prices for on-patent drugs tend to raise difficult political questions relating to equity and access for low-income or disadvantaged groups, and for setting priorities in allocating public health care budgets (Cockburn,2009b).

The prime question remains the same whether parallel trade is legal or not. To check the legality of parallel imports one has to go through the "exhaustion" principle, which is the sole basis of its legality.

Doctrine of First Sale "Principle of Exhaustion"

Patents grant exclusive legal rights to the holder of these rights over his/her design, innovation, invention etc. with the aim to promote R&D. These exclusive rights include right to publish, sell, distribute or made available to public at large. These exclusive rights, however, are not without limitation. Some of the rights can be extinguished by an authorized sale of a product. This is known as exhaustion or, alternatively, the first sale doctrine (Clugston, 2013). The monopoly granted by the IPRs laws are not unlimited, the principle of exhaustion reduce the monopoly to limited rights of patent holder. As United States Appellate Federal Judge Posner said, in the absence of exhaustion, if every time a car owner wished to resell his/her used car needed to request a license from the car maker, that would lead to an absurd situation of implying automatic compulsory licenses (Jack Walters & Sons Corp. v. Morton Building, Inc., 737 f.2d 698, 704 (7th cir. 1984).[10]

The principle of exhaustion or the doctrine of first sale imposes certain limits on IP owners' exclusive rights, wherein the owner is prevented from controlling the resale or re-distribution of a work that has already been sold by with his/her consent. The exhaustion doctrine in intellectual property law generally limits the rights of a patent, copyright or trademark owner ("IP Owner") to control the disposition of an article after the article has been sold by or under the authority of the IP Owner (Kobak,2005). According to the principle of exhaustion of intellectual property rights, the exclusive rights of the patentee to protect product are exhausted, and thus ends, when the product is first launched in the market. A patented item's initial authorized sale terminates all patent rights to that item. In other words, he/she cannot control the re-sale or re-distribution of the particular good that has already been sold once (Basheer & Kochupillai, 2008, p. 486). When a state or group of states applies this principle of exhaustion of intellectual property rights in a given territory, parallel importation is authorized to all residents in the state in question. In a state that does not recognize this principle, however, only the patent holder who has been registered has the right to import the protected product.[11]

The rationale behind the principle of exhaustion is that it enables the IP Owner to receive one fair reward for surrendering its right to withhold a product from the market but thereafter permits free disposition and movement of chattels; in this way, it is thought, IP rights will not unduly disrupt a modern and efficient system of distribution, and goods will not be encumbered with a maze of contractual restrictions and restraints on alienation (Jack Walters & Sons Corp. v. Morton Building, Inc., 737 f.2d 698, 704 7th cir. 1984). Generally, when a patent owner receives compensation for the use of his invention by the sale of a good, the purpose of patent law is fulfilled with respect to that good. Upon receiving compensation, the patent owner's rights to exclude others are exhausted and "the patent law affords no basis for restraining the use and enjoyment of the thing sold." Accordingly, a patent owner's voluntary introduction of a patented good into commerce without restriction prevents the patent owner from exercising his right to exclude others from using or reselling that good as long as it exists (Rinehart, 2010).

International Exhaustion

Generally said, those who favour the free movement of goods they have adopted the principle of international exhaustion in their IP laws. The basis of this policy is the free circulation and access to goods. This principle contrary to the other two set free the parallel imports. A majority of developing countries across the globe have adopted the principle of international exhaustion, which they believe shall enable them to pursue products, mainly medicines and drugs, from other markets at competitive prices eliminating the enforcement hindrances of the IP owner locally (Joshi, 2012). Economists argue in favour of international exhaustion because a system based on national exhaustion conflicts with the fundamental principle of free trade: though the system of national exhaustion imposes a non-tariff restriction to trade, the classical free-trade argument cannot be applied to parallel trade because in reality the business environment in which parallel imports takes place does not adhere to the basic market conditions under which free trade takes place: free entry and perfect competition (Rai, 2011a).

But the opponents express their concerns regarding quality and safety. Although parallel imports are authorized products, either made by the IPR owner or made under its authority, the importation is not authorized. As a result, the IPR owner cannot guarantee the quality or safety of the product. The unauthorized importer may not have used proper storage and handling techniques or may have even tampered with the goods in some way. In addition, where the imports are coming from a country with a different language, there are possible issues with instructions and warning labels (Clugston, 2013, p. 96).

National Exhaustion

In every intellectual property law, it is necessary to decide which steps in the chain of production and distribution of goods require the license of the right-owner: manufacture; first sale by the manufacture; subsequent sales and other dealings; export and import; use. In the past, legislators have often left the answer to the Courts. In many cases, both in British and in foreign laws, the rights are "exhausted" after first sale by the right-owner or with his consent. But often this is confined to first sales within the territory covered by the right-it amounts to a principle of domestic, rather than international exhaustion (Cornish, Llewelyn & Aplin, 2010). Under this policy of national exhaustion, the exclusive rights of the patentee terminate upon the first sale within the country but patentee can still exclude the parallel import from other countries. A policy of national exhaustion amounts to a government-enforced territorial restriction on international distribution. Countries following this regime choose to isolate their markets from unauthorized foreign competition in legitimate goods traded under recognized IPR protection. Thus, original manufacturers retain complete authority to distribute goods and services themselves or through dealers, including the right to exclude PI through border controls (Maskus, 2001b).

Those who favour National Exhaustion principle ensure some advantages: for example, in National Exhaustion regime firms will invest more in R&D and ultimately it will result into more innovations, National exhaustion will also take care of Licensees and authorized distributors that means no more free ridings on the investments made by licensees and distributors (Rai, 2011b).

Regional Exhaustion

Regional exhaustion is third way out, which delineate the area within which free movement of goods are permissible. But again, parallel imports outside the area would be infringement of policy. European Union is the perfect example of regional exhaustion. In the EU, the issue of parallel imports has been raised in many legal cases,[12] and the European Court of Justice (ECJ) has through its rulings, essentially adopted the principle of regional exhaustion (Chen & Maskus, 2005). Now, once a firm has put the drug on the market in any EU country, it may not prevent the sale of that drug within the EU by any other firm by claiming a violation of patent rights or trademarks, under most circumstances. Note the patent holder may still prevent the sale of products first marketed outside the EU; it remains illegal to import drugs from Africa, for example, without the permission of the patent holder. But the combination of large price differences within the EU, some of which exist because of price controls, and the inability of pharmaceutical firms to use intellectual property rights to prevent resale of their products has given rise to a substantial market in parallel imported products, now estimated to be €5bn annually (Kyle, 2009b).

LEGALITY OF PARALLEL IMPORT

The legality or illegality has to be settled by the rules and regulations dealing with the subject matter. One aspect of this paradox shows that Parallel Importing should not be banned rather promoted and the other side completely condemns this policy. Legality of Parallel Imports entirely depends on the principle of exhaustion and moreover it varies from country to country. Legal inconsistency over the parallel imports initiated the intense debate in various countries and within the World Trade Organisation (WTO). The WTO's agreement on Trade-Related Aspects of Intellectual Property Rights (TRIPS) provides flexibility to member countries to frame their own rules to settle the issue of parallel Importing. Article 6 which is titled as "Exhaustion" says, "For the purposes of dispute settlement under this Agreement, subject to the provisions of Articles 3 and 4 nothing in this Agreement shall be used to address the issue of the exhaustion of intellectual property rights." The meaning of Article 6 is made more clear by Article 5(d) of the Doha Convention which states that "the effect of the provisions in the TRIPS Agreement that are relevant to the exhaustion of intellectual property rights is to leave each member free to establish its own regime for such exhaustion without challenge (Basheer & Kochupillai, 2008).

TRIPS made it clear by granting privileges to the member countries to frame their own rules to deal with this issue. So the infringement of rules depends on the nature of exhaustion system adopted by the said country, If a country opts for national exhaustion of IPR, a rights holder there may exclude parallel imports, because intellectual property rights continue until such a time as a protected product is first sold in that market. If a country instead chooses international exhaustion of IPR, parallel imports cannot be blocked, because the rights of the patent, copyright, or trademark holder expire when a protected product is sold anywhere in the world (Grossman & Lai, 2008).

PARALLEL IMPORTS AND GLOBAL MARKET

Parallel Importing had essentially impacted the Global Market from various points of views. Both the welfare face of parallel imports and at some point, discouragement to R&D are impacting the trade policies of every country. We have major world economies like Europe, U.S.A and the emerging one India.

European Union

Countries of Europe have adopted a single market system under the shadow of European Union. Principle of regional exhaustion has been followed by the European Union, which allow the free flow of goods within the geographical limits of E.U. While parallel trade in pharmaceuticals remains illegal in most countries, it is now permitted within the European Union. This is part of the move to a single market for pharmaceuticals in the EU; other changes include harmonization of regulations for the approval of new drugs and the adoption of the Euro. In particular, Article 28 of the European Community (EC) Treaty bans most actions that would inhibit the free movement of goods between member states. Article 30 provides some exceptions. For example, a trademark owner may restrict resale of an imported product bearing his trademark if the original packaging has been substantially changed (Kyle, 2009, p. 361). The principle of regional exhaustion has been established based on these Articles by the ECJ (European Court of Justice) through a number of cases[13].

U.S.A.

The position in the United States is confusing than any other country regarding the principle of exhaustion. Numbers of Article published by various renowned authors claimed either U.S. follow the national exhaustion or international exhaustion, but the consensus is nowhere seen. However, a recent Supreme Court case[14] held that, in the area of copyright law, international exhaustion is recognized under United States law. Thus, a copyright owner cannot prevent the parallel importation of copyrighted products first sold in a foreign country.

Section 271 of the Patent Law Act reads that "whoever without authority makes, uses or sells any patented invention, within the United States during the term of the patent therefor, infringes the patent." Thus, owners of U.S. patents can claim infringement by unauthorized importers of their products. Court decisions in the United States have usually affirmed the rights of patent owners to restrict resale or parallel imports of their products, though not always. In *Curtiss Aeroplane & Motor Corp. v. United Aircraft Eng'g Corp.*[15] the court ruled that because the patent owner had not expressly forbidden resale into the U.S. by its licensee, the patent owner could not prevent parallel trade. *Jazz Photo v. International Trade Commission*[16] reestablished that U.S. patent owners could claim infringement by the import of goods legally purchased abroad, stating that "...[t]o invoke the protection of the first sale doctrine, the authorized first sale must have occurred under the United States patent."

India

Most of the Developing countries like India practice the principle of "international exhaustion". Indian pharmacy sector is emerging at very fast pace. From a market size of US$ 12.6 billion in 2009, the Indian pharmaceutical market will grow to US$ 55 billion by 2020, with the potential to reach US$ 70 billion in an aggressive growth scenario.[17] Since TRIPS has granted the discretion to all member countries to frame their own rule and regulations to tackle parallel imports, India has made two significant amendments in its patent laws. By the year 2002, Indian legislature introduced an amendment in section 107A(b) of Patents Act, 1970 which read as, "...importation of patented products by any person from a person who is duly authorized by the patentee to sell or distribute the product, shall not be considered as an infringement of patent rights." Under this amendment "any person" who imports the products needs to get permission from the patentee or any authorized person. By the year 2005, the Government of India removed the consent part from the statutory compliance provision, this time the 2002 amendment undergone a drastic change which read as "...importation of patented products by any person from a person who is duly authorized under the law to produce and sell or distribute the product." Therefore, in the contrast with the earlier provision under the 2002 Act, once the "first sale" of any product had been authorized by the patentee, a parallel importer could buy that product from any reseller and not necessarily from the one that had the express permission of the patentee to resell or distribute... to this extent, the 2005 amendment implement the principle of "international exhaustion" in its true spirit (Basheer & Kochupillai, 2008, p. 489).

India's trademark laws are not bringing any clarity; a controversial case is pending before the Hon'ble Supreme Court, which appeals against the order of Delhi High Court's Double Beanch[18]. The Court while recognising the principle of "international exhaustion" under the Trade Marks, 1999 allowed the Parallel Imports. Though the case is not essentially relating to pharmacy sector, but the judgment of the Supreme Court will surely affect the entire Trademark regime. The government of India has appointed a committee under the chairmanship of Rajesh Chandra which has submitted its report. The committee has focused on parallel imports in copyright area and suggested some amendments in the existing copyright laws.

CONCLUSION

The concept of Parallel imports is emerging as a complicated issue in the global market. The chapter has introduced the entire concept by outlining the controversies around it. Apart from the daily need goods, drugs and specially those of life saving are very important to human life. History is the witness of the story of South Africa. In developing countries, the practice of parallel imports is rampant and the reason is apparent to everyone. The welfare impact of parallel imports is not hidden to anyone, but the next step difficulty of incentivizing R&D is also noticeable. Some of the questions which need to be addressed with greater care are; whether parallel imports should be declared as illegal activity to prevent the loss in R&D? Whether it should be allowed to promote welfare in developing countries? Plenty of rich minds are already looking for the answers to these questions by trying to strike a balance between welfare impact of parallel imports and loss in the R&D.

Along with this major issue there is also some of the impact of parallel imports with needs to be addressed again with greater care. Many scholars apprehend that there is a large risk of Counterfeit products. Essentially Parallel imports of trademark products are prone to be counterfeit. Another issue regarding parallel imports is that parallel trade differs from country to country and therefore it is often difficult to file legal suit against parallel trade. The international trading blocs also agreed that if parallel trade is legally permitted, then it is difficult for the multinational companies to control it because the traders can always earn higher profit by engaging in such activities (Mazumdar & Meenakshi Rajeev,2010).

Some eminent scholars have suggested that instead of complete restraint on parallel imports, why not we see some neutral way. The idea of allowing parallel trading of life saving drugs is widely appreciated. But still discussions are taking place all over the world to remove the tension built around this issue.

REFERENCES

Basheer, S., & Kochupillai, M. (2008). Exhausting Patent Rights in India: Parallel Imports and TRIPS Compliance. *Journal of Intellectual Property Rights, 13*, 486-497.

Chen, Y., & Maskus, K. E. (2005). Vertical Pricing and Parallel Imports. *The Journal of International Trade & Economic Development, 14*(1), 1–18. doi:10.1080/0963819042000333225

Clugston, C.J. (2013). International Exhaustion, Parallel Imports, and the Conflict between the Patent and Copyright Laws of the United States. *Beijing Law Review,* (4), 95-99.

Cockburn, I. M. (2009). Intellectual property rights and Pharmaceuticals: Challenges and opportunities for economic research, *The Economic of Intellectual Property*. Retrieved from http://www.wipo.int/export/sites/www/ip- development/en/economics/pdf/wo_1012_e_ch_5.pdf

Cornish, W., Llewelyn, D. & Aplin T. (2010). Intellectual Property: Patents, Copyright, Trade Marks and Allied Rights.

Grossman, G.M. & Lai, E.L.-C. (2008). Parallel Imports and Price Controls. *RAND journal of Economics, 39*(2), 378-402.

Ho, C.M. (2011). Access to medicine in a global economy, international agreements on patents and related rights. Oxford University Press.

Joshi, D. (2012). A point of view on parallel imports. *Global Policy Essay*. Retrieved from http://www.globalpolicyjournal.com/sites/default/files/pdf/View%20Points%20on%20Imports%20-%20July%2012.pdf

Kobak, J. B., Jr. (2005). Exhaustion of intellectual property rights and international trade. *Global Economy Journal,* 5(1). Retrieved from http://www.hugheshubbard.com/ArticleDocuments/Exhaustion_IP_Rights_2003.pdf

Kyle, M.K. (2009). Parallel trade in pharmaceuticals: firm responses and competition policy. In B. Hawk (Ed.), International Antitrust Law & Policy: Fordham Competition Law 2009 (Ch. 13). New York: Juris Publishing.

Lewell, F. R. (2009, January). *The role of intellectual property rights, innovation and competition law in the European software industry* [Master's Thesis].

Maskus, K. E. (2001, April). Parallel imports in pharmaceuticals: implications for competition and prices in developing countries (Final Report to World Intellectual Property Organization).

Mazumdar, M., & Rajeev, M. (2010). Parallel Trade and its Implication on the Availability of Patented Drugs: A Theoretical Approach. *The Journal of World Intellectual Property*, *13*(4), 581–604.

Rai, R. K. (2011). Should the WTO harmonize parallel import laws? An analysis of exhaustion doctrine. *Journal of Intellectual Property Law & Practice*, *6*(12), 898–911. doi:10.1093/jiplp/jpr163

Rinehart, A. S. (2010). Contracting patents: A modern patent exhaustion doctrine. *Harvard Journal of Law & Technology*, (23): 2010.

ENDNOTES

1 Consonant with the etymological origin of the word, "innovation" implies the creation of something new. In this regard, innovation is often equated with invention. Invention is the first occurrence of an idea for a new product or process. Retrieved from http://www.schoolnet.org.za/conference/sessions/SKG/InnovationHandoutPacket.pdf

2 Innovation is the first attempt to carry invention out into practice. Innovation occurs when someone uses an invention or an idea to change how the world works, how people organize themselves, or how they conduct their lives. In this view innovation occurs whether or not the act of innovating succeeds in generating value for its champions. For more information visit at http://www.schoolnet.org.za/conference/sessions/SKG/InnovationHandoutPacket.pdf

3 Invention protection and economic development, Japan patent Office Asia-Pacific industrial property center, JIII,2011, Retrieved 4 Nov 2014 from http://www.training-jpo.go.jp/en/uploads/text_vtr/pdf/Invention%20Protection%20and%20Economic%20Development.pdf

4 "Patent" is an exclusive right granted for an invention, which is a product or a process that provides, in general, a new way of doing something, or offers a new technical solution to a problem. To get a patent, technical information about the invention must be disclosed to the public in a patent application. Patent is also a limited time monopoly granted by statutory laws over the invention or innovation made.

5 "Copyright" is a legal term used to describe the rights that creators have over their literary and artistic works. Works covered by copyright range from books, music, paintings, sculpture and films, to computer programs, databases, advertisements, maps and technical drawings.

6 "Trademarks" can be a word, phrase, symbol, or design or combination thereof which identifies and distinguishes the source of the goods or services from current or potential competitors and other firms.

7 An introduction to IPRs has given on WIPO website. For more information visit at http://www.wipo.int/about-ip/en/

8 The Agreement on Trade-related Aspects of Intellectual Property Rights of the WTO is commonly known as the TRIPS Agreement or simply TRIPS. TRIPS are one of the main agreements comprising the World Trade Organisation (WTO) Agreement. This Agreement was negotiated as part of the eighth round of multilateral trade negotiations in the period 1986-94 under General Agreement on Tariffs and Trade (GATT) commonly referred to as the Uruguay Round extending from 1986 to 1994. The TRIPS Agreement is a minimum standards agreement, which allows Members to provide more extensive protection of

intellectual property if they so wish. Members are left free to determine the appropriate method of implementing the provisions of the Agreement within their own legal system and practice.

9 The information is retrieved from the official website of World Health Organisation (WHO). For more information, visit http://www.who.int/trade/glossary/story002/en/

10 Jack Walters & Sons Corp. v. Morton Building, Inc., 737 f.2d 698, 704 (7th cir. 1984), The reference of this case has been given in the paper titled "Interface between exhaustion of intellectual property rights and competition law" prepared by WIPO. Retrieved from http://www.wipo.int/edocs/mdocs/mdocs/en/cdip_4/cdip_4_4rev_study_inf_2.pdf

11 Globalization and Access to Drugs. Perspectives on the WTO/TRIPS Agreement - Health Economics and Drugs Series, No. 007 (1998)(Revised). Retrieved from http://apps.who.int/medicinedocs/pdf/whozip35e/whozip35e.pdf

12 There are numbers of cases decided by the ECJ, but some of the key rulings are Merck v Stephar, (C-187/80); Dior v Evora, (C-337/95) and EMI v CBS, (C-51/75).

13 Some important cases are Glaxo Group v. Dowelhurst, Hoffman-La Roche v. Centrafarm, Pfizer v. Eurim-Pharma.

14 Kirtsaeng v. John Wiley & Sons, Inc 2013 USLEXIS 2371 (2013).

15 Curtiss Aeroplane & Motor Corp. v. United Aircraft Eng'g Corp., 266 F. 71 (2d Cir. 1920).

16 Jazz Camera Photo v. Int'l Trade Comm'n, 264 F.3d 1094 (Fed. Cir. 2001).

17 For more information visit at http://www.ibef.org/industry/pharmaceutical-india.aspx

18 Kapil Wadhwa & Ors. v. Samsung Electronics Co. Ltd. & Anr., FAO(OS) 93/2012 (Del. A.B. Sept. 7, 2012).

Chapter 6
Exclusions on Patentability: A Study

Parul Sharma
Lovely Professional University, India

Rajinder Kaur
Panjab University, India

ABSTRACT

Exclusion of patentability finds its justification in philanthropy and public welfare. Time and again this approach has been endorsed and upheld by the eminent jurists. However, the "US Supreme Court in the case of Diamond v. Chakrabarty" endorsed a controversial view holding that "anything under the sun made by man" is patentable, but the situation was however rectified subsequently in "Diamond v. Dier." The Boards have gone a step forward in being very selective while granting patents excluding "Plant and Animal varieties" and also other immoral procedures, for example the process of cloning human beings etc. from the scope of patentability. The chapter will take up the study relating to the provisions of exclusions in patentability in international and national regime. The chapter will further highlight the emerging grey areas on the exclusions of patentability.

DEVELOPMENT OF EXCLUSIONS

The exclusions pertaining to subject matter patentability has an interminable tale to narrate. It goes way back to 1844 where the French law excluded the pharmaceutical compositions of a kind and also the schemes relating to credit and finance from the scope of patentability. Following the trail, In August 1852, the Austrian law excluded

DOI: 10.4018/978-1-5225-2414-4.ch006

Copyright © 2017, IGI Global. Copying or distributing in print or electronic forms without written permission of IGI Global is prohibited.

'methods of food preparations, "beverages, and medicines', scientific principles or purely scientific theorems, inventions or improvements", and discoveries, for the reason of being antithetical to the interest of the state in compliance with the existing regulations or in conflict with Public health, morals or safety. Later in 1864 Article 6 of the Italian Patent law further strengthened this position.

In the common-law countries, a very general criteria for patentability was being followed, with regard to the "manner of new manufacture", pertaining to the scope of patentability. This had originated from the famous "Statute of Monopolies of 1623", which was one of the first acts relating to patents in the world. Through the years, statutes of monopoly have been interpreted in such a way that patents which are inconvenient or are opposed to public policy were specifically excluded from the scope of patentability.

The "United States of America" had deviated from the above stated general rule by advocating marginally a different model for a while but again confined itself to the general prevailing principle. "The Patent Act of 1793", had marginally deviated from the "Patent Act of 1870"by offering patents to "any person who has invented or discovered any new and useful art, machine, manufacture or composition of matter, or any new and useful improvement thereof..." By assuring its general compliance with the prevailing principle, it has particularly excluded aspects of the "natural world", "discoveries", "unembodied inventions", "handiwork of nature", "medical inventions, and business methods." This view also found support by the judicial pronouncements as the "US Supreme Court" had vouched this view in its 2010 Bilski decision. (Bently et al., n. d.).

Now according to Bently et al. (n. d.). It has become a more like a tradition in the United States to restrict to the three basic exclusions, namely:

- "Laws of Nature"
- "Physical phenomena"
- "Abstract Ideas"

In 2006, in "*Lab Corp v. Metabolite*", the US Supreme court rejected the grant of patent to an invention by stating that, "the patent was simply an attempt to gain a monopoly over a law of Nature". Later, in2007 the "Federal circuit court in the case of *re Comiskey*", the court found that "a purely mental process was outside the scope of patentability".

The exclusion of the above stated group of inventions had found justification in the rulings of courts primarily on two lines of reasoning that reinforces the policy intents of "promoting the progress of useful arts."

- Firstly, permitting an inventor to acquire a "monopoly" of a fundamental approach would attract an adverse response by confining the evolution of science by hindering exertion in the extensive domain of technology. (Treglia, 2008)
- The second line of reasoning finds support in the concept that a "Law of nature" or an "Abstract concept" do not qualify to be called an invention; for the reason of being nothing better than a mere discovery.

Though this shift has invited a number of controversies however the US Supreme Court came to the rescue of this approach in the year 2010 in the case of Bilskiv. Kappos. However, with regard to the statutory definition of subject- matter patentability, The United states actually relied upon the states not falling within its periphery. For Instance, Patentability for Jamaican Law referred to "some new and useful art, machine, manufacture, or composition of matter, not theretofore known or used within this Island, or some improvement in any invention or discovery". Newfoundland, furthermore, granted patents to those who had discovered or made "any new and useful art, machine, manufacture or composition of matter not theretofore known or used." Under Title XV section 1 of the Consolidated Statutes of Newfoundland· "Lower and Upper Canada" ended up adopting the same definition in the year 1824 and 1826 respectively, and, in turn, in "the Canadian Act Respecting Patents of Invention, 1869". Nevertheless, Canadian law vouched for specific exclusions from patentability by stating that, "no patent shall issue for an invention having an illicit object in view, nor for any mere scientific principle or abstract theorem." (Bently et al., n. d.).

With the passage of time, there has been a significant rise in the number of exclusions. Owing to the attention the issue of patentability had been garnishing, the subject had been under constant scrutiny as to "what field of technology should be excluded from patent protection". However, by 1987 many countries had narrowed down to the following exclusions on patentability:

- "Methods of treatment
- Animal Varieties
- Plant Varieties
- Biological processes
- Nuclear Technologies
- Computer programs"

According to Bently et al. (n. d.) the enhancement in the number of exclusions can find support in Social, economic, technological and to some extent, religious causes.

As regards the international legal framework, the 'Paris Convention' and the 'Patent Cooperation Treaty' (PCT) shy away from addressing the issue of patentability, however, "Article 4 quarter of the Paris Convention and Rules 39 and 67 of the Regulations under the PCT" do talk about some of the issue incidental to exclusions. "The Agreement on Trade Related Aspects of Intellectual Property Rights (TRIPS) under Paragraph 3 of Article 27 allows members to exclude diagnostic, therapeutic and surgical methods for the treatment of humans or animals from the scope of patentable subject matter." (Treglia, 2008)

An invention in order to secure a patent in its name, must qualify the pre-conditions of "Novelty, utility and non-obviousness". Apart from the above stated requisites, it must also hold technical advancement to the "Existing knowledge" or have an "Economic essence" or both. However, some inventions in spite of being in compliance with the above stated traits do not find place in the subject matter of patentability i.e. certain inventions are excluded from the scope of patentability for being:

- "Injurious to public health" or in violation of "Public morality" or "Public interest"
- Unfavorable to human, animal or plant life or health or to the environment.
- "Method of agriculture or horticulture"
- A process for the treatment of "human beings, animals or plants" including any process for "medicinal, surgical curative, prophylactic, diagnostic, therapeutic or other treatment of human beings or any process for a similar treatment of animals to render them free of disease or to increase their economic value or that of their products."
- "Mere discovery of a new form or property of a known substance" which does not result in the enhancement of the known efficacy of that substance
- "Traditional Knowledge" or any such duplication of traditional Knowledge.
- Inventions pertaining to atomic energy.

Apart from the above established exclusions, the journey of settling down to reasonable and acceptable guidelines has been full of ups and downs. For instance, for once in "*Diamond v. Chakrabarty*" in 1980 the court endorsed the controversial view that "anything under the sun made by man" is subject to patent protection. Subsequently decisions of the court have been more cautious as in the following year 1981 in "*Diamond v. Dier*" the US Supreme court observed that "laws of nature, natural phenomena and abstract ideas are beyond the scope of patent protection."

Methods of Medical Treatment

Methods of medical and veterinary treatment are particularly excluded from patentability under the "Article 53(c) EPC 2000", as it states that "a patent shall not be granted for methods of treatment of the human or animal body of surgery or therapy, and diagnostic methods practiced on Human or animal body." Similar changes were made in the UK to bring the Patents Act 1977 into line with EPC 2000. However, it is important to note the exclusion is confined to "methods *of treatment,*" and as such it doesn't preclude "any substance pertaining to surgical, therapeutic, or diagnostic fields and also their compositions (such as drugs), or apparatuses or products from the scope of patentability."

Patentability of Diagnostic Treatment

The scope of patentability from a significant time has been resting in the hands of the courts apart from the statutory laws and the subject indeed has flourished in the care of the judicial interpretations put forth by the honorable courts form time to time. However, in the last few years, not only did the US courts have avoided decisions on the scope of "Section 101 of the Patents Act" but also it did reject the chance to review the scope of patent protection for diagnostic methods. In '*Laboratory Corp v Metabolite Labs*(2006) the court not only refused to consider the issue of the scope of patent protection for methods of medical treatments particularly diagnostic methods; but it also refused to give a definitive answer whether such patents were worth allowing.'(Laakmann, 2012)

In *re Gram* (Fed. Cir. 1989) the federal circuit considered the issue with regard to patentability under section 101 of diagnostic methods in 1980 again and the decision excluded diagnostic methods from the scope of patentability. Later in "*re Meyer* (Fed Cir 1982)," the federal court held that "the claims demanding patent protection for diagnostic methods were for a "Mathematical algorithms" representing a mental process that had not been applied to physical element or process... the claimed method was thus not patentable." (McFarlane, Litts, & Robert, 2012)

The United Nations Supreme Court did not decide the issue of patentability of a medical method in *Laboratory Corp v Metabolite Labs*, (2006) (Breyer) however the issue came in for confrontation in "*Mayo Collaborative Services v Prometheus Labs.*" The Court in Prometheus held that "the patents claimed the correlations between certain thiopurine drug metabolite levels and therapeutic efficacy and toxicity. As a result, it found that these correlations were natural phenomena and not patentable inventions because the correlations resulted from a natural body process."

After some uncertainty, the nature and scope of the exclusion of diagnostic methods has been clarified by the decision of the "Enlarged Board of Appeal in Diagnostic methods (EBA2006)". In this decision, the Enlarged Board said that "methods of diagnosis typically consist of four subsidiary steps. These are:

1. **Examination:** Involving the collection of data (recording the case history),
2. **Comparison:** Comparing this data with normal values,
3. **Identification:** Identification any significant deviation from the norm (i.e. symptom), and
4. **Diagnosis:** The 'deductive medical or veterinary decision phase' where the diagnostic for curative purposes is made (which represents a purely intellectual or non-technical exercise)."

The Enlarged board further affirmed that, "In order to fall within the range of exclusions, an invention, apart from the deductive stage, must satisfy all four steps and that no distinction should be drawn between essential method steps that have a diagnostic character and non-essential steps that do not."

A general distinction is now drawn between the act of making a diagnosis (which involves using examination and data to reach a decision) and methods of data acquisition or data processing (the results of which may subsequently be used in diagnosis). If an invention only provides interim or preliminary results (data or information), the exclusion would only apply where an invention makes it immediately possible to decide on a particular course of medical treatment. As a result, a method of taking a sample or determining internal temperature or pH would not in itself identify a condition and as such would not be classified as a diagnostic method. This means that many diagnostic methods will no longer be caught by the exclusion despite the express language of the EPC 2000 and the UK Patents 1977 Act. (Bently et al., n. d.).

The (Indian) Patents Act, 1970 via 2003 amendment has specifically excluded "Diagnostic, therapeutic, medicinal or other methods for treatment of human beings or any process for a similar treatment of animals."

Exclusion of 'Animal Varieties'

The 'animal varieties' have been specifically excluded from the protection by "Para 3(f) of Schedule A2 to the Patent Act 1977/ Article 53(b)" is 'animal varieties' Also under "Section 3(j) of the Indian Patents Act. 1970" specifically puts 'animal varieties' outside the scope of patentability for the reason of not being an invention.

The meaning of 'Animal varieties' was considered by the 'Technical Board of Appeal in its 2006 decision in Harvard/Transgenic Animals'. The Technical Board of Appeal began by noting that the enlarged Board of Appeal's reasoning in relation to plant varieties in Novartis was applicable to the decision as to whether an invention fell within the animal variety exclusion. In Novartis, the Board held that held that "where a specific plant variety is not individually claimed, the claim will not be excluded from patentability under 53(b) EPC."

Opposition against PTO's animal patenting announcement was swift and strong. The arguments for excluding higher life forms from patentable subject matter can be summed up under five major heads:

- Interference with natural world
- Devaluation of human life
- Survival of family farms
- Commercialization of academic research
- Agriculture and laboratory animal suffering
- Genetic tapering with the higher animal life form

However, those in favor of animal patenting contend that the opposition against animal patenting is somewhat exaggerated as it fails to raise any novel animal welfare problems. In fact, our society routinely compromises the interests of animals in order to obtain a variety of benefits for human beings and even the harmful aspects of animal patenting is present in existing agricultural and scientific practices. Apart from that, the introduction of new techniques to agriculture is viewed as a speedier and more precise means of achieving the benefits of classical animal breeding. With the aid of such technical advancements Scientists have already made transgenic chickens resistant to one serious poultry virus by using a transferred gene to block the virus receptor sites.

Exclusion of Plant Varieties

Plants accompany animal varieties in the list of biological subject matters excluded from the scope of 'Patentability.' Bently (2011) states that one of the earliest decisions to contemplate upon the scope of 'Plant Variety exclusion' was "*Ciba- Geigy's Application* (EPO 1984)." The application in question claimed any plant-propagating material which had been chemically treated so as to make the material restraint to other agricultural chemicals. In deciding that the invention was not a 'plant variety', the 'Technical Board of Appeal' held that "plant varieties were limited to claims to individually characterized plants which would have the detailed taxonomy and the reproductive capacity which is required in general for a plant variety right." (Martin & San, 2009). The Board of Appeal also stressed that a defining feature of a plant variety was that it contained certain features that distinguished the variety in question from other varieties. These distinguishing features needed to be stable enough so that the essentials characteristics were passed on through subsequent generations. In so doing the Technical Board of Appeal highlighted the need for homogeneity between different generations. They also added that "it is perfectly sufficient for the exclusion to be …restricted… to cases in which plants are characterized precisely by the genetically determined peculiarities of their natural phenotype."

The next decision to scrutinize the scope of plant varieties exclusion was "*Plant Genetic Systems* (EPO 1995)." The claims in dispute related to plants, plant cells, and seeds that possessed a foreign gene which made them resistant to a type of herbicide. Given that modified plants were immune to the application of the weed-killer, farmers were able to spray (modified) crops safe in the knowledge that the weed-killer would only affect unmodified weeds. (Bently, 2011). The 'Technical board of Appeal' held that "while claims relating to plant cells are potentially patentable, claims which 'encompass' or are 'based on' a plant variety are not. Given that plant varieties are frequently used as the starting point for the production of genetically engineered would not have been patentable.' Given this it is not surprising that the PGS decision was subject to a considerable amount of criticism. This is because of two subsequent events have effectively overturned the PGS decision. These are the Biotechnology Directive and the 'decision of the Enlarged Board of Appeal in Novartis'.

"Article 4(2) of the Biotechnology Directive" provides that "inventions which concerns plants… shall be patentable if the technical feasibility of the invention is not confined to a particular plant… variety." Similar provisions have been introduced in the 1977 Act and the EPC 2000. (Bently, 2011)

A more or less similar stance was adopted by 'Enlarged Board of Appeal of the EPO in *Novartis'* (it related to plants that were genetically modified to render them resistant to fungi*)* In relation to the plant variety exclusion, the board found that "a claim wherein specific plant varieties are not individually claimed is not excluded from patentability under Article 53(b) EPC, even though it may embrace plant varieties.' In a way, the Enlarged Board overturned the PGS decision and held that a claim that encompasses more than one variety is not excluded under Article 53(b)." (Bently, Lionel, Sherman et al., 2009)

BIOLOGICAL PROCESSES

Biological processes have been specifically excluded from the protection as for being regarded as "essentially biological processes for the production of animals and plants." and it has been reconfirmed in the Biotechnological Directive, and by corresponding changes made to the 1977 act and to the EPC. Three aspects of this exclusion are worth emphasizing.

- As the exclusion are only applicable to the processes, it has no application to a product claim or a product-by-process claim. Consequently, in the Onco-mouse litigation it became immaterial for the patentability of the invention that the claims included circumstances where genetically modified rodents reproduced. The offspring of such an 'essentially biological processes' (if sexual reproduction is such a process) were products and hence fell outside the exclusion. (EPO, 1990)
- "The exclusion only applies where the process is for the 'production of animals or plants'. As such, the exclusion may not apply if the process results in the death or destruction of animals or plants." ('CAF. NRDC's Application,' 1961)
- 'Essentially biological processes' only attract exclusions. As in *Lubrizol*, where the Technical Board of Appeal had to decide whether a process of production high-quality hybrids was excluded from patentability on the ground that it was 'essentially biological.'

Exclusion of Inventions Contrary to Public Order and Morality

'Article 53(a) EPC 2000' provides that "European patents' shall not be granted in respect of inventions the commercial exploitation of which would be contrary to 'public order' or morality…" The essence of the morality exclusion under the EPC, first came into consideration in 1989 "*Onco-mouse decision.*" The case pertaining to patentability of a genetically modified mice who was likely to suffer from cancer, an outcome which the applicants believed to be utile in cancer research. The claimed faced a lot of opposition for being in contravention to Article 53(a) EPC. It was observed by TBA that "the genetic manipulation of mammalian animals is undeniably problematic, particularly in circumstances where the modifications necessarily cause suffering."

The TBA, while addressing the case for reconsideration to the Examination Division explained that "the application of Article 53(a) 'would seem to depend mainly on a careful weighing-up of the suffering of animals and possible risks to the environment and the usefulness of the invention to the mankind on the other." Putting this "Utilitarian balancing test" into application, the Examining Division held that the "Subject matter was patentable as finding a cure for cancer was highly desirable end and the mouse would assist in achieving this end." (Bently et al., n. d.).

The next occasion on which the application of 'Article 53(a) EPC' was considered was in the case of *Plant Genetic Systems* (1993). In the pertinent case, the opponents (Greenpeace) objected to the grant of a patent for a genetically engineered plant (Which rendered the plants resistant to herbicide) on the grounds that it was "inherently immoral" and also detrimental to environment. Following the "Cost-benefit test suggested in Onco-mouse", the opposition council submitted that "these risks should be balanced against the benefits likely to accrue from the invention." The 'Opposition Division' refused to apply the "utilitarian Cost-benefit analysis". The opposition division believed that it should not be routinely involved in considering ethical questions. (Sherman, 1995)

The approach advocated in the Plant Genetic systems decision was adopted by the Opposition Division in the "*Relaxin (Howard* Florey/ Relaxin 1995)" case. It was explicitly acknowledged in Relaxin when the opposition division said the question of whether "human genes should be patented is a controversial issue on which many persons have strong opinions… the EPO is not the right institution to decide on fundamental ethical questions." (Sherman, 1995)

The next development in this area came with the decision of the Board of Appeal in "*Plant Genetic Systems" (1995)* where the TBA concluded that claims for genetically modified seeds did not contravene Article 53(a). Although this ruling was highly criticized. (Laakmann, 2012). The fact that patent offices exist "at the crossroads between science and Public Policy", the Board of Appeal said that "Public order in Article 53(a) covers the protection of the public security, the physical integrity of individuals as a part of society, and protection of the environment." On this basis, the Board of Appeal said that, "where the exploitation of an invention was likely to breach Public peace or social order or seriously prejudice the environment, the invention would be excluded from patentability under Article 53(a) EPA."

Furthermore, in addition to the "General morality provisions in Article 53(a)/ section 1(3)", there are a number of specific types of biological invention that are deemed to be "immoral or contrary to public order." These are to be found in "EPC 2000 Rule 28" (formerly EPC 1973 Rule 23d) and para 3, "Schedule A2 of the Patents Act 1977.".

Processes for 'Cloning Human Beings'

Human being is defined as "any process, including techniques of embryo splitting, designed to create a human being with the same nuclear genetic information as another living or deceased human being. In particular, 'human being' may be defined in such a way as not to include 'human embryos and embryonic tissue.'(Bently et al. 2009). 'The UK Intellectual Property Office' has said (Citing Schedule A2 para) that "human totipotent cells would not be patentable, because the human body at the various stages of its formation and development is excluded from patentability". In contract the office is willing to grant patents for "human embryonic pluripotent stem cells." (Martin & San, 2009). However, the EPO has its stand clear by holding that methods in a cloning process which fused human and pig cells were contrary to morality. (Bently et al., 2009) As such, it seems that even if cloning of human embryos was not caught by EPC 2000 Rule 28(a) EPC 1973 Rule 23d (a) it would fall under the general prohibition in Article 53(a).

Use of Human Embryo in Industrial Purposes

October 18, 2011 the court of justice of the European Union in the year 2010 in "*Brustle v. Green Peace eV*" (C-34/10) gave an extensive interpretation of the Human embryo and patent's exclusion for uses of 'human embryos' for commercial or industrial uses. Recently in the Technion case, the 'European Patent Organization' (EPO) chose to follow the CJEU's decision even though there was no legal obligation to do so. Indeed with the Technion case has helped bring a certain level of uniformity of European Patent.

Enforcing the CJEU ruling in Brustle case, the German Federal Court ruled that the German patent of Prof. Brüstle could be maintained in an amended form and held that inventions are within the scope of patentability if the method of obtaining hESC from human embryos did not involve its destruction, irrespective of whether such methods are actually described in patent claims. On the basis of such interpretation of the CJEU ruling in Brustle and its implementation by the German Federal Court for his German patent, Prof. Brüstle has newly claimed for his European patent stating that he has obtained hESC without prior destruction of human embryos. However, the opposition division of the EPO revoked his European patent entirely on April 11, 2013 owing to fact that the non-destruction of human embryos did not find mention in the original patent application. Therefore, the opposition division of the EPO surprisingly avoided the question of proving the use of permitted methods for harvesting hESC. It should be noted that 'Prof. Brüstle' appealed in August 2013 but the decision of the technical board's regarding this European patent is still awaited.

Computer Related Programs and Computer-Related Inventions

Given that "computer programs are expressly excluded from patentability by Section 1(2)(c) of the Patents act, 1977/Article 52(2)(c), EPC 1973", it may come as a matter of surprise to learn that multifold patents have already been granted for "computer-related inventions." (Bently, 2011).

Given the fact that a computer program is cannot be granted a patent in the United Kingdom, following the acceptance of the whole contents approach it is clear that applications which contain a computer program are prima facie patentable, so long as the invention as a whole makes a technical contribution to the art. "In Kearney", (EPOR 1997) for instance the "Technical Board of Appeal" held that a "computer program" that alerted machine operators when their machine needed to be repaired or a worn tool needed to be replaced solved a technical problem and as such was patentable subject matter. Similarly, In Bosch the Board of Appeal said that a device for monitoring computer components was technical because it considerably reduced 'the operating time of the computer component and thus undoubtedly improved the effectiveness of the device. (Bainbridge, 2007)

In contrast, if it cannot be shown that an application that contains a computer program is technical, then it will not be patentable. This was the case, for example, in 1991 "*Gale's Application*", where the court of Appeal decided that "a ROM carrying a particular program was not distinguishable from the program itself and, as such, was patentable." This was again reiterated in "*Fujitsu's Àpplication (EPC 1997),*" "where the court of Appeal held that a computer-related invention that enabled chemists to produce digital models of hybrid chemicals was not patentable." (Bently, 2011)

The question of Scope of the exclusion of computer programs was considered in two decisions by the Technical Board of Appeal, both involving applications by IBM.

The invention in the First decision "IBM/Computer Programs (T935/97) was a method for allowing information in a data-processing system that was displayed in one window to be altered if that window was obscured by another window." The application included claims for software in itself, and for software recorded in a computer-readable medium. While some of the claims were acceptable, the Examining Division refused the application insofar as it was directed to a computer-program product. The second IBM decision (T1173/97) related to "resource recovery in a computer-program system," Again the examining Division rejected the application insofar as it claimed a computer-program product. (Bently et al., n. d.).

While it is clear that the IBM decisions mark a victory for the proponents of greater protection for information-technology-related inventions, ultimately the extent to which computer programs are patentable depends on how "technical character" is construed. Thus it would be safe to conclude that, so long as a computer program is technical, the medium in which it is recorded is irrelevant. (Bently et al., n. d.).

RATIONALE FOR EXCLUSIONS

When it comes to the subject of 'exclusions' the scarcity of material has been encountered from time to time in explaining "exclusions from patentability" or possible "exceptions to patentees' rights." Therefore, much of the explaining of the purpose of the exclusions on patentability falls upon the shoulders of the judicial bodies, allowing much room for interpretations. The problem with the courts providing with the rationale to exclusions came to light when the courts of different jurisdictions had distinct views to offer with regard to a subject set out for exclusion. For instance, in relation to the exclusion of "animals", it is a matter of public policy in Europe whereas in Canada (as held by 'The Supreme Court of Canada in the year 2002', in the case of *Harvard College v. Canada*) the animals are excluded from the subject of patentability as they didn't fall within the definition of invention.

Six Rationales to Exclusions From Patentability

Thus, different exclusions often have different rationales. Basically, six rationales can be cited to justify various exclusions from patentability.

Exclusions Clarifying the Term "Invention"

'Section 101 of Patents act of United States,' provides:

Whoever invents or discovers any new and useful process, machine, manufacture, or composition of matter, or any new and useful improvement thereof, may obtain a patent therefore...

Many legal systems have attempted to define the term "invention". In Antigua & Barbuda, According to Section 2(1)(ii), Act 23 Of 2003, an invention has been defined to include "an idea of an inventor which permits in practice the solution to a specific problem in the field of technology and an invention may be, or relate to, a product or a process." In Japan, referring to 'Section 2 (1) of the Patents act', an invention has been defined to include a "highly advanced creation of technical ideas by which a law of nature is utilized."

The other systems have failed to provide a positive definition to the term "invention". The European countries have found it exceptionally difficult to find a common definition of invention. Instead EPC has provided an illustrative list of matters that are deemed not to be inventions. Even the countries of "invention" often operate with exclusions, either by express statutory exclusions or with the aid of precedents.

In "*Diamond v. Chakrabarty*" the US Supreme Court in the year 1981 declared that:

Einstein could not patent his celebrated law that $E=MC^2$; nor could Newton have patented the law of gravity. Such discoveries are manifestations of nature free to all men and reserved exclusively to none.

Exclusions Reflecting Policy-Decisions in Other Parts of the Patent System

Sometimes exclusions from subject-matter patentability reflect policies that might find mention elsewhere in the patent system, for instance, novelty, non-obviousness or disclosure. Professor Duffy (2009) had an interesting insight to share on matter culled out from the US patent history. According to him, the exclusion of "new uses" as a matter of patentability reflects the lack of standards of non-obviousness, whereas the exclusion of life forms emulates difficulties with disclosure. He further argued that the exclusion of "abstract principles" from the scope of patentability was therefore not a question of 'principle' but reflected an inclination for categorical clarity.

Similar arguments were threshed out during the 1990s in Europe and more recently dealing with "software and business methods." By Professors James Bessen and Michael Meurer (2008), as they have contended that the 'adversities examining patent applications referring to computer software and business methods, as well as hardships in constructing clear boundaries around the subject matter of such claims imposes significant costs on businesses.' In an earlier invasion into this territory, Michael Meurer (2002) argued that these sorts of issues would rationalize a categorical ex ante exclusion:

Cost-savings justify the exclusion of business methods ...because a proper non-obviousness analysis (based on the economic trade-off) would deny patents to most business method patent innovations. (Michael Meurer, 2002)

Exclusions Reflecting the Fact That Protection Is Being Afforded Elsewhere

Literary, artistic and aesthetic works are beyond the scope of patentability for the fact they are protected under the copyright law. The 'Eurasian Patent system' seems to offer an analogical approach to the subject matters those are capable of protection by trademarks and designs law.

The objective behind such exclusions is twofold:

- Where the copyrights law is there to offer protection to a subject matter in such a case additional protection of Patent law is not mandated.
- Enhances production by saving the society of the additional burden led by the exclusions.

In the sight of the commentators, subject matter should find protection only under one regime. At times, emulating this view, Patent documentation has been excluded from the copyright protection by many legal systems and trade mark protection has been denied to technical subject matters.

These rationales to some people do appear farfetched, owing to the distinct intellectual property laws serve protection on different facets on intellectual subject matters and products. This is self-evident with regard to the trade mark/Patents interface, where patents deal with "manufacturing and sale" of an invention, trademark on the other hand offers protection to the features of an invention, with which the people tend to associate the invention with, and that indeed comes to operate as a trademark for the said invention. Thereby, where the scope and ambit of each intellectual property is distinct, denial of patent protection for the fact that the said "intellectual artefact" is also finds protection in copyright law appears to be skeptical in cases where copyright and patents are advancing protection to distinct facets of an "intellectual property." (Bently et al., n. d.).

Exclusions Reflecting Patent Law's Cost-Benefit Analysis

Some matters fall beyond the scope of patentability owing to the fact that their social costs of the legally enforceable rights surpass the benefits. These social costs are determined keeping social and economic contextual backgrounds for the same. There may be certain categories of inventions which do not regard artificial incentive as necessary to optimize investment. This is because a certain 'level of recognition', 'protection or reward' or 'sufficient economic incentives' are provided by the social norms without interfering in the marketplace, an obvious example for the same have long-exited from the world of "pure-science" been recognized and rewarded with naming rights- for instance, the right to name a planet or plant or have a scientific theory or medical syndrome named after one. The existence of such social norms render the patent rights avoidable.

The "Cost-effective "analysis, though, is not just about excluding inventions that "would occur anyway." It is also with regard to recognizing the costs that patents create- the social costs associated with the deadweight loss, transaction costs and so on.

But the costs that demand a serious thought are not only economic, there is also a need to it realize that patenting has the potential to transform particular environments from ones that operate with certain communal, altruistic sharing norms to ones in which individual private gain is maximized. If "methods of treatment" constitute an example of a situation where strong social norms find place in incentivizing creation and disclosure, it may also be an environment where the introduction of market norms has a serious impact on the benefits derived from those norms. Say, for example, that the diagnosis of certain illnesses might be greatly improved by doctors sharing informational resources concerning patients. Such a cooperative arrangement is likely to be much less costly in an environment where all believe they have a mutual project of improving health outcomes, compared to one where the effect of sharing information is to facilitate one gaining monopoly rights over a particular method of diagnosis. In *Lab Corp of America v Metabolite Labs., Inc*, Breyer J in the Supreme Court of the United States summed up the issue:

...the reason for this exclusion is that sometimes too much patent protection can impede rather than 'promote the Progress of Science and Useful Arts', the constitutional objective of patent and copyright protection. (Bently et al., n. d.).

Exclusions in Relation to Inventions that Are Positively Undesirable

Certain exclusions can base their justification on the basis of "undesirability" or simply being immoral or against the public policy. In such cases, it would be unacceptable to offer to artificial incentives to such inventions by awarding patents. The exclusion of immoral inventions has been regarded to be contrary to the requirement of utility by US Jurisprudence.

The exclusions from patentability on moral grounds are common but not universal. Though morality exclusion had been a "utility requirement" for United States, however this approach seems to have been taken a back seat. In "*Diamond v. Chakrabarty,*" the Supreme Court relied upon:

...a gruesome parade of horribles that might result from genetic research, but said that these concerns were a matter for Congress, implying that the morality of an invention was irrelevant if the subject matter otherwise fell within the statutory clause.

As observed in the case of Commissioner of Patents v. President and Fellows of Harvard College in 2002, by Binnie J, the 'Canadian Commissioner of Patents', similarly has "no discretion to refuse a patent on the grounds of morality, public interest, public order or any other ground if the statutory criteria are met...

A mutual protest towards the "exclusion of patentability" with regard to the "immoral subject matter" is that it fails to understand the significance of patenting. The grant of patent is neither considered as a "permission or positive authority to exploit the invention", nor as "an expression of approval or disapproval." For instance, to grant patents for "genetically-modified organisms" would not preclude anyone from experimenting with such organisms from complying with requisite regulatory controls. There is a "fundamental distinction ... between patentability of an invention and regulation of an activity associated with an invention." (Bently et al., n. d.).

Exclusions that Recognize Countervailing Policy Considerations

Certain class of exclusions are beyond the reach of the patent law, motivated by the goals aiming at the maximizing access to food and medicine. "The Patent law of Ghana", for example, excludes "products and processes excluded by law for national security, economy, health or any other national concern," while "Jordan" and "Moldova" exclude from "protection inventions necessary to protect the life and health of humans." "Kenya" similarly excludes "designated methods for the prevention or treatment of serious health hazards and life threatening diseases."

Such systems work on the principle that where the free profiteering of an invention is indispensable to promote public health and other vital social concerns, property rights should not be given preference over such concerns and also that the logic of patent law should give way to the greater social good. (Bently et al., n. d.).

CONCLUSION

The rationale of excluding inventions from the scope of patentability is multifold. However, time and again the courts have cited Public welfare and morality as being a major factor in deciding the scope of patentability. In 'Diamond v. Chakrabarty' where the 'U.S Supreme Court' endorsed a controversial view that "anything under the sun made by man" is subject to patent protection. The courts have been quick to rectify its stand Subsequently in Diamond v. Dier by holding that the "laws of nature, natural phenomena and abstract ideas are beyond the scope of patent protection". The Boards have gone a step forward in being very selective while granting patents as a result of which a number of subjects and substances have been excluded from the scope of patentability including "Animal and plant varieties" and other immoral procedures for example the process of cloning human beings etc. There is definitely criteria set for a subject to be capable of being awarded a patent for instance, the subject matter must be an invention within the meaning of the various statutes dealing with the patentability criteria of various states however the factor of Public welfare and morality stands above all.

REFERENCES

Bainbridge, D. (2007). Court of Appeal parts company with the EPO on software patents. *Computer Law & Security Report*, *23*(2), 199–204. doi:10.1016/j.clsr.2007.01.001

Bently, L. (2011). Exclusions from patentability and exceptions to Patentees Rights: Taking Exceptions Seriously. *Current Legal Practices*, *64*(1), 315–347. doi:10.1093/clp/cur011

Bently, L., Sherman, B., & Hubicki, S. (2009). Patent Issues in Biotechnology. doi:10.1002/9780470015902.a0005189.pub2

Bently, L., Sherman, B., Borges Barbosa, D., Grau-Kuntz, K., Basheer, S., Visser, C., & Gold, R. (2010). Exclusions from Patentability and Exceptions and Limitations to Patentees' Rights. WIPO, SCP/15/31-100. Retrieved from http://www.wipo.int/edocs/mdocs/scp/en/scp_15/scp_15_3-annex1.pdf

Bessen, J., & Meurer, M. (2008). Patent Failure: How Judges, Bureaucrats, and Lawyers Put Innovators at Risk. Princeton University Press. Retrieved from http://www.jstor.org/stable/j.ctt7sc3z

Duffy, J. F. (2009). Rules and standards on the forefront of patentability. *Wn & Mary Law Review*, *51*(2), 609–646.

Laakmann, A. B. (2012). An explicit policy lever for patent scope. *Michigan Telecommunications & Technology Law Review*, *19*(1), 44-97. Retrieved from http://repository.law.umich.edu/mttlr/vol19/iss1/2

Martin, B. S. (2009). Embryonic stem cells: the moral dilemma of patentability and funding. *Pharmaceutical Technology Europe*, *21*(9). Retrieved from https://hinxtongroup.files.wordpress.com/2010/10/san-martin_pharm-tech-europe_2009.pdf

McFarlane, R. A., & Litts, R. G. (2012). Business Methods and Patentable Subject Matter following In re Bilski: Is Anything under the Sun Made by Man Really Patentable. *Santa Clara High Tech. L. J.*, 26(1), 35-38. Retrieved from http://digitalcommons.law.scu.edu/chtlj/vol26/iss1/2

Meurer, M. (2002). Business Method Patents and Patent Floods. *Washington University Journal of Law and Policy*, *8*(1), 309.

Sherman, B. (1995). The ethics of patenting: Towards a transgenic patent system. *Medical Law Review*, *3*(3), 275–291. doi:10.1093/medlaw/3.3.275 PMID:11657691

Treglia, B. (2008). Patentable subject matter: separating abstract ideas and laws of nature from patentable inventions. *Jurimetrics Journal of Law & Science*, *48*(4), 427-456. Retrieved from http://www.jstor.org/stable/25767404

ADDITIONAL READING

Baldock, C., & Kingsbury, O. (2000). Where Did It Come from and Where Is It Going? The Biotechnology Directive and Its Relation to the EPC. *Biotechnology Law Report*, *19*(1), 7–17. doi:10.1089/073003100320957

Minssen, T., & Nordberg, A. (2015). The Impact of "Broccoli II" and "Tomatoes II" on European Patents in Conventional Breeding, GMOs, and Synthetic Biology: The Grand Finale of a Juicy Patents Tale? *Biotechnology Law Report*, *34*(3), 81-98.

Rogers, E.J. (2012). Patenting medical diagnostic methods: the mort strikes back. *Journal of Technology Law & Policy*, *17*.

Schellekens, M., & Vantsiouri, P. (2013). Patentability of Human Enhancements. *Law Innovation and Technology*, *5*(2), 190–213. doi:10.5235/17579961.5.2.190

Ventose, E. D. (2011). Patent protection for dosage regimes in Europe: A dissenting view. *Journal of Intellectual Property Law & Practice*, *6*(4), 238–253. doi:10.1093/jiplp/jpr003

Chapter 7
Product Patent in Pharmaceuticals and Compulsory Licensing

Jatinder Maan
Panjab University, India

Dinesh Kumar
Panjab University, India

ABSTRACT

The issue of patenting is a contentious issue. Different stakeholders hold opposite views. The pharmaceutical giants demand for stricter and longer Intellectual Property Protection for the promotion of research and development. They contend IP protection to be the "bedrock of their business". While the health activists and governments of developing nations want greater flexibility in intellectual property protection and shorter patent period protection. Article 31 of the TRIPs agreement provides certain flexibilities to cater to certain situations. The countries are free to determine the grounds to issue provisions like compulsory licensing. But despite the provisions very few countries have used them. Pharmaceuticals giants with the backing of developed countries always try to denounce the practice of compulsory licensing with economic and political pressure. This chapter explains the concept and significance of Intellectual Property with reference to Pharmaceuticals. It also traces the little history of TRIPs agreement and explains the concept of Compulsory Licensing with trends in its use. It also discusses the few instances where compulsory License has been issued in different countries and tries to find the reasons of non issuance of Compulsory License.

DOI: 10.4018/978-1-5225-2414-4.ch007

Copyright © 2017, IGI Global. Copying or distributing in print or electronic forms without written permission of IGI Global is prohibited.

INTRODUCTION

Over the last 50 years, the world has made some significant progress in medical research and development of new drugs to combat deadly diseases. The average life expectancy across the globe has increased from around 30 years a century ago to 65 years today. This has been made possible in large part by medicines. But at the same time due to rapid technological advances, industrial pollution, global warming, destruction of flora and fauna various new forms of diseases have emerged and people are at higher risk especially in developing and under developed countries because of poor health care facilities. The current regime of Intellectual property rights (IPRs) has further hit the health sector badly. Intellectual Property Rights received a major push with the formation of World Trade Organization (WTO) and its binding Trade related aspects of Intellectual Property (TRIPs) agreement. The TRIPs agreement made Intellectual Property (IP) protection binding in all fields of trade including food and health which was earlier excluded. Since then the most controversial aspect of World Trade Organization's TRIPs agreement is over the issue of patents for pharmaceutical drugs. . (Siddiqi, 2005)

The inherent tussle between profit-driven drug companies and welfare oriented governments seeking to ensure cheaper access to essential medicines has occupied the global centre stage after the ratification of the TRIPS agreement by the World Trade Organization. .(Sood, 2013) The Membership of WTO is conditional on the pre-condition of signing of its related agreements especially TRIPs. The countries will have to amend their IP laws to bring them in consonance with TRIPs agreement. Earlier many developing countries did not allow patent in pharmaceuticals, this represents a significant change in the pharmaceutical sector.

Worldwide, there is growing concern about the impact of the Patent system on the health sector of developing countries, on innovation and on investment, on prices of vital life saving drugs etc. Proponents believe this will lead to an increase in investment and in R&D, yet public health experts, consumer groups, health workers across the world and especially in poor countries have expressed concern about the impact of the TRIPS Agreement on the availability and prices of drugs (Jakarta, 2000). The local pharmaceutical industries in countries such as Brazil and India can no longer reverse-engineer patented foreign medicines and sell them at low prices in the markets of developing countries. .(Bond & Saggi, 2012a)

Intellectual Property and Pharmaceuticals

Continuous Innovation is necessary for the prosperity of individuals, companies and nations. But Innovation is not a simple and an isolated process. It involves numerous factors such as technical know-how, Intellectual property laws, governmental support,

University collaborations, risk taking behavior and availability of Investment capital. From the above referred Intellectual property was specifically created as a key driving force for stimulating innovation (Gupta, 2010).

The intellectual property rights system has been developed in order to achieve two contradictory aims:

- To promote the publication of ideas, inventions and creations, in order to make them available to others, who can then further improve them; this will nurture scientific progress or artistic inspiration;
- To provide an economic incentive for people to invent or to engage in creative efforts, by ensuring that the originator can reap the financial rewards of his/ her efforts by giving a temporary monopoly, in exchange for making his/her idea known to society.

The pharmaceutical industry across the world in particular is dependent upon Intellectual Property protection for its growth and sustainability. In the pharmaceutical sector, patents[1] are the most important form of IPR protection. In fact, the very existence of the Trade Related aspects of Intellectual Property Agreement (TRIPs) is mainly due to the pressure from the pharmaceutical companies on the US government, which in turn insisted that this issue should be on the agenda of the Uruguay Round negotiations.

There are several reasons for the importance of patents for the pharmaceutical industry:

- The costs of pharmaceutical Research & Development (hereinafter called R&D) are high. While the actual amount is being disputed, it is in any case significant.
- Usually, imitation is relatively easy; therefore the patent is important to protect the invention.
- It allows the company to make extra profits to further invest in developing of new drugs.

However before the signing of TRIPs agreement many countries did not grant patent protection for pharmaceutical products; this included a number of developed countries, such as Portugal and Spain, as well as many developing countries, for instance Brazil, India, Mexico and Egypt. Developing countries were reluctant to introduce Intellectual Property in various spheres, especially food products and patent in pharmaceuticals as majority of the Research and Development has taken place in developed countries and there are very few patents with the developing countries. (Bond & Saggi, 2012b)

The reason of coming into force of TRIPs was the intense pressure from the US. For the U.S. film and pharmaceutical industries in particular, intellectual property (copyright for the former, patents for the latter) represented the backbone of their industries (Drahos, 1999). So, the business consultants, lobbyists and lawyers started pushing the idea of linking Intellectual property with Trade. During the 1980's, to include the intellectual property issue as a negotiating issue in the Uruguay Round of trade talks the US industries started intense lobbying. In 1980s, the U.S.A. reshaped its trade law and brought enforcement strategy measures against countries having a weak IP enforcement mechanism. In 1984, the U.S.A. amended its Trade Act of 1974 to include intellectual property in the 'section 301'[2] trade process. The 1984 amendment had a sequel in the form of the Omnibus Trade and Competitiveness Act of 1988. This latter Act strengthened the 301 process by adding more processes called 'Regular 301', 'Special 301' and 'Super 301.' Essentially these provisions required the Office of the United States Trade Representative to identify problem countries, assess the level of abuse of US intellectual property interests and to enter into negotiations with those countries to remedy the problems. Ultimately, if this proved futile, the U.S.A. could impose trade sanctions. Countries caught up in the 301 process came to learn a simple truth. If they failed to act on intellectual property they would, sooner or later, face retaliatory action from the U.S.A.

It became difficult (politically and economically) for nations to avoid talks on Intellectual Property. At the launch of the Uruguay Round of Trade Talks, in 1986, Intellectual property was included as a negotiating Issue. On 15 April, 1994 the Uruguay concluded in Marrakach with the signing of the final act embodying the results of the Uruguay Round of Multilateral Trade Negotiations. More than 100 countries signed the Final Act. It contained a number of agreements, including the Agreement Establishing the World Trade Organization and the TRIPS Agreement.

The TRIPs agreement introduced the Intellectual property law into the international trading system for the first time and it remains the most comprehensive international agreement on Intellectual Property till date. It made the granting of patents for pharmaceutical product and process inventions[3] compulsory.[4]

Patents and Right to Health

As human beings, our health and the health of those we care about is a matter of daily concern. Regardless of our age, gender, socioeconomic or ethnic background, we consider our health to be our most basic and essential asset.[5] The right to health has been a fundamental part of our human rights and of our understanding of a life of dignity. It's a broad right covering freedom from hunger, adequate nutrition, clean surroundings, sanitation, access to clean water, right to health care in case of any disease etc. Right to Health care further includes access to essential medicines, equal and timely access to basic health services and the provision of health-related education and information.

Access to essential medicines as part of the right to the highest attainable standard of health ("the right to health") is also well-founded in international[6] and national laws[7].The authoritative General Comment 14 (2000) adopted by the UN Committee on Economic, Social and Cultural Rights, which monitors compliance with the ICESCR, authoritatively recognized access to medicines as a means of fulfilling the right to health.[8]Despite being fundamental right the health sector was brought under the ambit of trade. Stricter IP enforcements have been brought and developing countries have been forced to conform to those enforcements. According to the recent study by the UN body over 5 billion people worldwide lack access to essential medicines (UN News Centre, 2015).

Worldwide, there is growing concern about the impact of the Patent system on the health sector of developing countries as once granted the patent holder shall have the exclusive right to prevent third parties from making, using, offering for sale, selling or importing that product or process.[9] The term of protection available under TRIPs is twenty years counted from the filing date.[10]

The tendency to monopolize the knowledge and production, especially in pharmaceuticals has hit the health sector badly. Products to treat a range of diseases are denied to those who need them the most merely because they cannot pay for them.[11] It is denied to them not because these medicines cannot be produced at a reasonable cost, but because the few corporations treat knowledge as their property and sells these medicines at exorbitant prices. .(Sengupta, 2012)

However, The TRIPs also provide some exceptions to the general rule of IP Protection. Article 8 of the TRIPs provides that member countries while formulating and amending their Intellectual Property laws can design legislation which is in the best interest of the country. They can adopt measures necessary to protect public health and nutrition, and to promote the public interest in sectors of vital importance to their socio-economic and technological development also provide provisions needed to prevent the abuse of Intellectual property rights provided these provisions are consistent with the provisions of TRIPs agreement[12]. TRIPS also provides for a number of safeguards which may be used to protect public health and promote competition, such as compulsory licensing, parallel importing etc[13]. However, these safeguards can only be used if they have been incorporated in the national legislation. The objective to be achieved is to strike a between protecting intellectual property and promoting the well- being of the population. .(Alberto, 2005)

Compulsory License

A compulsory license is an involuntary contract between a willing buyer and an unwilling seller, which is enforced by a state government. (Matthews, 2010) Compulsory licensing is when a government allows someone else to produce the patented product or process without the consent of the patent owner (World Trade Organization, 2006). A compulsory license permits a nation (or a third party authorized by the nation) to use a patented invention without permission of the patent owner in exchange for payment of a government-determined royalty. The license is compulsory in that it is forced upon the patent owner. The patent owner is required to accept the government's compensation — which is likely far less than the patent owner could obtain in a free market. However, the issuance of Compulsory License does not mean that the patent has ceased to exist, patent remains in force. The patent holder holds the right to exclude all except the government License holder. But he looses the exclusive control over the market for its product because of Compulsory Licensing.

Article 31 of the TRIPs agreement deals with compulsory Licensing. The interesting fact is that the agreement nowhere uses the term Compulsory licensing but instead uses the phrase "other use without authorization of the right holder". Compulsory license can be issued in any field of IP but in the current chapter it is usually associated with pharmaceuticals.

The use of compulsory licensing has been recognized internationally for more than 125 years, however in recent years there has been a distinct expansion in scope. The Paris Convention, dating from 1883,[14] first recognized compulsory licensing as a means to address the abusive exercise of patent rights on "failure to work" grounds, thereby justifying issuance in limited cases.

Most countries have provisions for compulsory licenses, either under their patent law or, as in the US, through anti-trust legislation Under the TRIPs Agreement; countries have the right to issue such licenses. The TRIPs agreement does not limit the grounds -or reasons- for granting compulsory licenses, countries can use those grounds which are allowed by their national legislation. Countries have specified many different grounds for issuing compulsory licenses; these can include public health reasons. Other grounds are, for instance, emergency situations, epidemics, public non-commercial use, to remedy anti-competitive practices or to protect the environment. Nations are not limited to these common grounds — they are free to create new grounds for issuing licenses. It is entirely up to the national law to decide which are the grounds so there is a lot of flexibility. The German law, for example, simply states that compulsory licensing is allowed 'for reasons of public interest';

a broad description that can be used in many situations. Under US law, compulsory licenses can be issued to remedy anti-competitive practices and for use by the Federal Government; both these grounds are used extensively for issuing such licenses.

However, the TRIPS Agreement has provided certain conditions to be followed while granting Compulsory licenses under Article 31. Before Issuing CL the proposed user must try to obtain authorization from the patent holder on reasonable commercial terms.[15] The prerequisite of prior negotiation with the patentee for authorization may be waived under some circumstances like in cases of national emergency and other cases of extreme urgency or in cases of public non commercial use without prior negotiation but the patent holder be notified as soon as reasonably practicable. The TRIPs does not define the terms National Emergency, cases of extreme urgency and public non commercial use. This leaves the countries with discretion to determine what constitute national Emergency or cases of extreme urgency.

The Compulsory License must be predominantly for use with in the country.[16] It should be non exclusive and non assignable.[17] The scope and duration of the license shall be limited to the purpose for which it was authorized. The authorization shall be terminated, when the circumstances which led to it cease to exist and are unlikely to re occur.[18] The patent holder shall be paid adequate remuneration in the circumstances of each case[19]. TRIPs also give the right to the patent holder to challenge the decision of government to issue a compulsory license. In addition, the holder can also challenge the decision regarding the remuneration paid to him for compulsory License.[20]

The safeguards such as provisions for compulsory licensing are an essential element of IPR legislation, since they signal to the patent holder that, in the case of abuse of rights and/or non-availability of the product, a third party could be allowed to use the invention. As such, they reduce the risk of misuse of the monopoly rights conferred by a patent. However, to ensure that such safeguards can be used effectively, it is important to carefully state the grounds and conditions for their use in the national legislation.

Trends in Compulsory Licensing

It is interesting to observe that developing nations have seldom made use of the flexibility of the TRIPs agreement and whenever they have used the provisions it has been met with severe retaliation from the pharmaceuticals companies often with backing of state governments. For example during mid and late ninety –nineties, South Africa rapidly became the country with the highest absolute number of people living with HIV/AIDS. The overall adult prevalence rate approached the twenty percent mark, and approximately forty-five percent of military personnel were infected with HIV.11 However, with an average annual income of $2,600, most South Africans suffering from HIV/AIDS could not afford to pay for treatment with antiretroviral drugs, which at that time cost about $1,000 a month. Life expectancy at birth dropped significantly, and the number of orphans was increasing steadily

A new Section 15C was inserted into the South African Medicines and Related Substances Control Act (MRSCA) The controversial legislative proposal contained the explicit authorization of parallel imports of patented pharmaceuticals. The South African Ministry of Health imposed a compulsory license over a number of AIDS medications. As a result, thirty American pharmaceutical companies lobbied the U.S. government to sue the South African government for violation of TRIPS. South Africa was also removed from the "most favored member trade status" under the U.S. Special 301." ."(Ali, 2002)

This led to a great debate at the world level and in particular the US pharmaceutical industry became more concerned, which led to a number of events and tension between US and South Africa. The pharmaceutical companies were criticized for trying to restrict the access of medicines to people dying with AIDS. Finally the matter settled with Merck's price reductions for its AIDS drugs, Crixivan and Stocrin, Merck's new prices - $600 per patient per year for Crixivan, and $500 for Stocrin. (Fisher III & Rigamonti, 2005)

Similarly, on November 13, 1996, Senator Jose Sarney proposed Law No. 9,313, which enabled the Brazilian's universal and free access to antiretroviral through the National Health System. The Federal Government sanctioned the law. As part of the universal coverage the government began providing free antiretroviral, in an effort to prevent the spread of HIV/AIDS among its young and sexually active population, in particular (an estimated 730,000 people were living with HIV/AIDS) It also started local production of antiretroviral.

Article 68 of Brazil's patent law, allows for compulsory licensing when patent holders do not manufacture their products locally. So the government announced issuing of Compulsory License for Stocrin, Viracept, Crixavan as the prices of these imported drugs were very high.

Merck the patent holder of Efavirenze and Indinavir, agreed on price discounts of 59 percent for Efavirenze and 65 percent for Indinavir, and Roche,the patent holder of Viracpt, agreed to sell Viracept in Brazil at an additional 40% discount as long as Brazil does no issue a compulsory license for the drugs (Wetzler & Ayala, 2008).

In response to Brazil's actions, the US filed a complaint with the WTO in early 2001, accusing the government of violating TRIPS. But later because of international pressure the US withdrew the complaint in June 2001, saying it would pursue the issue in bilateral talks.

The spread of the AIDS pandemic, along with highly publicized cases such as Brazil and South Africa, contributed to increased awareness on an international level that patents threatened to severely restrict access to health in developing countries. The flexibilities provided under TRIPs for developing and under developed countries also needed to be reinforced. This awareness contributed to the outcome at Doha in November 2001, hailed as the development round of the WTO.

DOHA DECLARATION

In Nov. 2001, a separate declaration on TRIPS and Public Health was adopted by WTO ministerial conference at Doha. It reaffirmed the flexibility of TRIPs member states in circumventing patent rights for better access to essential commodities. They agreed that the TRIPS Agreement does not and should not prevent members from taking measures to protect public health. They underscored countries' ability to use the flexibilities that are built into the TRIPS Agreement, including compulsory licensing and parallel importing. And they agreed to extend exemptions on pharmaceutical patent protection for least-developed countries until 2016.

On the issue of Article 31(f) of the TRIPS Agreement which says that products made under compulsory licensing must be "predominantly for the supply of the domestic market". It has an impact on countries unable to make medicines and therefore wanting to import generics. They would find it difficult to find countries that can supply them with drugs made under compulsory licensing.

The Doha declaration para 6 recognized that WTO members with insufficient or no manufacturing capabilities in pharmaceutical sector could face difficulty in making effective use of compulsory License under TRIPs agreement.

This was resolved on 30 August 2003 when WTO members agreed on legal changes to make it easier for countries to import cheaper generics made under compulsory licensing if they are unable to manufacture the medicines themselves. It also provided a waiver of Article 31 (h) namely, remuneration for the importing country when remuneration is already paid in the exporting country. (Thapa, 2011)

Egypt

In 2002, Egyptian government first provided full patent protection to renowned Pfizer an American pharmaceuticals giant drug 'Viagra24' but only after two months, Egyptian government granted unlimited compulsory license in response to domestic pressure especially from local pharmaceutical manufacturers. The 12 local companies promised to produce a generic version of the drug at one-twentieth of Pfizer's market price of about $5.20 for each 50-milligram pill (Allam, 2002)

As a reaction to this decision, Pfizer cancelled its plan to construct an additional production facility in Egypt. Moreover, in the wake of the same issue, the Pharmaceutical Research and Manufacturers Association of America (hereinafter PhRMA27) told Egyptian representatives that pharmaceutical companies had cancelled their plans to invest $300 million in Egypt owing to weak intellectual property laws of the country. . (Abbas & Riaz, 2013)

Malaysia

Malaysia, in 2003 became the first Asian country to issue a government use license following the adoption of Doha Declaration. The government authorized the import of generic version of Antiretrovirals (Azt, ddl and combivir) to treat AIDS from Indian Company Cipla. After the issuance of License for one combination of drug- the cost fell by 83% and for another combination, a decline of 68% was registered.

According to the news reported in 2004, there were 59,000 people in Malaysia infected with HIV, and only 6000 were going for follow up in govt. hospitals and a few years ago only 1500 out of 4000 positive people on the verge of developing full blown AIDS were receiving treatment.

Thailand

In Nov. 2006 and Jan. 2007 The Thai Ministry of Public Health announced the Government Use of Patents on three patented drugs, i.e., Efavirenz (Stocrin®) of Merck Sharp and Dohme), Lopinavir+Ritonavir (Kaletra®) of Abbott Laboratory) and Clopidogrel (Plavix®) of Sanofi- Aventis), to treat HIV and Heart disease.

Abbott Laboratories, the maker of the AIDS drug Kaletra, took the radical step of withdrawing all of its new products from Thailand, depriving Thais of access to new drugs for rheumatoid arthritis, kidney disease, heart disease and high blood pressure (Fuller, 2007).But the Thai government remained firm and in 2007-2008, decided to grant compulsory License on four anti-cancer drugs. The drug Docetexel (trade name Taxotere), The drug Letrozole (trade name Femara), The drug Erlotinib (trade name Tarceva), The drug Imatinib (trade name Glivec). Cancer has been one of the top killers among Thai people for over a decade. It is the cause of more than 30,000 deaths annually in Thailand, with more than 100,000 new cases reported each year.

Thailand has implemented compulsory licensing for the following three cancer drugs -- Docetaxel, used mainly for the treatment of breast and lung cancer (sold as Taxotere by Sanofi Aventis); Erlotinib, used to treat lung cancer (sold as Tarceva by Roche); and Letrozole, used to treat breast cancer (sold as Femara by Novartis).

A fourth drug - imatinib for treating leukemia and other cancers (and sold as Glivec by Novartis) - was also to have been subjected to a compulsory license, but the license was not implemented after Novartis reportedly agreed to give its drugs free to a Thai public health programme (Shashikant, 2008).

Except the above mentioned Zimbabwe, Mozambique, Zambia, Ghana, Indonesia, Taiwan, China, Korea issued compulsory licenses for HIV/AIDS and pandemic Flu.

India

After India amended its law to make it TRIPS compliant, the government never invoked the provision of Compulsory License. It was only recently The Intellectual Property Appellate Board (IPAB) on 13 March 2013 upheld the grant of India's first compulsory licence (CL) to the Hyderabad-based Natco Pharma Limited, a generic drug maker, to produce and market Nexavar, a patented cancer drug of multinational pharma major Bayer Corporation (Sivaraman, 2013).

The German Pharmaceutical and Chemical giant, Bayer, obtained a patent in India in 2008 to produce an anti cancer drug (sorafnib tosylate). It produces the drug and market it under the brand name Nexavar, which is used in the treatment of patients diagnosed as being in the advanced stages of affliction with liver and kidney cancer, which cost Rs. 2.8 lakh for a pack of 120 tablets, equivalent to a month's dosage. On March 9, last year, the Controller of Patents, Mumbai, granted the first-ever compulsory licence to Natco to make 'sorofenib tosylate', a generic version of Bayer's high-priced anti-cancer drug Nexavar. Natco was told to sell the pack at Rs. 8,800.

CONCLUSION

The issue of Patent in pharmaceuticals has always been a complex one. As the developing countries are moving towards universal health coverage, the conflict among nations is rising. Pharmaceutical giants, supported by developed nations, assert for greater protection under the legislations of developing countries and ridicule the use of provisions like compulsory licenses.

But at the same time, pressure is building in the developing countries as the high priced patented drugs are restricting the access of needy people to the life saving drugs and putting an additional monetary burden on the governments of developing nations.

In the recent past many countries have issued compulsory licenses to deal with the situation, which have been accepted with great enthusiasm by the people. But, pharmaceutical giants have expressed their strong resentment by cutting down their investments and shutting their research facilities. The experience in each of the episodes of compulsory license of countries shows that developing countries are at higher risk of facing adverse situation. The ability to actually use TRIPS-consistent compulsory licenses also involves a lot of other issues except only the legal one. The issues involved are beyond TRIPS. In particular, the threat of retaliation by drug companies and major trading partners may make countries hesitant to issue them.

The issuance of First Compulsory license by India is a welcome step, considered the "Pharmacy of South" the grant of license will strengthen the stand of developing countries at international forums and provide the much needed relief to thousands of cancer patients of not only of India but world.

As we are making great technological advances in different fields, it is important that the humanity as such benefits from such development in science and technology. We need to strike a fine balance among the needs of hundreds and thousands of people, who are losing their precious lives because of money constraints and the needs of investors to boost innovation.

Even the UN Human Development Report soon after the formation of a WTO cautioned the world of the repercussions of the IP Protection.

The relentless march of intellectual property rights needs to be stopped and questioned. Developments in the new technologies are running far ahead of the ethical, legal, regulatory and policy frameworks needed to govern their use. More understanding is needed -in every country- of the economic and social consequences of the TRIPs Agreement. Many people have started to question the relationship between knowledge ownership and innovation. Alternative approaches to innovation, based on sharing, open access and communal innovation, are flourishing, disproving the claim that innovation necessarily requires patents. -UNDP Human Development Report 1999

REFERENCES

Abbas, Z., & Riaz, S. (2013), Flexibilities under Trips: Implementation Gaps between Theory and Practice, *Nordic Journal of Commercial Law*, 1.

Al-Ali, N. (2002). The Egyptian Pharmaceutical Industry After TRIPS — A Practitioner's View. *Fordham International Law Journal, 26*(2). Retrived from http://ir.lawnet.fordham.edu/cgi/viewcontent.cgi?article=1871&context=ilj last seen 2/12/2016

Allam, A. (2002). Seeking Investment, Egypt Tries Patent Laws. *The New York Times.* Retrieved from http://www.nytimes.com/2002/10/04/business/seeking-investment-egypt-tries-patent-laws.html

Bond, Eric and Saggi, kamal (2012). Compulsory licensing, price controls, and access to patented foreign products. Retrieved from http://www.wipo.int/edocs/mdocs/mdocs/en/wipo_ip_econ_ge_4_12/wipo_ip_econ_ge_4_12_ref_saggi.pdf

do Amaral, A. (2005). Compulsory Licensing and Access to Medicine in Developing Countries. *SELA (Seminario en Latinoamérica de Teoría Constitucional y Política) Papers Paper 47.* Retrieved from http://digitalcommons.law.yale.edu/yls_sela/47

Drahos, P. (1999). The Universality Of Intellectual Property Rights: Origins and Development. Retrieved from http://www.wipo.int/edocs/mdocs/tk/en/wipo_unhchr_ip_pnl_98/wipo_unhchr_ip_pnl_98_1.pdf

Fisher, W.W., III, & Dr. Rigamonti C. P. (2005). The South Africa AIDS Controversy A Case Study in Patent Law and Policy. Retrived from https://cyber.harvard.edu/people/tfisher/South%20Africa.pdf

Fuller, T. (2007). Thailand takes on drug industry, and may be winning. *The New York Times.* Retrieved November 22, 2016 from http://www.nytimes.com/2007/04/11/world/asia/11ihtpharma.4.5240049.html?pagewanted=all&_r=0

Gupta, M. S. (2010) Effect of patent law changes on the innovation strategy of Chinese and Indian Life Science companies as reflected in US patent filings. Retrieved September 24, 2016 from http://dspace.mit.edu/handle/1721.1/62524

Matthews, J. (2010). Renewing Healthy Competition: Compulsory Licenses and Why Abuses of the TRIPS Article 31 Standards Are Most Damaging to the United States Healthcare Industry. *J. Bus. Entrepreneurship & L.*, 1. Retrieved from http://digitalcommons.pepperdine.edu/jbel/vol4/iss1/5

Sengupta, A. (2012). Patent to Plunder. *Frontline, 29*(8).

Shashikant, S. (2008) Recent Thai compulsory licenses and the aftermath. *Choike.* Retrieved from http://www.choike.org/nuevo_eng/informes/6432.html

Siddiqi, A. (2005). Patents and Pharmaceutical Drugs The Need for Change. *SURG Spring.*

Sivaraman, R. (2013, March 4). Natco Pharma wins cancer drug case, Chennai. *The Hindu.* Retrieved December 11, 2016 from http://www.thehindu.com/business/companies/natco-pharma-wins-cancer-drug-case/article4475762.ece

Sood, M. (2013). Natco Pharma Ltd. V. Bayer Corporation and The Compulsory Licensing Regime In India. *NUJS L.Rev.,* 6(99).

Thapa, R. (2011). Waiver Solution in Public Health and Pharmaceutical Domain under TRIPs agreement. *Jorunal of Intellectual Property Rights, 16,* 470–476.

Timmermans, K., & Hutadjulu, T. (2000, May 2-4). The Trips Agreement and Pharmaceuticals. *Report of an ASEAN Workshop on the TRIPs Agreement and its Impact on Pharmaceuticals,* Jakarta. Retrieved March 26, 2016 from http://apps.who.int/medicinedocs/en/d/Jh1459e/

UN News Centre. (2015). *Over 5 billion people worldwide lacking access to essential medicines, says UN report.* Retrieved September 24, 2016 from http://www.un.org/apps/news/story.asp?NewsID=50230#.VgDhjdKqqko

Wetzler, J., & Ayala, A. (2008). Timeline on Brazil's Compulsory Licensing. retrieved November 22, 2016 from https://www.wcl.american.edu/pijip/download.cfm?downloadfile=9C0107B5-DE2F

World Trade Organization. (2006). Fact sheet: trips and pharmaceutical patents. *World Trade Organization.* Retrieved from https://www.wto.org/english/tratop_e/trips_e/factsheet_pharm02_e.htm

ENDNOTES

1 A patent is an exclusive right granted for an invention, which is a product or a process that provides, in general, a new way of doing something, or offers a new technical solution to a problem. To get a patent, technical information about the invention must be disclosed to the public in a patent application. From http://www.wipo.int/patents/en/

2 Section 301 of the Trade Act of 1974 19 U.S.C. 2411(1982) authorizes the President to take any action, including the imposition of or an increase in import fees and restrictions, in response to acts, policies, or practices of foreign governments or their instrumentalities which meet specified criteria. For more information refer Bello, Judith Hippler and Holmer, Alan F. (1985-

1986), Section 301 of the Trade Act of 1974: Requirements, Procedures, and Developments, *7 Nw. J. Int'l L. & Bus.* 633 Retrieved December 10, 2016 from http://scholarlycommons.law.northwestern.edu/cgi/viewcontent.cgi?article=1211&context=njilb

3 The difference between product and process patent is that a product patent confers monopoly rights over the product, regardless of the production method. A process patent, on the other hand confers rights over the process of the production of the product instead of the product itself. Production of the same product via a different production method, however, does not infringe a process patent and it is allowed.eg. The Indian Patents Act of 1970 allowed only process patents and did not allow product patents in case of Pharmaceuticals till 2005 amendment.

4 The obligations under TRIPS apply equally to all member states, however developing countries were allowed extra time to implement the applicable changes to their national laws, in two tiers of transition according to their level of development. The transition period for developing countries expired in 2005. The transition period for least developed countries to implement TRIPS was extended to 2013, and until 1 January 2016 for pharmaceutical patents, with the possibility of further extension.

5 *The Right to Health*, Fact Sheet No. 31, Office of the United Nations High Commissioner for Human Rights and World Health Organization, available at http://www.ohchr.org/Documents/Publications/Factsheet31.pdf

6 The right to health first emerged as a social right in the World Health Organization (WHO) Constitution (1946) and in the Article 25 of the Universal Declaration of Human Rights (1948). Article 12 of The International Covenant on Economic, Social, and Cultural Rights (ICESCR) of 1966, Art 12 of the Convention on the Elimination of All Forms of Discrimination Against Women, Art 24 of the Convention on the Rights of the Child, Art 5(e) of the International Convention on the Elimination of All Forms of Racial Discrimination

7 Articles 39(e),(f); 42 and 47 in part IV of the Constitution of India talks of state duty to maintain good health. Under Article 21 of the Indian Constitution the government is bound to take whatever steps necessary to ensure that everyone has access to health facilities, goods and services so that they can enjoy, as soon as possible, the highest attainable standard of physical and mental health. Refer Mohd. Ahmed (Minor) V.Union Of India & Ors. ..... In The High Court of Delhi at New Delhi W.P.(C) 7279/2013

8 Paragraph 43 of General Comment 14 stated clearly, for the first time, that state parties are obliged "to provide essential drugs, as from time to time defined under the WHO Action Programme on Essential Drugs" and "to ensure equitable distribution of all health facilities, goods and services."

9 TRIPS Art 28 (1)(a), (b)

10 TRIPS Art.33

11 In 2001 the annual cost of treating one HIV/AIDS patient was 10,000 US dollars. Some countries had to spend half of their GDP to procure those medicines. In 2003, an Indian company Cipla started selling the same medicine at $250 per annum. Even this price was high; the same drug came further down to $100 for a year's supply. Refer Sengupta, Amit (2012). *Patent to Plunder,* Vol.29 Number 8 Frontline, 4

12 TRIPS Art 8

13 TRIPS Art 31

14 Paris Convention for the Protection of Industrial Property, Art. 5(A), Mar. 20, 1883, 21 U.S.T. 1538 provides that: (1) Importation by the patentee into the country where the patent has been granted of articles manufactured in any of the countries of the Union shall not entail forfeiture of the patent. (2) Each country of the Union shall have the right to take legislative measures providing for the grant of compulsory licenses to prevent the abuses which might result from the exercise of the exclusive rights conferred by the patent, for example, failure to work. (3) Forfeiture of the patent shall not be provided for except in cases where the grant of compulsory licenses would not have been sufficient to prevent the said abuses. No proceedings for the forfeiture or revocation of a patent may be instituted before the expiration of two years from the grant of the first compulsory license. (4) A compulsory license may not be applied for on the ground of failure to work or insufficient working before the expiration of a period of four years from the date of filing of the patent application or three years from the date of the grant of the patent, whichever period expires last; it shall be refused if the patentee justifies his inaction by legitimate reasons. Such a compulsory license shall be non–exclusive and shall not be transferable, even in the form of the grant of a sub–license, except with that part of the enterprise or goodwill which exploits such license.

15 TRIPS Art. 31

16 TRIPS Art. 31 (f)

17 TRIPS Art. 31 (d),(e)

18 TRIPS Art. 31 (c)

19 TRIPS Art. 31 (h)

20 TRIPS Art. 31 (j)

Chapter 8 Compulsory Licensing of Patents in India

Shinu Vig
Amity Business School, India

Teena Bagga
Amity Business School, India

ABSTRACT

Compulsory licensing is defined generally as the granting of a license by a government to use a patent without the patent-holder's permission. As applied to international intellectual property rights, it allows governments to grant licenses for patent use in situations where the patent-holder is either not using the patent within the country or is not using it adequately. Most of the drugs for which compulsory licenses have been granted in India are used for treatment of life-threatening diseases. The pharmaceutical companies however object on the ground of violation of their patent rights. This chapter discusses the provisions for compulsory licensing in TRIPs and the India patent system.

INTRODUCTION

Compulsory licensing is defined generally as the granting of a license by a government to use a patent without the patent-holder's permission. As applied to international intellectual property rights, it allows governments to grant licenses for patent use in situations where the patent-holder is either not using the patent within the country or is not using it adequately. Although compulsory licensing is not a new concept, it recently has received considerable attention as pharmaceutical companies and

DOI: 10.4018/978-1-5225-2414-4.ch008

Copyright © 2017, IGI Global. Copying or distributing in print or electronic forms without written permission of IGI Global is prohibited.

activist groups seek to advance their respective political agendas over the right to drug access for life-threatening diseases. When governments issue compulsory licenses, the result is often a sharp decrease in prices, similar to the introduction of other competitive forces like generic drugs.' For this reason, many developing nations argue for the right to issue compulsory licenses for pharmaceuticals that are normally very expensive for their citizens." During the negotiations for the TRIPs agreement (Agreement on Trade Related Aspects of Intellectual Property), however, most developed nations argued for strict restrictions on compulsory licenses to safeguard their domestic industries. In this backdrop, this paper presents a discussion on the provisions for compulsory licensing in TRIPs and India patent system.

The Agreement on Trade Related Aspects of Intellectual Property (TRIPS)

TRIPs agreement was adopted at the conclusion of the Uruguay Round in Marrakesh in April 1994. TRIPs outlined a framework for minimum intellectual property standards that bind all WTO Member nations. TRIPS was significantly disparate from all earlier efforts that were made to achieve harmonization of intellectual property rights worldwide. As part of the founding of the WTO, TRIPS clearly tied intellectual property rights to trade. The TRIPS mandates minimum substantive patent protections for a wide range of inventions. Under TRIPS, member states of the WTO are not permitted to exclude any field of technology from patentability, including pharmaceuticals. Also, WTO members are required to provide a uniform term of twenty years of patent protection from the filing date of any invention. TRIPS further forbids parties from providing patent protection that differentiates between inventions based on place of invention or from requiring that inventions be produced locally. TRIPs introduced some remarkably new patent provisions in the international intellectual property law most significant out of them was that TRIPs allowed for compulsory licensing amidst several other provisions in its Article 31.

Article 31 of TRIPS, entitled "Other Use Without Authorization of the Right Holder," lays down the conditions under which WTO member countries can authorize compulsory licenses for patented inventions. This provision requires that WTO member countries first engage in negotiations for a reasonable period of time to obtain authorization from the patent holder on reasonable commercial terms and conditions before authorizing a compulsory license. In the case of a "national emergency" or other "circumstances of extreme urgency," these requirements can be waived by the WTO member country. Even in these circumstances, however, the WTO member country authorizing the compulsory license has a responsibility to inform the patent holder of its actions. The use of a compulsory licenses under

Article 31 must be "predominantly for the supply of the domestic market" of the authorizing WTO member country. Any authorization of a compulsory license is subject to the requirement that patentees receive "adequate remuneration...taking into account the economic value of the authorization."

Though TRIPs vividly authorized Member countries to legislate exceptions to the rights of' legitimate patent holders (TRIPs art. 30, 33) but the text of TRIPs contained ambiguities that required clarification (WTO, 2001). For example the text of TRIPS did not define the term "national emergency" anywhere. Such ambiguity in the language of TRIPs led to widely differing interpretations of language of Article 31 by developing and developed countries (Ford, 2000).

As a result of this the WTO Members sought guidance in the area of compulsory licensing. One major purpose of the fourth WTO Ministerial Conference held in Doha, Qatar in November 2001 hereinafter referred as 'Doha Conference' was to reduce any ambiguities relating to the compulsory licensing provisions of TRIPs. The ministerial text intended to discuss two major issues: the scope of the term "public health" and the ability of Members without adequate manufacturing capacities to seek the benefits of compulsory licensing ("third party compulsory license"). The result of the meeting in Doha was a Declaration on the TRIPs Agreement and Public Health (WTO, 2001).

Paragraph 5 of the Doha Declaration clarified the term 'national emergency' used in TRIPs. Under TRIPs, an instant way for a country to issue a compulsory license is to claim a national emergency. Both developing and developed countries sought to define the term "national emergency" because the text of TRIPs neglected to provide any clear interpretation. The Doha Declaration provides Members the "right to determine what constitutes a national emergency," and precisely elucidates that 'public health crises' such as HIV/AIDS, malaria, and "other epidemics," will be considered as national emergencies.

In compulsory licensing matters, TRIPS should be interpreted in a manner that respects the legitimate policy concerns of both developed and developing nations. When a compulsory license of a patent for a critical pharmaceutical is granted for public use in a developing country, where a pharmaceutical company has targeted no investment and has no expectation of profits, "adequate remuneration" in TRIPS Article 31(h) should be interpreted to mean "without compensation." At the same time, TRIPS Article 31(f) should be interpreted as not allowing production under compulsory license for export and gray market sale of the patented product. Such interpretations of TRIPS' provisions provide one possible means of resolving the general conflict between developed countries who seek stronger IPR protection for economic benefit, and developing countries who seek to acquire and apply new technology to address their citizens' pressing needs.

Need for Compulsory Licensing

Pharmaceutical companies across the globe have invested heavily in research and development and have invented new medicines to battle against chronic conditions and life-threatening diseases such as AIDS and cancer that have infested people all over the world. But these life-saving innovations are accompanied by a lack of accessibility caused by pharmaceutical companies' ever-rising drug prices that are exorbitant for the poorest countries, which unfortunately have some of the sickest populations. The preposterous prices of these drugs place a very heavy burden on the poor population which cannot afford these medicines.

Developing countries are posed with the strenuous challenge of ensuring access to medications for the prevention and treatment of chronic diseases. Developing countries are confronted with a number of difficulties such as the development of adequate supply chain networks, ensuring that national drug regulatory authorities prevent the marketing of unsafe or counterfeit drugs and also effective delivery of medication for chronic diseases to their populations. (Amir Attaran & Lee Gillespie, 2001). In many under developed and developing nations, the major obstacle to ensuring that population with chronic diseases can access essential medications is 'pricing of pharmaceutical drugs.(Hoen, 2002). In these countries any treatment program for a chronic disease or epidemic can become successful only when the price of medications is affordable.

In many developing countries, including China and India, deaths from chronic diseases now far outnumber those from either communicable diseases or injuries. Sub-Saharan Africa currently stands as the only World Bank region where deaths from infectious diseases outnumber deaths from chronic diseases. The rapid graying of the developing world promises to further accelerate the growth of the chronic disease burden in low- and middle-income countries, given the correlation between advanced age and the development of chronic disease. While chronic diseases increasingly pose a grave threat to people living in developing countries, infectious diseases have not ceased to pose a threat to these populations. Developing countries still face high rates of morbidity and mortality due to infectious diseases, including HIV/AIDS, malaria, and tuberculosis (UNAIDS, 2006). A number of infectious diseases, such as dengue, HIV/AIDS and tuberculosis, are easily transmitted in urban environments. Developing countries thus face a "double burden" of infectious and chronic disease—a burden that threatens to quickly exhaust limited resources available for the purchase of medicines.

Developing countries and non-governmental organizations ("NGOs") argue that strict enforcement of pharmaceutical patent holders' rights has resulted in high prices, which render unaffordable to poor countries drugs critical to the treatment of epidemics.' The concern stems from the fact that the patent holders' rights exclude others from selling or making their exact or substantially similar patented products for the term of the patent. This period of exclusivity provides the patent holder with the power to control the selling price of the patented product.- Critics contend that pharmaceutical companies, as patent holders, have abused this right in order to reap tremendous profits, despite a staggering loss of human life.(Correa, 2001) In response, proponents of strong patent rights assert that patents are not the major barrier to access to essential medicines; rather inaccessibility to critical medications results from inadequate infrastructure, absence of an effective drug distribution system, and poverty (Attaran and Lee Gillespie (2001).

There have been several examples of compulsory licensing procedures that led to agreements with major pharmaceutical companies, initiated in Malaysia (2004), Indonesia (2004), Brazil (2003 and 2007), Zambia (2004), Zimbabwe (2004), and Mozambique (2004). Moreover, compulsory licenses were threatened against Roche for the use of oseltamivir (Tamiflu) in Indonesia, India, Vietnam, and South Korea, in the period 2003–2006. As a result, Roche selected partners in those countries to assist in the manufacture of sufficient supplies of Tamiflu to combat Asian influenza. (Zimmerman et. al., 2014)

General Objections to Compulsory Licensing

Developed countries, specifically, the United States strongly opposes the issuance of compulsory licenses for several reasons. The United States has discouraged the use of compulsory licenses for various reasons, such as the promotion of scientific research and development in the industries in developing nations and the commitment to international treaties enforcing the policy of intellectual property rights. Yet, the constant complaint in this regard by the United States is that compulsory licenses violate international intellectual property law proscribed in the TRIPs agreement (Ford, 2000).

THE INDIAN SCENARIO

The Pharmaceutical Industry in India

The Indian pharma industry is on a good growth path and is likely to be in the top 10 global markets in value term by 2020, according to the PWC – CII report titled "India Pharma Inc: Gearing up for the next level of growth". The report highlights that high burden of disease, good economic growth leading to higher disposable income, improvements in healthcare infrastructure and improved healthcare financing are driving growth in the domestic market. Chronic diseases (including cardiovascular and respiratory diseases, mental disorders, diabetes, and cancers) and injuries are the leading causes of death and disability in India—their burden will continue to increase during the next 25 years as a consequence of the rapidly ageing population in India (WHO, 2011). The Indian pharmaceutical industry has been growing at a compounded annual growth rate (CAGR) of more than 15% over the last five years and has significant growth opportunities. However, for the industry to sustain this robust growth rate till 2020, companies will have to rethink their business strategy. They will have to adopt new business models and think of innovative ideas to service their evolving customers faster and better (PWC, 2013)

A recent study carried out a study of 1115 patented products of 16 MNCs, out of which only 140 were commercially worked, i.e., were marketed in India (12.6%). Again out of the 140 patented products worked in India, information about whether these were manufactured in India or not were available for only 92 products. Only 4 of these were manufactured in India. The remaining 88 patented products were being imported and marketed in India. (Chaudhari, 2014). For 88 patents as mentioned above, the MNCs are importing the products rather than manufacturing these in the country. If patented drugs are imported rather than being manufactured, India does not gain technologically but pays the price of higher costs of monopoly drugs and this seriously questions the propriety of having product patents in that case. What is worse is that while MNCs may not be keen to manufacture drugs in the country they are not hesitating to take legal action against those who try to do so. These companies can contribute to the technological progress of India by manufacturing these here but they are keener to enjoy monopoly markets and high prices rather than to contribute to technological progress.

Indian Patent System

An important event in the history of intellectual property in India was the passage of the Patents Act 1970 (which became effective in April, 1972). India explicitly excluded pharmaceutical products from patent protection, and provided limited patent protection for pharmaceutical products. This legislation prohibited the issuance of pharmaceutical product patents entirely, only issuing process patents for the method by which a company produced a given pharmaceutical product. It also provided pharmaceutical patents with a reduced patent term of only seven years, in contrast with the fourteen years of patent protection provided for other inventions.

The Patents Act, 1970 remained in force for about 24 years without any change till December 1994. An ordinance effecting certain changes in the Act was issued on 31 st December 1994, which ceased to operate after six months. Subsequently, another ordinance was issued in 1999. This ordinance was subsequently replaced by the Patents (Amendment) Act, 1999 that was brought into force retrospectively

Figure 1. The history of patent law in India

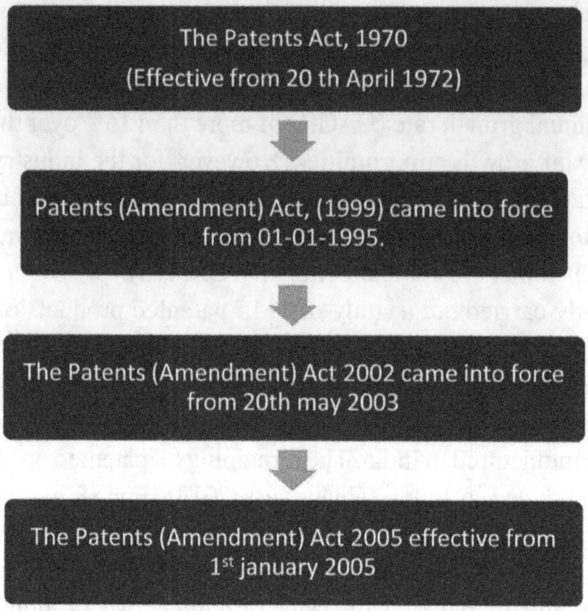

from 1st January, 1995. The amended Act provided for filing of applications for product patents in the areas of drugs, pharmaceuticals and agro chemicals though such patents were not allowed. However, such applications were to be examined only after 31-12-2004. Meanwhile, the applicants could be allowed Exclusive Marketing Rights (EMR) to sell or distribute these products in India, subject to fulfillment of certain conditions.

The second amendment to the 1970 Act was made through the Patents (Amendment) Act, 2002 (Act 38 0f 2002). This Act came into force on 20th May 2003 with the introduction of the new Patent Rules, 2003 by replacing the earlier Patents Rules, 1972. Consequently, the third amendment to the Patents Act 1970 was introduced through the Patents (Amendment) Ordinance, 2004 w.e.f. 1st January, 2005. This Ordinance was later replaced by the Patents (Amendment) Act 2005 (Act 15 of 2005) on 4th April, 2005 which was brought into force from 1-1-2005.

Compulsory Licensing in India

Under Indian Patent Act, 1970, the provision with regard to compulsory licensing is specifically given under Chapter XVI. This chapter is drafted along the lines of Article 31 of the TRIPS Agreement. The conditions which need to be fulfilled in order for a compulsory license to be granted are laid down under Sections 84 and

92 of the Act. As per Section 84, any person who is interested or already the holder of the license under the patent can make a request to the Controller for grant of Compulsory License on patent after three years from the date of grant of that patent on the existence of conditions mentioned in the Section 84 of the Patents Act, 1970. While granting the compulsory license, the Patent office will take into account few measures such as the nature of the invention, any measures already taken by the patentees or any licensee to make full use of the invention, ability of the applicant to work the invention to the public advantage and time elapsed since the grant of the patent i.e. worked or not worked.

Section 84(1) of Patents Act 1970 states that after the expiration of three years from the date of grant of patent any person may make an application for grant of compulsory license on three grounds:

1. The reasonable requirements of the public have not been satisfied or
2. The patented invention is not available to the public at an affordable price or
3. The patented invention is not worked in the territory of India.

Section 92A was inserted in the existing patent law through The Patents (Amendment) Act 2005. This section provides that Compulsory license shall be available for manufacture and export of patented pharmaceutical products to any country having insufficient or no manufacturing capacity in the pharmaceutical sector for the concerned product to address public health problems, provided compulsory license has been granted by such country or such country has, by notification or otherwise, allowed importation of the patented pharmaceutical products from India.

India granted its first compulsory license in the March 2012 to Natco Pharma Ltd. for producing generic version of Bayer Corporation's patented medicine Nexavar used in treatment of liver and kidney cancer. After this there have several other instances of compulsory licenses being granted for making available expensive drugs for treatment of cancer and other chronic diseases. The recent patent clashes in the Indian courts on two anti-cancer drugs Gleevac and Erlontinib highlight the issue. Gleevac is a patented drug of Novartis Ltd for the treatment of myeloid leukemia and was being sold in India for Rs. 1,20,000 ($ 2500) per patient per month (ppm) in India while Indian companies offer a generic for about Rs. 8,000 ($175) ppm. Another battle is being fought by Cipla, an Indian pharma company that sells Erlontinib a medicine for lung cancer for about Rs 50,000 for a year's need or about a third of the price of Tarceva marketed by the patent owner Roche.

The Controller-General of Patents should not hesitate invoking provisions of compulsory licensing (CL), and other flexibilities available under the TRIPS and Indian Patent Act (2005) whenever the drugs required by the poor remain out of reach (Satyanarayana, 2008). The Thailand government has shown the way as to how CL could be enforced with a pro-public interpretation of international patent laws. However there is also another view which holds that there should be a balance between the need for affordability of drugs and intellectual property (IP) protection. The intention of the government to ensure the availability of patented medicines at a reasonable price is noble but there are other ways of achieving the same goal. The indiscriminate use of compulsory licensing will undermine both the Indian as well as foreign pharmaceutical companies (PWC, 2013)

CONCLUSION

WTO Members must come to a clear understanding on the issues of public health and compulsory licensing for export. Developing countries need to accept limits on what constitutes a "public health" concern, while developed countries need to accept a more expansive definition of "third party." The millions of men, women, and children suffering from HIV/AIDS, cancer and other life-threatening diseases all over the world are awaiting a solution to this issue. Amendments or declarations to TRIPs that expand exceptions to patent rights in combination with safeguards to ensure limited exceptions will help preserve the balance between patent rights and the public good.

REFERENCES

Agreement on Trade Related Aspects of Intellectual Property Rights and Public Health (WT/MIN(01)IDEC/2). (2001, November 20).

Attaran, A., & Gillespie-White, L. (2001). *Do Patents for Antiretroviral Drugs Constrain Access to AIDS Treatment in Africa.*

Basheer, S. (2005). India's tryst with TRIPS: the patents (amendment) Act 2005. *Indian Journal of Law and Technology.*

Beall, R., & Kuhn, R. (2012). Trends in compulsory licensing of pharmaceuticals since the Doha Declaration: a database analysis. *PLoS Medicine*, *9*(1).

Bird, R. C. (2009). Developing Nations and the Compulsory License: Maximizing Access to Essential Medicines while Minimizing Investment Side Effects. *The Journal of Law, Medicine & Ethics*, *37*(2), 209–222. doi:10.1111/j.1748-720X.2009.00366.x PMID:19493067

Carlos, M. (2001). Correa, *Public Health and Patent Legislation in Developing Countries,* J. TECH. & INTELL. *PROP*, *1*, 3.

Chaudhuri, S. (2014). *Intellectual Property Rights and Innovation: MNCs in Pharmaceutical Industry in India after TRIPS*. New Delhi: Institute for Studies in Industrial Development.

Chien, C. (2003). Cheap drugs at what price to innovation: Does the compulsory licensing of pharmaceuticals hurt innovation? *Berkeley Technology Law Journal*, 18(3), 853–907.

Fink, C. (2000). How stronger patent protection in India might affect the behavior of transnational pharmaceutical industries. World Bank Policy Research Working Paper.

Ford, S. M. (1999). Compulsory licensing provisions under the TRIPS agreement: Balancing pills and patents. *Am. U. Int'l L. Rev.*, *15*, 941.

Koshy, S. (1995). Effect of TRIPs on Indian Patent Law: A Pharmaceutical Industry Perspective. *BUJ Sci. & Tech. L.*, *1*, 123.

Lanjouw, J. O. (1998). *The Introduction of Pharmaceutical Product Patents in India:" Heartless Exploitation of the Poor and Suffering"? (No. w6366)*. National Bureau of Economic Research. doi:10.3386/w6366

FM't Hoen, E. (2002). TRIPS, pharmaceutical patents and access to essential medicines: Seattle, Doha and beyond.

Murthy, D. (2001). Future of Compulsory Licensing: Deciphering the Doha Declaration on the TRIPs Agreement and Public Health, The. *Am. U. Int'l L. Rev.*, *17*, 1299.

PWC. (2013). Indian pharmaceutical market highlights 2013

Reichman, J. H. (2009). Comment: compulsory licensing of patented pharmaceutical inventions: evaluating the options. *The Journal of Law, Medicine & Ethics*, *37*(2), 247–263. doi:10.1111/j.1748-720X.2009.00369.x PMID:19493070

Saha, S. (2009). Patent law and TRIPS: Compulsory licensing of patents and pharmaceuticals. *Journal of the Patent and Trademark Office Society*, *91*, 364.

Sara, M. Ford, Note, Compulsor, Licensing Provisions Under the Satyanarayana, K. (2008). Towards equitable health care: Drug prices, and beyond. *The Indian Journal of Medical Research*, *127*(4), 301. PMID:18577784

Thorsteinsdóttir, H., Quach, U., Daar, A. S., & Singer, P. A. (2004). Conclusions: Promoting biotechnology innovation in developing countries. *Nature Biotechnology*, *22*(12s), DC48–DC52. doi:10.1038/nbt1204supp-DC48 PMID:15583685

Trade Organization. (2001). Annex IC, art. 66, para. 1, Legal Instruments-Results of the *TRIPS Agreement: Balancing Pills and Patients,* 15 AM. U. INT'L L. REV. 941, TRIPS COUNCIL. *Work (Reading, Mass.)*, 24.

UNAIDS. 2006 REPORT ON THE GLOBAL AIDS EPIDEMIC (2006). Retrieved from http://www.unaids.org/en/HIV_data/2006GlobalReport/default.asp

Uruguay Round vol. 31, 33 I.L.M. 81 (1994).

Van Zimmeren, E., Nicol, D., Gold, R., Carbone, J., Chandrasekharan, S., Baldwin, A. L., & Cook-Deegan, R. (2014). The BRCA patent controversies. *Breast Cancer Gene Research and Medical Practices: Transnational Perspectives in the Time of BRCA, 151.*

Watal, J. (2000). Pharmaceutical patents, prices and welfare losses: Policy options for India under the WTO TRIPS agreement. *World Economy*, *23*(5), 733–752. doi:10.1111/1467-9701.00299

WHO. (2011). Chronic diseases and injuries in India. *WHO.* Retrieved from http://www.who.int/choice/publications/Chronic_diseaseIndia.pdf

WTO. (n. d.) Doha Declaration Retrieved from https://www.wto.org/english/thewto_e/minist_e/min01_e/.../doha_presspack_e.pdf

WTO Ministerial Conference. (n. d.). Declaration on the TRIPs Agreement.

Chapter 9
An Interface Between Traditional Knowledge and Intellectual Property Rights (IPR):
An Indian Perspective

Nisha Dhanaraj
Amity Law School Delhi, India

Mamta Sharma
Gautam Buddha University, India

ABSTRACT

Traditional knowledge and Intellectual Property Rights (IPR), both are supplementary and complementary to each other. The aim of traditional knowledge is to promote community interest and protect indigenous rights against bio-piracy and bio-prospecting. On the other hand, IPR guarantees monopoly of a product or service to an organization and empowers it to profit from it. This article studies the present Indian IPR system to understand whether it is capable to handle traditional knowledge or should it be amended to incorporate a separate law to protect traditional knowledge. Besides, a large-scale commercialization and unauthorized use of traditional knowledge has been observed, which gives rise to the need to screen and protect it. This article also takes into consideration the Bonn guidelines and Indian Biodiversity Act 2002 and the issues related to traditional knowledge, and finds that the current issues cannot be resolved by the existing IPR regime.

DOI: 10.4018/978-1-5225-2414-4.ch009

Copyright © 2017, IGI Global. Copying or distributing in print or electronic forms without written permission of IGI Global is prohibited.

INTRODUCTION

There is a growing need to protect traditional knowledge (TK) and fortify it against issues such as bio-piracy, bio-prospecting and rights of indigenous people. Traditional knowledge needs to be protected for sustainable development and for maintaining intellectual property rights (IPR). As of now, traditional knowledge does not have an internationally accepted definition. World Intellectual Property Organization (WIPO) refers to it as "tradition-based literary, artistic, or scientific works, performances, inventions, scientific discoveries, designs, marks, names, and symbols, undisclosed information and all other tradition-based innovations and creations resulting from intellectual activity in the industrial, scientific, literary or artistic fields." "Tradition-based" refers to "knowledge systems, creations, innovations and cultural expressions, which have generally been transmitted from generation to generation and are generally regarded as pertaining to a particular people or its territory which are constantly evolving in response to a changing environment" (Inter-governmental Committee (IGC), 2002).

"Indigenous people' refers to a community that has a distinct identity or a tribe or nation that still preserves, conserves and protects its ancestral past. These people are essentially seen as a group which exists under relatively disadvantageous conditions due to bio-piracy and bio-prospecting. Bio-piracy refers to the misappropriation and commercialization of genetic resources and traditional knowledge of rural and indigenous people. It involves making profit from freely available natural products (plants, seeds, leaves etc.), or by copying techniques used daily for generations by local people or communities. It has generally been observed that pharmaceutical companies, cosmetic and agro-food firms fall under the categories of bio-pirates. These companies set up their own potent precincts on bio-diversity in order to create innovative products and then guarantee their monopoly through the IPR system. Once the procedure is fulfilled and protection is granted, the heritage or knowledge is acquired by a third person. So a grant of an IPR under such circumstances is essentially a violation of the rights of the indigenous people (Jha, 2009). Emerging economies such as India, South Africa, China, Indonesia and Philippines have a rich bio-diversity heritage, which they can exploit to attain a higher level of sustainable development.

Bio-piracy is a serious threat to our ecosystem. Therefore, protecting traditional rights of the indigenous people is extremely vital to ensure that they get justice. It is only when their TK is protected they would be able to preserve their heritage and use their skills to propagate growth of vital areas such as food security and the development of agriculture and medical treatment (Dutfield, 2003).

RESEARCH METHODOLOGY

The methodology adopted for this paper is a combination of descriptive research and doctrinal research. The descriptive research was taken as a tool to access the present situation of traditional knowledge existing in India. Doctrinal research is adopted to achieve the objectives of the research, i.e., to access the relationship between IPR and TK, to provide an overview of the debate on the protection of traditional knowledge at the international level; to study traditional knowledge in terms of property rights and sovereignty rights; to identify ways by which TK can be effectively protected both nationally and internationally; and to discover the relationship between traditional knowledge and Intellectual property laws in India. The study is primarily based on international conventions, treaties, national laws, policy papers and national instruments. Relevant decisions of national, regional and international courts have also been considered. Secondary sources such as journal and newspaper articles, books and web resources on the practice and policies related to protection of TK and Intellectual Property Rights have also been tapped to supplement the study.

The study also takes into consideration the case law method for bio-piracy and protection of traditional knowledge of various countries, communities and tribes to analyze the jurisdictional aspect and legality of the issues between developed and developing countries. It also takes into consideration the regimes of IPR pertaining to the protection of TK in various countries to recommend a model law, which is suitable to protect TK in India.

STATUS QUO OF IPR AND TK

The current international framework for the protection of traditional knowledge is prescribed by TRIPS, WIPO, UNCTAD, WTO and Convention on Biodiversity (COB) through intellectual property; however, these international documents pay very little attention towards developing countries. Our study reveals that developing countries are the source of 90 percent of the world's biological resource (Chauhan, 2001). It is little wonder that they demand protection for their traditional knowledge and the rights of their indigenous communities. In this context, many developing countries are taking the support of the sui generis system. India, which harbors the majority of the earth's species and is extremely biodiverse, has also faced some bitter experiences in the past related to some of its indigenous products such as turmeric, basmati and neem. These experiences have pushed the country to adopt hard-hitting polices and laws to protect its traditional knowledge. These laws include the Geographical Indications (Registration and Protection) Act, 1999, the Plant Varieties and Farmers Rights Act, 2001, and the Biodiversity Act, 2002.

The WIPO members in 2000 established an Intergovernmental Committee on Intellectual Property and Genetic Resources, Traditional Knowledge and Folklore (IGC). Further, in 2009, they agreed to develop an international legal instrument to include traditional knowledge, genetic resources and traditional cultural expressions (folklore) for efficient protection. In response to the pressure to protect the TK rights of its indigenous communities, India established the Traditional knowledge Digital Library (TKDL) in 2001 which is a collaborative project of Council of Scientific and Industrial Research (CSIR) and Department of Ayurveda, Yoga & Naturopathy, Unani, Siddha and Homeopathy (AYUSH). The TKDL allows the examiners of Patent Offices to search for information regarding substance or practice in order to grant patents. The authorities can also dismiss the grant of patent, if the substance or practice is already mentioned in the TKDL list as an Indian traditional knowledge.

PROTECTION OF TRADITIONAL KNOWLEDGE: LEGAL ISSUES

There are three areas in India, which are widely covered by traditional knowledge: technical know-how, skill, practices, and innovation relating to biodiversity, agriculture or health; traditional cultural expressions of folklore (including cultural manifestations such as music, art, designs, symbols and performances); and finally, genetic resources (genetic material of actual or potential value found in plants, animals and micro-organisms). All these fields demand protection through IPR, for example, if the area falls under the first category. In this case, it can seek protection under the Patent, Biodiversity Act, and the Plant Varity Act. If the area falls under the second category, then protection can be sought under the Copyright and Design Act, 2000. If the area falls under the third category, then the patent can be sought under the Plant Variety Act (Mgbeoji, 2006). Apart from these Acts, the Trade Marks Act and Geographical Indications Act also recognize and support the protection of TK under various domains of the IPR system.

The objectives of protecting TK are as follows:

- To improve the lives of TK holders and communities
- To benefit national economies
- To strengthen research and development linkages

- To help India become an inventive and creative society and a global leader in sustainable technologies
- To prevent bio-piracy or unauthorized acquisition through bio-prospecting
- To stop the unauthorized use of TK acquired by deception, knowingly or failure to fully disclose the commercial motive behind the acquisition

Given the above objectives, it becomes very important to protect traditional remedies and indigenous art and indigenous people's rights against misappropriation and exploitation. Now the next question is how to protect traditional knowledge rights? Under the IPR system, two types of protections can be sought. Firstly, to restrict outsiders from acquiring intellectual property rights over traditional knowledge. For this, the self-protective strategy can also be used to protect consecrated cultural expressions, manifestations, sacred symbols, signs, or words through registration.

The secondly is to seek rights for communities who are involved in the preserving and conserving of this traditional knowledge since a long time. A number of countries have also developed specific legislation or incorporated exclusive provisions for protecting TK in their local laws. Apart from that, many countries have taken an initiative to provide practical assistance and technical advice to enable these communities to make more effective use of existing intellectual property systems and participate more effectively in the IGC's negotiation (Intergovernmental Committee of WIPO on Intellectual Property and Genetic Resources, Traditional Knowledge and Folklore). On the other hand, international laws have developed and strengthened national and regional systems for the protection of traditional knowledge (policies, laws, information systems and practical tools) by providing their assistance, for example, WIPO's Creative Heritage Project work for Maasai of Laikipya Kenya where WIPO provided hands-on training to the community with a digital camera, sound recording equipments and a durable state-of-the-art laptop computer to document their cultural heritage. This work spread awareness about their rights. WIPO also helped to set up a Maasai Women Development Organization (MWEDO) to establish a "Maasai brand" for authenticating genuine products such as handicrafts made by the Maasai women. Despite WIPO's contribution, TK has been the subject of concern on the international platform but no effective legal measure has ever been devised to oblige the international community to respect TK as a protected property and the rights of the indigenous people. These indigenous communities have no means to protect their traditional knowledge so it is defensive protection which is more needed than positive protection against exploitation of traditional knowledge (Krystyna Swiderska, 2006).

THE ROLE OF BENEFIT-SHARING MECHANISM

The efforts of the international system with regards to TK are impressive, however, they are not adequate to ensure that TK is recognized at the international level. Therefore, the heritage of the indigenous communities in the developing world faces threat from the developed countries. Besides WIPO, the Convention on Biological Diversity (CBD) also helps to protect the knowledge, practices, and innovations of indigenous and local communities as per Article 8(j) of the CBD. The CBD is supported by the International Treaty on Plant Genetic Resources for Food and Agriculture (ITPGRFA), which commenced in 2001. The CBD and the ITPGRFA converse about the sovereign right of countries for the preservation of their traditional knowledge. Article 15 of the CBD provides a framework for national governments to implement Access and Benefit Sharing (ABS) mechanisms to regulate and protect knowledge and genetic resources in order to facilitate access and ensure the fair and equitable sharing of benefits.

Bonn Guidelines is a major achievement of COP VI (Conference of the parties VI/24 decision) held in the Hague, Netherland, in 2002, on access to genetic resources and the fair and equitable sharing of the benefits arising from their utilization (CBD, 2006). These Guidelines established a constructive step towards an evolutionary process in the implementation of relevant provisions of the Convention related to the access to genetic resources and benefit sharing amongst indigenous people.

However, these are kept under consideration by the COP for further refinement on the basis of developments related to fretful issues under the Convention, i.e., traditional knowledge and technology transfer.

Then there is the Nagoya Protocol, which is a supplementary agreement on "Access to Genetic Resources and the Fair and Equitable Sharing of Benefits Arising from their Utilization to the Convention on Biological Diversity". The provisions contained in the Nagoya Protocol like Art. 10, Art.14, Art.21, Art.25 and Art. 30 address issues related to genetic resources, global ABS, indigenous and local communities rights, resource mobilization, capacity building and development. The Nagoya Protocol on ABS was adopted on 29th October 2010 in Nagoya, Japan, and came into force on 12th October 2014. As per this protocol, the contracting parties are to acquire measures to ensure these communities prior informed consent, and fair and equitable benefit-sharing, keeping in mind community laws and procedures as well as customary use and exchange.

Being a signed member to the Convention on Bio Diversity (CBD) and Nagoya Protocol, India in pursuance of these international instruments, has set up its own Indian National Biodiversity Policy and Macro Level Action Strategy at the national level. Furthermore, the Jeevani (*Aarogyapachha*) case came into the public domain when indigenous rights were implemented by means of ABS by granting royalty to the Ḳani tribe against exploitation. In India, the main aim of the Biodiversity Act, 2002, is to regulate access to biological resources, to foster conservation and sustainable use of biological resources, to respect and protect knowledge of local communities related to biodiversity, and to implement the benefit sharing mechanism for example, all the foreign nationals and companies are required to have the permission of National Biodiversity Authority (NBA) before transferring biological material out of India (Sec. 6, Biological Diversity Act, 2002). It is also provided that the said provision shall not apply to the local people and communities of the area, including growers and cultivators of biodiversity, and *Vaidas* and who have been practicing indigenous medicine. In addition to this, Sec. 7 provides that no person, who is a citizen of India or a body corporate, association or organization, which is registered in India, shall obtain any biological resource for commercial utilization, or bio-survey and bio-utilization for commercial utilization except after giving prior intimation to the State Biodiversity Board concerned. This law is largely designed to counter bio-piracy. On the other hand, the Constitution of India also strengthens the rights related to environment through its provisions like Art. 21, Art. 48A and Art. 51A (g). The same was functionalized by the Supreme Court in *M.C. Mehta* v. *Kamal Nath*, (1997) case where it was held that the doctrine of public trust places an affirmative duty on the state as a trustee of certain public resources to protect resources like air, sea, water and the forests for the enjoyment of the general public.

PROTECTION OF TRADITIONAL KNOWLEDGE: AN ANALYSIS OF EXISTING INTELLECTUAL PROPERTY RIGHTS REGIME IN INDIA

The question of TK protection under the international IP regime was referred to in Clause 19 of the Doha Ministerial Declaration (IV), which instructs the Trade Related Intellectual Property Rights (TRIPs) Council to review Article 27.3(b), and examine the relationship between TRIPs and CBD and the protection of Traditional Knowledge (TK) and folklore, and other relevant new developments (Patrick, 2012).

Patent and TK

TRIPs does not mention traditional knowledge specifically as a protectable subject matter under its ambit, nor does it expressly deny the protection to TK as a form of IPR. So if the traditional knowledge concept fulfils the criteria of TRIPS, then protection can be granted to TK through the IPR system. So the issue that needs to be addressed is whether traditional knowledge can get protection within the regimes falling under the IPR system in India or not? Or is there an urgent need to prepare a new legislation which would deal with traditional knowledge, ownership, owner, term of protection, rights or community rights of indigenous people, royalty, infringement or even penalties and remedial measures? In India, patent protection is granted on the basis of (a) novelty, (b) inventive step and (c) industrial utility. These are the globally accepted pre-requisites for patents too. The concept of novelty is *sine quo non* of patents in relation to traditional knowledge also. Though the Indian Patent Act, 1970, does not define the term 'novelty', the Patents (Amendment) Act, 2005 demonstrates the concept of novelty when it defines the term 'new invention' under section 2 (l) as under: New invention means any invention or technology which has not been anticipated by publication in any document or used in the country or elsewhere in the world before the date of filing of patent application with complete specification, i.e., the subject matter has not fallen in public domain or that it does not form part of the state of the art. Novelty lies in the non-disclosure of the invention to the public. It presupposes that there should be no prior knowledge of the invention with the public. It requires the secrecy of the information for the purpose of claiming novelty. An invention may be anticipated either by (a) prior publication or by (b) prior use. But traditional knowledge does not qualify as it is already known and, being used for many years by the communities or people related to this prior art. The question then arises why TK related to invention should be protected under Indian patent laws when it is a subject of prior art?

In addition to this, the TRIPs agreement states that patents shall be available for any inventions, whether products or processes, in all fields of technology, provided that they are new, involve an inventive step and are capable of industrial application. To implement the same, India patent law is dealing with patentability and non-patentability under Sec 3 that all inventions are not patentable though they may otherwise satisfy all the conditions of patentability. A patent will be granted for an invention if the subject matter is open for patenting, or to put it in other words, if the invention does not fall under an excluded category. In reference to the above discussion, Section 3 (p) excludes from patentability of an invention which, in effect, is traditional knowledge or which is an aggregation or duplication of known properties or traditionally known component or components. Also sections 25 (1) (d) and 25 (2) (d) provide that if the subject of any claim of the complete specification is not an invention within the meaning of the Act, or is not patentable under the Act, then it can be opposed on that ground. For making a conduit of the above two provisions, sections 64 (1) (d) permits revocation of a patent if the subject of any claim of the complete specification is not an invention within the meaning of the Act.

A combined reading of these sections reiterates that there can be no patent protection in the country on traditional knowledge per se or which involves traditionally known component or components (Kalluri, 2012). These provisions again contradictory argument against patent protection of traditional knowledge in India.

Copyright and TK

In contrast to the above, copyright protection is not as worst to treat folklore, poetry, tales, culture, tradition, songs, art, garments, textile compositions, pictorial works, dance and presentations which are the part of cultural heritage under Indian copyright Act, 1957 still some issues are not settled for example that how the copyright protection can be given to literary, artistic, religious, dramatic and other traditions and productions created by the national or ethnic communities or unknown communities or unidentified authors or unidentified communities or lapsed communities or tribes. What will be the criteria of their royalty? Whether indigenous people are entitled to avail exclusive rights, neighboring rights or a moral right which is called the basis of protection given under the copyright Act, 1957? As the present Act is having Joint authorship, co-authorship rights, duration of protection still not suffice and lucid in relation to traditional knowledge, indigenous people or tribe rights subject.

Trade Mark and TK

Protection under the Trade Marks Act, 1999, can be availed through Collective mark given under chapter VIII, certification mark under Chapter IX where indigenous people or communities or tribes can obtain registration of their mark, sign, words, phrase, symbols and design to sell their products and services. At the international level, agencies such as WIPO's cultural heritage project and the United Nations help in creating this awareness and provide assistance to indigenous people to protect their traditional knowledge rights. However, this raises another dilemma - the protection as envisaged above, will that assure defensive protection against acts of passing off and if so then to what extent trademark protection should be granted to the indigenous community? Further, how and to what extent are the rights, as given under the Trade Marks Act, such as exclusive rights, Assignment and transmission (mentioned under chapter V of Trade Marks Act, 1999) applicable to indigenous communities? Although there is no doubt that if their mark has acquired recognition worldwide and there is a length and continuity of its use, then registration should be recognized by the concerned authorities also.

Geographical Indications and TK

Geographical Indications is the best form of protection for tangible traditional knowledge with traceable geographical origin. It is a *sui generis* system, using collective and certification marks as trademark but the difference lies in the fact that geographical indications identify a good as originating from a particular region, place, group or community. In contrast, a trademark identifies a good or service as originating from a particular company or proprietor. At the international level, WIPO, Lisbon Agreement (Sec. 2) and TRIPs (Sec. 22) which defines Geographical Indication and other characteristics, could be applied to other forms of traditional knowledge. A specific form of geographical indicator is called an appellation of origin. Appellations of origin specify the quality of a product based on its geographical environment. Geographical indications and appellations of origin can be used to enhance the commercial value of natural, traditional and craft products of all kinds if their particular characteristics are attributed to their geographical origin. The special characteristics of those products may be symbolized by the indication of source used to identify the products. The worst exploitation against protection of traditional geographical indications would make it possible to afford better protection to the economic interests of the communities and regions of origin of the products. Hence, the producers in the relevant region, indigenous or local community, can associate together to develop, maintain, register and protect their products bearing the geographical indication.

CONCLUSION

Recently, a draft Bill was prepared by a six-member committee headed by Dr. N.S. Gopal Krishnan, Director, Inter University Centre for IPR Studies, CUSAT, to propose the constitution of people's trusts for protection of TK at the ground level through Biodiversity Management Committees. This Bill was criticized by Mr. R.S. Praveen Raj, a former examiner with the India Patent Office and currently a scientist at the CSIR-National Institute for Interdisciplinary Science and Technology (NIIST). He stated, "We should be careful in creating registrable rights on TK." In his opinion, any attempt to codify community-held TK in the form of Traditional Knowledge Digital Libraries (TKDL) using "Prior Informed Consent" and "Access and Benefit Sharing" concepts would be a gross injustice to those communities if the knowledge was shared with patent offices (Kumar, 2015). This shows another facet of dealing with an interface between IPR and traditional knowledge. However,

(Traditional Knowledge Digital System) TKDS has been established in India which is useful to know the location of TK and the community that possesses the TK. It also provides a short description of the nature of TK and the community protocol but the information is not sufficient for their recognition. There is no doubt that TK protection in the IPR system is applicable in many countries but it's difficult to understand the rights of indigenous people, the criteria of registration in patent and trade mark since this subject is highly debatable. Apart from this, bio-piracy and bio-prospecting, which are the ultimate threats against the biodiversity, are not considered anywhere in the Indian Patent Act, 1999. Therefore, India should establish a proper, cogent and comprehensive legislation on traditional knowledge separately, rather compellingly, to make it as a part of different regimes of IPR. Further, this legislation should define the terms TK, indigenous people rights, duration of protection, license, succeeding interest and rights of communities, royalty, procedure of registration, bio-piracy and bio-prospecting and punishment. Many countries such as Africa and Philippines have ensured protection to their traditional knowledge through separate legislation and are further considering indigenous communities rights over their traditional knowledge. These rights extend to controlling access to ancestral lands, access to biological and genetic resources, and to indigenous knowledge related to these resources. If protection is not given at the earliest in India through separate legislation, the knowledge which is still secured in the hands of these groups would be easily misappropriated or commercialized.

REFERENCES

Andanda, P. (2012). Striking a Balance between Intellectual Property Protection of Traditional Knowledge, Cultural Preservation and Access to Knowledge. *E Journal of intellectual Property Rights, 17*, 23-27.

Biological Diversity Act (2002).

Chauhan, S. S. (2001). Bio Diversity, Biopiracy and Biopolitics: The global perspective. Delhi: Kalinga Publications.

Commission, I. P. R. (n. d.) Traditional Knowledge and Geographical Indications. In *Integrating Intellectual Property Rights and Development Policy* (Ch. 13, pp. 73-94). Retrieved from www.iprcommission.org/papers/pdfs/final_report/ch4final.pdf

COP 6 Decisions. (2002, April 7-19). Convention on Biodiversity and Decision of conference of the parties VI/24 decision. (n. d.) *Convention on Biological Diversity.* Retrieved from https://www.cbd.int/decisions/cop/?m=cop-06

Dutfield, G. (2003). *Trading in knowledge: Development perspectives on TRIPS, trade and sustainability*. Christophe Bellmann & Ricardo Melendez-Ortiz Press.

Hirwade, M., & Hirwade, A. (2012). Traditional Knowledge Protection: An Indian Prospective. *DESIDOC Journal of Library & Information Technology*, *32*(3), 33–35. doi:10.14429/djlit.32.3.2381

Jha, A. (2009). *Traditional Knowledge System in India*. Delhi: Atlantic Press.

Kalluri, S. (2012). Traditional knowledge and Patent strategy. *Journal of Intellectual Property Rights*, *17*, 430–436.

Kumar, T. N. (2015 August 28). Caution on classifying traditional knowledge under IPR. *The Hindu*. Kerala. Retrieved from http://www.thehindu.com/news/national/kerala/caution-on-classifying-traditional-knowledge-under-ipr/article7589338

Martens, P. (2012). Can traditional knowledge owners and producers in developing countries use geographical indications for protection and economic development gain? In *Proceedings of the Third biennial global conference July 12 - 14, 2012, National University of Singapore, Faculty of Law Centre for International Law, Society of International Economic Law, online proceedings working paper no.* 2012/04, 3- 16.

M.C. Mehta v. Kamal Nath (1997)1 SCC 388.

Mgbeoji, I. (2006). *Global biopiracy: patents, plants, and indigenous knowledge*. University of British Columbia Press.

Convention on Biological Diversity. (n. d.). Nagoya Protocol on Access and Benefit Sharing. Retrieved from https://www.cbd.int/abs/

Swamy, N. R. (2014). Protection of traditional knowledge in the present IPR regime: A mirage or a reality. Retrieved from http://www.iipa.org.in/new%20folder/dr.%20raju%20narayana%20swamy.pdf

Swiderska, K. (2006). *Banishing the biopirates: A new approach to protecting traditional knowledge*. International Institute for Environment and Development.

Varadarajan, D. (2011). A Trade Secret Approach to Protecting Traditional Knowledge. *The Yale journal of international law, 36*, 371-416.

Venkataraman, K. & Swarna Latha, S. (2008, July). Intellectual Property Rights, Traditional Knowledge and Biodiversity in India. *Journal of intellectual property Rights, 13*, 326-335.

WIPO. (2002, June 13-21). Intergovernmental committee on intellectual property and genetic resources, traditional knowledge and folklore third session held in Geneva. Retrieved from www.wipo.int/edocs/mdocs/tk/.../wipo.../wipo_grtkf_ic_3_9-main

Chapter 10 Colgate-Palmolive's Attempt of Patenting Toothpaste Formula

Neetika Mehta
University of Petroleum and Energy Studies, India

ABSTRACT

By creating a robust intellectual property structure, a high-quality job future can be secured and sustained. Therefore, promotion to innovation/invention requires adequate protection. The multinational giant Colgate- Palmolive can be seen caught up into legal dispute where accusation is over the company for having purloined an archaic formula to have its roots to ancient times, and also being used by Indians for generations. India foiled an attempt by consumer goods giant Colgate-Palmolive to patent a mouthwash formula containing herb extract by citing ancient texts that show it was traditionally used in ancient medicinal practices. Traditional Knowledge Digital Library of Council of Scientific & Industrial Research (CSIR-TKDL) had submitted proof in the form of references from ancient books, which said the herb and its extracts in Indian systems of medicine. The proactivness of Indian community to safeguard its traditional knowledge obstructed the profit-making strategy of the company.

DOI: 10.4018/978-1-5225-2414-4.ch010

Copyright © 2017, IGI Global. Copying or distributing in print or electronic forms without written permission of IGI Global is prohibited.

INTRODUCTION TO COLGATE-PALMOLIVE

A humble beginning of Colgate Palmolive dates back to 1806, when a young Englishman – William Colgate set up a starch, soap & candle business in New York City. It was made into legal entity in 1807 with smith Francis & Colgate. With demise of the founder Mr. Colgate in 1857, the company was renamed to Colgate & Co.

Manhattan to Mumbai

In 1937, Colgate Palmolive Pvt. Ltd. was incorporated in India. It successfully rolled out new products with well executed business plans. Variety of toothpaste, toothbrushes, shampoos and creams were introduced in the Indian market. By 1978, Colgate Palmolive consolidated presence in India. The launch of variety of products helped the company expand market leadership positions and gain new ones. In 1978, the Indian public was offered 60% equity in the company with shares being listed on the Bombay Stock Exchange. It was successfully placed as the Blue Chip Company on the Indian bourses.

1980-1990's was the era where company started manufacturing with state of the art facility. With its massive success, Colgate Palmolive USA reaffirms its commitment by raising its equity from 40% - 51%. Colgate started being considered as India's No.1 brand across all categories. (Company)

Colgate oral pharmaceutical products were launched across Asia Pacific region. With brilliant launch strategy, new innovative products and having had great advantage at early stage, Colgate Palmolive entered a new category of household surface. Owing to this raising popularity, Colgate Palmolive introduced the top of the line products to Indian consumers. As the social media and user generated reviews proliferation, the organization noticed the power of valuing its customers. Websites were launched along with toll free consumer helpline for easy access to the information about the company and its wide variety of products.

The company started witnessing the ultimate vote of consumer's confidence. Colgate maintained its status of the most trusted FMCG brand position in the tenth year of the Brand Equity survey. It was presented the "Hall of Fame" for being in the top 3 consistently for 10 years. It was voted as India's most trusted brand across various categories in the annual survey for Economic Times Brand Equity conducted by Nielsen. Colgate Palmolive was on its way of building on success, it was ranked the 3rd most admired company in India by the global business magazine fortune and management consultancy – Hay Group. (Colgate-Palmolive, 2010)

Colgate Palmolive was a company dedicated to provide with the best oral health solutions to the nation, it launched several innovative new products in the oral care as well as personal care segment. Promoting healthy habits nationwide through its annual national oral health awareness program, these camps were scaled up significantly with wider reach every year. Colgate Caligaurd and Colgate plus toothbrush were the first to receive the Indian Dental Association's seal of acceptance. Overseas, the company operates approximately 280 properties of which 80 are owned in over 70 countries. Major overseas facilities used by the Oral, Personal and Home Care segment are located in Australia (Sydney and the Gold Coast), Brazil, China, Colombia, France, Guatemala, Italy, Mexico, Poland, South Africa, Thailand, Venezuela and elsewhere throughout the world.

Colgate-Palmolive's chief manufacturing plant was located in Burlington, New Jersey, producing all of the fragrance and flavor oils for the company's facilities around the world. The company had numerous subsidiary organizations spanning 200 countries, but it is publicly listed in only two countries, the USA and India.

Ethical Record of Colgate-Palmolive

Colgate's Code of Conduct promotes the highest ethical standards in all of the company's business dealings.[1]Colgate has been benchmarking its performance and is being identified as ethical. Colgate Palmolive has been conferred various awards covering ethics and compliance programs, corporate responsibility including environmental policies and community involvement, and the "culture" of ethics at the firm. (HRA, 2014-07-13) Although once there were recommendations by Ethical Consumer Research Association to its customers suggesting to not buy its products as they were animal testing done. However, Colgate Palmolive was freed of all charges as it emerged out to be one of the first companies recognized by PETA (people for the ethical treatments of animals) under the new 'working for regulatory change' category for companies that test on animals only when mandated by the government regulations and are actively seeking alternatives to animal testing. (Company, Colgate-Palmolive Company Tops PETA's New List Recognizing Companies Working to End Government-Mandated Tests)

Through Colgate's partnership with water for people, over 10,000 people in India and Guatemala now have access to clean water and sanitation system. Colgate as also selected for CDP's Climate Disclosure Leadership Indices, ranked as one of the world's most ethical companies by Ethisphere Institute and was again named to the Dow Jones world and Youth America Sustainability Indices.

Colgate was named No.1 most trusted brand in India by the Economic Times Brand Equity. In 2015, Forbes named Colgate one of the world's most valuable brands, most innovative company among 25 most reputable companies (Colgate-Palmolive, 2013)

COLGATE-PALMOLIVE PATENT BREACH CASE

India foiled an attempt by consumer goods giant Colgate-Palmolive to patent a mouthwash formula containing herb extract by citing ancient texts that show it was traditionally used in ancient medicinal practices. Traditional Knowledge Digital Library of Council of Scientific & Industrial Research (CSIR-TKDL) had submitted proof in the form of references from ancient books, which said the herb and its extracts of Myristica Fragrans were used for oral diseases in Indian systems of medicine. In addition, other third party observations also made submission against the claim.

Indian Patent Office

History of Patent Laws in India can be traced back to 1856, where, Protection of intellectual property was based on the then British Law of 1852. It granted some privileges and rights to the new comers in the field of invention and manufacturing for period of 14 years. The Act was re-worked and after approval from the British Crown, it was introduced as Act XV in 1859. The difference between 'importers' and 'inventors' was well defined.

In 1872, the Act for Patent Laws was consolidated to provide protection rights relation to the design of the inventions and was renamed as "the Patterns and Design Protection Act" under Act XIII of 1872, which was further amended in 1883. For 30 years, the act had been in forced until in 1883, but then changes were made in the patent laws of United Kingdom. These changes were considered as integral, therefore were considered as the basis for modifications made to the Indian Patent Law. Hence, introducing the amended law in 1888. For the first time, Patent administration was brought under the management of the controller of Patents in 1911 with 'the Indian Patents and Design Act II of 1911. The entire above Act were neatly replaced by the particular Act.

Post-Independence, the Indian Judicial system realized the potential of the above act and suggested it needed some robust changes in order to achieve its aim of safeguarding the novelty of inventors. The word 'Licence of Right' was considered so that the controller could grant license to endorsement of patent. However, the Act of 1911continued to be applicable to design, but most of the patent rules were brought in force on April 20, 1972 with publication of the patent rules 1972.

Further changes were amended in the Act, issued in December 1994. The Amended Act provided for filling of applications for the patents in the areas of drugs, pharmaceuticals and agro chemicals though such patents were not allowed. Such applications were examined after December 31, 2004. Meanwhile the applications could be allowed Exclusive Marketing Rights (EMR) to sell or distribute these products in India; subject to fulfillment of certain conditions.

Characteristics

The section 3(d) of the Indian Patent Act encourages the organizations to focus on research invention instead of additional innovation.

Section 3(d) reads as follows:

The mere discovery of a new form of a known substance which does not result in the enhancement of the known efficacy of that substance or the mere discovery of any new property or new use for a known substance or of the mere use of the known process, machine or apparatus unless such known process results in a new product or employs at least one new reactant.

This means; in the clause, different derivatives, combinations salts, metabolites, polymorphs, practical's and their size, mixtures and complexes are considered as the same (through depicted in an interchanged way) until unless the efficacy of the portion/substance differs significantly in its pursuit.

The Indian Patent Office has 75 Patent Examiners, 70 Assistant Controllers, 7 Deputy Controllers, 1 Joint Controller, and 1 Senior Joint Controller, all of whom operate from four branches. Although the designations of the Controllers differ, all of them (with the exception of the Controller General) have equal authority in administering the Patents Act.

Amendment 1

On 26th March, 1999, Patents (Amendment) Act, 1999 came into force retrospective effect from 1st January, 1995. The main amendments are as follows:

Section 5(2) was introduced which provides for filing of applications for patent in the field of drugs, medicines and agro-chemicals. These applications were kept pending in the mailbox or black box. This mailbox was to be opened on 1st January 2005.

Provision of Exclusive Marketing Rights (EMR) was brought in by way of Chapter IV A. Thus, pipeline protection was provided for pharmaceutical and agro-chemical manufacturers whose applications for product were lying in black box.

Section 39 was omitted from the Act, thereby enabling the Indian residents to file the applications for in an outside India simultaneously.

Chapter II (A) was inserted in the Indian Patent Rules dealing with International Applications under PCT.

Amendment 2

The second phase of amendment was brought in by the Patents (Amendment) Act, 2002 which came into force on 20th May 2003. The main features of the amendments included:

1. Term of patent was extended from 14 to 20 years, wherein the date of patent was the date of filing of complete specification. Also, the difference in term of a drug/food patent and other patent was removed.
2. The definition of "invention" was made in conformity with the provisions of TRIPS Agreement by introducing the concept of inventive step, thereby enlarging the scope of invention.
3. Deferred examination system was introduced.
4. Introduction of the provision of publication of application after 18 months from the date of filing thereby bringing India at par with the rest of the world.
5. Microorganisms became patentable, whereas inventions relating to traditional knowledge were included in the list of *"what are not inventions"*.
6. The concept of unity of invention in accordance with EPC and PCT.
7. Section 39 was reintroduced thereby prohibiting the Indian residents to apply abroad without prior permission or first filing in India.
8. Provisions of Appellate Board were brought in by inserting section 116. All appeals to the decision of the Controller would be appealable before the Appellate Board. The Head Quarter of the Appellate Board is to be in Chennai.
9. Section 117 provided for Bolar provision for the benefit of agrochemical and pharmaceutical industry.

Amendment 3

The third and final amendment to the Patents Act, 1970 came by way of Patents (Amendment) Ordinance, 2004, which was later replaced by The Patent (Amendment) Act, 2005, and Patents (Amendment) Rules, 2006 with retrospective effect from 1st January, 2005. With the third amendment India met with the international obligations under the TRIPS. Significant achievements of this amendment were:

Deletion of section 5, opening of mailbox and grant of product patents. Thus, this amendment led to the dawn of the "product patent regime" in India.

Abolition of Exclusive Marketing Rights (EMR).

CURRENT POSITION

By creating a robust intellectual property structure, a high-quality job future can be secured and sustained. Therefore, promotion to innovation/invention requires adequate protection. According to reports, published by Global Intellectual Property Center (since 2012) India has been persistently lacking as compared to its counterparts of emerging economies. (ABC, 2014)

The Patent (Amendment) Act 2005, and Patent (Amendment) Rules 2006, India is taking positive steps to make the intellectual property highly effective and has brought its laws in line with agreement on Trade Related Aspects of Intellectual Property Rights (TRIPS).

Patent Requirements

Specifically, patented inventions must meet three characteristics: novel, useful and not obvious

- **Novel:** Being the foremost and first requirement of the invention to be patentable. The invention has to be an outcome of a pioneering research. The product/process must prove to be something which has different constitution elements, composition altogether. Just by discovering an innovative way of using the existing product/process in a different situation does not make it a patentable invention. Often, we see this as an example in the pharmaceutical world where, the existing drug or known composition can be used for treating a completely different disease.
- **Useful:** The invention must ensure its usability or be an objective of reality and must perform the act for which it has been invented.
- **Not Obvious:** It should be clearly evident that the invention is not prevailing in any form similar to something existing in order to be patentable.

Procedure for Grant of Patent in India

The first step to secure one's invention is to fill the application in the Indian Patent Office. A set of forms can be submitted online as well as in a true copy state (additional 10% fee is charged). The most important part of the procedure is drafting of patent specifications, one must be professionally skilled in patent laws as well as have technical knowledge. After submission of the forms, patent application number is allotted to the applicant. This may take up to 18 months from the priority date. Another option is by filling 'Form 9'; patent specifications can be published within one month from filling it. This gives the inventor rights of the patent but it is enforceable only after the patent is granted.

Further, 'Form 18' is a request application for examination of the patent. The examination will be done on its foremost criteria of novelty, inventiveness and industrial application based on which a first examination report (FER) shall be sent to the applicant.

Rule 24B (4) (ii) says, that within 12 months of the FER the applicant must respond to the objections raised by the examiner. Based on the satisfactory response the controller has the power to grant the application. This application will record a serial number, which will be accorded to patents under Indian Patent's Act 1970 (39 of 1970).[2]

Figure 1.

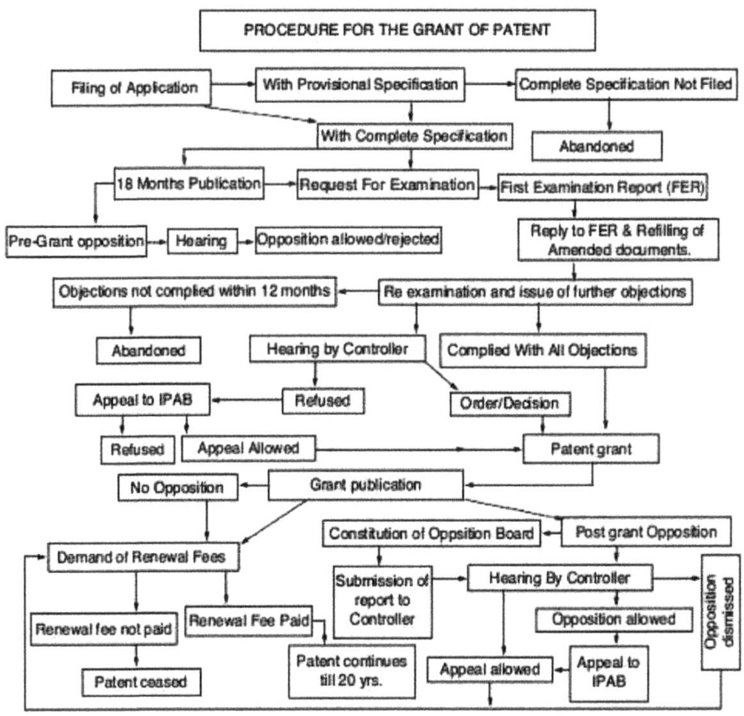

The Following Is Not a Patentable Invention

An invention of a method for the treatment of the human or animal body by surgery or therapy, or of a diagnosis practiced on the human or animal body. An invention that could encourage offensive, immoral or anti-social behavior, even if it satisfies the key criteria for patents.

COLGATE PALMOLIVE PATENT

The application for patent was filled by Colgate Palmolive which claimed the adequacy of the mouthwash formula. The application stated the formula offered enhanced taste, good whitening solution and upgraded teeth whitening agent such as hydrogen peroxide (H2O2); in consolidation with citric acid and phosphoric acid (H3PO4) respectively. Few other combinations added to the solution are sucralose and saccharin, an acidic polymer alkali, pyrophosphate salts, copolymers of maleic anhydride and methyl vinyl are one or more anti-calculus agents which were aligned.

Claims

Claim 1: The first claim made by Colgate Palmolive was the mouthwash solution is a composition of whitening agent in a significant amount. The split up of the whole combination shows the use of one peroxy compound, with combination of one or more whitening agent added to it. Further supplemented with two acids, first one being PKa of 4.5 and the second acid belong to a selected group of chloric acid, hydrochloric acid, nitric acid, phosphoric acid, sulfuric acid and sulfurous acid combined.

Claim 2: In accordance to Claim 1, the mouth was solution talks about the numerical composition of the two acids which are present along with the whitening agent i.e., hydrogen peroxide is 0.01-5%. The first acid has a PKa of 4-5. The second acid has a PKa 1.5-2.5 and PKa of 6.5-7.5 respectively.

Claim 3: It suggests the combination of citric acid and phosphoric acid as first and second acid respectively.

Claim 4: Conceded with any prior cases in mouthwash solution, the ratio present citric acid to phosphoric acid is present in 1:1 to 1:10.

Claim 5: In accordance to cases before in a mouth wash solution the significance of phosphoric acid is from 0.01 to 1.5%.

Claim 6: In accordance to the cases before in a mouth wash solution the significance of citric acid is from 0.01 to 0.5%.

Claim 7: A further combination of polymer which are preferred from poly-carboxyl ate polymers and polyvinyl methol ether/maleic anhydride (PVME/MA) copolymers. This combination is different from cases of any other mouthwash formula.

Claim 8: From diakali or tetralkali metal pyrophosphate salts they have selected an anti-calculus – effective amount of one or more pyrophosphate salts which claimed to be different from any of the prior cases of mouth wash solution.

Claim 9: In accordance to the claim made the mouthwash solution slew comprised of saccharin and sucralose.

Claim 10: A blend of menthol and methyl salicylate is claimed to be in accordance to the mouthwash solution in any prior claims.

Claim 11: In accordance to the claims previously, additional combination comprises of an anti-bacterial agent which is preferred from triclosan and cetylpyridinium chloride.

Claim 12: In addition to any of the previous cases the mouth wash formula comprises of the following components of concoction. Water 60-80% Polyphosphate salt 1.1-3%, Non-saccharide sweetener 0.01-0.05%, Saccharide sweetener 0.001-0.005%, Organic acid 0.6-2.0%, Polyhydric alcohol (humectants) 7-45%, Surfactant 0.5-2%, Whitening agent 0.5-5%, Flavorant 0.2-2%.

Claim 13: The mouthwash according to claim 13, which comprises: TABLE-US-00007 Water 60-80%, TSPP **0.**1-1%, TKPP 1-2%, Sodium saccharin 0.01-0.05%, Sucralose 0.001-0.005, Phosphoric acid 0.5-1.5%, Citric acid 0.1-0.5%, Humectants 0.1-0.5%, Surfactant 0.1-0.5%, Hydroxide peroxide 0.5-5%, Flavor 0.02-2%, PYME/MA (e.g. Gantrez ®) 1-2%.

Claim 14: A method of whitening teeth comprising administering a mouthwash according to any of the preceding claims to the oral cavity of subject in need thereof. Use of a mouthwash according to any of claims 1-14 in the manufacture of a medicament is for the whitening of teeth.

CASE BACKGROUND

As plutocratic western world gets saturated, the developing countries are seen as new promenades to earn larger profits and therefore are targeted with robust strategy. Deceptive western marketing style often commandeers the traditions of the developing world. The multinational giant Colgate- Palmolive can be seen caught up into legal dispute where accusation is over the company for having purloined an archaic formula to have its roots to ancient times, and also being used by Indians for generations. (Colgate Keeps Triclosan in Its $1B Total Brand, 2011)

Figure 2. Patent applications year on year from 2005 till 2015

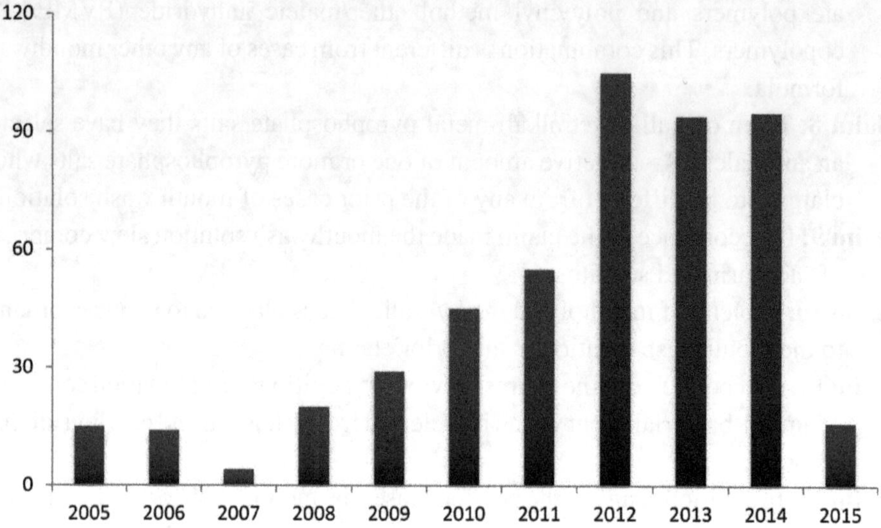

In June 2010, the MNC Colgate – Palmolive patented a formula called 'Red Herbal Dentifrice' in USA. The company called it to be the ultimate formula for solving dental problems and expected India to be a huge market for it. The ingredients of the formula were clove oil, camphor, black pepper3 and spearmint. These ingredients are the ones which have been used by the Indians as a solution to tooth problem for generations. (Today, 2006)

President of Association of Manufacturers of Ayurvedic Medicines (AMAM), Mr. Devender Triguna accused the tooth mixture of having ingredients to be classical in Ancient India. As claimed by the AMAM group, this formula has nothing new to offer Indians except for a fancier packaging. Thus, do not favor the patenting of it. Every common Indian household has used the formula as traditional remedy to dental problems.

The AMAM group has requested the government of India to intervene in the matter and question the organization to justify the patent. It was brought to public notice by the AMAM group that if the patent was not appropriately justified, it will be an example and open doors for other western organizations to ravage many other traditional formulas as their own in a modernized way. This will give the western organizations huge profits despite they are only manufacturing but invention dates back to ancient times.

Once the issue was raised, the organization Colgate – Palmolive has been in questions but no response has been received, according to WOFL FOX 35 report. (Reuters, 2011) The only response considered was the claim made by Colgate i.e., they have used an ingredient different from the ancient Indian formula. The claim that they have used Red Iron Oxide (a type of mineral) which is a groundbreaking invention for the toothpaste industry.

Free flow of knowledge has always been essential for the growth of a society. With the country becoming digital, Indian officials has worked towards setting of a 34 million web page. These webpages will document the ancient text which legitimately belongs to the country. It will help in preventing the foreign MNC to extract our traditional formulas to medicinal material without compensating the indigenous people and country. Colgate – Palmolive's pursuit to one such similar desire was obstructed by India, where the conglomerate wished to patent the mouth wash formula that accommodated herbs forever known and used by Indian folks. India had presented sufficient argument from ancient documents to verify the authenticity of these practices in India.

India has actively been creating the Traditional Knowledge Library (TKDL) for the decade. A battle for patent at the European Patent Registration Office was fought for almost 7 years when Colgate – Palmolive claimed a toothpowder formula in September 2008 encompassing extracts Indian common kitchen herbs which included cinnamon—often referred to as dalchini in India. The petition was strongly opposed by the Indian government. As a strong database had been maintained and presented b the Council of Scientific and Industrial Research (CSIR) in May 2011.

By mid-2015, judgment was drawn in favor of India by the European patent office. In 2010, Colgate – Palmolive filled its second application to the European patent office. It wanted to safeguard another composition which comprised of nutmeg, ginger, 'Bakul' tree, camphor, long pepper, Neem, and Clove. This mixture claimed to be a treatment to oral problems and diseases.

By June 2014, TKDL challenged the application for second patent. Sufficient evidences were shown to the patent office examiner. Many ancient texts were cited which clearly quoted the use of these particular extracts for the same oral problem as mentioned by Colgate. Hence, the plea filled by Colgate was rejected once again by European patent Office by March 2015.

The first case against Colgate was initiated in the tenure of Mr. V.K. Gupta, a former director of the TKDL group in CSIR. The Indian government has analyzed that 1500 cases have been target to Bio-Piracy. Strong actions have started being taken. Out of the 1500 cases identified, approximately 200 cases have been scrutinized by patent examiners and India has won 180 cases among them.

Yet another application was submitted in 2011 by the MNC to patent a composition claiming to be a pioneering solution to oral problems. This composition claimed to contain extracts from Myristica Fragrans or Nutmeg. Although the application for this patent has been withdrawn by the organization in 2015.

TKDL observed and accorded notified the used of Myristica Fragrns which dated its use in ancient civilization of the country. The fragrans alone or when combined in some mixture it proved to be useful to eliminate bad breath, it made teeth stronger, gingivitis was curable, fissures of the tongue and palate, excess salivation to name a few of oral problems. (Palmolive)

This herb has also been used in Indian medicine to solve problems like dryness of the mouth and different disease of Pharynx, lips, tongue and teeth.

MyristicFragrans is considered as a brilliant solution to its oral troubles and ample conformation can be testified in printed books of ayurveda'schakara-samhita (1000 BC, 4th Century) and books of unani, Qarabaadeen-Najm-al-Ghani (20th Century AD). The roots of this scintillating tree run widely from India and south East Asia to North Australia and Pacific islands. Sporadically it is refined to be used as a spice, often known as aril (mace) and seed (nutmeg).

The digital database, was devised and invigorated when India won a successful IPR battle on haldi (turmeric), neem and basmati rice. The database was equipped with texts from Ayurveda, Unani and Siddha formulations. These comprised of various medicinal properties of herbs in India.

DEFAULTS IN PATENT REGISTRATION

WIPO

World Intellectual Property was created for one goal i.e., to provide benefits to everyone with an efficient and accessible intellectual property system. It is one of the 17 exclusive agencies of the United Nations. WIPO is headquartered in Geneva, Switzerland and has currently 189 member states.

WIPO was created with aim to 'promote the protection of intellectual property throughout the world'. WIPO acknowledges the importance of Traditional Knowledge in one's culture. It has an intergovernmental committee which focuses on Intellectual property of Traditional Knowledge and folklore. Traditional Knowledge is understanding the skill and practices which have been constant in the society. These are well maintained and travelled through generations. These work as key ingredients in forming the cultural and spiritual identity.

Traditional Knowledge

Though inventions which are on the basis of Traditional Knowledge can be patented, or even preserved in variety of ways such as geographical indication protection, or protected as a trade secret but if that knowledge is wide/ orally known or has its references in ancient texts then it cannot be patented. For this organization must present robust information to get the invention patented. However, there is no definition which has been accepted at an international level. Another default we see when issue narrow's down to Traditional Knowledge, the policy framed are quite broad and diverse.

The two types of Intellectual property protection being popularly sought are:

- **Defensive Protection:** By defensive protection we cite to the strategies that protect the Traditional Knowledge from the third parties and they do not gain illegitimate IP rights. To ensure the above statement amendments have been continuously made in the WIPO administered patent system.

Further, to safeguard the Traditional Knowledge, countries are actively working on making a database which can be used as an evidence to put the claim for patent as a failed effort. WIPO has been of assistance to all its member states by providing them toolkit and practical assistance for creating and documenting their Traditional Knowledge.

- **Positive Protection:** Positive protection means granting of rights that empower communities to promote their conventional and traditional knowledge, control its uses and wrongfully benefit from its commercial exploitation. A few uses of conventional knowledge can be protected by the existing intellectual property system, and many countries have also developed specific legislation. However, any specific protection that is under national law may not hold for other nations, a reason why many indigenous and local communities and governments have been pressing for an international legal instrument.

In 2008, the intergovernmental committee had an intercessional review process during which certain gap analyses was done. For the same comments were invited from the accredited observers of the member states. These comments were, basically related to 2 broad concerns.

- The protection of Traditional Cultural Expression
- The protection of Traditional Knowledge

Specific technical and legal questions raised while addressing the Gap are:

- What form of protection is intended and what rights should be granted
- Who would own the rights and who would benefit from them
- What are the exceptions and limitations
- Should the rights operate retroactively
- How should the foreign rights be treated

Issues when discussed needed to be clear on the broader economic, cultural and social objectives. The biggest challenge is whether to address gaps at international, regional, national and or local levels?

There are also several initiatives underway to file traditional knowledge. In most cases the aim is to preserve or disseminate it, or to use it, for instance, in environmental management, instead of for the purpose of legal protection. Also, the documentation protects traditional knowledge, say, by giving a confidential or secret record of traditional knowledge reserved only for the relevant community. A few formal documentation and registries of traditional knowledge support the *sui generis* protection systems, while other traditional knowledge databases like India's database on traditional medicine play a defensive role in the protection within the current IP system. Such examples demonstrate the importance to ensure the documentation of traditional knowledge is linked to an intellectual property strategy and does not occur in a policy or legal vacuum.

Genetic Resources

Functional units of hereditary which are found in plants, animals, microbial in nature, their genetic material may be of some value. This is referred to as Genetic Resources. Since these resources are found in the nature and cannot be claimed as human creation so these resources cannot be patented. However, if some invention or completely different variety is created based on the genetics already found in universe then that innovation may be patented. IP has strongly been takes into consideration with respect to Genetic Resources. For the benefit sharing and access to knowledge WIPO has been working closely with Convention on Biological Diversity(CBD) and its Nagoya Protocol and the International Treaty on plat genetic Resources for food and Agriculture of the United Nations food and Agriculture Organization.

WIPO has consistently been working on strengthening its issues of negotiations on international legal instruments. At present 2 major points of discussion are:

- **Defensive Protection of Genetic Resources:** This work aims to prevent patents from being granted over genetic resources (and associated traditional knowledge) which do not fulfill the current requirements of being novel and inventive.
- "Bio piracy" is sometimes loosely used to describe biodiversity-related patents that do not meet patentability criteria or that do not comply with the CBD's obligations – but this term has no precise or agreed meaning.
- **Disclosure Requirements:** A number of countries have enacted domestic legislation putting into effect the CBD obligations that access to a country's genetic resources should depend on securing that country's prior informed consent and agreeing to fair and equitable benefit sharing. WIPO members want to make it mandatory for patent applications to show the source or origin of genetic resources, as well as evidence of prior informed consent and a benefit sharing agreement.

Complete disclosure must be made giving the evidence of the source of origin of the genetic resources, evidence of benefit sharing etc.

Traditional Cultural Expression: Folklore

Traditional Cultural Expression is entirely different from the Traditional Knowledge. It is a form or a method in which the Traditional Culture is expressed. It acts as a part of the society or a community where expression has been in practice for centuries. Expression of culture can be in wide variety of forms, for example – dance, songs, handicraft, tales etc.

The protection of Traditional Culture has certain aim:

- It must recognize values, folklore and creativity must benefit the cultural community and in large must benefit humanity.
- It must promote respect for traditional folklore. It must recognize the value and respect the community that has preserved and maintained the expression.
- IP rights must present misusage of the traditional culture of expression.
- Innovation and creativity can be boosted by preserving the Traditional Culture.

Folklore have been created centuries ago and passed down through generations. The purpose was simple i.e., to contribute to economic development, reassure cultural diversification and preserve the heritage in a community. Different forms that exist are copyrights, geographical indications, appellation of origins, etc. If the folklore has been recognized as legitimate, then that particular community may use it for free.

One of the major reasons for the non-implementation of provisions stated by many developing countries is that there is often no attempt to recognize an ownership right in folklore by a community.

When we speak in special reference to India. India is a place of contrast between cities of skyscrapers, atomic power plants, all sorts of modern technology and small tribal/village settlements.

The tribal/village settlements prove India's rich and preserved heritage in various forms like craft, art, various languages, beliefs etc,. For a culture that is so vivid and vast, a robust legal framework where the concern of giving ownership rights to whom and benefit sharing must be clearly stated. (Associates)

Also, the acute lack of awareness is a big default, they lack the awareness about copyrights act and more importantly the performer's rights. Under the Copyright Act in 1994, a certain amount of protection is offered to the performers. However, the act does not provide any provisions of protection of folklore. Article 29 of the constitution recognizes as a 'fundamental right' (Part III) the protection of the cultural minorities.

Controversies Related to IPRs

Although, Convention on Biological Diversity provides for access and sharing of biological resources on one hand and Trade Related Aspects of Intellectual Property Rights provides for exclusion of plant and animal material from patenting, yet, there has been a spurt in the arena of IPRs, which periodically give rise to controversies. Some such controversies are as given below:

- The patenting of ancient herbal remedies, for instance, the US Patent (No. 5,401,504) given to the healing properties of turmeric, known for centuries to Indians.
- The US Plant Patent (No. 5751) on the "Ayahuasca Plant", which is considered sacred and used for medicinal purposes by Amazon's indigenous people.
- The patenting of crop varieties whose name is similar to those grown for centuries in certain geographical areas, for instance, the term Basmati used by US Firm Rice-Tec Corporation (Patent No. 5,663,484). The term Basmati is used for certain varieties of rice grown in Northern India.
- The patenting of human genetic material, for instance, on the human cell line of Hagahai tribesmen from Papua New Guinea (US Patent No. 5,397,696).

Outcomes of the Colgate-Palmolive Case

The rejection of this patent by the European Patent Office comes as a major milestone in the Intellectual Properties legal space. There are direct short term and long-term implications on the future of international patenting laws and the related stakeholders.

Impact on Colgate

For a start, Colgate-Palmolive are struck with quite a blow, losing their chance to patent the formula, which has a direct impact on their product and market strategy. The company's plan had been to ride on the success of the mouthwash formula to gain a competitive advantage over other players, which has been foiled now. Colgate-Palmolive will now have to think of some alternative and innovative strategy to keep its hold over the mouthwash segment of the oral care market. This patent if granted would have allowed Colgate to introduce some new variety to its mouthwash product portfolio and cater to the increasingly health conscious consumers.

Impact on Other Companies

This judgment also serves as a deterrent for any third party to blindly copy the traditional Indian recipes, and make profits on an already used medicine. Not only India, but many civilizations had their own traditional healing methods and formulas, which are still being used in places around the world. Multinationals will always try to capitalize through such methods, and a case like this will now force them to think rationally before trying to patent such formulas.

Role of TKDL

Intellectual Property Law's and protection of Traditional Knowledge has recently drawn attention worldwide. This has laid emphasis on protecting the cultural heritage and favoring appropriate measures to protect it for the benefit of the Society. Traditional Knowledge is not a person's invention but information gathered and passed from generation. Importance of traditional Knowledge and preserving it in an extremely systematic way was acknowledge at international level along with the Colgate- Palmolive Case.

The Indian community was much appreciated at International level for enduring a pioneering initiative of creating a Traditional Knowledge from being misused. The success of creating TKDL by India was widely covered in newspapers, television and Scientific journals. In 2003, The director General, WIPO appreciated India's efforts and recognized India's exemplary initiative.

India's medical Knowledge is widely available in local languages such as Sanskrit, Hindi, Urdu, Arabic, Tamil, etc., it was not accessible by the patent examiners at International Patent Offices to examine the claims. TKDL has successful in scientifically converting and structuring up to 0.29 million medical formulation from ancient text. With help of information technology tools text on Ayurveda, unanimedicine, siddha, etc., have been converted not only in English but Japanese, French, German and Spanish as well. It acts as an impeccable link between this rare collection of knowledge and the International Patent Examiner.

TKDL is made available to nine International Patent offices and access agreement ensures protection of India's interest against any possible misuse. Hence, the impact is widely visible. Approximate 200 patent applications by the pharmaceutical companies from USA, UK, Spain, Italy, etc., have either been withdrawn or amended because of the evidences present in TKDL for no cost. Hence it not only saved time bit lots of money as well.

Owing to the growing success of TKDL, the TK-rich countries have displayed their interest in creating a similar platform to safeguard their cultural Knowledge. Interestingly, agreeing to it WIPO in collaboration with CSIR and DIPP (Ministry of Commerce and Industry) has organized an "International study visit to TKDL" for 19 nations who displayed their interest in replicating the TKDL model.

The nation is quite confident that there is still a body like Traditional Knowledge Digital Library which will not let our ancient medicines and herbs be used by foreign companies for their profit, without a putting up fight. It is not only for this case, but Traditional Knowledge Digital Library has been active in fighting many patents of a similar nature, where traditional Indian knowledge was being put forth as an invention by some foreign companies. (Taplin & Nowak, 2010)

GLOBALIZATION OF PATENT LAW

The component globalization, laws, and Intellectual Property together form a complex structure. There are different viewpoints related to patenting of it. Some views them as one's creativity but some view them as tools to serve economic and monopolistic interest, while largely it feels it is not much significant in the digital era of free and easily available information.

The term globalization is used boarded. Big corporate to refer the free flow of information regardless. With this case of Colgate – Palmolive we can understand the moneymaking strategy devised based on information from one part of the world and redeem benefits in another. The proactivness of Indian community to safeguard its traditional knowledge obstructed the profit-making strategy of the company. This incident proves thoughts about how big corporations evade the local knowledge from some part of the world, patent it and gulp down all the profit based on that knowledge without even acknowledging the contribution of that community.

Impact on FMCG Market

In a broader view, considering the Fast-Moving Consumer Goods segment, the patent and trademark laws are very significant in driving the future market growth. With technological advances, there is less differentiation among the product varieties, so companies look for any alternative to gain a competitive advantage, and trying to leverage the ancient knowledge and wisdom of various civilizations is one of the ways the industries are trying to increase their market share.

Opinions on the Case

It is observed that in a minimum span of two years, in Europe alone, the country has achieved success in bringing about a situation for cancellation or withdrawal of about 36 applications to patent our traditionally inherited medicinal formulations. The key to the success of protecting our traditional formulations has been driven by Traditional Knowledge Digital Library (TKDL), a database made to incorporate a variety of medicinal formulations in multiple languages. This is a tool that has helped the officials who examine patents in searching and relating the formulations documented in different languages. TDKL serves as a massive data silo for traditional medical wisdom India has. This tool also has ensured the connection of linguistic gap between the knowledge that is traditional, documents in languages such as Sanskrit, Urdu, Arabic, Persian and Tamil which are directly used in the intellectual property offices in the country. As previously discussed, this tool has evolved as a critical assistant to prevent any traditional value hijack from the country.

The only country to have set up a formal institutional mechanism, the TKDL to ensure protection of its traditional knowledge. The system enables regular, fast and almost negligible fee for cancellation or withdrawal of patent applications relation to our country's traditional knowledge.

There have been enough instances where various traditional knowledge has been hijacked under disguises. The MNCs should understand the impact of such a decision would have on the company in the country. These companies should have involved in long-term and short term plans to incorporate traditional values through the formal approach and paying royalty and legally be clean.

These misappropriations were clearly seen with EPO (European Patent Office) allowing an American company and the US dept. of Agriculture (USDA)to patent hydrophobic Neem oil in 1994. This granted was opposed in 1995 by international NGOs and delegates of prime Indian farmer associations stating that India realized the medicinal properties of Neem many hundred years ago. Then subsequent revoking and challenging until when EPO rejected the challenge made by the American company and USDA in 2006.

The impact of these issues on the consumer sentiments related to Colgate-Palmolive is very less. As these cases discussed are generally not completely exposed or made comprehensible to the public. The ultimate information, i.e. rejected or approved, is only valued at the customer end.

Had the product been launched it would have definitely improved the status of Colgate-Palmolive in the oral care market as the company holds about 40- 50% of Indian oral care markets. The company considering its stature should have involved more R&D and formally registered the oral mix. It has been observed that the average R&D investment amongst Indian industries is about 0.7% which is considered generally very low according to the international standards. The incompetency amongst markets and the patents laws that are inclined towards protectionism has caused this lack of R&D investments. This phenomenon is prevalent in the pharmaceutical market.

The case correlates with defensive protection of genetic resources, which aim at preventing patents being granted over resources, which do not fulfill the existing requirements of novelty and inventiveness. This case is a classic example of the defensive protection of traditional knowledge and genetic resources. The herb extract, which is being patented for a mouthwash formula contains a variety of nutmeg. This herb, as claimed by the TKDL, is already a known Indian traditional cure for oral diseases since ancient civilization. TKDL submitted a restraining application against Colgate-Palmolive's patent application. With the help of supporting proofs, in the form of ancient Indian texts, TKDL was able to prove that the patent application is not an invention, and consequently the patent application was rejected.

REFERENCES

Australian Broadcasting Corporation ABC. (2014, March 11). Body Shop withdraws products from China over animal testing.

Choudhary, K., & Ritiraj. (n. d.). *India: The Trickle Down Effect of Product Patent India and On The Developing World.* Singh and Associates.

Colgate-Palmolive. (2010, June 26). *Legal/Privacy.* Retrieved from http://www.colgate.co.in/app/Colgate/IN/Corp/LegalPrivacy.cvsp

Colgate-Palmolive. (2013, February 21). *Form 10-K, Annual Report.* Retrieved March 27, 2013, from secdatabase.com

Colgate-Palmolive Company. (n. d.). *Colgate-Palmolive Company Tops PETA's New List Recognizing Companies Working to End Government-Mandated Tests.* Retrieved May 31, 2012, from peta.org

Colgate-Palmolive Company. (n. d.). *Legal/Privacy*. Retrieved from http://www.colgate.co.in/app/Colgate/IN/Corp/LegalPrivacy.cvsp

Duggan, M., Garthwaite, C., & Goyal, A. (2014, September). *The Market Impact of Pharmaceutical Product Patents in Developing Countries Evidence from India.* Stanford.

HRA. (2014, July 13). *Choosing Cruelty Free.* Human Research Australia.

Knowmore. (n. d.). Colgate-Palmolive. Retrieved Feb 25, 2009 from knowmore.org

Neff, J. (2011). Colgate Keeps Triclosan in Its $1B Total Brand. *Adage*. Retrieved from http://adage.com/article/news/colgate-triclosan-total-toothpaste-brand/148408/

Reuters. (2011, March 23). Colgate buys Sanex from Unilever for $940 million. United States of America. Retrieved from http://www.reuters.com/article/colgate-unilever-idUSL3E7EN1Z920110323

Spring, C. (2012, February 23). *NIOSH and NHCA present 2012 Safe-in-Sound Excellence in Hearing Loss Prevention Awards.* Retrieved from Centers for Disease Control and Prevention: https://www.cdc.gov/niosh/updates/upd-02-23-12.html

Taplin, R., & Nowak, A. Z. (Eds.). (2010). *Intellectual Property, Innovation, Management in Emerging Economies*. London, New York: Routledge Taylor and Francis Group.

USA Today. (2006, March 22). Colgate expands reach of quirky toothpaste.

WBIR. (2008, July 3). Colgate-Palmolive plant in Morristown goes green. Retrieved February 25 2009 from http://www.wbir.com/news/local/story.aspx?storyid=55329

Chapter 11
Various Tools Available to Access Patent Information in India

Teena Bagga
Amity Business School, India

Shinu Vig
Amity Business School, India

ABSTRACT

The 21st century has seen the emergence of global economy where world has moved from information to knowledge. Innovation and Creativity indeed has become the necessity for organizations to gain competitive advantage. The sustenance of this competitive advantage requires the protection of Intellectual Property (IP) which an individual or an organization possesses. In order to protect their Intellectual Property, Innovators needs to apply for patents. A patent which is an exclusive right granted for an invention needs to be novel. Hence, one of the important steps in patent filing process is "searching", which is very much required to see whether the concept or product has been already patented and publicly made available before claiming the originality. To get a patent, technical information about the invention must be disclosed to the public in a patent application. This information is available from both free and fee-based sources across globe. This chapter attempts to presents different databases and tools available in India for Patent Search.

DOI: 10.4018/978-1-5225-2414-4.ch011

Copyright © 2017, IGI Global. Copying or distributing in print or electronic forms without written permission of IGI Global is prohibited.

INTRODUCTION

If you are in need of patent information what will you do? What are the tools available for obtaining patent information in India? These are some of the questions, the answers to which have become more important especially in a country like India which is growing at a rapid pace. A Patent is a protected innovation right, identifying with developments and is the concede of restrictive right, for constrained period, gave by the Government to the patentee, in return of full revelation of his creation, for barring others, from making, utilizing, offering, bringing in the licensed item or process delivering that item for those reasons. The main motivation behind this framework is to empower creations by advancing their assurance and use in order to add to the improvement of ventures, which thusly, adds to the advancement of mechanical development and to the exchange and spread of innovation. In easier words, we can say, a patent is a legal monopoly granted for a limited time to the owner of an invention, this way it empowers the owner of an invention and prevent others to manufacture, use, import or sell the patented invention.

India is a major market with a population of 1.21 billion people (2011 census), the second most populous country in the world and is a rapidly growing economy (Amit, Binal, & Sandhya). The number of patents being filed in India is increasing year by year, from 1st April 2015 – 31st March 2016, no of Application filed in India were 44258 and number of Patent granted were 5890 only! (PatSeer, 2016).

Figure 1. Number of patents applied and granted in India
Source: thelogicalindian.com/news/government-launches-imprint-india-to-encourage-research-know-about-the-initiative

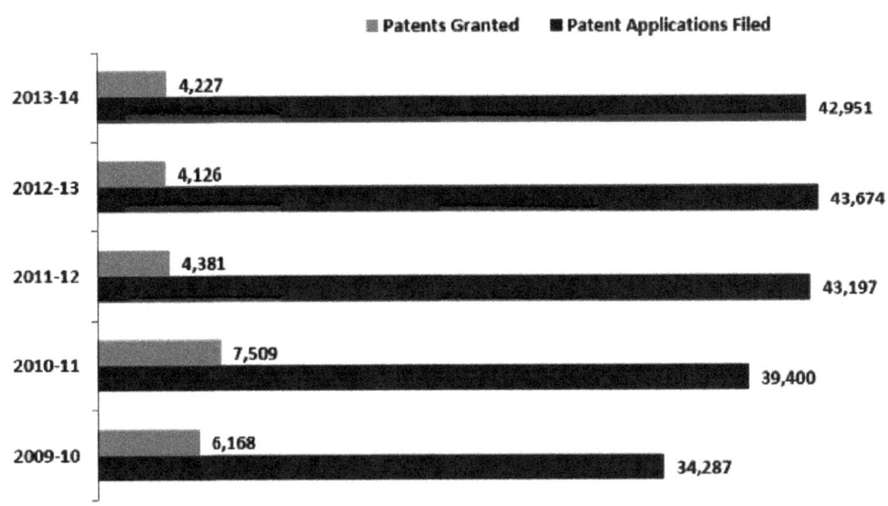

Patent right is regional in nature and a patent got in one nation is not enforceable in other nation. Hence, the innovators/their trustees are required to record isolate patent applications in various nations for getting the patent in various nations. Thus the necessity of robust sources from where information about various patents can be obtained has increased manifold.

PATENT INFORMATION

Patent information today is available from both free and fee-based sources across globe. These sites allow users to search and retrieve patents for that authority and often, other countries. A search of a country's official Web site sometimes yields the most thorough results for that authority's pending and issued patents. Unfortunately, in India, government Web site may not be well suited for advanced searching as a fee-based service is essential for the professional searcher.

The best sources available for Indian Researchers/Innovators are:

1. Websites, which provide extensive coverage of International and National patent documents such as *patentscope.wipo.int.* by World Intellectual Property Organization.
2. Some other major sources for patent information in India include various intellectual property firms.
3. In addition, a good option is website like anov.com that helps in patent validation and then help in filing a patent too.
4. 'Google patents' also, is a favorite place for applicants where lot of free information is available.
5. Every organisation too has its own IP cell so even that can be a source of information.
6. Patent attorneys or advocates in patent office likewise act as intermediaries to provide the patent information.

In the recent past, patent information services have undergone a huge revolution, and it's still continuing. The detailing aspect of available patent literature is becoming larger, with growing availability of full-text records content for main emerging markets and, with the intense support of machine translation, greater access to these records in English. Simultaneously, public access to the primary patent content and information from global patent offices has opened gates of the market to new entrants and increased pressure on the incumbent players to continuously add value with new tools and premium services. Now, a basic shift in the method that intellectual property is maintained in the corporate world is driving further innovation.

Applying for patents has traditionally been a defensive, tactical activity aimed at minimizing risk, but, increasingly, the intellectual property portfolio is seen as a strategically important bonus to be actively leveraged and exploited. At the heart of both existing and emerging patent information services is the patent research and analysis platform.

PATENTABILITY SEARCH

Prior to filing an application for any patent, patentability searches are performed to determine whether the concept or product has been patented and publicly made available, as a published work, anywhere in the world before a determined date that might be relevant to a patent's claims of originality. A patentability search is predominantly required to either determine ways to pursue patent protection without treading on an unknown prior work. Basic criterions such as novelty and obviousness are focused upon while searching as the invention part is already an essential prerequisite for any patent. One should avoid being either in a hurry or so short sighted and reluctant towards the facts and carefully organize and study the search results. In simple words, Patent search is the process by which prior inventions or ideas are examined, with the goal being to find information that bears close similarity to a given patent or proposed invention.

The motives for performing a patent search are many. Though, the primary reason is to determine whether or not the invention has already been patented i.e for the novelty, the other reasons can be classified into three stages and they are:

1. **Pre Patent Filing:**
    a. To determine the originality by Innovator or Consultant
    b. For writing patent applications.
    c. Learn more about inventions in the area of interest.
2. **During Patent Processing:**
    a. To determine the originality by Patent Examiner
    b. Avoid patent infringement
3. **Post Patent Filing:**
    a. Understand competition
    b. Competitor tracking
    c. To invalidate the granted patent

Hence before discussing and comparing various databases to access patent information, the understanding of search methodology used by these data bases is must. The documents which are searched during a patent search generally include:

1. List of already granted Indian, U.S. and other foreign patents databases.
2. Various published patent applications
3. Non-patent literature, such as the Web
4. Related product literature
5. Numerous scientific journals and databases.
6. Trade journal articles Publications (including data books and catalogs)
7. Public discussions (conference and seminar)
8. Trade shows
9. Brochures of various Products, devices & equipment.

PATENT SEARCH TYPES

There are various different types of patent searches, and each of these require different search strategy. These different types are (Vinita, 2012):

1. Patentability searches (also called novelty searches)
2. Infringement searches (also called Clearance, Freedom to Operate, or Right To Use searches)
3. Validity searches (also called Invalidity, or Enforcement Readiness searches),
4. State of the Art searches (also called Collection searches).

The most basic and primary search is originality/novelty search which is referred as a Patentability Search. Whenever an inventor invents something which he is interested in patenting, the patenting search is conducted to check if anyone has beforehand invented something alike to determine whether the invention is original, valid and can be patented.

There are no date constraints in patentability searches i.e., if you find prior art that reads on the invention, it does not matter whether the prior art is from yesterday or 100 years ago – it is relevant. The reason behind is that according to patent law: Anything that has already been disclosed to the public, in any manner, at any time, cannot be patented. Patentability searches are constrained upon time, budget and on the public availability of information. One should search patents and published applications for patents in all major patent offices and countries.

What to be searched in a Patentability Search? – Full text specification and claims of granted patents and published patents from all major patent offices of the world (World wide database). So, in patentability searches one should search

- Full patent specifications (Although the specifications provided might be pretty lengthy. Also, it might be possible that they may serve only as a minor reference for defining the terms that are mentioned in the claims. Quite frequently, it has been observed that patent applicants attempt to question limitations of their own specifications included into their own claims.)
- Claims (Although the claims are merely interpreted under the specifications and limitations risen from the application of them and are not read into the claims. Hence, the wording of the claim, as mentioned, and the way it could be interpreted basically define the scope of the invention and remain as the enforceable part of a patent.)
- Technical and non-technical publications (such as product brochures etc.)

Under infringement searches the objective is clearly to compare written claims as a set against the claims of relevant and in-force patents. Hypothetical claims could be drafted via a written description. Patent claims are subjected to the subject matter of disclosure and can depending on hypothetical or relevant the claim may be. Searches must be directed towards the claims and patent documents of various countries and patent authorities. The scope should be broader.

Though patents almost every time offer exclusive rights to the patent holders, but they do not exactly provide the right to practice the invention in an environment where another patent constitutes the claimed subject.

A validity search is conducted in order to generate the evidence that patents were granted erroneously due to either overlooking or the concealment of the facts about the prior art during the examination process. These searches are then looked upon as the potential infringement of patents or potentially profitable business opportunity. In validity searches one should search for claims or drawings of patents based on whether they are utility patents or design patents respectively.

Under Clearance searches, which are required in order to avoid ant alleged infringements while using, making or selling a process or any product, organizations seek assurance regarding business decisions enforced and buttressed by patent information in public domain. For this a clearance opinion, forecasting the infringement potential of a patent's claims, is drafted.

Clearance search is broader than infringement search as the search is more worldwide rather than region specific for the technological claim. Need for licensing and free use are to be checked.

These searches determine:

- Who else has been practicing the same literature at some other nation
- Existence of multiple patenting and hence validity of patents.
- Information regarding potentially unexploited markets

One can consider clearance searches as a blend of patentability and encroachment in terms of the broadness of patent and non-patent writing that needs to re-seen, and in addition consideration that you ought to provide for enforceable patent claims. Unless generally coordinated, the expert clearance searches include an audit of worldwide licenses and distributed patent applications, both lapsed and unexpired, and all accessible non-patent writing. The target is to realize what exists in people in public domain and, in this way, is allowed to utilize.

Under the "State-of-the-Art Searches", the searcher does not concentrate on a solitary innovation, however, collects all references that identify with a characterized technical field. At the point when assembled, the specialized references ought to mirror the present "condition of the craftsmanship." The hunt as a rule results in an expansive arrangement of references. The broadness and profundity of the hunt rely on upon how nearly the technology was characterized

These are conducted when:

- To determine direction of the research activities
- Marketing of technology
- Assisting them with licensing activities
- Assist patentability opinions

Under the "State-of-the-Art Searches", one needs to search:

- Global patents
- Published patent applications
- Conduct patent landscape searches

One exceptionally complete best in class pursuit is a 'patent landscape' study. The patent landscape inquiry is a more profound investigation of patent and non-patent references after culmination of the best in class. The study regularly brings about the categorization of patents into key disclosures versus incremental changes, a visual presentation of patenting after some time periods, the history of an innovation's improvement, and even examinations of inventor collaborations. The patent landscape study may further distinguish key creative bunches over characterized durations of time.

The patent landscape study helps in:

- Monitoring markets of interest
- Identify gaps and enhance your innovative work
- Determine which of your forthcoming patents will have noteworthy business esteem
- Confirm which innovations are currently in the general population area
- Better comprehend current contenders and recognize future ones

INDIAN PATENT STRUCTURE

Patent Application filed in Indian Patent have following structure:

- Title of invention
- Name of applicant(s) nationality and address
- Name of inventor(s), nationality and address
- Preamble of application
- Field of invention
- Background of Invention
- Object of invention
- Summary of Invention
- Detailed description
- Claims
- Figures (if any)
- Abstract

After 18 months of filling patent application, Patent Office publish the application in the Patent office journal having the following details (Patent Office Patent Office, 2016):

- Application Number
- Date of Application
- Date of Publication
- Title Of Invention of International Patent Classification (IPC)
- Name and Address of The Applicant
- Name of Inventors or Priority Details (if any)
- Abstract

Patent Search of Indian patents can be possible using by using any of above mentioned field. Using above mentioned fields one can search Indian Patents from the Indian Patent office database which is available free online. However, certain more details are there which are not available online and hence are non-searchable fields. To access these additional details (mentioned below), full text of patent articles need to be purchased from patent office.

- Field of invention
- Background of Invention
- Object of invention
- Summary of Invention
- Detailed description
- Claims
- Figures (if any)

PATENTS SEARCH TOOLS

Numerous databases both free and paid are available for accessing patent information. Free databases provide basic information, whereas paid databases provide facilities like Data mining, Data Processing & Data Analysis. In addition, paid databases facilitate "Patent Landscape Search". Some of the databases are detailed below:

Indian Patent Office

The Indian Patent Office is one of the important tools which provide access to patent information in India. Controller General of Patents, Designs and Trade Marks i.e., CGPDTM administers the Indian Patent Office (Intellectual Property India, 2016). Designs, Indian law of Patents and Trade Marks are administered by this office. The main advantage of it is that it is very user friendly and it provides search facility for two types of databases:

- Indian patent application published after 18 months (but yet not granted) from 1st January 2005 onwards.
- Indian Patents granted from 1st January 1912 onwards.

In addition, it also provides search facility according to the particular patent office [i.e. Delhi, Mumbai, Chennai, Kolkata or All]. But it does not provide search for detailed description or claims and provides search for limited field only for published as well as granted Indian Patent application. [viz. title, date of filing, date of publication, name of applicant, name of inventor, Abstract etc.]

Big Patents India

Big patents India is one of the tools to access patent information. If one can think about what Big Patents India is: It was an open searchable database of "post-TRIPS India's patent applications and patents already issued", that was introduced by the website bigpatents.com, Patrick Crosby of XB Labs and Bhaven Sampat from Columbia University in the Mailman School of Public Health. By using proprietary algorithms developed by XB Labs, the bulk of data was parsed from Indian patent journals first came in January 2005 (Basheer, 2007). Hand coding by Digital Divide Data, a non-profit social enterprise is done for the data that is not parsable through programming by offering data entry services. But this tool is no longer available from November 2012 (Intellogist).

NIC

One more tool which provides access to patent information in India is National Informatics Centre. The National Informatics Centre (NIC) of India is an organisation in Science and Technology of Union Government of the India in Information-and-Communication-Technology (ICT) applications and Information services (NIC). NIC is also a part in the department of Electronics and Information Technology in the Indian Ministry of Communications and Information Technology. It plays a major role in steering the applications of e – governance in the departments of government at national, state and at district levels. It also enables improvement in wider transparency of the government services. And almost all the Indian-government websites are developed / managed by NIC. The NIC also publishes E-Governance named as Patent Informatics which is a sub category under Informatics, in both print and PDF format. This publication is available at Informatics website.

MCPaIRS

In recent times, in accordance with the rising demands and needs of the growing international patent market in which India is an improving player with modern technology, Molecular Connections (an information solutions company which was founded by professionals who have expertise in drug-discovery, IP, publishing and IT), introduced an online solution named MCPaIRS (MCPaIRS). It is a full-text access to Indian patent applications and also to grant patents, as well as legal information with a pretty good user-friendly interface. MCPaIRS offers its services in free as well as charging on basic, regular, and premium subscription models. Users can hereby sign up via any of the above methods and they have to fill a request form for the trial access of the site. The main advantages of MCPaIRS are:

- This database provides extensive XML having records of full-text granted Indian patents and patent in the application stage. (over 300,000 Indian patent applications and granted patents)
- Legal status information for each of the patents is also included within each document.
- The database is updated weekly.
- Backup files having data of full-text Indian patent s from 2000-2011. Front files, since 2012 and onwards are updated.
- Bibliographic information provided for Indian patent applications and granted patents in database since 1981-1999
- Regional language such as Hindi & international language such as French or Chinese language patents are translated by internal translators for easy reference. For this many English synonyms are also added to regional terms present inside the patent
- Legal status data for the patents
- Here more than 1.7 million drawings in TIFF format are provided.

MCDESiGN

MCDESiGN is an extensive collection of well crafted, user friendly, fully searchable knowledgebase of Design patents of India. Mcdesign is used by a diverse set of users namely from science, engineering or commerce background for scientific, technical and business based purposes. To get access to the database one needs to sign up in the link provided on the home page to register for the MCDESiGN database. MCDESiGN updates itself in every seven days.

MCDESiGN offers their users many different methods for conducting a search on their site. The simplest of them all is done by the “Expert Search box” on the MCDESiGN homepage (MCDESiGN).

TKDL

Though not a patent information system, TKDL is a database representing the rich heritage of India in the field of medical care. The need for TKDL was felt after the CSIR- "Council of Scientific and Industrial Research" of patents had to file a case in which the patents on turmeric (US Patent No. 5401540), neem (EPO Patent No, 0436257) and basmati were revoked. Although the case was won, it took 2 years for the cancellation of the patent for turmeric and 5 years for that of Neem.

INDIA due to its ancient heritage has a vast amount of information related to various fields which are transmitted through expressions in the form of poems, music, drams, cooking habits etc. In relation to medicine, India is ranked 7th in pant diversity and about 95% of the medicinal products being used in INDIA are plant based.

It was found that Grant of wrong patents at international level was occurring mostly due to nonexistence of information, or in cases information was available it was in a form that couldn't be accessed by an outsider. As a result, it was estimated that leading up to year 2001 about 2,000 patents relating to Indian medicinal systems had been granted around the world.

Consequently, a task force was formed comprising of specialists from CCRAS, Banaras Hindu University, IT experts from National Informatics Centre (NIC) as well as scientists of CSIR.

The TKRC is modelled on WIPO's International Patent Classification. It consists of some 27,000 different subgroups for Ayurveda and yoga; for example in the case of Ayurveda, the information has been retrieved from fifteen well known Ayurvedic books which are being referred at undergraduate and postgraduate level courses in Ayurveda and are also well-known to Ayurvedic practitioners. The information has also been translated into different languages like English, French, German, Japanese and Spanish.

Agreements were signed with EPO in February 2009, with United Kingdom Trademark & Patent Office and with the U.S. Patent and Trademark Office (USPTO) in January 2010 for sharing this data. India has access agreements with the patent offices of Australia, Canada, and Germany. Negotiations are also on-going with the patent offices of New Zealand and Japan where agreement in principle has already been reached. Since July 2009, 215 patent applications relating to Indian medicinal systems against which information is available in TKDL have been identified. Of these 36 have already been rejected and it is expected that some 179 cases that are currently in the balance will either be rejected by the EPO or will be withdrawn by the applicants. A study has shown that at the EPO there has been a decline of forty-four in the number of patent applications filed concerning Indian medicinal systems, particularly related to medicinal plants. What this translates to is that with patent examiners around the world getting access to the TKDL database, all those cases of unethical patent claims, which had taken years and also incurred expenditure for each case can now be avoided.

Since 2008 attempts are being made to include in the database 1,500 postures in yoga. The need for taking such a step was felt because many reports of false gurus trying to patent this ancient knowledge in their own countries were brought to light. For example, in 2007 as many as 131 yoga related patents were traced in the US alone. As a result, the government of India took up the issue with the USPTO. After that, a team of yoga gurus from nine schools working with government officials and 200 numbers of scientists from the CSIR scanned 35 ancient texts including the Hindu epics, the Mahabharata and the Gita, and Patanjali's Yoga Sutras to register each pose. Till date more than 1500 asanas have been added (General Knowledge Today, 2013).

So far India, the only country, has set up an institutional mechanism like TKDL to protect its information. Many other countries like Mexico, Srilanka and Brazil have taken a cue from this initiative to safeguard traditional knowledge and information in their countries.

iPAIRS/InPASS

The Indian Patent Information Retrieval System was a free search portal launched by the Indian Patent Office. IPAIRS (Intellogist, n. d.). allowed a search to be conducted in all the Indian Patents and Patent Applications. This system however didn't allowed users to perform a full-text search. The Patent Office hence developed a new search tool, InPASS. InPASS, "Indian Patent Advanced Search System", is a new facility for patent search; it was launched on 27th February, 2015. It allows a full-text search to be conducted in all the Indian Patents and Patent Applications (Intepat IP Services Pvt. Ltd.). Numerous functionalities have been improved in this advanced search system. With this, the IPAIRS, the Indian Patent Information Retrieval System that was launched in 2010 has now officially been withdrawn. The Controller General of Patents, Designs and Trademarks (CGPDTM), has been working towards improving the procedures in Indian patent office. INPASS (BananaIP Counsels) supports wild-cards, truncation as well as Boolean operators in all the fields of the ST.36 compliant data available with the Patent Office, thereby enabling the stakeholders to conduct an advanced search in the Indian Patent Database.

MCPaIRS

MCPaIRS is another subscription-based Indian patent full-text database created by Molecular Connections Ltd. This pioneering Indian Patent Database, addresses the need of having a searchable, enriched and indexed full text Patents published from India. The data is hand-curated by domain experts and provided in an easy to use web interface. Data coverage starts from 1912 to till date. This database provides XML records of full-text granted patents and patent application, along with legal status information. This database is updated weekly. It provides two different search forms. Quick Search where Users can enter keywords or phrases, or users can create more complex queries utilizing field prefixes, Boolean operators, proximity operators, and wild card operators. The Quick Search therefore doubles as both a keyword search form and a command-line interface. Whereas Advanced Search allows users to enter keywords or dates in text boxes associated with specific fields. Available fields include title, abstract, full text, applicant(s), inventor(s), filing date, grant date, priority date, patent number, application number, publication number, and IPC code. Boolean operators may be used within the fielded forms. The Results are displayed with query details and number of results included above the results list. Keywords are highlighted in the results list, and the title, application/patent numbers, applicants, inventors, and an abstract are listed for each result. From the results page, users can: Filter results by year, select individual or multiple results via check box to be exported (CSV or HTML format), Select to order individual results, Select the result title to load the full-text page and Select to view the legal status for individual results (mcpairs)

EKASWA A, B, and C Databases

These are the first Indian patent searchable databases available in CD-ROM and Web. This First Indian Patent Searchable Database Ekaswa is a set of three separate databases, Ekaswa A, Ekaswa B, and Ekaswa C, available through the Patent Facilitating Centre (PFC) Technology Information, Forecasting, and Assessment Council. The "PFC Technology Information, Forecasting and Assessment Council was set up by the Indian Department of Science and Technology to provide patent information to promote research and development, and to monitor developments in the area of [intellectual property rights] for policy makers, scientists, industry, etc." According to the PFC website, the three databases consist of (Patent Facilitating Centre):

Ekaswa A: "Patent applications filed in India as published in the issues of the Gazette of India (Part III, Section 2) from January 1995 to December 2004." Within the Ekaswa A Database, searchable fields include Application Number, Applicant, Title, Date of Filing, Gazette Date, Convention Date, Convention Country, Convention (Yes, No, or Any), and Class (General, Chemicals, Drugs, Electrical, Electronics, Materials, or Mechanical). Results can be sorted by Date of Filing, Title, or Applicant.

Ekaswa B: "Patent applications notified for opposition in the Gazette of India (Part III, Section 2) published from January 1995 to December 2004." Within the Ekaswa B Database, searchable fields include Patent Number, Application Number, Applicant, Title, Inventor(s), Gazette Date, and Opposition Office, Results can be sorted by Patent Number, Title, or Applicant.

Ekaswa C: "Patent applications published in official Journal of Patent office published from January 2005 onwards." Within the Ekaswa C Database, searchable fields include Application Number, Applicant, Title, Inventors, Date of Filing, Journal Date, Priority Date, Priority Country, and Priority (Yes, No, or Any). Results can be sorted by Patent Number, Title, or Applicant.

INPAT

The Intellectual Property Management Division (formerly Patents Unit) was set up at CSIR Headquarters at the very inception of the Council in 1942. Division has also excelled in establishing in-house patent search systems; it developed a computerised database on Indian patents (INPAT) for the first time in the country and has also acquired an international patent database on microfiche. INPAT contains bibliographic information in respect of patents published under the Indian Patents Act, 1970, i.e., from the year 1972 onwards. This database is being updated regularly. INPAT is also available on-line through SIRNET.

INPAT is a bibliographic database, which provides information on 52,624 patents granted in India during 1975-2002. The information on a patent in the database comprises: patent title, applicant(s) name(s), inventor(s) name(s), patent number, application number, application date, publication date, international classification code, and country. The database can be searched by various parameters including keyword(s) from title, applicant(s) name(s), inventor(s) name(s), patent number, subject code or subject, application number, application date, publication date, country, and any combination of the above parameters (NISCAIR).

REFERENCES

Amit, G., Binal, V., & Sandhya, T. (n. d.). Indian economy. *Incredible India*. Retrieved from http://www.iseindia.com/pdf/Sample%20Economic%20Report%20on%20Indian%20Economy.pdf

Banana IP. (n. d.). Patent: InPASS: New Patent Full-Text Search Tool from IPO. Retrieved October 29, 2016, from http://www.bananaip.com/ip-news-center/inpass-new-patent-full-text-search-tool-from-ipo/

Basheer, S. (2007). Big patents arrive in India!! First useful patent database. *SpicyIP*. Retrieved 10 23, 2016 from http://spicyip.com/2007/03/big-patents-arrive-in-india-first.html

General Knowledge Today. (2013). *Traditional Knowledge Digital Library (TKDL)*. Retrieved 10 20, 2016, from http://www.gktoday.in/tkdl/

Gujarat Technological University. (n. d.). Patent Search Methodology.

Intellectual Property India. (2016). Retrieved from http://www.ipindia.nic.in/

Intellogist. (n. d.). India BigPatents. Retrieved 10 25, 2016, from http://www.intellogist.com/wiki/India_BigPatents

Intellogist. (n. d.). IPairs. Retrieved 10 29, 2016, from http://www.intellogist.com/wiki/IPairs

Intepat IP Services Pvt Ltd. (n. d.). How to Conduct Patent Search in India? Retrieved 10 28, 2016, from https://www.intepat.com/blog/patent/conduct-indian-patent-search/

MCDESiGN. (n. d.). About MCDESiGN. Retrieved 10 27, 2016, from http://www.mcdesign.co.in/home.do

MCPaIRS. (n. d.). About MCPaIRS. Retrieved 10 27, 2016, from http://mcpairs.com/app/Mcpairs.jsp

NIC. (n. d.). Patent Granted Years 2012-2013 to 2014-2015. Retrieved 10 24, 2016, from http://www.dbtindia.nic.in/patents-granted-year-2012-2013/

NISCAIR. (n. d.). Information Products. Retrieved 10 30, 2016, from http://www.niscair.res.in/aboutus/AnnRep05/Information%20Products.pdf

Patent Facilitating Centre. (n. d.). Free Online Access to First Indian Patent Searchable Database. Retrieved 10 29, 2016, from http://pfc.org.in/db/db.htm

Patent Office Patent Office. (2016). Official Journal Of The Patent Office (41/2016). Retrieved from http://www.ipindia.nic.in/writereaddata/Portal/IPOJournal/1_383_1/Part1.pdf

PatSeer. (2016). India patent trends for 2015-2016. Retrieved 11 29, 2016, from http://patseer.com/2016/07/india-patent-trends-for-2015-2016/

Vinita, J. (2012). Types of patent searches. Retrieved 10 29, 2016, from http://birac.nic.in/webcontent/pat1.pdf

Related References

To continue our tradition of advancing information science and technology research, we have compiled a list of recommended IGI Global readings. These references will provide additional information and guidance to further enrich your knowledge and assist you with your own research and future publications.

Aas, I. H. (2013). Improving patient safety with telemedicine: Exploring organizational factors. In A. Moumtzoglou & A. Kastania (Eds.), *E-health technologies and improving patient safety: Exploring organizational factors* (pp. 56–70). Hershey, PA: Medical Information Science Reference; doi:10.4018/978-1-4666-2657-7.ch004

Aboelfotoh, M. H., Martin, P., & Hassanein, H. (2013). Ubiquitous multimedia data access in electronic health care systems. In D. Tjondronegoro (Ed.), *Tools for mobile multimedia programming and development* (pp. 191–227). Hershey, PA: Information Science Reference; doi:10.4018/978-1-4666-4054-2.ch011

Abreu, J. F., Almeida, P., & Silva, T. (2013). iNeighbour TV: A social TV application to promote wellness of senior citizens. In R. Martinho, R. Rijo, M. Cruz-Cunha, & J. Varajão (Eds.), Information systems and technologies for enhancing health and social care (pp. 1-19). Hershey, PA: Medical Information Science Reference. doi:10.4018/978-1-4666-3667-5.ch001

Aceti, V., & Luppicini, R. (2013). Exploring the effect of mhealth technologies on communication and information sharing in a pediatric critical care unit: A case study. In J. Tan (Ed.), *Healthcare information technology innovation and sustainability: Frontiers and adoption* (pp. 88–108). Hershey, PA: Medical Information Science Reference; doi:10.4018/978-1-4666-2797-0.ch006

Adami, I., Antona, M., & Stephanidis, C. (2014). Ambient assisted living for people with motor impairments. In G. Kouroupetroglou (Ed.), *Disability informatics and web accessibility for motor limitations* (pp. 76–104). Hershey, PA: Medical Information Science Reference; doi:10.4018/978-1-4666-4442-7.ch003

Adeyemo, O. (2013). The nationwide health information network: A biometric approach to prevent medical identity theft. In I. Management Association (Ed.), User-driven healthcare: Concepts, methodologies, tools, and applications (pp. 1636-1649). Hershey, PA: Medical Information Science Reference. doi:10.4018/978-1-4666-2770-3.ch081

Åkerberg, A., Lindén, M., & Folke, M. (2013). Pedometer cell phone applications and future trends in measuring physical activity. In R. Martinho, R. Rijo, M. Cruz-Cunha, & J. Varajão (Eds.), *Information systems and technologies for enhancing health and social care* (pp. 324–339). Hershey, PA: Medical Information Science Reference; doi:10.4018/978-1-4666-3667-5.ch021

Al Hamouche, V. (2014). Making quality control decisions in radiology department: A decision support system for radiographers' performance appraisal using PACS. In C. El Morr (Ed.), *Research perspectives on the role of informatics in health policy and management* (pp. 48–61). Hershey, PA: Medical Information Science Reference; doi:10.4018/978-1-4666-4321-5.ch004

Al-Khudairy, S. (2014). Caring for our aging population: Using CPOE and telehomecare systems as a response to health policy concerns. In C. El Morr (Ed.), *Research perspectives on the role of informatics in health policy and management* (pp. 153–166). Hershey, PA: Medical Information Science Reference; doi:10.4018/978-1-4666-4321-5.ch010

Albuquerque, C. (2013). The study of social needs as a strategic tool for the innovation of the social care sector: The contribution of new technologies. In M. Cruz-Cunha, I. Miranda, & P. Gonçalves (Eds.), *Handbook of research on ICTs for human-centered healthcare and social care services* (pp. 347–365). Hershey, PA: Medical Information Science Reference; doi:10.4018/978-1-4666-3986-7.ch018

Alexandrou, D. A., & Pardalis, K. V. (2013). SEMantic PATHways: Modeling, executing, and monitoring intra-organizational healthcare business processes towards personalized treatment. In A. Moumtzoglou & A. Kastania (Eds.), *E-health technologies and improving patient safety: Exploring organizational factors* (pp. 98–123). Hershey, PA: Medical Information Science Reference; doi:10.4018/978-1-4666-2657-7.ch007

Algarín, A. D., Demurjian, S. A., Ziminski, T. B., Sánchez, Y. K., & Kuykendall, R. (2014). Securing XML with role-based access control: Case study in health care. In A. Ruiz-Martinez, R. Marin-Lopez, & F. Pereniguez-Garcia (Eds.), *Architectures and protocols for secure information technology infrastructures* (pp. 334–365). Hershey, PA: Information Science Reference; doi:10.4018/978-1-4666-4514-1.ch013

Alhaqbani, B., & Fidge, C. (2013). A medical data trustworthiness assessment model. In I. Management Association (Ed.), User-driven healthcare: Concepts, methodologies, tools, and applications (pp. 1425-1445). Hershey, PA: Medical Information Science Reference. doi:10.4018/978-1-4666-2770-3.ch071

Almeida, L., Menezes, P., & Dias, J. (2013). Augmented reality framework for the socialization between elderly people. In M. Cruz-Cunha, I. Miranda, & P. Gonçalves (Eds.), *Handbook of research on ICTs for human-centered healthcare and social care services* (pp. 430–448). Hershey, PA: Medical Information Science Reference; doi:10.4018/978-1-4666-3986-7.ch023

Amer, M. B., Amawi, M., & El-Khatib, H. (2013). A novel neural fuzzy approach for diagnosis of potassium disturbances. In J. Tan (Ed.), *Healthcare information technology innovation and sustainability: Frontiers and adoption* (pp. 208–218). Hershey, PA: Medical Information Science Reference; doi:10.4018/978-1-4666-2797-0.ch013

Andersen, S. T., & Jansen, A. (2013). Innovation in ICT-based health care provision. In J. Tan (Ed.), *Healthcare information technology innovation and sustainability: Frontiers and adoption* (pp. 58–72). Hershey, PA: Medical Information Science Reference; doi:10.4018/978-1-4666-2797-0.ch004

Angjellari-Dajci, F., Lawless, W. F., Stachura, M. E., Wood, E. A., & DiBattisto, C. (2013). Economic evaluations for service delivery in autism spectrum disorders: benefit-cost analysis for emerging telehealth systems. In M. Cruz-Cunha, I. Miranda, & P. Gonçalves (Eds.), *Handbook of research on ICTs and management systems for improving efficiency in healthcare and social care* (pp. 16–42). Hershey, PA: Medical Information Science Reference; doi:10.4018/978-1-4666-3990-4.ch002

Archibald, D., MacDonald, C. J., Hogue, R., & Mercer, J. (2013). Accessing knowledge from the bedside: Introducing the tablet computer to clinical teaching. In C. Rückemann (Ed.), *Integrated information and computing systems for natural, spatial, and social sciences* (pp. 96–109). Hershey, PA: Information Science Reference; doi:10.4018/978-1-4666-2190-9.ch005

Archondakis, S. (2013). Static telecytological applications for proficiency testing. In V. Gulla, A. Mori, F. Gabbrielli, & P. Lanzafame (Eds.), *Telehealth networks for hospital services: New methodologies* (pp. 228–239). Hershey, PA: Medical Information Science Reference; doi:10.4018/978-1-4666-2979-0.ch015

Arling, P. A., Doebbeling, B. N., & Fox, R. L. (2013). Improving the implementation of evidence-based practice and information systems in healthcare: A social network approach. In J. Tan (Ed.), *Healthcare information technology innovation and sustainability: Frontiers and adoption* (pp. 247–270). Hershey, PA: Medical Information Science Reference; doi:10.4018/978-1-4666-2797-0.ch016

Arriaga, P., Esteves, F., & Fernandes, S. (2013). Playing for better or for worse?: Health and social outcomes with electronic gaming. In M. Cruz-Cunha, I. Miranda, & P. Gonçalves (Eds.), *Handbook of research on ICTs for human-centered healthcare and social care services* (pp. 48–69). Hershey, PA: Medical Information Science Reference; doi:10.4018/978-1-4666-3986-7.ch003

Arslan, P. (2014). Collaborative participation in personalized health through mobile diaries. In K. Rızvanoğlu & G. Çetin (Eds.), *Research and design innovations for mobile user experience* (pp. 150–181). Hershey, PA: Information Science Reference; doi:10.4018/978-1-4666-4446-5.ch009

Assis-Hassid, S., Reychav, I., Pliskin, J. S., & Heart, T. H. (2013). The effects of electronic medical record (EMR) use in primary care on the physician-patient relationship. In M. Cruz-Cunha, I. Miranda, & P. Gonçalves (Eds.), *Handbook of research on ICTs for human-centered healthcare and social care services* (pp. 130–150). Hershey, PA: Medical Information Science Reference; doi:10.4018/978-1-4666-3986-7.ch007

Azar, A. T. (2013). Overview of biomedical engineering. In I. Management Association (Ed.), Bioinformatics: Concepts, methodologies, tools, and applications (pp. 1-28). Hershey, PA: Medical Information Science Reference. doi:10.4018/978-1-4666-3604-0.ch001

Azar, A. T., & Eljamel, M. S. (2014). Medical robotics. In I. Management Association (Ed.), Robotics: Concepts, methodologies, tools, and applications (pp. 1116-1147). Hershey, PA: Information Science Reference. doi:10.4018/978-1-4666-4607-0.ch054

Baladrón, C., Aguiar, J. M., Calavia, L., Carro, B., & Sánchez-Esguevillas, A. (2014). Learning on the move in the web 2.0: New initiatives in m-learning. In *K-12 education: Concepts, methodologies, tools, and applications* (pp. 1693–1714). Hershey, PA: Information Science Reference; doi:10.4018/978-1-4666-4502-8.ch097

Bauer, K. A. (2013). Caught in the web: The internet and the demise of medical privacy. In I. Management Association (Ed.), User-driven healthcare: Concepts, methodologies, tools, and applications (pp. 1252-1272). Hershey, PA: Medical Information Science Reference. doi:10.4018/978-1-4666-2770-3.ch063

Belsis, P., Skourlas, C., & Gritzalis, S. (2013). Secure electronic healthcare records management in wireless environments. In M. Khosrow-Pour (Ed.), *Interdisciplinary advances in information technology research* (pp. 202–219). Hershey, PA: Information Science Reference; doi:10.4018/978-1-4666-3625-5.ch015

Benito, R. V., Vega-Colado, C., Coco, M. B., Cuadrado, R., Torres-Zafra, J. C., Sánchez-Pena, J. M., & López-Miguel, A. et al. (2013). New electro-optic and display technology for visually disabled people. In M. Cruz-Cunha, I. Miranda, & P. Gonçalves (Eds.), *Handbook of research on ICTs for human-centered healthcare and social care services* (pp. 687–718). Hershey, PA: Medical Information Science Reference; doi:10.4018/978-1-4666-3986-7.ch036

Bergenti, F., Poggi, A., & Tomaiuolo, M. (2013). Using multi-agent systems to support e-health services. In M. Cruz-Cunha, I. Miranda, & P. Gonçalves (Eds.), *Handbook of research on ICTs for human-centered healthcare and social care services* (pp. 549–567). Hershey, PA: Medical Information Science Reference; doi:10.4018/978-1-4666-3986-7.ch029

Berler, A., & Apostolakis, I. (2014). Normalizing cross-border healthcare in Europe via new e-prescription paradigms. In C. El Morr (Ed.), *Research perspectives on the role of informatics in health policy and management* (pp. 168–208). Hershey, PA: Medical Information Science Reference; doi:10.4018/978-1-4666-4321-5.ch011

Bernardi, R. (2013). Information technology and resistance to public sector reforms: A case study in Kenya. In I. Management Association (Ed.), User-driven healthcare: Concepts, methodologies, tools, and applications (pp. 14-33). Hershey, PA: Medical Information Science Reference. doi:10.4018/978-1-4666-2770-3.ch002

Bernhard, S., Al Zoukra, K., & Schtte, C. (2013). From non-invasive hemodynamic measurements towards patient-specific cardiovascular diagnosis. In *Data mining: Concepts, methodologies, tools, and applications* (pp. 2069–2093). Hershey, PA: Information Science Reference; doi:10.4018/978-1-4666-2455-9.ch106

Best, C., O'Neill, B., & Gillespie, A. (2013). Assistive technology for cognition: Enabling activities of daily living. In M. Cruz-Cunha, I. Miranda, & P. Gonçalves (Eds.), *Handbook of research on ICTs for human-centered healthcare and social care services* (pp. 112–129). Hershey, PA: Medical Information Science Reference; doi:10.4018/978-1-4666-3986-7.ch006

Bhattacharya, P., Asanga, A. P., & Biswas, R. (2013). Stomodeum to proctodeum: Email narratives on clinical problem solving in gastroenterology. In I. Management Association (Ed.), User-driven healthcare: Concepts, methodologies, tools, and applications (pp. 1073-1091). Hershey, PA: Medical Information Science Reference. doi:10.4018/978-1-4666-2770-3.ch054

Boboc, C., & Ţiţan, E. (2014). Migration of medical doctors, health, medical education, and employment in eastern and central Europe. In A. Driouchi (Ed.), *Labor and health economics in the Mediterranean region: Migration and mobility of medical doctors* (pp. 158–191). Hershey, PA: Medical Information Science Reference; doi:10.4018/978-1-4666-4723-7.ch007

Botella, C., Baños, R. M., Etchemendy, E., Castilla, D., García-Palacios, A., & Alcañiz, M. (2013). An e-health system for promoting wellbeing in the elderly: The butler system. In I. Management Association (Ed.), User-driven healthcare: Concepts, methodologies, tools, and applications (pp. 838-852). Hershey, PA: Medical Information Science Reference. doi:10.4018/978-1-4666-2770-3.ch042

Bradai, N., Chaari, L., & Kamoun, L. (2013). A comprehensive overview of wireless body area networks (WBAN). In J. Rodrigues (Ed.), *Digital advances in medicine, e-health, and communication technologies* (pp. 1–32). Hershey, PA: Medical Information Science Reference; doi:10.4018/978-1-4666-2794-9.ch001

Brown, K. E., Bayley, J., & Newby, K. (2013). Serious game for relationships and sex education: Application of an intervention mapping approach to development. In S. Arnab, I. Dunwell, & K. Debattista (Eds.), *Serious games for healthcare: Applications and implications* (pp. 135–166). Hershey, PA: Medical Information Science Reference; doi:10.4018/978-1-4666-1903-6.ch007

Brown, M. (2013). Will comparative effectiveness research lead to healthcare rationing? In I. Management Association (Ed.), User-driven healthcare: Concepts, methodologies, tools, and applications (pp. 1487-1507). Hershey, PA: Medical Information Science Reference. doi:10.4018/978-1-4666-2770-3.ch074

Burlamaqui, A. M., Azevedo, S. O., Silva, I. R., Silva, S. R., Souto da Silva, G. H., & Benjamim, X. C. … Felix de Castro, A. (2013). Low cost t-health and t-social with ginga: Experience with mime TV, ImFine, and iFunnyCube interactive TV programs. In M. Cruz-Cunha, I. Miranda, & P. Gonçalves (Eds.), Handbook of research on ICTs for human-centered healthcare and social care services (pp. 303-318). Hershey, PA: Medical Information Science Reference. doi:10.4018/978-1-4666-3986-7.ch015

Burns, J., Blanchard, M., & Metcalf, A. (2013). Bridging the digital divide in Australia: The potential implications for the mental health of young people experiencing marginalisation. In *Digital literacy: Concepts, methodologies, tools, and applications* (pp. 772–793). Hershey, PA: Information Science Reference; doi:10.4018/978-1-4666-1852-7.ch040

Buyurgan, N., Rardin, R. L., Jayaraman, R., Varghese, V. M., & Burbano, A. (2013). A novel GS1 data standard adoption roadmap for healthcare providers. In J. Tan (Ed.), *Healthcare information technology innovation and sustainability: Frontiers and adoption* (pp. 41–57). Hershey, PA: Medical Information Science Reference; doi:10.4018/978-1-4666-2797-0.ch003

Cabrita, M. D., & Cabrita, M. (2014). Applying social marketing to healthcare: Challenges and opportunities. In A. Kapoor & C. Kulshrestha (Eds.), *Dynamics of competitive advantage and consumer perception in social marketing* (pp. 78–97). Hershey, PA: Business Science Reference; doi:10.4018/978-1-4666-4430-4.ch004

Carroll, J. M., & Rosson, M. B. (2013). Community networks: Infrastructure and models for therapeutic support. In M. Cruz-Cunha, I. Miranda, & P. Gonçalves (Eds.), *Handbook of research on ICTs for human-centered healthcare and social care services* (pp. 187–207). Hershey, PA: Medical Information Science Reference; doi:10.4018/978-1-4666-3986-7.ch010

Castiglioni, I., Gilardi, M. C., & Gallivanone, F. (2013). E-health decision support systems for the diagnosis of dementia diseases. In A. Moumtzoglou & A. Kastania (Eds.), *E-health technologies and improving patient safety: Exploring organizational factors* (pp. 84–97). Hershey, PA: Medical Information Science Reference; doi:10.4018/978-1-4666-2657-7.ch006

Catley, C., Smith, K., McGregor, C., James, A., & Eklund, J. M. (2013). A framework for multidimensional real-time data analysis: A case study for the detection of apnoea of prematurity. In A. Gangopadhyay (Ed.), *Methods, models, and computation for medical informatics* (pp. 16–35). Hershey, PA: Medical Information Science Reference; doi:10.4018/978-1-4666-2653-9.ch002

Chaari, L., & Kamoun, L. (2013). QoS concepts and architecture over wireless body area networks for healthcare applications. In J. Rodrigues (Ed.), *Digital advances in medicine, e-health, and communication technologies* (pp. 114–130). Hershey, PA: Medical Information Science Reference; doi:10.4018/978-1-4666-2794-9.ch007

Chamberlin, B., Maloney, A., Gallagher, R. R., & Garza, M. L. (2013). Active video games: Potential for increased activity, suggestions for use, and guidelines for implementation. In S. Arnab, I. Dunwell, & K. Debattista (Eds.), *Serious games for healthcare: Applications and implications* (pp. 191–212). Hershey, PA: Medical Information Science Reference; doi:10.4018/978-1-4666-1903-6.ch009

Charisi, A., Korvesis, P., & Megalooikonomou, V. (2013). Similarity searching of medical image data in distributed systems: Facilitating telemedicine applications. In A. Gangopadhyay (Ed.), *Methods, models, and computation for medical informatics* (pp. 58–77). Hershey, PA: Medical Information Science Reference; doi:10.4018/978-1-4666-2653-9.ch004

Chattopadhyay, A., Malhotra, K., & Chatterjee, S. (2013). Ethical guidelines for the quality assessment of healthcare. In I. Management Association (Ed.), User-driven healthcare: Concepts, methodologies, tools, and applications (pp. 1332-1347). Hershey, PA: Medical Information Science Reference. doi:10.4018/978-1-4666-2770-3.ch066

Chen, J. Y., Xu, H., Shi, P., Culbertson, A., & Meslin, E. M. (2013). Ethics and privacy considerations for systems biology applications in predictive and personalized medicine. In I. Management Association (Ed.), Bioinformatics: Concepts, methodologies, tools, and applications (pp. 1378-1404). Hershey, PA: Medical Information Science Reference. doi:10.4018/978-1-4666-3604-0.ch071

Chen, Y. (2013). Construction of digital statistical atlases of the liver and their applications to computer-aided diagnosis. In J. Wu (Ed.), *Technological advancements in biomedicine for healthcare applications* (pp. 68–79). Hershey, PA: Medical Information Science Reference; doi:10.4018/978-1-4666-2196-1.ch008

Cheng, B., Stanley, R. J., De, S., Antani, S., & Thoma, G. R. (2013). Automatic detection of arrow annotation overlays in biomedical images. In J. Tan (Ed.), *Healthcare information technology innovation and sustainability: Frontiers and adoption* (pp. 219–236). Hershey, PA: Medical Information Science Reference; doi:10.4018/978-1-4666-2797-0.ch014

Cherian, E. J., & Ryan, T. W. (2014). Incongruent needs: Why differences in the iron-triangle of priorities make health information technology adoption and use difficult. In C. El Morr (Ed.), *Research perspectives on the role of informatics in health policy and management* (pp. 209–221). Hershey, PA: Medical Information Science Reference; doi:10.4018/978-1-4666-4321-5.ch012

Chowdhry, N., Ashraf, A., Chowdhry, B., Baloch, A., Ansari, A., & De Meer, H. (2013). Grid for post operative care through wireless sensor networks. In I. Management Association (Ed.), User-driven healthcare: Concepts, methodologies, tools, and applications (pp. 514-531). Hershey, PA: Medical Information Science Reference. doi:10.4018/978-1-4666-2770-3.ch026

Chun, S. A., Kwon, J. H., & Lee, H. (2013). Social credential-based role recommendation and patient privacy control in medical emergency. In A. Gangopadhyay (Ed.), *Methods, models, and computation for medical informatics* (pp. 215–237). Hershey, PA: Medical Information Science Reference; doi:10.4018/978-1-4666-2653-9.ch013

Cohen, J. F., Bancilhon, J., & Sergay, S. (2013). An empirical study of patient willingness to use self-service technologies in the healthcare context. In M. Cruz-Cunha, I. Miranda, & P. Gonçalves (Eds.), *Handbook of research on ICTs and management systems for improving efficiency in healthcare and social care* (pp. 378–395). Hershey, PA: Medical Information Science Reference; doi:10.4018/978-1-4666-3990-4.ch019

Constantinides, P. (2013). The development of the English national health information infrastructure. In I. Management Association (Ed.), User-driven healthcare: Concepts, methodologies, tools, and applications (pp. 968-991). Hershey, PA: Medical Information Science Reference. doi:10.4018/978-1-4666-2770-3.ch049

Constantinides, P. (2013). The development of a regional health information infrastructure in Greece. In I. Management Association (Ed.), User-driven healthcare: Concepts, methodologies, tools, and applications (pp. 992-1017). Hershey, PA: Medical Information Science Reference. doi:10.4018/978-1-4666-2770-3.ch050

Corrigan, D., Hederman, L., Khan, H., Taweel, A., Kostopoulou, O., & Delaney, B. (2013). An ontology-driven approach to clinical evidence modelling implementing clinical prediction rules. In A. Moumtzoglou & A. Kastania (Eds.), *E-health technologies and improving patient safety: Exploring organizational factors* (pp. 257–284). Hershey, PA: Medical Information Science Reference; doi:10.4018/978-1-4666-2657-7.ch016

Corritore, C. L., Kracher, B., Wiedenbeck, S., & Marble, R. (2013). Foundations of trust for e-health. In I. Management Association (Ed.), User-driven healthcare: Concepts, methodologies, tools, and applications (pp. 1167-1193). Hershey, PA: Medical Information Science Reference. doi:10.4018/978-1-4666-2770-3.ch059

Costa, Â., Andrade, F., & Novais, P. (2013). Privacy and data protection towards elderly healthcare. In M. Cruz-Cunha, I. Miranda, & P. Gonçalves (Eds.), *Handbook of research on ICTs for human-centered healthcare and social care services* (pp. 330–346). Hershey, PA: Medical Information Science Reference; doi:10.4018/978-1-4666-3986-7.ch017

Coughlan, J., & Brinkman, W. (2013). Design considerations for delivering e-learning to surgical trainees. In J. Rodrigues (Ed.), *Digital advances in medicine, e-health, and communication technologies* (pp. 341–350). Hershey, PA: Medical Information Science Reference; doi:10.4018/978-1-4666-2794-9.ch020

D'Abundo, M. L. (2013). Electronic health record implementation in the United States healthcare industry: Making the process of change manageable. In V. Wang (Ed.), *Handbook of research on technologies for improving the 21st century workforce: Tools for lifelong learning* (pp. 272–286). Hershey, PA: Information Science Publishing; doi:10.4018/978-1-4666-2181-7.ch018

D'Abundo, M. L. (2013). Electronic health record implementation in the United States healthcare industry: Making the process of change manageable. In I. Management Association (Ed.), User-driven healthcare: Concepts, methodologies, tools, and applications (pp. 382-395). Hershey, PA: Medical Information Science Reference. doi:10.4018/978-1-4666-2770-3.ch019

D'Andrea, A., Ferri, F., & Grifoni, P. (2013). RFID technologies in the health sector. In A. Moumtzoglou & A. Kastania (Eds.), *E-health technologies and improving patient safety: Exploring organizational factors* (pp. 140–147). Hershey, PA: Medical Information Science Reference; doi:10.4018/978-1-4666-2657-7.ch009

D'Astolfo, C. (2014). Investing in a "rehabilitation model" to improve the decision-making process in long-term care. In C. El Morr (Ed.), *Research perspectives on the role of informatics in health policy and management* (pp. 37–47). Hershey, PA: Medical Information Science Reference; doi:10.4018/978-1-4666-4321-5.ch003

Daniel, V. M. (2013). Genomics and genetic engineering: Playing God? In I. Management Association (Ed.), Bioinformatics: Concepts, methodologies, tools, and applications (pp. 249-267). Hershey, PA: Medical Information Science Reference. doi:10.4018/978-1-4666-3604-0.ch013

Dasgupta, S. S. (2013). Cyber capability framework: A tool to evaluate ICT for development projects. In M. Cruz-Cunha, I. Miranda, & P. Gonçalves (Eds.), *Handbook of research on ICTs for human-centered healthcare and social care services* (pp. 399–406). Hershey, PA: Medical Information Science Reference; doi:10.4018/978-1-4666-3986-7.ch021

Davis, S. A. (2013). Global telemedicine and ehealth: Advances for future healthcare – Using a systems approach to integrate healthcare functions. In V. Gulla, A. Mori, F. Gabbrielli, & P. Lanzafame (Eds.), *Telehealth networks for hospital services: New methodologies* (pp. 15–32). Hershey, PA: Medical Information Science Reference; doi:10.4018/978-1-4666-2979-0.ch002

Deng, M., Petkovic, M., Nalin, M., & Baroni, I. (2013). Home healthcare in cloud computing. In M. Cruz-Cunha, I. Miranda, & P. Gonçalves (Eds.), *Handbook of research on ICTs and management systems for improving efficiency in healthcare and social care* (pp. 614–634). Hershey, PA: Medical Information Science Reference; doi:10.4018/978-1-4666-3990-4.ch032

DeVany, M., Knobloch-Ludwig, K., Penticoff, M., Assimacopoulos, A., & Speedie, S. (2013). Telehealth implementation: The voice of experience. In S. Sarnikar, D. Bennett, & M. Gaynor (Eds.), *Cases on healthcare information technology for patient care management* (pp. 126–139). Hershey, PA: Medical Information Science Reference; doi:10.4018/978-1-4666-2671-3.ch008

Ding, W., Qiu, P., Liu, Y., & Feng, W. (2013). Current omics technologies in biomarker discovery. In I. Management Association (Ed.), Bioinformatics: Concepts, methodologies, tools, and applications (pp. 465-497). Hershey, PA: Medical Information Science Reference. doi:10.4018/978-1-4666-3604-0.ch027

Dingli, A., Abela, C., & D'Ambrogio, I. (2013). PINATA: Taking e-health a step forward. In A. Moumtzoglou & A. Kastania (Eds.), *E-health technologies and improving patient safety: Exploring organizational factors* (pp. 173–195). Hershey, PA: Medical Information Science Reference; doi:10.4018/978-1-4666-2657-7.ch012

Dogra, D. P., Nandam, K., Majumdar, A. K., Sural, S., Mukhopadhyay, J., Majumdar, B., & Mukherjee, S. et al. (2013). A tool for automatic hammersmith infant neurological examination. In J. Rodrigues (Ed.), *Digital advances in medicine, e-health, and communication technologies* (pp. 301–311). Hershey, PA: Medical Information Science Reference; doi:10.4018/978-1-4666-2794-9.ch017

Doyle, J., Bertolotto, M., & Wilson, D. (2013). Towards multimodal mobile GIS for the elderly. In *Digital literacy: Concepts, methodologies, tools, and applications* (pp. 590–609). Hershey, PA: Information Science Reference; doi:10.4018/978-1-4666-1852-7.ch031

Dragoni, A. F. (2013). Health services through digital terrestrial television. In V. Gulla, A. Mori, F. Gabbrielli, & P. Lanzafame (Eds.), *Telehealth networks for hospital services: New methodologies* (pp. 207–227). Hershey, PA: Medical Information Science Reference; doi:10.4018/978-1-4666-2979-0.ch014

Dragoni, A. F. (2013). Virtual carer: A first prototype. In V. Gulla, A. Mori, F. Gabbrielli, & P. Lanzafame (Eds.), *Telehealth networks for hospital services: New methodologies* (pp. 290–299). Hershey, PA: Medical Information Science Reference; doi:10.4018/978-1-4666-2979-0.ch019

Driouchi, A. (2014). Introduction to labor and health economics: Mobility of medical doctors in the Mediterranean region. In A. Driouchi (Ed.), *Labor and health economics in the Mediterranean region: Migration and mobility of medical doctors* (pp. 1–22). Hershey, PA: Medical Information Science Reference; doi:10.4018/978-1-4666-4723-7.ch001

Driouchi, A. (2014). Medical knowledge, north-south cooperation, and mobility of medical doctors. In A. Driouchi (Ed.), *Labor and health economics in the Mediterranean region: Migration and mobility of medical doctors* (pp. 376–395). Hershey, PA: Medical Information Science Reference; doi:10.4018/978-1-4666-4723-7.ch015

Driouchi, A. (2014). Skilled human resources in the health sectors and impacts of new health technologies on health workforce in developing economies. In A. Driouchi (Ed.), *Labor and health economics in the Mediterranean region: Migration and mobility of medical doctors* (pp. 23–50). Hershey, PA: Medical Information Science Reference; doi:10.4018/978-1-4666-4723-7.ch002

Duan, X., Wang, X., & Huang, Q. (2013). Medical manipulators for surgical applications. In J. Wu (Ed.), *Technological advancements in biomedicine for healthcare applications* (pp. 111–122). Hershey, PA: Medical Information Science Reference; doi:10.4018/978-1-4666-2196-1.ch012

Dugdale, A. (2013). Australian patient organizations: Using digital technologies to engage health citizen communities in health policy. In I. Management Association (Ed.), User-driven healthcare: Concepts, methodologies, tools, and applications (pp. 853-869). Hershey, PA: Medical Information Science Reference. doi:10.4018/978-1-4666-2770-3.ch043

Dunwell, I., & Jarvis, S. (2013). A serious game for on-the-ward infection control awareness training: Ward off infection. In S. Arnab, I. Dunwell, & K. Debattista (Eds.), *Serious games for healthcare: Applications and implications* (pp. 233–246). Hershey, PA: Medical Information Science Reference; doi:10.4018/978-1-4666-1903-6.ch011

Durant, K. T., McCray, A. T., & Safran, C. (2013). Identifying temporal changes and topics that promote growth within online communities: A prospective study of six online cancer forums. In A. Gangopadhyay (Ed.), *Methods, models, and computation for medical informatics* (pp. 78–97). Hershey, PA: Medical Information Science Reference; doi:10.4018/978-1-4666-2653-9.ch005

El-Farargy, N. (2013). Refresher training in clinical psychology supervision: A blended learning approach. In A. Benson, J. Moore, & S. Williams van Rooij (Eds.), *Cases on educational technology planning, design, and implementation: A project management perspective* (pp. 295–317). Hershey, PA: Information Science Reference; doi:10.4018/978-1-4666-4237-9.ch016

Enquist, H. (2013). From idea to use: lessons learned from a participatory ICT healthcare case study. In I. Management Association (Ed.), User-driven healthcare: Concepts, methodologies, tools, and applications (pp. 1037-1053). Hershey, PA: Medical Information Science Reference. doi:10.4018/978-1-4666-2770-3.ch052

Ervin, K. (2014). Legal and ethical considerations in the implementation of electronic health records. In J. Krueger (Ed.), *Cases on electronic records and resource management implementation in diverse environments* (pp. 193–210). Hershey, PA: Information Science Reference; doi:10.4018/978-1-4666-4466-3.ch012

Escayola, J., Trigo, J., Martínez, I., Martínez-Espronceda, M., Aragüés, A., Sancho, D., . . . García, J. (2013). Overview of the ISO/IEEE11073 family of standards and their applications to health monitoring. In I. Management Association (Ed.), User-driven healthcare: Concepts, methodologies, tools, and applications (pp. 357-381). Hershey, PA: Medical Information Science Reference. doi:10.4018/978-1-4666-2770-3.ch018

Facelli, J. C., Hurdle, J. F., & Mitchell, J. A. (2013). Medical informatics and bioinformatics. In I. Management Association (Ed.), Bioinformatics: Concepts, methodologies, tools, and applications (pp. 195-221). Hershey, PA: Medical Information Science Reference. doi:10.4018/978-1-4666-3604-0.ch010

Fakhar, A. (2014). Beyond brain drain: A case study of the benefits of cooperation on medical immigration. In A. Driouchi (Ed.), *Labor and health economics in the Mediterranean region: Migration and mobility of medical doctors* (pp. 294–313). Hershey, PA: Medical Information Science Reference; doi:10.4018/978-1-4666-4723-7.ch012

Falan, S. L., Han, B., Zoeller, L. H., Tarn, J. M., & Roach, D. M. (2013). Sustaining healthcare through waste elimination: A taxonomic analysis with case illustrations. In J. Tan (Ed.), *Healthcare information technology innovation and sustainability: Frontiers and adoption* (pp. 18–39). Hershey, PA: Medical Information Science Reference; doi:10.4018/978-1-4666-2797-0.ch002

Farinha, C., & Mira da Silva, M. (2013). Identifying requirements for healthcare information systems with focus groups. In M. Cruz-Cunha, I. Miranda, & P. Gonçalves (Eds.), *Handbook of research on ICTs for human-centered healthcare and social care services* (pp. 491–510). Hershey, PA: Medical Information Science Reference; doi:10.4018/978-1-4666-3986-7.ch026

Fernando, J. (2013). The protocols of privileged information handling in an e-health context: Australia. In I. Management Association (Ed.), User-driven healthcare: Concepts, methodologies, tools, and applications (pp. 737-759). Hershey, PA: Medical Information Science Reference. doi:10.4018/978-1-4666-2770-3.ch036

Ferreira, L., Teixeira, A., & Cunha, J. P. (2013). Medical information extraction in European Portuguese. In M. Cruz-Cunha, I. Miranda, & P. Gonçalves (Eds.), *Handbook of research on ICTs for human-centered healthcare and social care services* (pp. 607–626). Hershey, PA: Medical Information Science Reference; doi:10.4018/978-1-4666-3986-7.ch032

Fitzpatrick, J. (2013). An exploration of the experiences of migrant women: Implications for policy development of effective user driven health care delivery systems. In I. Management Association (Ed.), User-driven healthcare: Concepts, methodologies, tools, and applications (pp. 954-967). Hershey, PA: Medical Information Science Reference. doi:10.4018/978-1-4666-2770-3.ch048

Fitzpatrick, J., & Ako, W. (2013). Developing community ontologies in user driven healthcare. In I. Management Association (Ed.), User-driven healthcare: Concepts, methodologies, tools, and applications (pp. 655-672). Hershey, PA: Medical Information Science Reference. doi:10.4018/978-1-4666-2770-3.ch032

Flores, A. E., Win, K. T., & Susilo, W. (2013). Secure exchange of electronic health records. In I. Management Association (Ed.), IT policy and ethics: Concepts, methodologies, tools, and applications (pp. 1059-1079). Hershey, PA: Information Science Reference. doi:10.4018/978-1-4666-2919-6.ch048

Flores, A. E., Win, K. T., & Susilo, W. (2013). Secure exchange of electronic health records. In I. Management Association (Ed.), User-driven healthcare: Concepts, methodologies, tools, and applications (pp. 1403-1424). Hershey, PA: Medical Information Science Reference. doi:10.4018/978-1-4666-2770-3.ch070

Forrestal, E. J., Cellucci, L. W., Zeng, X., Kennedy, M. H., & Smith, D. (2013). Health information technology collaboration in community health centers: The community partners HealthNet, Inc. In S. Sarnikar, D. Bennett, & M. Gaynor (Eds.), *Cases on healthcare information technology for patient care management* (pp. 171–196). Hershey, PA: Medical Information Science Reference; doi:10.4018/978-1-4666-2671-3.ch011

Frederico, C. (2013). Nutrition games. In S. Arnab, I. Dunwell, & K. Debattista (Eds.), *Serious games for healthcare: Applications and implications* (pp. 167–190). Hershey, PA: Medical Information Science Reference; doi:10.4018/978-1-4666-1903-6.ch008

Freitas, L., Pereira, R. T., Pereira, H. G., Martini, R., Mozzaquatro, B. A., Kasper, J., & Librelotto, G. (2013). Ontological representation and an architecture for homecare pervasive systems. In R. Martinho, R. Rijo, M. Cruz-Cunha, & J. Varajão (Eds.), *Information systems and technologies for enhancing health and social care* (pp. 215–234). Hershey, PA: Medical Information Science Reference; doi:10.4018/978-1-4666-3667-5.ch015

Frigo, C. A., & Pavan, E. E. (2014). Prosthetic and orthotic devices. In *Assistive technologies: Concepts, methodologies, tools, and applications* (pp. 549–613). Hershey, PA: Information Science Reference; doi:10.4018/978-1-4666-4422-9.ch028

Fukami, T., & Wu, J. (2013). Image fusion method and the efficacy of multimodal cardiac images. In J. Wu (Ed.), *Technological advancements in biomedicine for healthcare applications* (pp. 47–54). Hershey, PA: Medical Information Science Reference; doi:10.4018/978-1-4666-2196-1.ch006

Furdu, I., & Patrut, B. (2013). ICT applications and solutions in healthcare: Present and perspectives. In M. Cruz-Cunha, I. Miranda, & P. Gonçalves (Eds.), *Handbook of research on ICTs and management systems for improving efficiency in healthcare and social care* (pp. 559–576). Hershey, PA: Medical Information Science Reference; doi:10.4018/978-1-4666-3990-4.ch029

Gabbrielli, F. (2013). Telemedicine R&D influencing incoming strategies and organization models. In V. Gulla, A. Mori, F. Gabbrielli, & P. Lanzafame (Eds.), *Telehealth networks for hospital services: New methodologies* (pp. 250–264). Hershey, PA: Medical Information Science Reference; doi:10.4018/978-1-4666-2979-0.ch017

Gaivéo, J. M. (2013). Security of ICTs supporting healthcare activities. In M. Cruz-Cunha, I. Miranda, & P. Gonçalves (Eds.), *Handbook of research on ICTs for human-centered healthcare and social care services* (pp. 208–228). Hershey, PA: Medical Information Science Reference; doi:10.4018/978-1-4666-3986-7.ch011

Gallo, C. (2013). A multichannel framework for multimedia content deployment in e-health environments. In M. Cruz-Cunha, I. Miranda, & P. Gonçalves (Eds.), *Handbook of research on ICTs and management systems for improving efficiency in healthcare and social care* (pp. 872–891). Hershey, PA: Medical Information Science Reference; doi:10.4018/978-1-4666-3990-4.ch045

Gao, Y., Yang, W., Yang, J., Satoshi, T., & Wu, J. (2013). Neural mechanisms of audiovisual integration in integrated processing for verbal perception and spatial factors. In J. Wu (Ed.), *Biomedical engineering and cognitive neuroscience for healthcare: Interdisciplinary applications* (pp. 327–336). Hershey, PA: Medical Information Science Reference; doi:10.4018/978-1-4666-2113-8.ch034

Garzo, A., Carmien, S. P., & Madina, X. (2013). Mapping input technology to ability. In I. Management Association (Ed.), User-driven healthcare: Concepts, methodologies, tools, and applications (pp. 480-501). Hershey, PA: Medical Information Science Reference. doi:10.4018/978-1-4666-2770-3.ch024

Gatzidis, C. (2013). First-person shooter game engines and healthcare: An examination of the current state of the art and future potential. In S. Arnab, I. Dunwell, & K. Debattista (Eds.), *Serious Games for Healthcare: Applications and Implications* (pp. 76–89). Hershey, PA: Medical Information Science Reference; doi:10.4018/978-1-4666-1903-6.ch004

Gaughan, M. (2013). The hybridized nature of America's health care system: Medicare as a case of both market and public failure. In M. Merviö (Ed.), *Healthcare management and economics: Perspectives on public and private administration* (pp. 154–164). Hershey, PA: Medical Information Science Reference; doi:10.4018/978-1-4666-3982-9.ch012

Gavgani, V. Z. (2013). Information therapy (ix) service and patients' preference. In A. Gangopadhyay (Ed.), *Methods, models, and computation for medical informatics* (pp. 117–125). Hershey, PA: Medical Information Science Reference; doi:10.4018/978-1-4666-2653-9.ch007

Gavgani, V. Z. (2013). Ubiquitous information therapy service through social networking libraries: An operational web 2.0 service model. In I. Management Association (Ed.), User-driven healthcare: Concepts, methodologies, tools, and applications (pp. 673-688). Hershey, PA: Medical Information Science Reference. doi:10.4018/978-1-4666-2770-3.ch033

Germaine-McDaniel, N. S. (2013). The emerging hispanic use of online health information in the United States: Cultural convergence or dissociation? In I. Management Association (Ed.), User-driven healthcare: Concepts, methodologies, tools, and applications (pp. 1607-1621). Hershey, PA: Medical Information Science Reference. doi:10.4018/978-1-4666-2770-3.ch079

Gholson, J., & Tennyson, H. (2013). One system of care, one electronic chart. In S. Sarnikar, D. Bennett, & M. Gaynor (Eds.), *Cases on healthcare information technology for patient care management* (pp. 55–69). Hershey, PA: Medical Information Science Reference; doi:10.4018/978-1-4666-2671-3.ch003

Ghosh, B. (2013). Healthcare systems using clinical data: Addressing data interoperability challenges. In S. Sarnikar, D. Bennett, & M. Gaynor (Eds.), *Cases on healthcare information technology for patient care management* (pp. 208–223). Hershey, PA: Medical Information Science Reference; doi:10.4018/978-1-4666-2671-3.ch013

Gibson, L., Sloan, D., & Moncur, W. (2013). E-health and digital inclusion. In I. Management Association (Ed.), User-driven healthcare: Concepts, methodologies, tools, and applications (pp. 197-210). Hershey, PA: Medical Information Science Reference. doi:10.4018/978-1-4666-2770-3.ch011

Gillies, A. C., & Howard, J. (2013). Information as change agent or barrier in health care reform? In J. Tan (Ed.), *Healthcare information technology innovation and sustainability: Frontiers and adoption* (pp. 1–17). Hershey, PA: Medical Information Science Reference; doi:10.4018/978-1-4666-2797-0.ch001

Glusker, A., & Hoelscher, E. (2014). Transitioning from print to online-only resources: The experience of a medium-sized healthcare organization library. In J. Krueger (Ed.), *Cases on electronic records and resource management implementation in diverse environments* (pp. 226–242). Hershey, PA: Information Science Reference; doi:10.4018/978-1-4666-4466-3.ch014

Gofuku, A., Fukumori, S., & Sato, K. (2013). A mirror visual feedback therapy system applying virtual reality technology. In J. Wu (Ed.), *Biomedical engineering and cognitive neuroscience for healthcare: Interdisciplinary applications* (pp. 73–80). Hershey, PA: Medical Information Science Reference; doi:10.4018/978-1-4666-2113-8.ch008

Gomes, C., Sperandio, F., Peles, A., Borges, J., Brito, A. C., & Almada-Lobo, B. (2013). An operating theater planning decision support system. In R. Martinho, R. Rijo, M. Cruz-Cunha, & J. Varajão (Eds.), *Information systems and technologies for enhancing health and social care* (pp. 69–86). Hershey, PA: Medical Information Science Reference; doi:10.4018/978-1-4666-3667-5.ch005

Grissom, T. E., DuKatz, A., Kordylewski, H. A., & Dutton, R. P. (2013). Bring out your data: The evolution of the national anesthesia clinical outcomes registry (NACOR). In A. Gangopadhyay (Ed.), *Methods, models, and computation for medical informatics* (pp. 126–145). Hershey, PA: Medical Information Science Reference; doi:10.4018/978-1-4666-2653-9.ch008

Gudes, O., Kendall, E., Yigitcanlar, T., Han, J. H., & Pathak, V. (2013). Developing a competitive city through healthy decision-making. In I. Management Association (Ed.), User-driven healthcare: Concepts, methodologies, tools, and applications (pp. 808-822). Hershey, PA: Medical Information Science Reference. doi:10.4018/978-1-4666-2770-3.ch040

Gugerty, B., & Maranda, M. J. (2013). The promises and challenges of health information technology. In I. Management Association (Ed.), User-driven healthcare: Concepts, methodologies, tools, and applications (pp. 57-76). Hershey, PA: Medical Information Science Reference. doi:10.4018/978-1-4666-2770-3.ch004

Guimarães, C., Antunes, D. R., García, L. S., & Fernandes, S. (2013). Information challenges of the deaf in their health and social care needs. In M. Cruz-Cunha, I. Miranda, & P. Gonçalves (Eds.), *Handbook of research on ICTs for human-centered healthcare and social care services* (pp. 93–111). Hershey, PA: Medical Information Science Reference; doi:10.4018/978-1-4666-3986-7.ch005

Guinalíu, M., Marta, J., & Subero, J. M. (2013). Social networks as a tool to improve the life quality of chronic patients and their relatives. In M. Cruz-Cunha, I. Miranda, & P. Gonçalves (Eds.), *Handbook of research on ICTs for human-centered healthcare and social care services* (pp. 172–186). Hershey, PA: Medical Information Science Reference; doi:10.4018/978-1-4666-3986-7.ch009

Gullà, V. (2013). Leading the technological innovation in healthcare systems: The telematic medicine approach. In V. Gulla, A. Mori, F. Gabbrielli, & P. Lanzafame (Eds.), *Telehealth networks for hospital services: New methodologies* (pp. 134–153). Hershey, PA: Medical Information Science Reference; doi:10.4018/978-1-4666-2979-0.ch009

Gullà, V., & Cancellotti, C. (2013). Telemedicine in emergency: A first aid hospital network experience. In V. Gulla, A. Mori, F. Gabbrielli, & P. Lanzafame (Eds.), *Telehealth networks for hospital services: New methodologies* (pp. 240–248). Hershey, PA: Medical Information Science Reference; doi:10.4018/978-1-4666-2979-0.ch016

Guo, M., Yu, Y., Yang, J., & Wu, J. (2013). The crossmodal between the visual and tactile for motion perception. In J. Wu (Ed.), *Biomedical engineering and cognitive neuroscience for healthcare: Interdisciplinary applications* (pp. 99–108). Hershey, PA: Medical Information Science Reference; doi:10.4018/978-1-4666-2113-8.ch011

Habib, M. K. (2014). Web-based multi-user distributed and collaborative environment supporting emergency and relief activities. In I. Management Association (Ed.), Crisis management: Concepts, methodologies, tools and applications (pp. 425-445). Hershey, PA: Information Science Reference. doi:10.4018/978-1-4666-4707-7.ch019

Hafeez-Baig, A., & Gururajan, R. (2013). Phenomena of adoption of wireless handheld devices: A case of healthcare setting. In H. Muga & K. Thomas (Eds.), *Cases on the diffusion and adoption of sustainable development practices* (pp. 20–43). Hershey, PA: Information Science Reference; doi:10.4018/978-1-4666-2842-7.ch002

Haida, M. (2013). Implications of NIRS brain signals. In J. Wu (Ed.), *Biomedical engineering and cognitive neuroscience for healthcare: Interdisciplinary applications* (pp. 120–128). Hershey, PA: Medical Information Science Reference; doi:10.4018/978-1-4666-2113-8.ch013

Han, D., & Braun, K. L. (2013). Promoting active ageing through technology training in Korea. In *Digital literacy: Concepts, methodologies, tools, and applications* (pp. 572–589). Hershey, PA: Information Science Reference; doi:10.4018/978-1-4666-1852-7.ch030

Haniff, D. (2013). Usability engineering and e-health. In I. Management Association (Ed.), User-driven healthcare: Concepts, methodologies, tools, and applications (pp. 1446-1468). Hershey, PA: Medical Information Science Reference. doi:10.4018/978-1-4666-2770-3.ch072

Hareva, D. H., Okada, H., & Oka, H. (2013). Ecological momentary assessment using a mobile phone. In J. Wu (Ed.), *Technological advancements in biomedicine for healthcare applications* (pp. 398–407). Hershey, PA: Medical Information Science Reference; doi:10.4018/978-1-4666-2196-1.ch039

Harnett, B. (2013). Patient centered medicine and technology adaptation. In I. Management Association (Ed.), User-driven healthcare: Concepts, methodologies, tools, and applications (pp. 77-98). Hershey, PA: Medical Information Science Reference. doi:10.4018/978-1-4666-2770-3.ch005

Hatton, J. D., Schmidt, T. M., & Jelen, J. (2013). Adoption of electronic health care records: Physician heuristics and hesitancy. In R. Martinho, R. Rijo, M. Cruz-Cunha, & J. Varajão (Eds.), *Information systems and technologies for enhancing health and social care* (pp. 148–165). Hershey, PA: Medical Information Science Reference; doi:10.4018/978-1-4666-3667-5.ch010

Heinrichs, L., Fellander-Tsai, L., & Davies, D. (2013). Clinical virtual worlds: The wider implications for professional development in healthcare. In K. Bredl & W. Bösche (Eds.), *Serious games and virtual worlds in education, professional development, and healthcare* (pp. 221–240). Hershey, PA: Information Science Reference; doi:10.4018/978-1-4666-3673-6.ch014

Heinrichs, W. L., Davies, D., & Davies, J. (2013). Virtual worlds in healthcare: Applications and implications. In S. Arnab, I. Dunwell, & K. Debattista (Eds.), *Serious games for healthcare: Applications and implications* (pp. 1–22). Hershey, PA: Medical Information Science Reference; doi:10.4018/978-1-4666-1903-6.ch001

Hirata, M., Yanagisawa, T., Matsushita, K., Sugata, H., Kamitani, Y., & Suzuki, T. … Yoshimine, T. (2013). Brain–machine interface using brain surface electrodes: Real-time robotic control and a fully implantable wireless system. In J. Wu (Ed.), Technological advancements in biomedicine for healthcare applications (pp. 362-374). Hershey, PA: Medical Information Science Reference. doi:10.4018/978-1-4666-2196-1.ch036

Hocine, N., & Gouaïch, A. (2013). Difficulty and scenario adaptation: An approach to customize therapeutic games. In S. Arnab, I. Dunwell, & K. Debattista (Eds.), *Serious games for healthcare: Applications and implications* (pp. 107–134). Hershey, PA: Medical Information Science Reference; doi:10.4018/978-1-4666-1903-6.ch006

Hoonakker, P., Cartmill, R. S., Carayon, P., & Walker, J. M. (2013). Development and psychometric qualities of the SEIPS survey to evaluate CPOE/EHR implementation in ICUs. In J. Tan (Ed.), *Healthcare information technology innovation and sustainability: Frontiers and adoption* (pp. 161–179). Hershey, PA: Medical Information Science Reference; doi:10.4018/978-1-4666-2797-0.ch010

Hoshi, K. (2013). Reframing dichotomies: Human experiential design of healthcare technologies. In I. Management Association (Ed.), User-driven healthcare: Concepts, methodologies, tools, and applications (pp. 1303-1331). Hershey, PA: Medical Information Science Reference. doi:10.4018/978-1-4666-2770-3.ch065

Høstgaard, A. M. (2013). End-user participation in health IT development: The EUPHIT method. In I. Management Association (Ed.), User-driven healthcare: Concepts, methodologies, tools, and applications (pp. 608-629). Hershey, PA: Medical Information Science Reference. doi:10.4018/978-1-4666-2770-3.ch030

Igrejas, G., Amaral, J. S., & Rodrigues, P. J. (2013). Fall detection systems to be used by elderly people. In M. Cruz-Cunha, I. Miranda, & P. Gonçalves (Eds.), *Handbook of research on ICTs for human-centered healthcare and social care services* (pp. 449–473). Hershey, PA: Medical Information Science Reference; doi:10.4018/978-1-4666-3986-7.ch024

Inomata, C., & Nitta, S. (2013). Nursing in integrative medicine and nurses' engagement in caring-healing: A discussion based on the practice and study of music therapy and nursing care for patients with neurodegenerative disorders. In J. Wu (Ed.), *Technological advancements in biomedicine for healthcare applications* (pp. 235–239). Hershey, PA: Medical Information Science Reference; doi:10.4018/978-1-4666-2196-1.ch025

Ishaq, G. M., Hussain, P. T., Iqbal, M. J., & Mushtaq, M. B. (2013). Risk-benefit analysis of combination vs. unopposed HRT in post-menopausal women. In I. Management Association (Ed.), Bioinformatics: Concepts, methodologies, tools, and applications (pp. 1424-1440). Hershey, PA: Medical Information Science Reference. doi:10.4018/978-1-4666-3604-0.ch073

Iwaki, S. (2013). Multimodal neuroimaging to visualize human visual processing. In J. Wu (Ed.), *Biomedical engineering and cognitive neuroscience for healthcare: Interdisciplinary applications* (pp. 274–282). Hershey, PA: Medical Information Science Reference; doi:10.4018/978-1-4666-2113-8.ch028

Ji, Z., Sugi, T., Goto, S., Wang, X., & Nakamura, M. (2013). Multi-channel template extraction for automatic EEG spike detection. In J. Wu (Ed.), *Biomedical engineering and cognitive neuroscience for healthcare: Interdisciplinary applications* (pp. 255–265). Hershey, PA: Medical Information Science Reference; doi:10.4018/978-1-4666-2113-8.ch026

Jiang, Y., Wang, S., Tan, R., Ishida, K., Ando, T., & Fujie, M. G. (2013). Motor cortex activation during mental imagery of walking: An fNIRS study. In J. Wu (Ed.), *Biomedical engineering and cognitive neuroscience for healthcare: Interdisciplinary applications* (pp. 29–37). Hershey, PA: Medical Information Science Reference; doi:10.4018/978-1-4666-2113-8.ch004

Johnson, K., & Tashiro, J. (2013). Interprofessional care and health care complexity: Factors shaping human resources effectiveness in health information management. In I. Management Association (Ed.), User-Driven Healthcare: Concepts, Methodologies, Tools, and Applications (pp. 1273-1302). Hershey, PA: Medical Information Science Reference. doi:10.4018/978-1-4666-2770-3.ch064

Jose, J. (2013). Pharmacovigilance: Basic concepts and applications of pharmacoinformatics. In I. Management Association (Ed.), Bioinformatics: Concepts, methodologies, tools, and applications (pp. 1453-1473). Hershey, PA: Medical Information Science Reference. doi:10.4018/978-1-4666-3604-0.ch075

Kalina, J., & Zvárová, J. (2013). Decision support systems in the process of improving patient safety. In A. Moumtzoglou & A. Kastania (Eds.), *E-health technologies and improving patient safety: Exploring organizational factors* (pp. 71–83). Hershey, PA: Medical Information Science Reference; doi:10.4018/978-1-4666-2657-7.ch005

Kalina, J., & Zvárová, J. (2013). Decision support systems in the process of improving patient safety. In I. Management Association (Ed.), Bioinformatics: Concepts, methodologies, tools, and applications (pp. 1113-1125). Hershey, PA: Medical Information Science Reference. doi:10.4018/978-1-4666-3604-0.ch057

Kamath, J. R., & Donahoe-Anshus, A. L. (2013). Electronic health record: Adoption, considerations and future direction. In I. Management Association (Ed.), User-driven healthcare: Concepts, methodologies, tools, and applications (pp. 34-56). Hershey, PA: Medical Information Science Reference. doi:10.4018/978-1-4666-2770-3.ch003

Karamagkioli, K. Z., & Karamagioli, E. (2013). European e-health framework: Towards more "patient-friendly" healthcare services? In I. Management Association (Ed.), User-driven healthcare: Concepts, methodologies, tools, and applications (pp. 760-775). Hershey, PA: Medical Information Science Reference. doi:10.4018/978-1-4666-2770-3.ch037

Kardaras, D. K., & Karakostas, B. (2013). Case studies in customization of e-health services. In I. Management Association (Ed.), User-driven healthcare: Concepts, methodologies, tools, and applications (pp. 1018-1036). Hershey, PA: Medical Information Science Reference. doi:10.4018/978-1-4666-2770-3.ch051

Kastania, A. N. (2013). Evaluation considerations for e-health systems. In I. Management Association (Ed.), User-driven healthcare: Concepts, methodologies, tools, and applications (pp. 1126-1140). Hershey, PA: Medical Information Science Reference. doi:10.4018/978-1-4666-2770-3.ch057

Kato, P. M. (2013). The role of the researcher in making serious games for health. In S. Arnab, I. Dunwell, & K. Debattista (Eds.), *Serious games for healthcare: Applications and implications* (pp. 213–231). Hershey, PA: Medical Information Science Reference; doi:10.4018/978-1-4666-1903-6.ch010

Katsura, S. (2013). Preservation and reproduction of human motion based on a motion-copying system. In J. Wu (Ed.), *Technological advancements in biomedicine for healthcare applications* (pp. 375–384). Hershey, PA: Medical Information Science Reference; doi:10.4018/978-1-4666-2196-1.ch037

Kikuchi, T. (2013). Human-friendly mechatronics systems with functional fluids and elastomers. In J. Wu (Ed.), *Technological advancements in biomedicine for healthcare applications* (pp. 94–101). Hershey, PA: Medical Information Science Reference; doi:10.4018/978-1-4666-2196-1.ch010

Kimura, T., Miura, T., Shinohara, K., & Doi, S. (2013). Visual attention in 3-D space while moving forward. In J. Wu (Ed.), *Biomedical engineering and cognitive neuroscience for healthcare: Interdisciplinary applications* (pp. 81–88). Hershey, PA: Medical Information Science Reference; doi:10.4018/978-1-4666-2113-8.ch009

Kldiashvili, E. (2013). Implementation of telecytology in Georgia. In V. Gulla, A. Mori, F. Gabbrielli, & P. Lanzafame (Eds.), *Telehealth networks for hospital services: New methodologies* (pp. 341–361). Hershey, PA: Medical Information Science Reference; doi:10.4018/978-1-4666-2979-0.ch022

Kolovou, L. T., & Lymberopoulos, D. K. (2013). The concept of interoperability for AAL systems. In I. Management Association (Ed.), User-driven healthcare: Concepts, methodologies, tools, and applications (pp. 1364-1385). Hershey, PA: Medical Information Science Reference. doi:10.4018/978-1-4666-2770-3.ch068

Koppar, A. R., & Sridhar, V. (2013). Malaria parasite detection: Automated method using microscope color image. In J. Rodrigues (Ed.), *Digital advances in medicine, e-health, and communication technologies* (pp. 289–300). Hershey, PA: Medical Information Science Reference; doi:10.4018/978-1-4666-2794-9.ch016

Kotsonis, E., & Eliakis, S. (2013). Information security standards for health information systems: The implementer's approach. In I. Management Association (Ed.), User-driven healthcare: Concepts, methodologies, tools, and applications (pp. 225-257). Hershey, PA: Medical Information Science Reference. doi:10.4018/978-1-4666-2770-3.ch013

Krishnaswamy, K., & Oates, T. (2014). Pathway to independence: Past, present, and beyond via robotics. In G. Kouroupetroglou (Ed.), *Disability informatics and web accessibility for motor limitations* (pp. 153–201). Hershey, PA: Medical Information Science Reference; doi:10.4018/978-1-4666-4442-7.ch005

Kuehler, M., Schimke, N., & Hale, J. (2013). Privacy considerations for electronic health records. In I. Management Association (Ed.), User-driven healthcare: Concepts, methodologies, tools, and applications (pp. 1387-1402). Hershey, PA: Medical Information Science Reference. doi:10.4018/978-1-4666-2770-3.ch069

Kurita, Y., Ikeda, A., Nagata, K., Okajima, M., & Ogasawara, T. (2013). Biomedical robotics for healthcare. In J. Wu (Ed.), *Technological advancements in biomedicine for healthcare applications* (pp. 160–169). Hershey, PA: Medical Information Science Reference; doi:10.4018/978-1-4666-2196-1.ch017

Lakkaraju, S., & Lakkaraju, S. (2013). Mobile device application in healthcare. In S. Sarnikar, D. Bennett, & M. Gaynor (Eds.), *Cases on healthcare information technology for patient care management* (pp. 276–307). Hershey, PA: Medical Information Science Reference; doi:10.4018/978-1-4666-2671-3.ch016

Laskowski, M. (2013). A prototype agent based model and machine learning hybrid system for healthcare decision support. In J. Rodrigues (Ed.), *Digital advances in medicine, e-health, and communication technologies* (pp. 230–253). Hershey, PA: Medical Information Science Reference; doi:10.4018/978-1-4666-2794-9.ch013

Lee, T. (2014). Mobile healthcare computing in the cloud. In J. Rodrigues, K. Lin, & J. Lloret (Eds.), *Mobile networks and cloud computing convergence for progressive services and applications* (pp. 275–294). Hershey, PA: Information Science Reference; doi:10.4018/978-1-4666-4781-7.ch015

Lelardeux, C., Alvarez, J., Montaut, T., Galaup, M., & Lagarrigue, P. (2013). Healthcare games and the metaphoric approach. In S. Arnab, I. Dunwell, & K. Debattista (Eds.), *Serious games for healthcare: Applications and implications* (pp. 23–49). Hershey, PA: Medical Information Science Reference; doi:10.4018/978-1-4666-1903-6.ch002

Lhotska, L., Bursa, M., Huptych, M., Chudacek, V., & Havlik, J. (2013). Interoperability of medical devices and information systems. In M. Cruz-Cunha, I. Miranda, & P. Gonçalves (Eds.), *Handbook of research on ICTs for human-centered healthcare and social care services* (pp. 749–762). Hershey, PA: Medical Information Science Reference; doi:10.4018/978-1-4666-3986-7.ch039

Li, X., Lin, Z., & Wu, J. (2013). Language processing in the human brain of literate and illiterate subjects. In J. Wu (Ed.), *Biomedical engineering and cognitive neuroscience for healthcare: Interdisciplinary applications* (pp. 201–209). Hershey, PA: Medical Information Science Reference; doi:10.4018/978-1-4666-2113-8.ch021

Liao, H. (2013). Biomedical information processing and visualization for minimally invasive neurosurgery. In J. Wu (Ed.), *Technological advancements in biomedicine for healthcare applications* (pp. 36–46). Hershey, PA: Medical Information Science Reference; doi:10.4018/978-1-4666-2196-1.ch005

Libreri, C., & Graffigna, G. (2014). How web 2.0 shapes patient knowledge sharing: The case of diabetes in Italy. In C. El Morr (Ed.), *Research perspectives on the role of informatics in health policy and management* (pp. 238–260). Hershey, PA: Medical Information Science Reference; doi:10.4018/978-1-4666-4321-5.ch014

Lin, C., Huang, Y., Li, C., & Jalleh, G. (2013). Key health information systems outsourcing issues from six hospital cases. In I. Management Association (Ed.), User-driven healthcare: Concepts, methodologies, tools, and applications (pp. 824-837). Hershey, PA: Medical Information Science Reference. doi:10.4018/978-1-4666-2770-3.ch041

Lin, L., Chen, Y., Wu, J., & Tennyson, R. D. (2013). What skill/knowledge is important to a nursing professional? In P. Ordóñez de Pablos (Ed.), *Business, technology, and knowledge management in Asia: Trends and innovations* (pp. 234–249). Hershey, PA: Business Science Reference; doi:10.4018/978-1-4666-2652-2.ch018

Liu, G. (2014). Using case costing data and case mix for funding and benchmarking in rehabilitation hospitals. In C. El Morr (Ed.), *Research perspectives on the role of informatics in health policy and management* (pp. 62–78). Hershey, PA: Medical Information Science Reference; doi:10.4018/978-1-4666-4321-5.ch005

Lixun, Z., Dapeng, B., & Lei, Y. (2013). Design of and experimentation with a walking assistance robot. In J. Wu (Ed.), *Technological advancements in biomedicine for healthcare applications* (pp. 123–127). Hershey, PA: Medical Information Science Reference; doi:10.4018/978-1-4666-2196-1.ch013

Lui, K. (2013). The health informatics professional. In I. Management Association (Ed.), User-driven healthcare: Concepts, methodologies, tools, and applications (pp. 120-141). Hershey, PA: Medical Information Science Reference. doi:10.4018/978-1-4666-2770-3.ch007

Ma, X., Chen, G., & Xiao, J. (2013). Understanding weight change behaviors through online social networks. In A. Gangopadhyay (Ed.), *Methods, models, and computation for medical informatics* (pp. 189–214). Hershey, PA: Medical Information Science Reference; doi:10.4018/978-1-4666-2653-9.ch012

Makikawa, M., Okada, S., Fujiwara, Y., & Esaki, M. (2013). Sleep monitoring system equipped with a flexible non-contact ECG, respiration, and body motion sensor. In J. Wu (Ed.), *Technological advancements in biomedicine for healthcare applications* (pp. 287–297). Hershey, PA: Medical Information Science Reference; doi:10.4018/978-1-4666-2196-1.ch030

Malindretos, G. (2013). Distribution and logistics outsourcing in the pharmaceutical sector. In D. Folinas (Ed.), *Outsourcing management for supply chain operations and logistics service* (pp. 202–222). Hershey, PA: Business Science Reference; doi:10.4018/978-1-4666-2008-7.ch012

Manvi, S. S., & B., M. R. (2013). A survey on health care services using wireless sensor networks. In M. Cruz-Cunha, I. Miranda, & P. Gonçalves (Eds.), *Handbook of research on ICTs for human-centered healthcare and social care services* (pp. 587-606). Hershey, PA: Medical Information Science Reference. doi:10.4018/978-1-4666-3986-7.ch031

Marshall, S., & Hogan, J. (2013). The use of medical simulation to improve patient safety. In A. Moumtzoglou & A. Kastania (Eds.), *E-health technologies and improving patient safety: Exploring organizational factors* (pp. 155–172). Hershey, PA: Medical Information Science Reference; doi:10.4018/978-1-4666-2657-7.ch011

Martin, J., & McKay, E. (2013). Mental health, post-secondary education, and information communications technology. In J. Lannon & E. Halpin (Eds.), *Human rights and information communication technologies: Trends and consequences of use* (pp. 196–213). Hershey, PA: Information Science Reference; doi:10.4018/978-1-4666-1918-0.ch012

Martin, J., & McKay, E. (2014). Mental health, post-secondary education, and information communications technology. In *Assistive technologies: Concepts, methodologies, tools, and applications* (pp. 1209–1226). Hershey, PA: Information Science Reference; doi:10.4018/978-1-4666-4422-9.ch063

Martin, V. (2013). Developing a library collection in bioinformatics: Support for an evolving profession. In I. Management Association (Ed.), Bioinformatics: Concepts, methodologies, tools, and applications (pp. 130-150). Hershey, PA: Medical Information Science Reference. doi:10.4018/978-1-4666-3604-0.ch007

Masayuki, K., Eiji, K., Tetsuo, T., & Nozomu, M. (2013). Evaluation of olfactory impairment in Parkinson's disease using near-infrared spectroscopy. In J. Wu (Ed.), *Biomedical engineering and cognitive neuroscience for healthcare: Interdisciplinary applications* (pp. 293–302). Hershey, PA: Medical Information Science Reference; doi:10.4018/978-1-4666-2113-8.ch030

Mazzanti, I., Maolo, A., & Antonicelli, R. (2013). E-health and telemedicine in the elderly: State of the art. In V. Gulla, A. Mori, F. Gabbrielli, & P. Lanzafame (Eds.), *Telehealth Networks for Hospital Services: New Methodologies* (pp. 33–43). Hershey, PA: Medical Information Science Reference; doi:10.4018/978-1-4666-2979-0.ch003

Mazzanti, I., Maolo, A., & Antonicelli, R. (2014). E-health and telemedicine in the elderly: State of the art. In *Assistive technologies: Concepts, methodologies, tools, and applications* (pp. 693–704). Hershey, PA: Information Science Reference; doi:10.4018/978-1-4666-4422-9.ch034

McCrossan, B. A., & Casey, F. A. (2013). The role of telemedicine in paediatric cardiology. In V. Gulla, A. Mori, F. Gabbrielli, & P. Lanzafame (Eds.), *Telehealth networks for hospital services: New methodologies* (pp. 44–88). Hershey, PA: Medical Information Science Reference; doi:10.4018/978-1-4666-2979-0.ch004

McGaha, J. (2013). Implementation issues on a national electronic health record network. In I. Management Association (Ed.), User-driven healthcare: Concepts, methodologies, tools, and applications (pp. 1236-1251). Hershey, PA: Medical Information Science Reference. doi:10.4018/978-1-4666-2770-3.ch062

McGinnes, S., & Burke, M. (2013). Hoping for the best: A qualitative study of information technology in primary care. In M. Cruz-Cunha, I. Miranda, & P. Gonçalves (Eds.), *Handbook of research on ICTs and management systems for improving efficiency in healthcare and social care* (pp. 1088–1108). Hershey, PA: Medical Information Science Reference; doi:10.4018/978-1-4666-3990-4.ch057

Medhekar, A., Wong, H. Y., & Hall, J. (2014). Innovation in medical tourism service marketing: A case of India. In A. Goyal (Ed.), *Innovations in services marketing and management: Strategies for emerging economies* (pp. 49–66). Hershey, PA: Business Science Reference; doi:10.4018/978-1-4666-4671-1.ch003

Medhekar, A., Wong, H. Y., & Hall, J. (2014). Medical tourism: A conceptual framework for an innovation in global healthcare provision. In A. Goyal (Ed.), *Innovations in services marketing and management: Strategies for emerging economies* (pp. 148–169). Hershey, PA: Business Science Reference; doi:10.4018/978-1-4666-4671-1.ch009

Menciassi, A., & Laschi, C. (2014). Biorobotics. In I. Management Association (Ed.), Robotics: Concepts, methodologies, tools, and applications (pp. 1613-1643). Hershey, PA: Information Science Reference. doi:10.4018/978-1-4666-4607-0.ch079

Mendes, D., & Rodrigues, I. P. (2013). A semantic web pragmatic approach to develop clinical ontologies, and thus semantic interoperability, based in HL7 v2.xml messaging. In R. Martinho, R. Rijo, M. Cruz-Cunha, & J. Varajão (Eds.), *Information systems and technologies for enhancing health and social care* (pp. 205–214). Hershey, PA: Medical Information Science Reference; doi:10.4018/978-1-4666-3667-5.ch014

Mendoza-González, R., Martin, M. V., & Rodríguez-Martínez, L. C. (2013). Identifying the essential design requirements for usable e-health communities in mobile devices. In I. Management Association (Ed.), User-driven healthcare: Concepts, methodologies, tools, and applications (pp. 533-552). Hershey, PA: Medical Information Science Reference. doi:10.4018/978-1-4666-2770-3.ch027

Mettler, T. (2013). Transformation of the hospital supply chain: How to measure the maturity of supplier relationship management systems in hospitals? In J. Tan (Ed.), *Healthcare information technology innovation and sustainability: Frontiers and adoption* (pp. 180–192). Hershey, PA: Medical Information Science Reference; doi:10.4018/978-1-4666-2797-0.ch011

Miesenberger, K., Nussbaum, G., & Ossmann, R. (2014). AsTeRICS: A framework for including sensor technology into AT solutions for people with motor disabilities. In G. Kouroupetroglou (Ed.), *Assistive technologies and computer access for motor disabilities* (pp. 154–179). Hershey, PA: Medical Information Science Reference; doi:10.4018/978-1-4666-4438-0.ch006

Miller, K., & Sankaranarayanan, S. (2013). Applications of policy based agents in wireless body sensor mesh networks for patient health monitoring. In J. Rodrigues (Ed.), *Digital advances in medicine, e-health, and communication technologies* (pp. 85–101). Hershey, PA: Medical Information Science Reference; doi:10.4018/978-1-4666-2794-9.ch005

Mohammadian, M., & Jentzsch, R. (2013). User and data classification for a secure and practical approach for patient-doctor profiling using an RFID framework in hospital. In S. Sarnikar, D. Bennett, & M. Gaynor (Eds.), *Cases on healthcare information technology for patient care management* (pp. 224–253). Hershey, PA: Medical Information Science Reference; doi:10.4018/978-1-4666-2671-3.ch014

Monguet, J. M., Huerta, E., Fernández, J., Ferruzca, M., & Badillo, S. (2013). E-health business models prototyping by incremental design. In I. Management Association (Ed.), User-driven healthcare: Concepts, methodologies, tools, and applications (pp. 776-790). Hershey, PA: Medical Information Science Reference. doi:10.4018/978-1-4666-2770-3.ch038

Montazemi, A. R., Pittaway, J. J., & Keshavjee, K. (2013). State of IS integration in the context of patient-centered care: A network analysis and research directions. In J. Tan (Ed.), *Healthcare information technology innovation and sustainability: Frontiers and adoption* (pp. 127–144). Hershey, PA: Medical Information Science Reference; doi:10.4018/978-1-4666-2797-0.ch008

Mori, A. R., Contenti, M., & Verbicaro, R. (2013). Policies on telemedicine-enhanced hospital services: Prioritization criteria for the interventions at regional level. In V. Gulla, A. Mori, F. Gabbrielli, & P. Lanzafame (Eds.), *Telehealth networks for hospital services: New methodologies* (pp. 1–14). Hershey, PA: Medical Information Science Reference; doi:10.4018/978-1-4666-2979-0.ch001

Morita, A. (2013). The quantitative EEG change in Parkinson's disease. In J. Wu (Ed.), *Biomedical engineering and cognitive neuroscience for healthcare: Interdisciplinary applications* (pp. 225–234). Hershey, PA: Medical Information Science Reference; doi:10.4018/978-1-4666-2113-8.ch023

Moromugi, S., & Ishimatsu, T. (2013). A strength training machine with a dynamic resistance control function based on muscle activity level. In J. Wu (Ed.), *Technological advancements in biomedicine for healthcare applications* (pp. 102–110). Hershey, PA: Medical Information Science Reference; doi:10.4018/978-1-4666-2196-1.ch011

Morrow, D., & Chin, J. (2013). Technology as a bridge between health care systems and older adults. In R. Zheng, R. Hill, & M. Gardner (Eds.), *Engaging older adults with modern technology: Internet use and information access needs* (pp. 59–79). Hershey, PA: Information Science Reference; doi:10.4018/978-1-4666-1966-1.ch004

Morrow, D., & Chin, J. (2013). Technology as a bridge between health care systems and older adults. In I. Management Association (Ed.), User-driven healthcare: Concepts, methodologies, tools, and applications (pp. 99-119). Hershey, PA: Medical Information Science Reference. doi:10.4018/978-1-4666-2770-3.ch006

Mostafa, R., Hasan, G. M., Kabir, A. A., & Rahman, M. A. (2013). Proposed framework for the deployment of telemedicine centers in rural Bangladesh. In J. Rodrigues (Ed.), *Digital advances in medicine, e-health, and communication technologies* (pp. 254–270). Hershey, PA: Medical Information Science Reference; doi:10.4018/978-1-4666-2794-9.ch014

Motoi, K., Ogawa, M., Yamakoshi, T., & Yamakoshi, K. (2013). Fusion physiological sensing system for healthcare. In J. Wu (Ed.), *Technological advancements in biomedicine for healthcare applications* (pp. 298–313). Hershey, PA: Medical Information Science Reference; doi:10.4018/978-1-4666-2196-1.ch031

Motorny, S. P. (2013). Big information technology bet of a small community hospital. In S. Sarnikar, D. Bennett, & M. Gaynor (Eds.), *Cases on healthcare information technology for patient care management* (pp. 70–94). Hershey, PA: Medical Information Science Reference; doi:10.4018/978-1-4666-2671-3.ch004

Moumtzoglou, A. (2013). Health 2.0 and medicine 2.0: Safety, ownership and privacy issues. In I. Management Association (Ed.), User-driven healthcare: Concepts, methodologies, tools, and applications (pp. 1508-1522). Hershey, PA: Medical Information Science Reference. doi:10.4018/978-1-4666-2770-3.ch075

Moumtzoglou, A. (2013). Risk perception as a patient safety dimension. In A. Moumtzoglou & A. Kastania (Eds.), *E-health technologies and improving patient safety: Exploring organizational factors* (pp. 285–299). Hershey, PA: Medical Information Science Reference; doi:10.4018/978-1-4666-2657-7.ch017

Msanjila, S. S. (2013). Emerging ICT challenges on provision of online HIV/AIDS advisory services. In M. Cruz-Cunha, I. Miranda, & P. Gonçalves (Eds.), *Handbook of research on ICTs for human-centered healthcare and social care services* (pp. 248–269). Hershey, PA: Medical Information Science Reference; doi:10.4018/978-1-4666-3986-7.ch013

Müller, A. (2013). Improving the identification of medication names by increasing phonological awareness via a language-teaching computer game (medicina). In S. Arnab, I. Dunwell, & K. Debattista (Eds.), *Serious games for healthcare: Applications and implications* (pp. 283–295). Hershey, PA: Medical Information Science Reference; doi:10.4018/978-1-4666-1903-6.ch014

Murakami, S., Kim, H., Tan, J. K., Ishikawa, S., & Aoki, T. (2013). The development of a quantitative method for the detection of periarticular osteoporosis using density features within ROIs from computed radiography images of the hand. In J. Wu (Ed.), *Technological advancements in biomedicine for healthcare applications* (pp. 55–67). Hershey, PA: Medical Information Science Reference; doi:10.4018/978-1-4666-2196-1.ch007

Nadathur, S. G., & Warren, J. R. (2013). Formal-transfer in and out of stroke care units: An analysis using Bayesian networks. In J. Tan (Ed.), *Healthcare information technology innovation and sustainability: Frontiers and adoption* (pp. 193–207). Hershey, PA: Medical Information Science Reference; doi:10.4018/978-1-4666-2797-0.ch012

Naidoo, V., & Naidoo, Y. (2014). Home telecare, medical implant, and mobile technology: Evolutions in geriatric care. In C. El Morr (Ed.), *Research perspectives on the role of informatics in health policy and management* (pp. 222–237). Hershey, PA: Medical Information Science Reference; doi:10.4018/978-1-4666-4321-5.ch013

Nakagawa, S. (2013). Bone-conducted ultrasonic perception: An elucidation of perception mechanisms and the development of a novel hearing aid for the profoundly deaf. In J. Wu (Ed.), *Technological advancements in biomedicine for healthcare applications* (pp. 148–159). Hershey, PA: Medical Information Science Reference; doi:10.4018/978-1-4666-2196-1.ch016

Nakai, M., & Niinomi, M. (2013). Recent progress in mechanically biocompatible titanium-based materials. In J. Wu (Ed.), *Technological advancements in biomedicine for healthcare applications* (pp. 206–212). Hershey, PA: Medical Information Science Reference; doi:10.4018/978-1-4666-2196-1.ch022

Nakakuki, T., & Okada-Hatakeyama, M. (2013). Methods for the analysis of intracellular signal transduction systems. In J. Wu (Ed.), *Technological advancements in biomedicine for healthcare applications* (pp. 347–353). Hershey, PA: Medical Information Science Reference; doi:10.4018/978-1-4666-2196-1.ch034

Nalin, M., Verga, M., Sanna, A., & Saranummi, N. (2013). Directions for ICT research in disease prevention. In M. Cruz-Cunha, I. Miranda, & P. Gonçalves (Eds.), *Handbook of research on ICTs for human-centered healthcare and social care services* (pp. 229–247). Hershey, PA: Medical Information Science Reference; doi:10.4018/978-1-4666-3986-7.ch012

Nap, H. H., & Diaz-Orueta, U. (2013). Rehabilitation gaming. In S. Arnab, I. Dunwell, & K. Debattista (Eds.), *Serious games for healthcare: Applications and implications* (pp. 50–75). Hershey, PA: Medical Information Science Reference; doi:10.4018/978-1-4666-1903-6.ch003

Narushima, T., & Ueda, K. (2013). Calcium phosphate coating on titanium by RF magnetron sputtering. In J. Wu (Ed.), *Technological advancements in biomedicine for healthcare applications* (pp. 223–233). Hershey, PA: Medical Information Science Reference; doi:10.4018/978-1-4666-2196-1.ch024

Nava-Muñoz, S., & Morán, A. L. (2013). A review of notifications systems in elder care environments: Challenges and opportunities. In M. Cruz-Cunha, I. Miranda, & P. Gonçalves (Eds.), *Handbook of research on ICTs for human-centered healthcare and social care services* (pp. 407–429). Hershey, PA: Medical Information Science Reference; doi:10.4018/978-1-4666-3986-7.ch022

Nganji, J. T., & Nggada, S. H. (2014). Adoption of blended learning technologies in selected secondary schools in Cameroon and Nigeria: Challenges in disability inclusion. In N. Ololube (Ed.), *Advancing technology and educational development through blended learning in emerging economies* (pp. 159–173). Hershey, PA: Information Science Reference; doi:10.4018/978-1-4666-4574-5.ch009

Nikolov, S., Vera, J., & Wolkenhauer, O. (2013). Bifurcation analysis of a model accounting for the 14-3-3s signalling compartmentalisation. In I. Management Association (Ed.), Bioinformatics: Concepts, methodologies, tools, and applications (pp. 851-859). Hershey, PA: Medical Information Science Reference. doi:10.4018/978-1-4666-3604-0.ch046

Nishiguchi, H. (2013). Description of and applications for a motion analysis method for upper limbs. In J. Wu (Ed.), *Technological advancements in biomedicine for healthcare applications* (pp. 1–10). Hershey, PA: Medical Information Science Reference; doi:10.4018/978-1-4666-2196-1.ch001

Nokata, M. (2013). Small medical robot. In J. Wu (Ed.), *Technological advancements in biomedicine for healthcare applications* (pp. 170–179). Hershey, PA: Medical Information Science Reference; doi:10.4018/978-1-4666-2196-1.ch018

Noritsugu, T. (2013). Wearable power assist robot driven with pneumatic rubber artificial muscles. In J. Wu (Ed.), *Technological advancements in biomedicine for healthcare applications* (pp. 139–147). Hershey, PA: Medical Information Science Reference; doi:10.4018/978-1-4666-2196-1.ch015

Noteboom, C. (2013). Physician interaction with EHR: The importance of stakeholder identification and change management. In S. Sarnikar, D. Bennett, & M. Gaynor (Eds.), *Cases on healthcare information technology for patient care management* (pp. 95–112). Hershey, PA: Medical Information Science Reference; doi:10.4018/978-1-4666-2671-3.ch005

O'Hanlon, S. (2013). Avoiding adverse consequences of e-health. In A. Moumtzoglou & A. Kastania (Eds.), *E-health technologies and improving patient safety: Exploring organizational factors* (pp. 13–26). Hershey, PA: Medical Information Science Reference; doi:10.4018/978-1-4666-2657-7.ch002

Ogawa, K., Nishio, S., Minato, T., & Ishiguro, H. (2013). Android robots as telepresence media. In J. Wu (Ed.), *Biomedical engineering and cognitive neuroscience for healthcare: Interdisciplinary applications* (pp. 54–63). Hershey, PA: Medical Information Science Reference; doi:10.4018/978-1-4666-2113-8.ch006

Ohashi, M., Sakimura, N., Fujimoto, M., Hori, M., & Kurata, N. (2013). Technical perspective of authentication policy extension for the adaptive social services and e-health care management. In M. Cruz-Cunha, I. Miranda, & P. Gonçalves (Eds.), *Handbook of research on ICTs for human-centered healthcare and social care services* (pp. 719–726). Hershey, PA: Medical Information Science Reference; doi:10.4018/978-1-4666-3986-7.ch037

Ohta, Y., & Uchida, M. (2013). Non-contact pulse monitoring using live imaging. In J. Wu (Ed.), *Technological advancements in biomedicine for healthcare applications* (pp. 240–246). Hershey, PA: Medical Information Science Reference; doi:10.4018/978-1-4666-2196-1.ch026

Ohuchida, K., & Hashizume, M. (2013). Biomedical robotics for healthcare. In J. Wu (Ed.), *Technological advancements in biomedicine for healthcare applications* (pp. 200–205). Hershey, PA: Medical Information Science Reference; doi:10.4018/978-1-4666-2196-1.ch021

Oikonomou, D., Moulianitis, V., Lekkas, D., & Koutsabasis, P. (2013). DSS for health emergency response: A contextual, user-centred approach. In R. Biswas (Ed.), *Clinical solutions and medical progress through user-driven healthcare* (pp. 51–69). Hershey, PA: Medical Information Science Reference; doi:10.4018/978-1-4666-1876-3.ch006

Okamoto, S., Hirotomi, T., Aoki, K., & Hosomi, Y. (2013). Evaluation of walking motions with the aid of walkers using acceleration sensors. In J. Wu (Ed.), *Biomedical engineering and cognitive neuroscience for healthcare: Interdisciplinary applications* (pp. 346–354). Hershey, PA: Medical Information Science Reference; doi:10.4018/978-1-4666-2113-8.ch036

Okamura, H. (2013). Rehabilitation of elderly people with dementia. In J. Wu (Ed.), *Biomedical engineering and cognitive neuroscience for healthcare: Interdisciplinary applications* (pp. 235–242). Hershey, PA: Medical Information Science Reference; doi:10.4018/978-1-4666-2113-8.ch024

Olvera-Lobo, M., & Gutiérrez-Artacho, J. (2013). Searching health information in question-answering systems. In M. Cruz-Cunha, I. Miranda, & P. Gonçalves (Eds.), *Handbook of research on ICTs for human-centered healthcare and social care services* (pp. 474–490). Hershey, PA: Medical Information Science Reference; doi:10.4018/978-1-4666-3986-7.ch025

Padovani, E., Orelli, R. L., Agnoletti, V., & Buccioli, M. (2013). Low cost and human-centered innovations in healthcare services: A case of excellence in Italy. In S. Saeed & C. Reddick (Eds.), *Human-centered system design for electronic governance* (pp. 239–252). Hershey, PA: Information Science Reference; doi:10.4018/978-1-4666-3640-8.ch014

Paninchukunnath, A. (2014). Healthcare services delivery in India: special reference to mother and child health. In A. Goyal (Ed.), *Innovations in services marketing and management: Strategies for emerging economies* (pp. 170–189). Hershey, PA: Business Science Reference; doi:10.4018/978-1-4666-4671-1.ch010

Paparountas, T., Nikolaidou-Katsaridou, M. N., Rustici, G., & Aidinis, V. (2013). Data mining and meta-analysis on DNA microarray data. In I. Management Association (Ed.), Bioinformatics: Concepts, methodologies, tools, and applications (pp. 1196-1236). Hershey, PA: Medical Information Science Reference. doi:10.4018/978-1-4666-3604-0.ch062

Parentela, G., Mancini, P., Naccarella, F., Feng, Z., & Rinaldi, G. (2013). Telemedicine, the European space agency, and the support to the african population for infectious disease problems: Potentiality and perspectives for Asia countries and China. In V. Gulla, A. Mori, F. Gabbrielli, & P. Lanzafame (Eds.), *Telehealth networks for hospital services: New methodologies* (pp. 89–96). Hershey, PA: Medical Information Science Reference; doi:10.4018/978-1-4666-2979-0.ch005

Paterson, G. I., MacDonald, J. M., & Mensink, N. N. (2014). The administrative policy quandary in Canada's health service organizations. In C. El Morr (Ed.), *Research perspectives on the role of informatics in health policy and management* (pp. 116–134). Hershey, PA: Medical Information Science Reference; doi:10.4018/978-1-4666-4321-5.ch008

Penchovsky, R. (2013). Engineering gene control circuits with allosteric ribozymes in human cells as a medicine of the future. In I. Management Association (Ed.), Bioinformatics: Concepts, methodologies, tools, and applications (pp. 860-883). Hershey, PA: Medical Information Science Reference. doi:10.4018/978-1-4666-3604-0.ch047

Pereira, O. R., Caldeira, J. M., & Rodrigues, J. J. (2013). An advanced and secure symbian-based mobile approach for body sensor networks interaction. In J. Rodrigues (Ed.), *Digital advances in medicine, e-health, and communication technologies* (pp. 33–48). Hershey, PA: Medical Information Science Reference; doi:10.4018/978-1-4666-2794-9.ch002

Petkovic, M., & Ibraimi, L. (2013). Privacy and security in e-health applications. In I. Management Association (Ed.), User-driven healthcare: Concepts, methodologies, tools, and applications (pp. 1141-1166). Hershey, PA: Medical Information Science Reference. doi:10.4018/978-1-4666-2770-3.ch058

Peyton, L., & Hu, J. (2013). Identity management and audit trail support for privacy protection in e-health networks. In I. Management Association (Ed.), User-driven healthcare: Concepts, methodologies, tools, and applications (pp. 1112-1125). Hershey, PA: Medical Information Science Reference. doi:10.4018/978-1-4666-2770-3.ch056

Pham, D. V., Halgamuge, M. N., Nirmalathas, T., & Moran, B. (2013). A centralized real-time e-healthcare system for remote detection and prediction of epileptic seizures. In I. Management Association (Ed.), User-driven healthcare: Concepts, methodologies, tools, and applications (pp. 326-356). Hershey, PA: Medical Information Science Reference. doi:10.4018/978-1-4666-2770-3.ch017

Phua, C., Roy, P. C., Aloulou, H., Biswas, J., Tolstikov, A., & Foo, V. S. ... Xu, D. (2014). State-of-the-art assistive technology for people with dementia. In Assistive technologies: Concepts, methodologies, tools, and applications (pp. 1606-1625). Hershey, PA: Information Science Reference. doi:10.4018/978-1-4666-4422-9.ch085

Pino, A. (2014). Augmentative and alternative communication systems for the motor disabled. In G. Kouroupetroglou (Ed.), *Disability informatics and web accessibility for motor limitations* (pp. 105–152). Hershey, PA: Medical Information Science Reference; doi:10.4018/978-1-4666-4442-7.ch004

Portela, F., Cabral, A., Abelha, A., Salazar, M., Quintas, C., Machado, J., & Santos, M. F. et al. (2013). Knowledge acquisition process for intelligent decision support in critical health care. In R. Martinho, R. Rijo, M. Cruz-Cunha, & J. Varajão (Eds.), *Information systems and technologies for enhancing health and social care* (pp. 55–68). Hershey, PA: Medical Information Science Reference; doi:10.4018/978-1-4666-3667-5.ch004

Previtali, P. (2013). Grid technology for archive solutions in health care organizations. In A. Moumtzoglou & A. Kastania (Eds.), *E-health technologies and improving patient safety: Exploring organizational factors* (pp. 148–154). Hershey, PA: Medical Information Science Reference; doi:10.4018/978-1-4666-2657-7.ch010

Purkayastha, S. (2013). Design and implementation of mobile-based technology in strengthening health information system: Aligning mhealth solutions to infrastructures. In I. Management Association (Ed.), User-driven healthcare: Concepts, methodologies, tools, and applications (pp. 689-713). Hershey, PA: Medical Information Science Reference. doi:10.4018/978-1-4666-2770-3.ch034

Qi, G., & Wu, J. (2013). Functional role of the left ventral occipito-temporal cortex in reading. In J. Wu (Ed.), *Biomedical engineering and cognitive neuroscience for healthcare: Interdisciplinary applications* (pp. 192–200). Hershey, PA: Medical Information Science Reference; doi:10.4018/978-1-4666-2113-8.ch020

Queirós, A., Alvarelhão, J., Silva, A. G., Teixeira, A., & Pacheco da Rocha, N. (2013). A conceptual framework for the design and development of AAL services. In M. Cruz-Cunha, I. Miranda, & P. Gonçalves (Eds.), *Handbook of research on ICTs for human-centered healthcare and social care services* (pp. 568–586). Hershey, PA: Medical Information Science Reference; doi:10.4018/978-1-4666-3986-7.ch030

Ravka, N. (2014). Informatics and health services: The potential benefits and challenges of electronic health records and personal electronic health records in patient care, cost control, and health research – An overview. In C. El Morr (Ed.), *Research perspectives on the role of informatics in health policy and management* (pp. 89–114). Hershey, PA: Medical Information Science Reference; doi:10.4018/978-1-4666-4321-5.ch007

Reibling, N., & Wendt, C. (2013). Regulating patients' access to healthcare services. In M. Merviö (Ed.), *Healthcare management and economics: Perspectives on public and private administration* (pp. 53–68). Hershey, PA: Medical Information Science Reference; doi:10.4018/978-1-4666-3982-9.ch005

Reis, C. I., Freire, C. S., Fernández, J., & Monguet, J. M. (2013). Patient centered design: Challenges and lessons learned from working with health professionals and schizophrenic patients in e-therapy contexts. In R. Martinho, R. Rijo, M. Cruz-Cunha, & J. Varajão (Eds.), *Information systems and technologies for enhancing health and social care* (pp. 120–135). Hershey, PA: Medical Information Science Reference; doi:10.4018/978-1-4666-3667-5.ch008

Remmers, H., & Hülsken-Giesler, M. (2013). e-Health technologies in home care nursing: Recent survey results and subsequent ethical issues. In I. Management Association (Ed.), User-driven healthcare: Concepts, methodologies, tools, and applications (pp. 396-420). Hershey, PA: Medical Information Science Reference. doi:10.4018/978-1-4666-2770-3.ch020

Ricketts, M. (2014). Making health information personal: How anecdotes bring concepts to life. In S. Hai-Jew (Ed.), *Packaging digital information for enhanced learning and analysis: Data visualization, spatialization, and multidimensionality* (pp. 1–36). Hershey, PA: Information Science Reference; doi:10.4018/978-1-4666-4462-5.ch001

Rocha, Á. (2013). Evolution of information systems and technologies maturity in healthcare. In J. Tan (Ed.), *Healthcare information technology innovation and sustainability: Frontiers and adoption* (pp. 238–246). Hershey, PA: Medical Information Science Reference; doi:10.4018/978-1-4666-2797-0.ch015

Rodríguez-Gómez, D., & Gairín, J. (2014). Communities of practice in the Catalan public administration: Promoting their improvement. In Y. Al-Bastaki & A. Shajera (Eds.), *Building a competitive public sector with knowledge management strategy* (pp. 383–402). Hershey, PA: Business Science Reference; doi:10.4018/978-1-4666-4434-2.ch018

Rodríguez-Solano, C., Lezcano, L., & Sicilia, M. (2013). Automated generation of SNOMED CT subsets from clinical guidelines. In R. Martinho, R. Rijo, M. Cruz-Cunha, & J. Varajão (Eds.), *Information systems and technologies for enhancing health and social care* (pp. 190–204). Hershey, PA: Medical Information Science Reference; doi:10.4018/978-1-4666-3667-5.ch013

Rosu, S. M., & Dragoi, G. (2014). E-health sites development using open source software and OMT methodology as support for family doctors' activities: A Romanian case study. In M. Cruz-Cunha, F. Moreira, & J. Varajão (Eds.), *Handbook of research on enterprise 2.0: Technological, social, and organizational dimensions* (pp. 72–88). Hershey, PA: Business Science Reference; doi:10.4018/978-1-4666-4373-4.ch004

Roy, N., Das, S. K., & Julien, C. (2013). Resolving and mediating ambiguous contexts in pervasive environments. In I. Management Association (Ed.), User-driven healthcare: Concepts, methodologies, tools, and applications (pp. 630-654). Hershey, PA: Medical Information Science Reference. doi:10.4018/978-1-4666-2770-3.ch031

Russo, M. R. (2014). Emergency management professional development: Linking information communication technology and social communication skills to enhance a sense of community and social justice in the 21st century. In I. Management Association (Ed.), Crisis management: Concepts, methodologies, tools and applications (pp. 651-665). Hershey, PA: Information Science Reference. doi:10.4018/978-1-4666-4707-7.ch031

Sabone, M. B., Mogobe, K. D., & Sabone, T. G. (2013). ICTS and their role in health promotion: A preliminary situation analysis in selected botswana rural communities. In I. Management Association (Ed.), User-driven healthcare: Concepts, methodologies, tools, and applications (pp. 211-224). Hershey, PA: Medical Information Science Reference. doi:10.4018/978-1-4666-2770-3.ch012

Saha, P. (2014). Systemic enterprise architecture as future: Tackling complexity in governments in the cusp of change. In P. Saha (Ed.), *A systemic perspective to managing complexity with enterprise architecture* (pp. 1–70). Hershey, PA: Business Science Reference; doi:10.4018/978-1-4666-4518-9.ch001

Saijo, Y. (2013). Biomedical application of multimodal ultrasound microscope. In J. Wu (Ed.), *Technological advancements in biomedicine for healthcare applications* (pp. 27–35). Hershey, PA: Medical Information Science Reference; doi:10.4018/978-1-4666-2196-1.ch004

Santos, M., Bastião, L., Costa, C., Silva, A., & Rocha, N. (2013). Clinical data mining in small hospital PACS: Contributions for radiology department improvement. In R. Martinho, R. Rijo, M. Cruz-Cunha, & J. Varajão (Eds.), *Information systems and technologies for enhancing health and social care* (pp. 236–251). Hershey, PA: Medical Information Science Reference; doi:10.4018/978-1-4666-3667-5.ch016

Santos, M. F., Portela, F., Miranda, M., Machado, J., Abelha, A., Silva, Á., & Rua, F. (2013). Grid data mining strategies for outcome prediction in distributed intensive care units. In R. Martinho, R. Rijo, M. Cruz-Cunha, & J. Varajão (Eds.), *Information systems and technologies for enhancing health and social care* (pp. 87–101). Hershey, PA: Medical Information Science Reference; doi:10.4018/978-1-4666-3667-5.ch006

Santos, R. J., Bernardino, J., & Vieira, M. (2013). A hypotension surveillance and prediction system for critical care. In M. Cruz-Cunha, I. Miranda, & P. Gonçalves (Eds.), *Handbook of research on ICTs and management systems for improving efficiency in healthcare and social care* (pp. 341–355). Hershey, PA: Medical Information Science Reference; doi:10.4018/978-1-4666-3990-4.ch017

Sanz, P. R., Mezcua, B. R., & Pena, J. M. (2013). ICTs for orientation and mobility for blind people: A state of the art. In M. Cruz-Cunha, I. Miranda, & P. Gonçalves (Eds.), *Handbook of research on ICTs for human-centered healthcare and social care services* (pp. 646–669). Hershey, PA: Medical Information Science Reference; doi:10.4018/978-1-4666-3986-7.ch034

Sarabdeen, J. (2013). Legal issues in e-healthcare systems. In I. Management Association (Ed.), User-driven healthcare: Concepts, methodologies, tools, and applications (pp. 1194-1219). Hershey, PA: Medical Information Science Reference. doi:10.4018/978-1-4666-2770-3.ch060

Sarbadhikari, S. N. (2013). Unlearning and relearning in online health education. In I. Management Association (Ed.), User-driven healthcare: Concepts, methodologies, tools, and applications (pp. 1348-1363). Hershey, PA: Medical Information Science Reference. doi:10.4018/978-1-4666-2770-3.ch067

Sasayama, T., Hamada, S., & Kobayashi, T. (2013). Application of prewhitening beamformer with linear constraints for correlated EEG signal source estimation. In J. Wu (Ed.), *Biomedical engineering and cognitive neuroscience for healthcare: Interdisciplinary applications* (pp. 243–254). Hershey, PA: Medical Information Science Reference; doi:10.4018/978-1-4666-2113-8.ch025

Sato, T., & Minato, K. (2013). Differences in analysis methods of the human uncinate fasciculus using diffusion tensor MRI. In J. Wu (Ed.), *Biomedical engineering and cognitive neuroscience for healthcare: Interdisciplinary applications* (pp. 162–170). Hershey, PA: Medical Information Science Reference; doi:10.4018/978-1-4666-2113-8.ch017

Satoh, J. (2013). Molecular network analysis of target RNAs and interacting proteins of TDP-43, a causative gene for the neurodegenerative diseases ALS/FTLD. In I. Management Association (Ed.), Bioinformatics: Concepts, methodologies, tools, and applications (pp. 964-985). Hershey, PA: Medical Information Science Reference. doi:10.4018/978-1-4666-3604-0.ch052

Satoh, J. (2013). Molecular network analysis of target RNAs and interacting proteins of TDP-43, a causative gene for the neurodegenerative diseases ALS/FTLD. In J. Wu (Ed.), *Technological advancements in biomedicine for healthcare applications* (pp. 314–335). Hershey, PA: Medical Information Science Reference; doi:10.4018/978-1-4666-2196-1.ch032

Schafer, S. B. (2013). Fostering psychological coherence: With ICTs. In M. Cruz-Cunha, I. Miranda, & P. Gonçalves (Eds.), *Handbook of research on ICTs for human-centered healthcare and social care services* (pp. 29–47). Hershey, PA: Medical Information Science Reference; doi:10.4018/978-1-4666-3986-7.ch002

Schmeida, M., & McNeal, R. (2013). Bridging the inequality gap to accessing medicare and medicaid information online: An empirical analysis of e-government success 2002 through 2010. In J. Gil-Garcia (Ed.), *E-government success around the world: Cases, empirical studies, and practical recommendations* (pp. 60–78). Hershey, PA: Information Science Reference; doi:10.4018/978-1-4666-4173-0.ch004

Scholl, J. C., & Olaniran, B. A. (2013). ICT use and multidisciplinary healthcare teams. In M. Cruz-Cunha, I. Miranda, & P. Gonçalves (Eds.), *Handbook of research on ICTs for human-centered healthcare and social care services* (pp. 627–645). Hershey, PA: Medical Information Science Reference; doi:10.4018/978-1-4666-3986-7.ch033

Serenko, N. (2013). The impact of genetic testing and genetic information on ethical, legal and social issues in North America: The framework. In I. Management Association (Ed.), Bioinformatics: Concepts, methodologies, tools, and applications (pp. 1317-1333). Hershey, PA: Medical Information Science Reference. doi:10.4018/978-1-4666-3604-0.ch067

Serrano, M., Elmisery, A., Foghlú, M. Ó., Donnelly, W., Storni, C., & Fernström, M. (2013). Pervasive computing support in the transition towards personalised health systems. In J. Rodrigues (Ed.), *Digital advances in medicine, e-health, and communication technologies* (pp. 49–64). Hershey, PA: Medical Information Science Reference; doi:10.4018/978-1-4666-2794-9.ch003

Shaw, V., & Braa, J. (2013). "Developed in the south": An evolutionary and prototyping approach to developing scalable and sustainable health information systems. In I. Management Association (Ed.), User-driven healthcare: Concepts, methodologies, tools, and applications (pp. 583-607). Hershey, PA: Medical Information Science Reference. doi:10.4018/978-1-4666-2770-3.ch029

Shi, J., Upadhyaya, S., & Erdem, E. (2013). Health information exchange for improving the efficiency and quality of healthcare delivery. In I. Management Association (Ed.), User-driven healthcare: Concepts, methodologies, tools, and applications (pp. 714-736). Hershey, PA: Medical Information Science Reference. doi:10.4018/978-1-4666-2770-3.ch035

Shibata, T. (2013). A human-like cognitive computer based on a psychologically inspired VLSI brain model. In J. Wu (Ed.), *Technological advancements in biomedicine for healthcare applications* (pp. 247–266). Hershey, PA: Medical Information Science Reference; doi:10.4018/978-1-4666-2196-1.ch027

Shimada, S. (2013). Self-body recognition and its impairment. In J. Wu (Ed.), *Biomedical engineering and cognitive neuroscience for healthcare: Interdisciplinary applications* (pp. 156–161). Hershey, PA: Medical Information Science Reference; doi:10.4018/978-1-4666-2113-8.ch016

Shimogonya, Y., Ishikawa, T., Yamaguchi, T., Kumamaru, H., & Itoh, K. (2013). Computational study of the hemodynamics of cerebral aneurysm initiation. In J. Wu (Ed.), *Technological advancements in biomedicine for healthcare applications* (pp. 267–277). Hershey, PA: Medical Information Science Reference; doi:10.4018/978-1-4666-2196-1.ch028

Shimonomura, K. (2013). A neuromorphic robot vision system to predict the response of visual neurons. In J. Wu (Ed.), *Technological advancements in biomedicine for healthcare applications* (pp. 193–199). Hershey, PA: Medical Information Science Reference; doi:10.4018/978-1-4666-2196-1.ch020

Shrestha, S. (2013). Clinical decision support system for diabetes prevention: An illustrative case. In S. Sarnikar, D. Bennett, & M. Gaynor (Eds.), *Cases on healthcare information technology for patient care management* (pp. 308–329). Hershey, PA: Medical Information Science Reference; doi:10.4018/978-1-4666-2671-3.ch017

Siddiqui, Z. S., & Jonas-Dwyer, D. R. (2013). Mobile learning in health professions education: A systematic review. In J. Keengwe (Ed.), *Pedagogical applications and social effects of mobile technology integration* (pp. 193–205). Hershey, PA: Information Science Reference; doi:10.4018/978-1-4666-2985-1.ch011

Silvana de Rosa, A., Fino, E., & Bocci, E. (2014). Addressing healthcare on-line demand and supply relating to mental illness: Knowledge sharing about psychiatry and psychoanalysis through social networks in Italy and France. In A. Kapoor & C. Kulshrestha (Eds.), *Dynamics of competitive advantage and consumer perception in social marketing* (pp. 16–55). Hershey, PA: Business Science Reference; doi:10.4018/978-1-4666-4430-4.ch002

Siqueira, S. R., Rocha, E. C., & Nery, M. S. (2013). Brazilian occupational therapy perspective about digital games as an inclusive resource to disabled people in schools. In I. Management Association (Ed.), User-driven healthcare: Concepts, methodologies, tools, and applications (pp. 918-937). Hershey, PA: Medical Information Science Reference. doi:10.4018/978-1-4666-2770-3.ch046

Sliedrecht, S., & Kotzé, E. (2013). Patients with a spinal cord injury inform and co-construct services at a spinal cord rehabilitation unit. In I. Management Association (Ed.), User-driven healthcare: Concepts, methodologies, tools, and applications (pp. 1054-1072). Hershey, PA: Medical Information Science Reference. doi:10.4018/978-1-4666-2770-3.ch053

Smedberg, Å. (2013). E-health communities for learning healthy habits: How to consider quality and usability. In I. Management Association (Ed.), User-driven healthcare: Concepts, methodologies, tools, and applications (pp. 310-325). Hershey, PA: Medical Information Science Reference. doi:10.4018/978-1-4666-2770-3.ch016

Smedberg, Å., & Sandmark, H. (2013). Dynamic stress management: Self-help through holistic system design. In I. Management Association (Ed.), User-driven healthcare: Concepts, methodologies, tools, and applications (pp. 1469-1486). Hershey, PA: Medical Information Science Reference. doi:10.4018/978-1-4666-2770-3.ch073

Sobol, M., & Prater, E. (2013). Adoption, usage and efficiency: Benchmarking healthcare IT in private practices. In J. Tan (Ed.), *Healthcare information technology innovation and sustainability: Frontiers and adoption* (pp. 145–159). Hershey, PA: Medical Information Science Reference; doi:10.4018/978-1-4666-2797-0.ch009

Sobrinho, Á. A., Dias da Silva, L., Melo de Medeiros, L., & Pinheiro, M. E. (2013). A mobile assistant to aid early detection of chronic kidney disease. In R. Martinho, R. Rijo, M. Cruz-Cunha, & J. Varajão (Eds.), *Information systems and technologies for enhancing health and social care* (pp. 309–323). Hershey, PA: Medical Information Science Reference; doi:10.4018/978-1-4666-3667-5.ch020

Soomlek, C., & Benedicenti, L. (2013). Agent-based wellness indicator. In V. Gulla, A. Mori, F. Gabbrielli, & P. Lanzafame (Eds.), *Telehealth networks for hospital services: New methodologies* (pp. 300–330). Hershey, PA: Medical Information Science Reference; doi:10.4018/978-1-4666-2979-0.ch020

Spadaro, L., Timpano, F., Marino, S., & Bramanti, P. (2013). Telemedicine and Alzheimer disease: ICT-based services for people with Alzheimer disease and their caregivers. In V. Gulla, A. Mori, F. Gabbrielli, & P. Lanzafame (Eds.), *Telehealth networks for hospital services: New methodologies* (pp. 191–206). Hershey, PA: Medical Information Science Reference; doi:10.4018/978-1-4666-2979-0.ch013

Springer, J. A., Beever, J., Morar, N., Sprague, J. E., & Kane, M. D. (2013). Ethics, privacy, and the future of genetic information in healthcare information assurance and security. In I. Management Association (Ed.), Bioinformatics: Concepts, methodologies, tools, and applications (pp. 1405-1423). Hershey, PA: Medical Information Science Reference. doi:10.4018/978-1-4666-3604-0.ch072

Stachura, M. E., Wood, J., Angjellari-Dajci, F., Grayson, J., Astapova, E. V., Tung, H., . . . Lawless, W. (2013). Representing organizational conservation of information: A review of telemedicine and e-health in Georgia. In I. Management Association (Ed.), User-driven healthcare: Concepts, methodologies, tools, and applications (pp. 1220-1235). Hershey, PA: Medical Information Science Reference. doi:10.4018/978-1-4666-2770-3.ch061

Stefaniak, J. E. (2013). Resuscitating team roles within wayburn health system. In A. Ritzhaupt & S. Kumar (Eds.), *Cases on educational technology implementation for facilitating learning* (pp. 130–145). Hershey, PA: Information Science Reference; doi:10.4018/978-1-4666-3676-7.ch008

Sugiura, M. (2013). A cognitive neuroscience approach to self and mental health. In J. Wu (Ed.), *Biomedical engineering and cognitive neuroscience for healthcare: Interdisciplinary applications* (pp. 1–10). Hershey, PA: Medical Information Science Reference; doi:10.4018/978-1-4666-2113-8.ch001

Supnithi, T., Buranarach, M., Thatphithakkul, N., Junsirimongkol, B., Wongrochananan, S., Kulnawan, N., & Jiamjarasrangsi, W. (2014). A self-management service framework to support chronic disease patients' self-management. In M. Kosaka & K. Shirahada (Eds.), *Progressive trends in knowledge and system-based science for service innovation* (pp. 425–450). Hershey, PA: Business Science Reference; doi:10.4018/978-1-4666-4663-6.ch023

Takahashi, K., & Watanabe, K. (2013). Crossmodal interactions in visual competition. In J. Wu (Ed.), *Biomedical engineering and cognitive neuroscience for healthcare: Interdisciplinary applications* (pp. 64–72). Hershey, PA: Medical Information Science Reference; doi:10.4018/978-1-4666-2113-8.ch007

Tamiya, T., Kawanishi, M., Miyake, K., Kawai, N., & Guo, S. (2013). Neurosurgical operations using navigation microscope integration system. In J. Wu (Ed.), *Technological advancements in biomedicine for healthcare applications* (pp. 128–138). Hershey, PA: Medical Information Science Reference; doi:10.4018/978-1-4666-2196-1.ch014

Tan, R., Wang, S., Jiang, Y., Ishida, K., & Fujie, M. G. (2013). Motion control of an omni-directional walker for walking support. In J. Wu (Ed.), *Biomedical engineering and cognitive neuroscience for healthcare: Interdisciplinary applications* (pp. 20–28). Hershey, PA: Medical Information Science Reference; doi:10.4018/978-1-4666-2113-8.ch003

Tanaka, H., & Furutani, M. (2013). Sleep management promotes healthy lifestyle, mental health, QOL, and a healthy brain. In J. Wu (Ed.), *Biomedical engineering and cognitive neuroscience for healthcare: Interdisciplinary applications* (pp. 211–224). Hershey, PA: Medical Information Science Reference; doi:10.4018/978-1-4666-2113-8.ch022

Tang, C., & Carpendale, S. (2013). Human-centered design for health information technology: A qualitative approach. In I. Management Association (Ed.), User-driven healthcare: Concepts, methodologies, tools, and applications (pp. 158-179). Hershey, PA: Medical Information Science Reference. doi:10.4018/978-1-4666-2770-3.ch009

Tang, X., Gao, Y., Yang, W., Zhang, M., & Wu, J. (2013). Audiovisual integration of natural auditory and visual stimuli in the real-world situation. In J. Wu (Ed.), *Biomedical engineering and cognitive neuroscience for healthcare: Interdisciplinary applications* (pp. 337–344). Hershey, PA: Medical Information Science Reference; doi:10.4018/978-1-4666-2113-8.ch035

Targowski, A. (2013). Well-being, wisdom, health, and IT: From the big-picture to the small-picture. In M. Cruz-Cunha, I. Miranda, & P. Gonçalves (Eds.), *Handbook of research on ICTs for human-centered healthcare and social care services* (pp. 1–28). Hershey, PA: Medical Information Science Reference; doi:10.4018/978-1-4666-3986-7.ch001

Tayabali, S., & Martin, C. M. (2013). The need to transform the core values of medical care and health organizations. In R. Biswas (Ed.), *Clinical solutions and medical progress through user-driven healthcare* (pp. 85–92). Hershey, PA: Medical Information Science Reference; doi:10.4018/978-1-4666-1876-3.ch009

Taylor, B. W. (2014). Decision-making and decision support in acute care. In C. El Morr (Ed.), *Research perspectives on the role of informatics in health policy and management* (pp. 1–18). Hershey, PA: Medical Information Science Reference; doi:10.4018/978-1-4666-4321-5.ch001

Teixeira, C., Pinto, J. S., Ferreira, F., Oliveira, A., Teixeira, A., & Pereira, C. (2013). Cloud computing enhanced service development architecture for the living usability lab. In R. Martinho, R. Rijo, M. Cruz-Cunha, & J. Varajão (Eds.), *Information systems and technologies for enhancing health and social care* (pp. 33–53). Hershey, PA: Medical Information Science Reference; doi:10.4018/978-1-4666-3667-5.ch003

Teixeira, L., Saavedra, V., Ferreira, C., & Santos, B. S. (2013). The role of ICTs in the management of rare chronic diseases: The case of hemophilia. In M. Cruz-Cunha, I. Miranda, & P. Gonçalves (Eds.), *Handbook of research on ICTs and management systems for improving efficiency in healthcare and social care* (pp. 635–649). Hershey, PA: Medical Information Science Reference; doi:10.4018/978-1-4666-3990-4.ch033

Teoh, S. Y., Singh, M., & Chong, J. (2013). An overview of e-health development in Australia. In I. Management Association (Ed.), User-driven healthcare: Concepts, methodologies, tools, and applications (pp. 901-917). Hershey, PA: Medical Information Science Reference. doi:10.4018/978-1-4666-2770-3.ch045

Tiwari, S., & Srivastava, R. (2014). Research and developments in medical image reconstruction methods and its applications. In R. Srivastava, S. Singh, & K. Shukla (Eds.), *Research developments in computer vision and image processing: Methodologies and applications* (pp. 274–312). Hershey, PA: Information Science Reference; doi:10.4018/978-1-4666-4558-5.ch014

Tobolcea, I. (2013). The psychosocial impact of ICT efficiency on speech disorders-treatment. In M. Cruz-Cunha, I. Miranda, & P. Gonçalves (Eds.), *Handbook of research on ICTs for human-centered healthcare and social care services* (pp. 70–92). Hershey, PA: Medical Information Science Reference; doi:10.4018/978-1-4666-3986-7.ch004

Toda, T., Chen, P., Ozaki, S., Fujita, K., & Ideguchi, N. (2013). A simple web-based image database system for facilitating medical care in dermatological clinics. In I. Management Association (Ed.), User-driven healthcare: Concepts, methodologies, tools, and applications (pp. 502-513). Hershey, PA: Medical Information Science Reference. doi:10.4018/978-1-4666-2770-3.ch025

Toda, T., Chen, P., Ozaki, S., Fujita, K., & Ideguchi, N. (2013). A simple web-based image database system for facilitating medical care in dermatological clinics. In J. Wu (Ed.), *Technological advancements in biomedicine for healthcare applications* (pp. 385–397). Hershey, PA: Medical Information Science Reference; doi:10.4018/978-1-4666-2196-1.ch038

Trudeau, S. (2013). CoRDS registry: An HIT case study concerning setup and maintenance of a disease registry. In S. Sarnikar, D. Bennett, & M. Gaynor (Eds.), *Cases on healthcare information technology for patient care management* (pp. 197–207). Hershey, PA: Medical Information Science Reference; doi:10.4018/978-1-4666-2671-3.ch012

Tseng, R., & Yi-Luen Do, E. (2013). The role of information and computer technology for children with autism spectrum disorder and the facial expression wonderland (FEW). In A. Gangopadhyay (Ed.), *Methods, models, and computation for medical informatics* (pp. 98–116). Hershey, PA: Medical Information Science Reference; doi:10.4018/978-1-4666-2653-9.ch006

Uchitomi, H., Suzuki, K., Nishi, T., Hove, M. J., Miyake, Y., Orimo, S., & Wada, Y. (2013). Gait rhythm of Parkinson's disease patients and an interpersonal synchrony emulation system based on cooperative gait. In J. Wu (Ed.), *Biomedical engineering and cognitive neuroscience for healthcare: Interdisciplinary applications* (pp. 38–53). Hershey, PA: Medical Information Science Reference; doi:10.4018/978-1-4666-2113-8.ch005

Usher, W., & San Too, L. (2013). E-health knowledge management by australian university students. In I. Management Association (Ed.), User-driven healthcare: Concepts, methodologies, tools, and applications (pp. 938-953). Hershey, PA: Medical Information Science Reference. doi:10.4018/978-1-4666-2770-3.ch047

Van Genderen, E. (2014). Intensive care. In V. Jham & S. Puri (Eds.), *Cases on consumer-centric marketing management* (pp. 53–67). Hershey, PA: Business Science Reference; doi:10.4018/978-1-4666-4357-4.ch006

Van Leuven, N., Newton, D., Leuenberger, D. Z., & Esteves, T. (2014). Reaching citizen 2.0: How government uses social media to send public messages during times of calm and times of crisis. In I. Management Association (Ed.), Crisis management: Concepts, methodologies, tools and applications (pp. 839-857). Hershey, PA: Information Science Reference. doi:10.4018/978-1-4666-4707-7.ch041

Vasudevan, V., & Rao, H. (2013). E-discovery and health care IT: An investigation. In I. Management Association (Ed.), User-driven healthcare: Concepts, methodologies, tools, and applications (pp. 1622-1635). Hershey, PA: Medical Information Science Reference. doi:10.4018/978-1-4666-2770-3.ch080

Vat, K. H. (2013). Conceiving community knowledge records as e-governance concerns in wired healthcare provision. In I. Management Association (Ed.), User-driven healthcare: Concepts, methodologies, tools, and applications (pp. 1093-1111). Hershey, PA: Medical Information Science Reference. doi:10.4018/978-1-4666-2770-3.ch055

Venkatasubramanian, K. K., Nabar, S., Gupta, S. K., & Poovendran, R. (2013). Cyber physical security solutions for pervasive health monitoring systems. In I. Management Association (Ed.), User-driven healthcare: Concepts, methodologies, tools, and applications (pp. 447-465). Hershey, PA: Medical Information Science Reference. doi:10.4018/978-1-4666-2770-3.ch022

Victan, H. (2013). Emerging trends in user-driven healthcare: Negotiating disclosure in online health community organizations. In I. Management Association (Ed.), User-driven healthcare: Concepts, methodologies, tools, and applications (pp. 1589-1606). Hershey, PA: Medical Information Science Reference. doi:10.4018/978-1-4666-2770-3.ch078

Vidal, B., Pereira, J. M., & Santos, G. (2013). SimBody: An interactive simulator for health education. In S. Arnab, I. Dunwell, & K. Debattista (Eds.), *Serious games for healthcare: Applications and implications* (pp. 265–282). Hershey, PA: Medical Information Science Reference; doi:10.4018/978-1-4666-1903-6.ch013

Vivekananda-Schmidt, P. (2013). Ethics in the design of serious games for healthcare and medicine. In S. Arnab, I. Dunwell, & K. Debattista (Eds.), *Serious games for healthcare: Applications and implications* (pp. 91–106). Hershey, PA: Medical Information Science Reference; doi:10.4018/978-1-4666-1903-6.ch005

Wahbeh, A. (2013). Application of handheld computing and mobile phones in diabetes self-care. In S. Sarnikar, D. Bennett, & M. Gaynor (Eds.), *Cases on healthcare information technology for patient care management* (pp. 254–275). Hershey, PA: Medical Information Science Reference; doi:10.4018/978-1-4666-2671-3.ch015

Waidyanatha, N., & Dekker, S. (2013). The RTBP – Collective intelligence driving health for the user. In R. Biswas (Ed.), *Clinical solutions and medical progress through user-driven healthcare* (pp. 70–78). Hershey, PA: Medical Information Science Reference; doi:10.4018/978-1-4666-1876-3.ch007

Waidyanatha, N., Dubrawski, A. M. G., & Gow, G. (2013). Affordable system for rapid detection and mitigation of emerging diseases. In J. Rodrigues (Ed.), *Digital advances in medicine, e-health, and communication technologies* (pp. 271–288). Hershey, PA: Medical Information Science Reference; doi:10.4018/978-1-4666-2794-9.ch015

Walker, D. (2013). How would a ban on prescriber-identifying information impact pharmaceutical marketing? In M. Merviö (Ed.), *Healthcare management and economics: Perspectives on public and private administration* (pp. 141–153). Hershey, PA: Medical Information Science Reference; doi:10.4018/978-1-4666-3982-9.ch011

Wang, B., Yan, T., & Wu, J. (2013). Neuronal function in the cortical face perception network. In J. Wu (Ed.), *Biomedical engineering and cognitive neuroscience for healthcare: Interdisciplinary applications* (pp. 171–182). Hershey, PA: Medical Information Science Reference; doi:10.4018/978-1-4666-2113-8.ch018

Wang, Y., & Wang, Q. (2013). Evaluating the IEEE 802.15.6 2.4GHz WBAN proposal on medical multi-parameter monitoring under WiFi/bluetooth interference. In J. Rodrigues (Ed.), *Digital advances in medicine, e-health, and communication technologies* (pp. 312–325). Hershey, PA: Medical Information Science Reference; doi:10.4018/978-1-4666-2794-9.ch018

Watanabe, T., & Miura, N. (2013). Functional electrical stimulation (FES) control for restoration and rehabilitation of motor function. In J. Wu (Ed.), *Technological advancements in biomedicine for healthcare applications* (pp. 80–93). Hershey, PA: Medical Information Science Reference; doi:10.4018/978-1-4666-2196-1.ch009

Watanabe, Y., Tanaka, H., & Hirata, K. (2013). Evaluation of cognitive function in migraine patients: A study using event-related potentials. In J. Wu (Ed.), *Biomedical engineering and cognitive neuroscience for healthcare: Interdisciplinary applications* (pp. 303–310). Hershey, PA: Medical Information Science Reference; doi:10.4018/978-1-4666-2113-8.ch031

Watfa, M. K., Kaur, M., & Daruwala, R. F. (2013). RFID applications in e-healthcare. In I. Management Association (Ed.), User-driven healthcare: Concepts, methodologies, tools, and applications (pp. 259-287). Hershey, PA: Medical Information Science Reference. doi:10.4018/978-1-4666-2770-3.ch014

Wesorick, B. (2013). Essential steps for successful implementation of the EHR to achieve sustainable, safe, quality care. In A. Moumtzoglou & A. Kastania (Eds.), *E-health technologies and improving patient safety: Exploring organizational factors* (pp. 27–55). Hershey, PA: Medical Information Science Reference; doi:10.4018/978-1-4666-2657-7.ch003

Whitaker, R. (2013). Securing health-effective medicine in practice: A critical perspective on user-driven healthcare. In R. Biswas (Ed.), *Clinical solutions and medical progress through user-driven healthcare* (pp. 35–50). Hershey, PA: Medical Information Science Reference; doi:10.4018/978-1-4666-1876-3.ch005

Wickramasinghe, N., Troshani, I., Hill, S. R., Hague, W., & Goldberg, S. (2013). A transaction cost assessment of a pervasive technology solution for gestational diabetes. In J. Tan (Ed.), *Healthcare information technology innovation and sustainability: Frontiers and adoption* (pp. 109–126). Hershey, PA: Medical Information Science Reference; doi:10.4018/978-1-4666-2797-0.ch007

Wilkowska, W., & Ziefle, M. (2013). User diversity as a challenge for the integration of medical technology into future smart home environments. In I. Management Association (Ed.), User-driven healthcare: Concepts, methodologies, tools, and applications (pp. 553-582). Hershey, PA: Medical Information Science Reference. doi:10.4018/978-1-4666-2770-3.ch028

Willis, E., Wang, Y., & Rodgers, S. (2013). Online health communities and health literacy: Applying a framework for understanding domains of health literacy. In I. Management Association (Ed.), User-driven healthcare: Concepts, methodologies, tools, and applications (pp. 180-196). Hershey, PA: Medical Information Science Reference. doi:10.4018/978-1-4666-2770-3.ch010

Wu, Q., Li, C., Takahashi, S., & Wu, J. (2013). Visual-tactile bottom-up and top-down attention. In J. Wu (Ed.), *Biomedical engineering and cognitive neuroscience for healthcare: Interdisciplinary applications* (pp. 183–191). Hershey, PA: Medical Information Science Reference; doi:10.4018/978-1-4666-2113-8.ch019

Yamaguchi, S., Onoda, K., & Abe, S. (2013). Feedback-related negativity and its clinical implications. In J. Wu (Ed.), *Biomedical engineering and cognitive neuroscience for healthcare: Interdisciplinary applications* (pp. 283–292). Hershey, PA: Medical Information Science Reference; doi:10.4018/978-1-4666-2113-8.ch029

Yan, B., Lei, Y., Tong, L., & Chen, K. (2013). Functional neuroimaging of acupuncture: A systematic review. In J. Wu (Ed.), *Biomedical engineering and cognitive neuroscience for healthcare: Interdisciplinary applications* (pp. 142–155). Hershey, PA: Medical Information Science Reference; doi:10.4018/978-1-4666-2113-8.ch015

Yang, J. (2014). Towards healthy public policy: GIS and food systems analysis. In C. El Morr (Ed.), *Research perspectives on the role of informatics in health policy and management* (pp. 135–152). Hershey, PA: Medical Information Science Reference; doi:10.4018/978-1-4666-4321-5.ch009

Yang, J., Li, Q., Gao, Y., & Wu, J. (2013). Temporal dependency of multisensory audiovisual integration. In J. Wu (Ed.), *Biomedical engineering and cognitive neuroscience for healthcare: Interdisciplinary applications* (pp. 320–326). Hershey, PA: Medical Information Science Reference; doi:10.4018/978-1-4666-2113-8.ch033

Yang, J. J., Liu, J. F., Kurokawa, T., Kitamura, N., Yasuda, K., & Gong, J. P. (2013). Tough double-network hydrogels as scaffolds for tissue engineering: Cell behavior in vitro and in vivo test. In J. Wu (Ed.), *Technological advancements in biomedicine for healthcare applications* (pp. 213–222). Hershey, PA: Medical Information Science Reference; doi:10.4018/978-1-4666-2196-1.ch023

Yang, W., Gao, Y., & Wu, J. (2013). Effects of selective and divided attention on audiovisual interaction. In J. Wu (Ed.), *Biomedical engineering and cognitive neuroscience for healthcare: Interdisciplinary applications* (pp. 311–319). Hershey, PA: Medical Information Science Reference; doi:10.4018/978-1-4666-2113-8.ch032

Yano, Y. (2013). An EMG control system for an ultrasonic motor using a PSoC microcomputer. In J. Wu (Ed.), *Technological advancements in biomedicine for healthcare applications* (pp. 11–17). Hershey, PA: Medical Information Science Reference; doi:10.4018/978-1-4666-2196-1.ch002

Yap, K. Y. (2013). The evolving role of pharmacoinformatics in targeting drug-related problems in clinical oncology practice. In I. Management Association (Ed.), User-driven healthcare: Concepts, methodologies, tools, and applications (pp. 1541-1588). Hershey, PA: Medical Information Science Reference. doi:10.4018/978-1-4666-2770-3.ch077

Yokoi, H., Kato, R., Mori, T., Yamamura, O., & Kubota, M. (2013). Functional electrical stimulation based on interference-driven PWM signals for neuro-rehabilitation. In J. Wu (Ed.), *Technological advancements in biomedicine for healthcare applications* (pp. 180–192). Hershey, PA: Medical Information Science Reference; doi:10.4018/978-1-4666-2196-1.ch019

York, A. M., & Nordengren, F. R. (2013). E-learning and web 2.0 case study: The role of gender in contemporary models of health care leadership. In H. Yang & S. Wang (Eds.), *Cases on formal and informal e-learning environments: Opportunities and practices* (pp. 292–313). Hershey, PA: Information Science Reference; doi:10.4018/978-1-4666-1930-2.ch016

Yu, W. D., & Bhagwat, R. (2013). Modeling emergency and telemedicine health support system: A service oriented architecture approach using cloud computing. In J. Rodrigues (Ed.), *Digital advances in medicine, e-health, and communication technologies* (pp. 187–213). Hershey, PA: Medical Information Science Reference; doi:10.4018/978-1-4666-2794-9.ch011

Yu, Y., Yang, J., & Wu, J. (2013). Cognitive functions and neuronal mechanisms of tactile working memory. In J. Wu (Ed.), *Biomedical engineering and cognitive neuroscience for healthcare: Interdisciplinary applications* (pp. 89–98). Hershey, PA: Medical Information Science Reference; doi:10.4018/978-1-4666-2113-8.ch010

Zaheer, S. (2014). Implementation of evidence-based practice and the PARIHS framework. In C. El Morr (Ed.), *Research perspectives on the role of informatics in health policy and management* (pp. 19–36). Hershey, PA: Medical Information Science Reference; doi:10.4018/978-1-4666-4321-5.ch002

Zalzala, A., Chia, S., Zalzala, L., Sahu, S., Vaghasiya, S., & Karimi, A. (2013). Rural e-health infrastructure development. In I. Management Association (Ed.), User-driven healthcare: Concepts, methodologies, tools, and applications (pp. 870-900). Hershey, PA: Medical Information Science Reference. doi:10.4018/978-1-4666-2770-3.ch044

Zapirain, B. G., & Zorrilla, A. M. (2013). Independent living support for disabled and elderly people using cell phones. In M. Cruz-Cunha, I. Miranda, & P. Gonçalves (Eds.), *Handbook of research on ICTs for human-centered healthcare and social care services* (pp. 379–397). Hershey, PA: Medical Information Science Reference; doi:10.4018/978-1-4666-3986-7.ch020

Zgodavová, K., & Bourek, A. (2013). Potential of web based learning in managing for the sustained success of a healthcare organization based on IMPROHEALTH® project. In I. Management Association (Ed.), User-driven healthcare: Concepts, methodologies, tools, and applications (pp. 1523-1540). Hershey, PA: Medical Information Science Reference. doi:10.4018/978-1-4666-2770-3.ch076

Zhao, X., Zuo, M. J., & Moghaddass, R. (2013). Generating indicators for diagnosis of fault levels by integrating information from two or more sensors. In I. Management Association (Ed.), User-driven healthcare: Concepts, methodologies, tools, and applications (pp. 288-309). Hershey, PA: Medical Information Science Reference. doi:10.4018/978-1-4666-2770-3.ch015

Zhou, X., & Ren, X. (2013). Speed-accuracy tradeoff models of target-based and trajectory-based movements. In J. Wu (Ed.), *Biomedical engineering and cognitive neuroscience for healthcare: Interdisciplinary applications* (pp. 355–368). Hershey, PA: Medical Information Science Reference; doi:10.4018/978-1-4666-2113-8.ch037

Zouag, N., & Driouchi, A. (2014). Trends and prospects of the Moroccan health system: 2010-2030. In A. Driouchi (Ed.), *Labor and health economics in the mediterranean region: Migration and mobility of medical doctors* (pp. 314–336). Hershey, PA: Medical Information Science Reference; doi:10.4018/978-1-4666-4723-7.ch013

Zvikhachevskaya, A., & Mihaylova, L. (2013). Advanced video distribution for wireless e-healthcare systems. In I. Management Association (Ed.), User-driven healthcare: Concepts, methodologies, tools, and applications (pp. 421-446). Hershey, PA: Medical Information Science Reference. doi:10.4018/978-1-4666-2770-3.ch021

Compilation of References

A Patent System for the 21st Century. (n. d.). Washington. The National academics Press.

Abbas, Z., & Riaz, S. (2013), Flexibilities under Trips: Implementation Gaps between Theory and Practice, *Nordic Journal of Commercial Law*, 1.

Access Campaign. (n. d.). The impact of patents on access to medicines. *Access Campaign.* Retrieved July 31, 2016 from http://www.msfaccess.org/content/impact-patents-access-medicines

Agreement on Trade Related Aspects of Intellectual Property Rights and Public Health (WT/MIN(01)IDEC/2). (2001, November 20).

Al-Ali, N. (2002). The Egyptian Pharmaceutical Industry After TRIPS — A Practitioner's View. *Fordham International Law Journal*, *26*(2). Retrived from http://ir.lawnet.fordham.edu/cgi/viewcontent.cgi?article=1871&context=ilj last seen 2/12/2016

Allam, A. (2002). Seeking Investment, Egypt Tries Patent Laws. *The New York Times.* Retrieved from http://www.nytimes.com/2002/10/04/business/seeking-investment-egypt-tries-patent-laws.html

Amit, G., Binal, V., & Sandhya, T. (n. d.). Indian economy. *Incredible India.* Retrieved from http://www.iseindia.com/pdf/Sample%20Economic%20Report%20on%20Indian%20Economy.pdf

Andanda, P. (2012). Striking a Balance between Intellectual Property Protection of Traditional Knowledge, Cultural Preservation and Access to Knowledge. *E Journal of intellectual Property Rights, 17*, 23-27.

Arnold, C. M. (2007). Protecting Intellectual Property in the Developing World: Next Stop—Thailand. Retrieved 11 July 2016 from http://scholarship.law.duke.edu/cgi/viewcontent.cgi?article=1156&context=dltr

Attaran, A., & Gillespie-White, L. (2001). *Do Patents for Antiretroviral Drugs Constrain Access to AIDS Treatment in Africa.*

Auerbach, J. I. (2006). Patent Law Principles & Strategies. *Edell, Shapiro & Finnan, LLC.* Retrieved 14 August 2016 from http://euro.ecom.cmu.edu/program/law/08-732/Patents/PatentLawPrinciples.pdf

Australian Broadcasting Corporation ABC. (2014, March 11). Body Shop withdraws products from China over animal testing.

Bainbridge, D. (2007). Court of Appeal parts company with the EPO on software patents. *Computer Law & Security Report*, *23*(2), 199–204. doi:10.1016/j.clsr.2007.01.001

Banana IP. (n. d.). Patent: InPASS: New Patent Full-Text Search Tool from IPO. Retrieved October 29, 2016, from http://www.bananaip.com/ip-news-center/inpass-new-patent-full-text-search-tool-from-ipo/

Bar-Shalom, A., & Cook-Deegan, R. (2002). Patents and Innovation in Cancer Therapeutics: Lessons from CellPro. *The Milbank Quarterly*, *80*(40). PMID:12532643

Basheer, S. (2005). India's tryst with TRIPS: the patents (amendment) Act 2005. *Indian Journal of Law and Technology.*

Basheer, S. (2007). Big patents arrive in India!! First useful patent database. *SpicyIP*. Retrieved 10 23, 2016 from http://spicyip.com/2007/03/big-patents-arrive-in-india-first.html

Basheer, S., & Kochupillai, M. (2008). Exhausting Patent Rights in India: Parallel Imports and TRIPS Compliance. *Journal of Intellectual Property Rights, 13*, 486-497.

Basics of the economics of monopoly". Retrieved August 8, 2016, from http://image.slidesharecdn.com/monopolywebinar-150529100216-lva1-app6892/95/basics-of-the-economics-of-monopoly-23-638.jpg?cb=1432893806

BBCNews, (2017). TPP: What is it and why does it matter? Retrieved from http://www.bbc.com/news/business-32498715

Beall, R., & Kuhn, R. (2012). Trends in compulsory licensing of pharmaceuticals since the Doha Declaration: a database analysis. *PLoS Medicine*, *9*(1).

Bengaluru, N. V. (2014) Patent expiries valued at $170 bn set Indian pharma to accelerate its complex generic programmes. *Pharmabix.com.* Retrieved from http://www.pharmabiz.com/NewsDetails.aspx?aid=85348&sid=1

Bennett, W. J. (2014). Indian Pharmaceutical Patent Law and the Effects of Novartis Ag v. Union of India. *Washington University Global Studies Law Review*, *13*(3).

Benoliel, D., & Chirwa, T. J. (n. d.). The Impact of Pharmaceutical Patents on Health Expenditures in Least-Developed Countries. Retrieved July 31, 2016 from http://weblaw.haifa.ac.il/he/Faculty/BenOliel/Publications/BenolielChirwa.pdf

Bently, L., Sherman, B., & Hubicki, S. (2009). Patent Issues in Biotechnology. doi:10.1002/9780470015902.a0005189.pub2

Bently, L., Sherman, B., Borges Barbosa, D., Grau-Kuntz, K., Basheer, S., Visser, C., & Gold, R. (2010). Exclusions from Patentability and Exceptions and Limitations to Patentees' Rights. WIPO, SCP/15/31-100. Retrieved from http://www.wipo.int/edocs/mdocs/scp/en/scp_15/scp_15_3-annex1.pdf

Bently, L. (2011). Exclusions from patentability and exceptions to Patentees Rights: Taking Exceptions Seriously. *Current Legal Practices*, *64*(1), 315–347. doi:10.1093/clp/cur011

Bessen, J., & Meurer, M. (2008). Patent Failure: How Judges, Bureaucrats, and Lawyers Put Innovators at Risk. Princeton University Press. Retrieved from http://www.jstor.org/stable/j.ctt7sc3z

Biological Diversity Act (2002).

Bird, R. C. (2009). Developing Nations and the Compulsory License: Maximizing Access to Essential Medicines while Minimizing Investment Side Effects. *The Journal of Law, Medicine & Ethics*, *37*(2), 209–222. doi:10.1111/j.1748-720X.2009.00366.x PMID:19493067

Bond, Eric and Saggi, kamal (2012). Compulsory licensing, price controls, and access to patented foreign products. Retrieved from http://www.wipo.int/edocs/mdocs/mdocs/en/wipo_ip_econ_ge_4_12/wipo_ip_econ_ge_4_12_ref_saggi.pdf

Bronnenberg, B. J., Dubé, J. P., Gentzkow, M., & Shapiro, J. M. (2015). Do Pharmacists Buy Bayer? Informed Shoppers and the Brand Premium. Retrieved Dec. 21, 2016 from https://www.brown.edu/Research/Shapiro/pdfs/generics.pdf

Brown, D. A. (2009). Protecting Intellectual Property Right from the Start. *Eurostat.* Retrieved 22 July 2016 from http://ec.europa.eu/eurostat/statistics-explained/index.php/Patent_statistics

Carlos, M. (2001). Correa, *Public Health and Patent Legislation in Developing Countries,* J. TECH. & INTELL. *PROP*, *1*, 3.

Chakroun, N. (2016). *Patents for Development Improved Patent Information Disclosure and Access for Incremental Innovation*. United Kingdom: Edward Elgar Publishing.

Chang, H. J. (2013, April 13). Company profits depend on the 'welfare payments' they get from society. The Guardian. Retrieved July 31, 2016, from <https://www.theguardian.com/commentisfree/2013/apr/05/company-profits-welfare-payments-society>

Chaudhuri, S. (2014). *Intellectual Property Rights and Innovation: MNCs in Pharmaceutical Industry in India after TRIPS*. New Delhi: Institute for Studies in Industrial Development.

Chauhan, S. S. (2001). Bio Diversity, Biopiracy and Biopolitics: The global perspective. Delhi: Kalinga Publications.

Chen, Y., & Maskus, K. E. (2005). Vertical Pricing and Parallel Imports. *The Journal of International Trade & Economic Development*, *14*(1), 1–18. doi:10.1080/0963819042000333225

Chien, C. (2003). Cheap drugs at what price to innovation: Does the compulsory licensing of pharmaceuticals hurt innovation? *Berkeley Technology Law Journal*, 18(3), 853–907.

Choudhary, K., & Ritiraj. (n. d.). *India: The Trickle Down Effect of Product Patent India and On The Developing World.* Singh and Associates.

Clugston, C.J. (2013). International Exhaustion, Parallel Imports, and the Conflict between the Patent and Copyright Laws of the United States. *Beijing Law Review,* (4), 95-99.

Cockburn, I. M. (2009). Intellectual property rights and Pharmaceuticals: Challenges and opportunities for economic research, *The Economic of Intellectual Property.* Retrieved from http://www.wipo.int/export/sites/www/ip-development/en/economics/pdf/wo_1012_e_ch_5.pdf

Colgate-Palmolive Company. (n. d.). *Colgate-Palmolive Company Tops PETA's New List Recognizing Companies Working to End Government-Mandated Tests.* Retrieved May 31, 2012, from peta.org

Colgate-Palmolive Company. (n. d.). *Legal/Privacy.* Retrieved from http://www.colgate.co.in/app/Colgate/IN/Corp/LegalPrivacy.cvsp

Colgate-Palmolive. (2010, June 26). *Legal/Privacy.* Retrieved from http://www.colgate.co.in/app/Colgate/IN/Corp/LegalPrivacy.cvsp

Colgate-Palmolive. (2013, February 21). *Form 10-K, Annual Report.* Retrieved March 27, 2013, from secdatabase.com

Commission, I. P. R. (n. d.) Traditional Knowledge and Geographical Indications. In *Integrating Intellectual Property Rights and Development Policy* (Ch. 13, pp. 73-94). Retrieved from www.iprcommission.org/papers/pdfs/final_report/ch4final.pdf

Convention on Biological Diversity. (n. d.). Nagoya Protocol on Access and Benefit Sharing. Retrieved from https://www.cbd.int/abs/

COP 6 Decisions. (2002, April 7-19). Convention on Biodiversity and Decision of conference of the parties VI/24 decision. (n. d.) *Convention on Biological Diversity.* Retrieved from https://www.cbd.int/decisions/cop/?m=cop-06

Cornish, W., Llewelyn, D. & Aplin T. (2010). Intellectual Property: Patents, Copyright, Trade Marks and Allied Rights.

D&B. (n. d.) Pharmaceuticals – Indian regulatory & policy environment. *D&B.* Retrieved from http://www.dsir.gov.in/reports/isr1/Pharmaceuticals/7_5.pdf

Danzon, P. M., & Towse, A. (2003). Differential pricing for pharmaceuticals: Reconciling access, R&D and patents. *International Journal of Health Care Finance and Economics, 3*(3), 183–205. doi:10.1023/A:1025384819575 PMID:14625999

Davit, B. M., Nwakama, P. E., Buehler, G. J., Conner, D. P., Haidar, S. H., Patel, D. T., ... & Woodcock, J. (2009). Comparing generic and innovator drugs: a review of 12 years of bioequivalence data from the United States Food and Drug Administration. *Annals of Pharmacotherapy, 43*(10), 1583-1597.

DiMasi, J. A. (1995). Success Rates for New Drugs entering Clinical Testing in the United States. *Clinical Pharmacology and Therapeutics*, *58*(1), 1–14. doi:10.1016/0009-9236(95)90066-7 PMID:7628176

DiMasi, J. A., Caglarcan, E., & Wood-Armany, M. (2001). Emerging role of pharmacoeconomics in the research and development decision-making process. *PharmacoEconomics*, *19*(7), 753–766. doi:10.2165/00019053-200119070-00004 PMID:11548911

DiMasi, J. A., Hansen, R. W., & Grabowski, H. G. (2003). Hansen, & Grabowski (2003). The price of innovation: New estimates of drug development costs. *Journal of Health Economics*, *22*(2), 151–185. doi:10.1016/S0167-6296(02)00126-1 PMID:12606142

do Amaral, A. (2005). Compulsory Licensing and Access to Medicine in Developing Countries. *SELA (Seminario en Latinoamérica de Teoría Constitucional y Política) Papers Paper 47*. Retrieved from http://digitalcommons.law.yale.edu/yls_sela/47

Drahos, P. (1999). The Universality Of Intellectual Property Rights: Origins and Development. Retrieved from http://www.wipo.int/edocs/mdocs/tk/en/wipo_unhchr_ip_pnl_98/wipo_unhchr_ip_pnl_98_1.pdf

Duffy, J. F. (2009). Rules and standards on the forefront of patentability. *Wn & Mary Law Review*, *51*(2), 609–646.

Duggan, M., Garthwaite, C., & Goyal, A. (2014, September). *The Market Impact of Pharmaceutical Product Patents in Developing Countries Evidence from India*. Stanford.

Dunne, S., Shannon, B., Dunne, C., & Cullen, W. (2013). A review of the differences and similarities between generic drugs and their originator counterparts, including economic benefits associated with usage of generic medicines, using Ireland as a case study. *BMC Pharmacol Toxicol*, *14*(1), 1. doi:10.1186/2050-6511-14-1 PMID:23289757

Durham, A. A. (1999). *Patents Law Essentials: A Concise Guide*. London: Greenwood Publishing Group.

Dutfield, G. (2003). *Trading in knowledge: Development perspectives on TRIPS, trade and sustainability*. Christophe Bellmann & Ricardo Melendez-Ortiz Press.

Encaoua, D. (2005). The economics of patents: from natural rights to policy instruments.

Fein, A. J. (2015). Profits in the 2015 Fortune 500: Manufacturers vs. Wholesalers, PBMs, and Pharmacies. Retrieved August 8, 2016 from http://www.drugchannels.net/2015/06/profits-in-2015-fortune-500.html

Fink, C. (2000). How stronger patent protection in India might affect the behavior of transnational pharmaceutical industries. World Bank Policy Research Working Paper.

Fisher, W.W., III, & Dr. Rigamonti C. P. (2005). The South Africa AIDS Controversy A Case Study in Patent Law and Policy. Retrived from https://cyber.harvard.edu/people/tfisher/South%20Africa.pdf

FM't Hoen, E. (2002). TRIPS, pharmaceutical patents and access to essential medicines: Seattle, Doha and beyond.

Ford, S. M. (1999). Compulsory licensing provisions under the TRIPS agreement: Balancing pills and patents. *Am. U. Int'l L. Rev.*, *15*, 941.

Fuller, T. (2007). Thailand takes on drug industry, and may be winning. *The New York Times*. Retrieved November 22, 2016 from http://www.nytimes.com/2007/04/11/world/asia/11ihtpharma.4.5240049.html?pagewanted=all&_r=0

Gaffney, A. (2014). EU regulators concerned about drug data fraud by Indian company. *Regulatory Affairs Professional Society*. Retrieved from http://www.raps.org/Regulatory-Focus/News/2014/12/08/20924/EU-Regulators-Concerned-About-Drug-Data-Fraud-by-Indian-Company/

General Knowledge Today. (2013). *Traditional Knowledge Digital Library (TKDL)*. Retrieved 10 20, 2016, from http://www.gktoday.in/tkdl/

Ghai, D. (2010). Patent protection and Indian pharmaceutical industry. *International Journal of Pharmaceutical Sciences Review and Researches*, *3*(2). Retrieved from http://www.globalresearchonline.net/journalcontents/Volume3issue2/Article%20008.pdf

Golden, J. M. (2008) The Federal Circuit and the D.C. Circuit: Comparative Trials of Two Semi Specialized Courts. Retrieved 24 November 2016 from http://www.gwlr.org/wp-content/uploads/2012/08/78-3-Golden1.pdf

Goldsmith, B. (2015). Is the end of AIDS in sight? *World Economic Forum*. Retrieved August 5, 2016 from https://www.weforum.org/agenda/2015/12/is-the-end-of-aids-in-sight/

Gov.uk. (n. d.). Intellectual property and your work. Retrieved 24 September 2016 from https://www.gov.uk/intellectual-property-an-overview/what-ip-is

Grossman, G.M. & Lai, E.L.-C. (2008). Parallel Imports and Price Controls. *RAND journal of Economics, 39*(2), 378-402.

Gujarat Technological University. (n. d.). Patent Search Methodology.

Gupta, M. S. (2010) Effect of patent law changes on the innovation strategy of Chinese and Indian Life Science companies as reflected in US patent filings. Retrieved September 24, 2016 from http://dspace.mit.edu/handle/1721.1/62524

Hall, B. H. (2007). Contribution to the New Palgrave: A Dictionary of Economics. Retrieved 22 June 2016 from http://web.mit.edu/e-club/hadzia/the-importance-of-patents.html

Harrison, S. S., & Sullivan, H. P. (2011). *Other Boardroom Revised How Leading Companies Realise Value From Their Intellectual Property*. Hoboken: Wiely & Sons. Inc.

Hirwade, M., & Hirwade, A. (2012). Traditional Knowledge Protection: An Indian Prospective. *DESIDOC Journal of Library & Information Technology*, *32*(3), 33–35. doi:10.14429/djlit.32.3.2381

Ho, C.M. (2011). Access to medicine in a global economy, international agreements on patents and related rights. Oxford University Press.

HRA. (2014, July 13). *Choosing Cruelty Free.* Human Research Australia.

Huskamp, H. A. (2006). Prices, Profits, and Innovation: Examining Criticisms Of New Psychotropic Drugs' Value. *Healthaffairs.org.* Retrieved August 8, 2016 from http://content.healthaffairs.org/content/25/3/635.full#xref-ref-15-1

Ibis. (n. d.). Astra pharma receives USFDA approval for Vadodara plant. *IBIS.* Retrieved from http://pharma.industry-focus.net/usfda-approvals.html

India Brand Equity Foundation. (2015). Indian Pharmaceutical Industry. Retrieved Jan. 19, 2017 from http://www.ibef.org/industry/pharmaceutical-india.aspx and http://www.ibef.org/download/Pharmaceuticals-March-2015.pdf

Indxx. (2016). Generic Drugs: Revolutionary Change in the Global Pharmaceutical Industry. Retrieved Dec. 8, 2016 from http://www.nasdaq.com/article/generic-drugs-revolutionary-change-in-the-global-pharmaceutical-industry-cm576603#ixzz4YqQmvtoK

Intellectual Property India. (2016). Retrieved from http://www.ipindia.nic.in/

Intellectual Property India. (n. d.). *Office of the Controller General of Patents, Designs & Trade Marks. Government of India.* Retrieved from: http://ipindia.nic.in/

Intellogist. (n. d.). India BigPatents. Retrieved 10 25, 2016, from http://www.intellogist.com/wiki/India_BigPatents

Intellogist. (n. d.). IPairs. Retrieved 10 29, 2016, from http://www.intellogist.com/wiki/IPairs

Intepat IP Services Pvt Ltd. (n. d.). How to Conduct Patent Search in India? Retrieved 10 28, 2016, from https://www.intepat.com/blog/patent/conduct-indian-patent-search/

Jha, A. (2009). *Traditional Knowledge System in India.* Delhi: Atlantic Press.

Joshi, D. (2012). A point of view on parallel imports. *Global Policy Essay.* Retrieved from http://www.globalpolicyjournal.com/sites/default/files/pdf/View%20Points%20on%20Imports%20-%20July%2012.pdf

Kaitin, K. I., & DiMasi, J. A. (2000). Measuring the Place of New Drug Development in the User Free Era. *Drug Information Journal*, 34(3), 673–680.

Kalluri, S. (2012). Traditional knowledge and Patent strategy. *Journal of Intellectual Property Rights*, *17*, 430–436.

Kesselheim, A. S., Misono, A. S., Lee, J. L., Stedman, M. R., Brookhart, M. A., Choudhry, N. K., & Shrank, W. H. (2008). Clinical equivalence of generic and brand name drugs used in cardiovascular disease: A systematic review and meta-analysis. *Journal of the American Medical Association, 300*(21), 2514–2526. doi:10.1001/jama.2008.758 PMID:19050195

Khaliq, I., & Winarski, T. (2014) USF School of Law. *Patent Licensing and Monetization Law.* Retrieved 21 July 2016 from http://www.uspto.gov/sites/default/files/inventors/edu-inf/BasicPatentGuide.pdf

Knowmore. (n. d.). Colgate-Palmolive. Retrieved Feb 25, 2009 from knowmore.org

Kobak, J. B., Jr. (2005). Exhaustion of intellectual property rights and international trade. *Global Economy Journal,* 5(1). Retrieved from http://www.hugheshubbard.com/ArticleDocuments/Exhaustion_IP_Rights_2003.pdf

Kobori, S. (2002). TRIPS and the Primacy of Public Health. *Asia-Pacific Review, 9*(1), 10–19. doi:10.1080/13439000220141550

Koshy, S. (1995). Effect of TRIPs on Indian Patent Law: A Pharmaceutical Industry Perspective. *BUJ Sci. & Tech. L., 1*, 123.

Kumar, T. N. (2015 August 28). Caution on classifying traditional knowledge under IPR. *The Hindu.* Kerala. Retrieved from http://www.thehindu.com/news/national/kerala/caution-on-classifying-traditional-knowledge-under-ipr/article7589338

Kuosmanen, L. (2016). *TRIPS and Pharmaceutical Patents: Effects on Access to Essential Medicine and Innovation* [Thesis]. Helsinki Metropolia University of Applied Sciences. Retrieved July 31, 2016, from http://www.theseus.fi/bitstream/handle/10024/112464/Kuosmanen_Lauri.pdf?sequence=1

Kyle, M.K. (2009). Parallel trade in pharmaceuticals: firm responses and competition policy. In B. Hawk (Ed.), International Antitrust Law & Policy: Fordham Competition Law 2009 (Ch. 13). New York: Juris Publishing.

Laakmann, A. B. (2012). An explicit policy lever for patent scope. *Michigan Telecommunications & Technology Law Review, 19*(1), 44-97. Retrieved from http://repository.law.umich.edu/mttlr/vol19/iss1/2

Lanjouw, J. O. (1998). *The Introduction of Pharmaceutical Product Patents in India:" Heartless Exploitation of the Poor and Suffering"? (No. w6366).* National Bureau of Economic Research. doi:10.3386/w6366

Levine, D. (n. d.). On ABC Special with Peter Jennings (2002). Bitter Medicine: Pills, Profit, and the Public Health. Retrieved August 8, 2016 from http://www.dklevine.com/archive/bitter-medicine.htm

Levy, R. & Wickelgren, A. (2001). Competition Policy Issues for Regulators: A U.S. Perspective on Pharmaceutical Industry Cases before the Federal Trade Commission. In H. Kettler (Ed.), *Consolidation and Competition in the Pharmaceutical Industry* (pp. 106-117). London: Office of Health Economics.

Lewell, F. R. (2009, January). *The role of intellectual property rights, innovation and competition law in the European software industry* [Master's Thesis].

Lybecker, K. M. (2011). The Economics of Access to Medicines: Meeting the Challenges of Pharmaceutical Patents, Innovation, and Access for Global Health. An Article from the Symposium: Developments and Challenges in International Intellectual Property Law. *Harvard International Law Journal Online, 53*, 25-26.

M.C. Mehta v. Kamal Nath (1997)1 SCC 388.

Martens, P. (2012). Can traditional knowledge owners and producers in developing countries use geographical indications for protection and economic development gain*?* In *Proceedings of the Third biennial global conference July 12 - 14, 2012, National University of Singapore, Faculty of Law Centre for International Law, Society of International Economic Law, online proceedings working paper no.* 2012/04, 3- 16.

Martin, B. S. (2009). Embryonic stem cells: the moral dilemma of patentability and funding. *Pharmaceutical Technology Europe*, *21*(9). Retrieved from https://hinxtongroup.files.wordpress.com/2010/10/san-martin_pharm-tech-europe_2009.pdf

Martinez, C., & Gullec, D. (2004). Overview of recent changes and comparison of patent regimes in the United Retrieved 23 October 2016 from https://www.researchgate.net/publication/250615452_Overview_of_recent_changes_and_comparison_of_patent_regimes_in_the_United_States_Japan_and_Europe

Maskus, K. E. (2001, April). Parallel imports in pharmaceuticals: implications for competition and prices in developing countries (Final Report to World Intellectual Property Organization).

Massey., ... (1994). Distributed intelligence engineering casualty and damage control management system using an AC power line carrier-current lan. Retrieved 11 November 2016 from http://www.patents.com/us-5349644.html

Matthews, J. (2010). Renewing Healthy Competition: Compulsory Licenses and Why Abuses of the TRIPS Article 31 Standards Are Most Damaging to the United States Healthcare Industry. *J. Bus. Entrepreneurship & L.*, 1. Retrieved from http://digitalcommons.pepperdine.edu/jbel/vol4/iss1/5

Maxwell (2010). *Maxwell on the Interpretation of Statutes.* Lexis Nexis

Mazumdar, M., & Rajeev, M. (2010). Parallel Trade and its Implication on the Availability of Patented Drugs: A Theoretical Approach. *The Journal of World Intellectual Property*, *13*(4), 581–604.

MCDESiGN. (n. d.). About MCDESiGN. Retrieved 10 27, 2016, from http://www.mcdesign.co.in/home.do

McFarlane, R. A., & Litts, R. G. (2012). Business Methods and Patentable Subject Matter following In re Bilski: Is Anything under the Sun Made by Man Really Patentable. *Santa Clara High Tech. L. J.*, 26(1), 35-38. Retrieved from http://digitalcommons.law.scu.edu/chtlj/vol26/iss1/2

MCPaIRS. (n. d.). About MCPaIRS. Retrieved 10 27, 2016, from http://mcpairs.com/app/Mcpairs.jsp

Médecins Sans Frontières (MSF). (2013). Global Fund: Proposed shake-up to drug pricing framework risks middle-income countries paying more. Retrieved Jan. 19, 2017 from http://www.msf.org/en/article/global-fund-proposed-shake-drug-pricing-framework-risks-middle-income-countries-paying-more

Merrill, S. A., Levin, R. C., & Myers, M. B. (Eds.). (2003) Committee on Intellectual Property Rights in the Knowledge-Based Economy; Board on Science, Technology, and Economic Policy; Policy and Global Affairs; National Research Council.

Meurer, M. (2002). Business Method Patents and Patent Floods. *Washington University Journal of Law and Policy*, *8*(1), 309.

Mgbeoji, I. (2006). *Global biopiracy: patents, plants, and indigenous knowledge*. University of British Columbia Press.

Moon, S., Jambert, E., Childs, M., & Schoen-Angerer, T. V. (2011). A win-win solution?: A critical analysis of tiered pricing to improve access to medicines in developing countries. *Globalization and Health*, *7*(1), 39. doi:10.1186/1744-8603-7-39 PMID:21992405

Moursund, D. (2005). Introduction to Information and Communication Technology in Education. *Introduction to Information and Communication Technology in Education*. Retrieved 16 August 2016 from http://pages.uoregon.edu/moursund/Books/ICT/ICTBook.pdf

Murthy, D. (2001). Future of Compulsory Licensing: Deciphering the Doha Declaration on the TRIPs Agreement and Public Health, The. *Am. U. Int'l L. Rev.*, *17*, 1299.

Narayan, P. (2013). *Intellectual Property Law*. Mumbai, India: Eastern Book Company.

Neff, J. (2011). Colgate Keeps Triclosan in Its $1B Total Brand. *Adage*. Retrieved from http://adage.com/article/news/colgate-triclosan-total-toothpaste-brand/148408/

NIC. (n. d.). Patent Granted Years 2012-2013 to 2014-2015. Retrieved 10 24, 2016, from http://www.dbtindia.nic.in/patents-granted-year-2012-2013/

NISCAIR. (n. d.). Information Products. Retrieved 10 30, 2016, from http://www.niscair.res.in/aboutus/AnnRep05/Information%20Products.pdf

Patent Facilitating Centre. (n. d.). Free Online Access to First Indian Patent Searchable Database. Retrieved 10 29, 2016, from http://pfc.org.in/db/db.htm

Patent Office Patent Office. (2016). Official Journal Of The Patent Office (41/2016). Retrieved from http://www.ipindia.nic.in/writereaddata/Portal/IPOJournal/1_383_1/Part1.pdf

Patents, R. (n.d.) Protecting Industrial Property Right. Retrieved 13 July 2016 from http://kipi.go.ke/index.php/regional-patents-aripo

PatSeer. (2016). India patent trends for 2015-2016. Retrieved 11 29, 2016, from http://patseer.com/2016/07/india-patent-trends-for-2015-2016/

Peters, D. M. (2006) Understanding Patent Pledges: An overview of legal considerations. Open Source Development Labs. Inc. Retrieved 12 August 2016 from http://www.patent-commons.org/publications/OSDL_Whitepaper_Final_final_4-12-06.pdf

PharmaPhorum. (n. d.) Articles. Retrieved from http://www.pharmaphorum.com/articles

Poltorak, A. I., & Lerner, P. J. (Eds.). (2001). *Essentials of Intellectual Property, Law, Economics and Strategy*. Hoboken: Wiley John Wiley & Sons, Inc.

Press Trust of India. (2013). Ranbaxy import ban: USFDA found suspected hair, oil in tablets. Retrieved from http://www.business-standard.com/article/companies/ranbaxy-import-ban-usfda-found-suspected-hair-oil-in-tablets-113091800573_1.html

PWC. (2013). Indian pharmaceutical market highlights 2013

Rahalkar H (2012). Historical Overview of Pharmaceutical Industry and Drug Regulatory Affairs. *Pharmaceutical Regulatory Affairs*, *11*. doi:10.4172/2167-7689.S11-002

Rai, R. K. (2011). Should the WTO harmonize parallel import laws? An analysis of exhaustion doctrine. *Journal of Intellectual Property Law & Practice*, *6*(12), 898–911. doi:10.1093/jiplp/jpr163

Rao, V. G. (2013). *Intellectual Property Rights in India*. India: SSDN Pub.

Reichman, J. H. (2009). Comment: compulsory licensing of patented pharmaceutical inventions: evaluating the options. *The Journal of Law, Medicine & Ethics*, *37*(2), 247–263. doi:10.1111/j.1748-720X.2009.00369.x PMID:19493070

Reuters. (2011, March 23). Colgate buys Sanex from Unilever for $940 million. United States of America. Retrieved from http://www.reuters.com/article/colgate-unilever-idUSL3E7EN1Z920110323

Reuters. (2015). Ranbaxy sued for manipulating USFDA rules. *The Times of India*. Retrieved 11 October 2016 from http://timesofindia.indiatimes.com/india/Ranbaxy-sued-for-manipulating-USFDA-rules/articleshow/47289866.cms

Rinehart, A. S. (2010). Contracting patents: A modern patent exhaustion doctrine. *Harvard Journal of Law & Technology*, (23): 2010.

RNCOS. (2018). US Generic Drug Market Outlook 2018. Retrieved Jan. 19, 2017 from http://www.rncos.com/Market-Analysis-Reports/US-Generic-Drug-Market-Outlook-2018-IM731.htm

Rossi, M. A., & Pammolli, F. (n. d.). Intellectual Property. Technological Regimes and Market Dynamics. Retrieved 23 November 2016 from http://www.who.int/intellectualproperty/submissions/IP-tech-reg-final.pdf

Saha, S. (2009). Patent law and TRIPS: Compulsory licensing of patents and pharmaceuticals. *Journal of the Patent and Trademark Office Society*, *91*, 364.

Sara, M. Ford, Note, Compulsor, Licensing Provisions Under the Satyanarayana, K. (2008). Towards equitable health care: Drug prices, and beyond. *The Indian Journal of Medical Research*, *127*(4), 301. PMID:18577784

Satyanarayana, K. (2005). TRIPS, patens & HIV/AIDS drugs. *The Indian Journal of Medical Research*, *121*, 211–214. Retrieved from http://icmr.nic.in/ijmr/2005/April/editorial2.pdf PMID:15817937

Sengupta, A. (2012). Patent to Plunder. *Frontline*, *29*(8).

Shashikant, S. (2008) Recent Thai compulsory licenses and the aftermath. *Choike*. Retrieved from http://www.choike.org/nuevo_eng/informes/6432.html

Sherman, B. (1995). The ethics of patenting: Towards a transgenic patent system. *Medical Law Review*, *3*(3), 275–291. doi:10.1093/medlaw/3.3.275 PMID:11657691

Siddiqi, A. (2005). Patents and Pharmaceutical Drugs The Need for Change. *SURG Spring*.

Singal, G. L., Nanda, A., & Kotwani, A. (2011). A comparative evaluation of price and quality of some branded versus branded-generic medicines of the same manufacturer in India. *Indian Journal of Pharmacology*, *43*(2), 131-136.

Sivaraman, R. (2013, March 4). Natco Pharma wins cancer drug case, Chennai. *The Hindu*. Retrieved December 11, 2016 from http://www.thehindu.com/business/companies/natco-pharma-wins-cancer-drug-case/article4475762.ece

Sood, M. (2013). Natco Pharma Ltd. V. Bayer Corporation and The Compulsory Licensing Regime In India. *NUJS L.Rev.*, 6(99).

Spring, C. (2012, February 23). *NIOSH and NHCA present 2012 Safe-in-Sound Excellence in Hearing Loss Prevention Awards*. Retrieved from Centers for Disease Control and Prevention: https://www.cdc.gov/niosh/updates/upd-02-23-12.html

Swamy, N. R. (2014). Protection of traditional knowledge in the present IPR regime: A mirage or a reality. Retrieved from http://www.iipa.org.in/new%20folder/dr.%20raju%20narayana%20swamy.pdf

Swiderska, K. (2006). *Banishing the biopirates: A new approach to protecting traditional knowledge*. International Institute for Environment and Development.

Taplin, R., & Nowak, A. Z. (Eds.). (2010). *Intellectual Property, Innovation, Management in Emerging Economies*. London, New York: Routledge Taylor and Francis Group.

Thapa, R. (2011). Waiver Solution in Public Health and Pharmaceutical Domain under TRIPs agreement. *Jorunal of Intellectual Property Rights*, *16*, 470–476.

The Economist. (2014). The New Drugs War. Retrieved July 31, 2016 from http://www.economist.com/news/leaders/21592619-patents-drugs-are-interests-sick-well-industry-protection-should-not

The Guardian. (2001). Pharmaceutical Industry: Sector Overview. Retrieved August 8, 2016 from https://corporatewatch.org/company-profiles/pharmaceutical-industry

The Indian Express. (n. d.). USFDA alerts to have no impact on pharmacy exports. Retrieved from http://indianexpress.com/article/business/business-others/usfda-alerts-to-have-no-impact-on-pharmacy-exports/

Thorsteinsdóttir, H., Quach, U., Daar, A. S., & Singer, P. A. (2004). Conclusions: Promoting biotechnology innovation in developing countries. *Nature Biotechnology*, *22*(12s), DC48–DC52. doi:10.1038/nbt1204supp-DC48 PMID:15583685

Timmermans, K., & Hutadjulu, T. (2000, May 2-4). The Trips Agreement and Pharmaceuticals. *Report of an ASEAN Workshop on the TRIPs Agreement and its Impact on Pharmaceuticals*, Jakarta. Retrieved March 26, 2016 from http://apps.who.int/medicinedocs/en/d/Jh1459e/

Trade Organization. (2001). Annex IC, art. 66, para. 1, Legal Instruments-Results of the *TRIPS Agreement: Balancing Pills and Patients,* 15 AM. U. INT'L L. REV. 941, TRIPS COUNCIL. *Work (Reading, Mass.)*, 24.

Treglia, B. (2008). Patentable subject matter: separating abstract ideas and laws of nature from patentable inventions. *Jurimetrics Journal of Law & Science*, *48*(4), 427-456. Retrieved from http://www.jstor.org/stable/25767404

Tufts Center for the Study of Drug Development. (2014). Cost to Develop and Win Marketing Approval for a New Drug Is $2.6 Billion. Retrieved Nov. 18, 2016 from http://csdd.tufts.edu/news/complete_story/pr_tufts_csdd_2014_cost_study

U.S Food & Drug Administration. (n. d.). How Drugs are Developed and Approved. Retrieved 11 November 2016 from http://www.fda.gov/Drugs/DevelopmentApprovalProcess/HowDrugsareDevelopedandApproved/

UN News Centre. (2015). *Over 5 billion people worldwide lacking access to essential medicines, says UN report*. Retrieved September 24, 2016 from http://www.un.org/apps/news/story.asp?NewsID=50230#.VgDhjdKqqko

UNAIDS. (2016) Fact Sheet 2016 UNAIDS. *Global Statistics*. Retrieved August 5, 2016, from http://www.unaids.org/sites/default/files/media_asset/UNAIDS_FactSheet_en.pdf

UNAIDS. 2006 REPORT ON THE GLOBAL AIDS EPIDEMIC (2006). Retrieved from http://www.unaids.org/en/HIV_data/2006GlobalReport/default.asp

Uruguay Round vol. 31, 33 I.L.M. 81 (1994).

USA Food and Drug Administration. (n. d.). Facts about Generic Drugs. Retrieved from http://www.fda.gov/Drugs/ResourcesForYou/Consumers/BuyingUsingMedicineSafely/UnderstandingGenericDrugs/ucm167991.htm

USA Today. (2006, March 22). Colgate expands reach of quirky toothpaste.

USPTO. (2014). General Information Concerning Patents. Retrieved 15 November 2016 from http://Www.Uspto.Gov/Patents-Getting-Started/General-Information-concerning-patents

USPTO. (2014). General information concerning patents. United States Patent and Trademark Office. Department of commerce. Retrieved 23 July 2016 from http://www.uspto.gov/sites/default/files/inventors/edu-inf/BasicPatentGuide.pdf

Van Zimmeren, E., Nicol, D., Gold, R., Carbone, J., Chandrasekharan, S., Baldwin, A. L., & Cook-Deegan, R. (2014). The BRCA patent controversies. *Breast Cancer Gene Research and Medical Practices: Transnational Perspectives in the Time of BRCA, 151.*

Varadarajan, D. (2011). A Trade Secret Approach to Protecting Traditional Knowledge. *The Yale journal of international law, 36*, 371-416.

Venkataraman, K. & Swarna Latha, S. (2008, July). Intellectual Property Rights, Traditional Knowledge and Biodiversity in India. *Journal of intellectual property Rights, 13*, 326-335.

Vinita, J. (2012). Types of patent searches. Retrieved 10 29, 2016, from http://birac.nic.in/webcontent/pat1.pdf

Waning, B., Kaplan, W., King, A. C., Lawrence, D. A., Leufkens, H. G., & Fox, M. P. (2009). Global strategies to reduce the price of antiretroviral medicines: Evidence from transactional databases. *Bulletin of the World Health Organization*, *87*(7), 520–528. doi:10.2471/BLT.08.058925 PMID:19649366

Watal, J. (2000). Pharmaceutical patents, prices and welfare losses: Policy options for India under the WTO TRIPS agreement. *World Economy*, *23*(5), 733–752. doi:10.1111/1467-9701.00299

WBIR. (2008, July 3). Colgate-Palmolive plant in Morristown goes green. Retrieved February 25 2009 from http://www.wbir.com/news/local/story.aspx?storyid=55329

Wetzler, J., & Ayala, A. (2008). Timeline on Brazil's Compulsory Licensing. retrieved November 22, 2016 from https://www.wcl.american.edu/pijip/download.cfm?downloadfile=9C0107B5-DE2F

WHO. (2011). Chronic diseases and injuries in India. *WHO.* Retrieved from http://www.who.int/choice/publications/Chronic_diseaseIndia.pdf

WIPO. (2002, June 13-21). Intergovernmental committee on intellectual property and genetic resources, traditional knowledge and folklore third session held in Geneva. Retrieved from www.wipo.int/edocs/mdocs/tk/.../wipo.../wipo_grtkf_ic_3_9-main

WIPO. (n. d.). WIPO Guide To Using patent information. Retrieved 26 August 2016 from http://www.wipo.int/edocs/pubdocs/en/patents/434/wipo_pub_l434_03.pdf

World Trade Organization. (2006). Fact sheet: trips and pharmaceutical patents. *World Trade Organization.* Retrieved from https://www.wto.org/english/tratop_e/trips_e/factsheet_pharm02_e.htm

WTO Ministerial Conference. (n. d.). Declaration on the TRIPs Agreement.

WTO. (n. d.) Doha Declaration Retrieved from https://www.wto.org/english/thewto_e/minist_e/min01_e/.../doha_presspack_e.pdf

Zacharias, N., & Farias, S. (2002). Patents and the Indian Pharmaceutical Industry. Retrieved Jan. 19, 2017 from http://www.nishithdesai.com/fileadmin/user_upload/pdfs/Patents_and_the_Indian_Pharmaceutical_Industry.pdf

Zdravko. (2015). Industries you should look at in 2016! *P&BC Consulting*. Retrieved February 8, 2017 from http://pbconsulting.co/industries-you-should-look-at-in-2016/

About the Contributors

Rajinder Kaur, Professor of Law, has completed her graduation, post-graduation in Law and her Doctorate of Philosophy from Panjab University, Chandigarh. She has thirteen years of teaching experience. She owes to her credit more than 35 research papers and two books at national and international level. She has co-authored three case studies published with Richard Ivey Publications listed with Harvard Business Publishing and available in Chinese language. She is also a reviewer in national and international Journals. She has contributed as a content writer in UGC ePathshala- A MHRD project and also helped the Punjab State Legal Aid to develop a curriculum for undergraduates' students to create legal awareness.

* * *

Dinesh Kumar is an Assistant Professor in the Department of Laws, Panjab University, Chandigarh, India. He has done his Ph.D. from Panjab University. He has published articles in international and national journals and participated in various international and national conferences, workshops. In the recent past, he was invited to present paper and participate in a two week program on *Law, Social Thought and Global Governance* organized by BIARI, Brown University, U.S.A., and was awarded a fellowship by the United Nations to participate in *Regional Course in International Law* held at Seoul National University, Republic of Korea. He is actively involved in teaching and research on Human Rights Obligations of MNCs.

Jatinder Maan is a Junior Research Fellow at Panjab University, Chandigarh and currently pursuing his research in Doctorate on Keyword Advertising and Trademark Infringement in Cyber Space. The author has always remained keen in diverse contemporary socio-legal issues and written on a considerable length street vendors and right to work, Sentencing Policy in India and e-Governance. His work on street vendors and right to work in India is appreciated bagged the third prize in 4th MARG Essay Competition.

Rita graduated in Law in 2011from Maharshi Dayanand University at Rohtak and got the post-graduation degree in Law in 2014 from Punjab University. She is pursuing her Ph.D. with the area of specialization named *"Impact of countervailing duties, Sanitary and Phytosanitary measures on Indian trade with special reference to WTO"*. She worked as Teaching Assistant at University Institute of Legal Studies, Punjab University and assisted in teaching International Trade Law. She also wrote the Case study and Teaching notes on *"Nestle India: Maggi Noodles at war with the Regulators"* Richard Ivey Publications (3-21-2016) pages 9, Richard Ivey School of Business Foundation at Western University of Ontario, Canada, Product No.9B16M034 and Product No.8B16M034, Peer Reviewed, Index with the world best Business School listed in *Harvard Business Review.* She also wrote another paper titled as "*Transparency in Judicial Appointments: illusion or reality*" has been published in book named Law and Good Governance.

Parul Sharma is working as an Assistant Professor in Lovely Professional University, Phagwara, Punjab. She was a LL.M student at the University Institute of Legal Studies, Panjab University. She has won the Best Memorial prize in the National Trial Advocacy Moot Court Competition organized by Surana and Surana international Attorneys at RGNUL, 2014. She has successfully submitted her dissertation on the topic *Role of Directors in Corporate governance in India: A Critical Analysis.* She has written and submitted her term paper on the topic "*Role of Independent Directors in corporate governance: A Study*. She has published in various reputed legal journals. Her area of research includes Corporate and Commercial Laws.

Gurjinder Singh is a Junior Research Fellow at Panjab University, Chandigarh and currently pursuing his research on Competition Law. The author has always remained keen in diverse contemporary socio-legal issues and written on a considerable length. He has worked on the issues of capital punishment, Corporate Social Responsibility, Issues relating to third gender and their working conditions, interaction of competition law and pharmaceutical industry etc. His work on Third gender and their right to work is appreciated by National Law School, Assam, India in their first Law Review Journal.

Naina Singh is pursuing her LL.M. from University Institute of Legal Studies, Panjab University. She has also participated and organized moots during her Graduation in Law. Her area of specialization in post graduate course is Law, Health and Technology. She has opted for this specialization in LL.M. due to her graduation in Microbial and Food Technology and was even awarded a Gold Medal by Panjab University for standing First in Bachelor of Science (Microbial and Food Technology). As a part of the curriculum in she was acquainted with the innovative and rapidly developing field of Intellectual Property Rights. Her topic of the dissertation is the conflict of Parody in Intellectual Property.

Surabhi Singh completed her Master in Business Administration from Amity University, Noida with a major in Human Resources and received her M.Phil. from Jodhpur National University. She teaches post-graduate (MBA) students in subjects related to Business Administration. Additionally, she spends her time researching on various business issues related to Indian industry.

Index

N

O

P

R

S

T

U

V

Purchase Print + Free E-Book or E-Book Only*

Purchase a print book through the IGI Global Online Bookstore and receive the e-book for free or purchase the e-book only! Shipping fees apply.

www.igi-global.com

Recommended Reference Books

ISBN: 978-1-4666-4546-2
© 2014; 486 pp.
List Price: $292

ISBN: 978-1-4666-6260-5
© 2014; 485 pp.
List Price: $260

ISBN: 978-1-4666-6611-5
© 2015; 528 pp.
List Price: $204

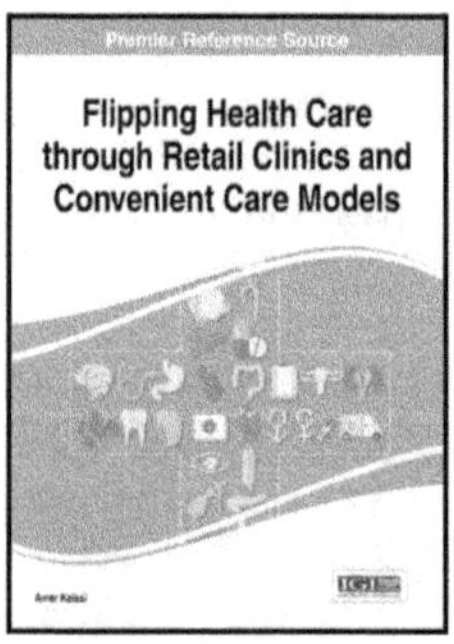

ISBN: 978-1-4666-6355-8
© 2015; 306 pp.
List Price: $196

ISBN: 978-1-4666-6118-9
© 2014; 342 pp.
List Price: $196

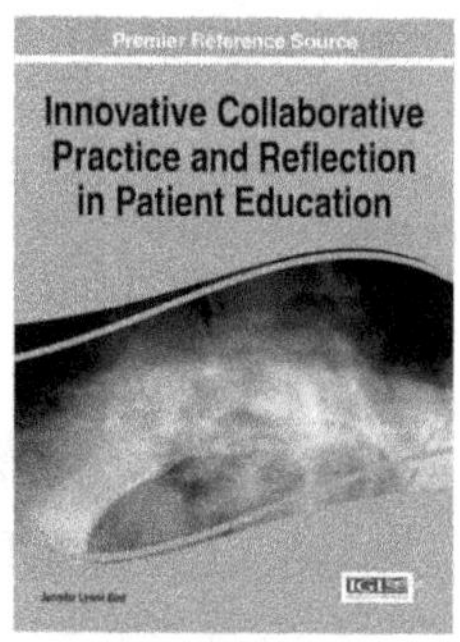

ISBN: 978-1-4666-7524-7
© 2015; 308 pp.
List Price: $180

*IGI Global now offers the exclusive opportunity to receive a free e-book with the purchase of the publication in print, or purchase any e-book publication only. You choose the format that best suits your needs. This offer is only valid on purchases made directly through IGI Global's Online Bookstore and not intended for use by book distributors or wholesalers. Shipping fees will be applied for hardcover purchases during checkout if this option is selected.

Should a new edition of any given publication become available, access will not be extended on the new edition and will only be available for the purchased publication. If a new edition becomes available, you will not lose access, but you would no longer receive new content for that publication (i.e. updates). The free e-book is only available to single institutions that purchase printed publications through IGI Global. Sharing the free e-book is prohibited and will result in the termination of e-access.

Publishing Information Science and Technology Research Since 1988

IGI GLOBAL DISSEMINATOR OF KNOWLEDGE

www.igi-global.com | Sign up at www.igi-global.com/newsletters | facebook.com/igiglobal | twitter.com/igiglobal

Stay Current on the Latest Emerging Research Developments

Become an IGI Global Reviewer for Authored Book Projects

The overall success of an authored book project is dependent on quality and timely reviews.

In this competitive age of scholarly publishing, constructive and timely feedback significantly decreases the turnaround time of manuscripts from submission to acceptance, allowing the publication and discovery of progressive research at a much more expeditious rate. Several IGI Global authored book projects are currently seeking highly qualified experts in the field to fill vacancies on their respective editorial review boards:

Applications may be sent to:
development@igi-global.com

Applicants must have a doctorate (or an equivalent degree) as well as publishing and reviewing experience. Reviewers are asked to write reviews in a timely, collegial, and constructive manner. All reviewers will begin their role on an ad-hoc basis for a period of one year, and upon successful completion of this term can be considered for full editorial review board status, with the potential for a subsequent promotion to Associate Editor.

If you have a colleague that may be interested in this opportunity, we encourage you to share this information with them.

www.igi-global.com

InfoSci®-Books

A Database for Progressive Information Science and Technology Research

Maximize Your Library's Book Collection!

Invest in IGI Global's InfoSci®-Books database and gain access to hundreds of reference books at a fraction of their individual list price.

The InfoSci®-Books database offers unlimited simultaneous users the ability to precisely return search results through more than 80,000 full-text chapters from nearly 3,900 reference books in the following academic research areas:

Business & Management Information Science & Technology • Computer Science & Information Technology
Educational Science & Technology • Engineering Science & Technology • Environmental Science & Technology
Government Science & Technology • Library Information Science & Technology • Media & Communication Science & Technology
Medical, Healthcare & Life Science & Technology • Security & Forensic Science & Technology • Social Sciences & Online Behavior

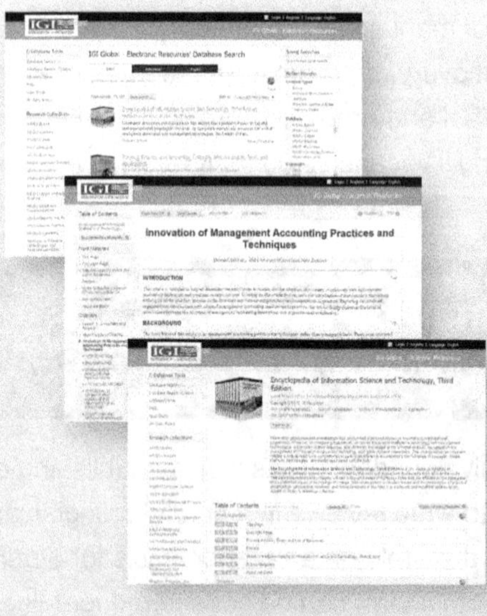

Peer-Reviewed Content:
- Cutting-edge research
- No embargoes
- Scholarly and professional
- Interdisciplinary

Award-Winning Platform:
- Unlimited simultaneous users
- Full-text in XML and PDF
- Advanced search engine
- No DRM

Librarian-Friendly:
- Free MARC records
- Discovery services
- COUNTER4/SUSHI compliant
- Training available

To find out more or request a free trial, visit: www.igi-global.com/eresources

IGI Global
DISSEMINATOR OF KNOWLEDGE
www.igi-global.com

IGI Global
DISSEMINATOR OF KNOWLEDGE
www.igi-global.com

IGI Global Proudly Partners with

eContent Pro

Professional & Marketing Services

Enhance Your Manuscript with
eContent Pro's Professional and Academic
Copy Editing Service

Additional Services

Expert Translation

eContent Pro Translation provides professional translation services across key languages around the world. Our expert translators will work to provide a clear-cut translation of your document, while maintaining your original meaning and ensuring that your document is accurately and professionally translated.

Professional Proofreading

eContent Pro Proofreading provides fast, high-quality, affordable proofreading that will optimize the accuracy and readability of your document, ensuring that its contents are communicated in the clearest way possible to your readers.

IGI Global Authors Save 20% on eContent Pro's Services!

Scan the QR Code to Receive Your 20% Discount

The 20% discount is applied directly to your eContent Pro shopping cart when placing an order through IGI Global's referral link. Use the QR code to access this referral link. eContent Pro has the right to end or modify any promotion at any time.

Email: customerservice@econtentpro.com

econtentpro.com

IRMA INTERNATIONAL

Information Resources Management Association

Become an IRMA Member

Members of the **Information Resources Management Association (IRMA)** understand the importance of community within their field of study. The Information Resources Management Association is an ideal venue through which professionals, students, and academicians can convene and share the latest industry innovations and scholarly research that is changing the field of information science and technology. Become a member today and enjoy the benefits of membership as well as the opportunity to collaborate and network with fellow experts in the field.

IRMA Membership Benefits:

- **One FREE Journal Subscription**
- **30% Off Additional Journal Subscriptions**
- **20% Off Book Purchases**
- Updates on the latest events and research on Information Resources Management through the IRMA-L listserv.
- Updates on new open access and downloadable content added to Research IRM.
- A copy of the Information Technology Management Newsletter twice a year.
- A certificate of membership.

IRMA Membership $195

Scan code or visit **irma-international.org** and begin by selecting your free journal subscription.

Membership is good for one full year.

www.irma-international.org

Encyclopedia of Information Science and Technology, Third Edition (10 Vols.)

Mehdi Khosrow-Pour, D.B.A. (Information Resources Management Association, USA)
ISBN: 978-1-4666-5888-2; **EISBN:** 978-1-4666-5889-9; © 2015; 10,384 pages.

The **Encyclopedia of Information Science and Technology, Third Edition** is a 10-volume compilation of authoritative, previously unpublished research-based articles contributed by thousands of researchers and experts from all over the world. This discipline-defining encyclopedia will serve research needs in numerous fields that are affected by the rapid pace and substantial impact of technological change. With an emphasis on modern issues and the presentation of potential opportunities, prospective solutions, and future directions in the field, it is a relevant and essential addition to any academic library's reference collection.

Take An Extra 30% Off[1]

[1] 30% discount offer cannot be combined with any other discount and is only valid on purchases made directly through IGI Global's Online Bookstore (www.igi-global.com/books), not intended for use by distributors or wholesalers. Offer expires December 31, 2016.

Free Lifetime E-Access with Print Purchase

Take 30% Off Retail Price:

Hardcover with Free E-Access:[2] $2,765
List Price: ~~$3,950~~

E-Access with Free Hardcover:[2] $2,765
List Price: ~~$3,950~~

E-Subscription Price:

One (1) Year E-Subscription: $1,288
List Price: ~~$1,840~~

Two (2) Year E-Subscription: $2,177
List Price: ~~$3,110~~

Recommend this Title to Your Institution's Library: www.igi-global.com/books

[2] IGI Global now offers the exclusive opportunity to receive free lifetime e-access with the purchase of the publication in print, or purchase any e-access publication and receive a free print copy of the publication. You choose the format that best suits your needs. This offer is only valid on purchases made directly through IGI Global's Online Bookstore and not intended for use by book distributors or wholesalers. Shipping fees will be applied for hardcover purchases during checkout if this option is selected.

The lifetime of a publication refers to its status as the current edition. Should a new edition of any given publication become available, access will not be extended on the new edition and will only be available for the purchased publication. If a new edition becomes available, you will not lose access, but you would no longer receive new content for that publication (i.e. updates). Free Lifetime E-Access is only available to single institutions that purchase printed publications through IGI Global. Sharing the Free Lifetime E-Access is prohibited and will result in the termination of e-access.

www.ingramcontent.com/pod-product-compliance
Lightning Source LLC
LaVergne TN
LVHW061537290926
849162LV00004B/826